To *Nancy Webb MacKay*
For never looking back . . .

THE VISUAL PRODUCTION
OF NATION AND PEOPLE

LOOKING FOR
AMERICA

Edited by ARDIS CAMERON

Editorial material and organization © 2005 by Ardis Cameron

BLACKWELL PUBLISHING

350 Main Street, Malden, MA 02148-5020, USA
108 Cowley Road, Oxford OX4 1JF, UK
550 Swanston Street, Carlton, Victoria 3053, Australia

First published 2005 by Blackwell Publishing Ltd

Library of Congress Cataloging-in-Publication Data

Looking for America : the visual production of nation and people / edited by
Ardis Cameron.
     p. cm.
Includes bibliographical references and index.
ISBN 1-4051-1465-7 (hardback : alk. paper) — ISBN 1-4051-1466-5
(pbk. : alk. paper) 1. United States—Civilization—20th century. 2. Visual
communication—Social aspects—United States—History—20th century.
3. Arts and society—United States—History—20th century. 4. National
characteristics, American. 5. United States—Social conditions—20th century.
I. Cameron, Ardis.

E169.1.L8194 2005
973.91′022′2—dc22

2004016922

A catalogue record for this title is available from the British Library.

Set in 10 on 12.5pt Minion
by Kolam Information Services Pvt. Ltd, Pondicherry, India
Printed and bound in the United Kingdom
by MPG Books Ltd, Bodmin, Cornwall

The publisher's policy is to use permanent paper from mills that operate a
sustainable forestry policy, and which has been manufactured from pulp
processed using acid-free and elementary chlorine-free practices. Furthermore,
the publisher ensures that the text paper and cover board used have met
acceptable environmental accreditation standards.

For further information on
Blackwell Publishing, visit our website:
www.blackwellpublishing.com

Contents

Acknowledgments

Books are collective acts that depend upon the kindness, expertise, generosity, and comradeship of many people. Debts like this are never adequately repaid; rather they just grow. For their incredible sleuthing skills, their computer wizardry, their artistry, their humor and good will, I'd like especially to thank Thelma Gilbert, Leanda Shrimpton, Lisa Eaton, Ken Provencher, Annie Lenth, Rosemary Osmond, Madeleine Winterfalcon, and Patrick Corey. My thanks especially to Madeleine for her sustained good humor and invaluable skills.

For their willingness to share their knowledge and get things back sooner than was fair or reasonable, my great thanks to Elspeth Brown and Andrea Volpe. Both were there at the beginning; their encouragement an essential ingredient, their talent generously offered. Jayne Fargnoli was also there when it counted most. Her style, insight, and sheer smarts made her both a helpful editor and a savvy collaborator. I'm grateful she took another look.

Much of this book took shape in heated discussions following sessions at the North American Labor History Conference at Wayne State University, and so my many thanks to Liz Faue, Melissa Dabakis, Ellen Todd, Fran Schor, and Larry Peterson.

Many others contributed in a dozen different ways, including the library staff at the University of Southern Maine, especially Casandra Fitzherbert, Zip Kellogg, and Loraine Lowell, and, as always, Kevin Granahan, the Harry Potter of computing services.

The encouragement and support of Alice Kessler-Harris, Mari Jo Buhle, Judith Smith, Jacquelyn Dowd Hall, Nancy Hewitt, Karen Sacks, Sue Porter-Benson, Steven Lawson, Patsy Yeager, and Joan Scott can never be repaid and is never taken for granted; their work and friendship are "a stay against confusion."

For teaching me the art and pain of seeing in a silent world, I remain always in debt to Michie O'Day, and to Sylvia Tate, who signs us all in and makes community happen. And, lastly, my deepest thanks to Joan Scott and Nancy MacKay for their perceptive readings, generosity of spirit, and willingness to temper the intensity of scholarship with good food, great wine, and love for a certain island in Maine.

Text Acknowledgments

The editor and publisher gratefully acknowledge the permission granted to reproduce the copyright material in this book:

Texts

Epigraph: Paul Simon, lyrics from America. © 1968 by Paul Simon. Reprinted with permission of the publisher: Paul Simon Music.

Chapter 2: Andrea L. Volpe, "Cartes de Visite Portrait Photographs and the Culture of Class Formation," in Burton J. Bledstein and Robert D. Johnston (eds.), *The Middling Sorts: Explorations in the History of the American Middle Class*. New York: Routledge, 2001: 157–69. © 2001 by Routledge. Reprinted with permission of Routledge/Taylor & Francis Books, Inc.

Chapter 3: Shawn Michelle Smith, "Photographing the 'American Negro': Nation, Race, and Photography at the Paris Exposition of 1900," in Smith, *American Archives: Gender, Race, and Class in Visual Culture*. Princeton, NJ: Princeton University Press, 1999: 157–86. © 1999 by Princeton University Press. Reprinted with permission of Princeton University Press.

Chapter 4: Laura Wexler, "Techniques of the Imaginary Nation: Engendering Family Photography," in Reynolds J. Scott-Childress (ed.), *Race and the Production of Modern American Nationalism*. New York: Garland, 1999: 359–81. Reprinted with permission of Routledge/Taylor & Francis Books, Inc.

Chapter 5: Jacquelyn Dowd Hall, "Private Eyes, Public Women: Images of Class and Sex in the Urban South, Atlanta, Georgia, 1913–1915," in Ava Baron (ed.), *Work Engendered: Toward a New History of American Labor*. Ithaca: Cornell University Press, 1991: 243–72. © 1991 by Cornell University. Reprinted with permission of the publisher, Cornell University Press.

Chapter 6: Paula Rabinowitz, "Margaret Bourke-White's Red Coat; or, Slumming in the Thirties," in Rabinowitz, *They Must Be Represented: The Politics of Documentary*. London and New York: Verso, 1994: 56–74. © 1994 by Verso. Reprinted with permission of the publisher.

Chapter 7: Wendy Kozol, "'The Kind of People Who Make Good Americans': Nationalism and *Life's* Family Ideal," in Kozol, *Life's America: Family and Nation in Postwar Photojournalism*. Philadelphia: Temple University Press, 1994: 51–95. © 1994 by Temple University Press. Reprinted with permission of the publisher.

Chapter 9: Mary Beth Haralovich, "Sit-coms and Suburbs: Positioning the 1950s Homemaker," *Quarterly Review of Film and Video*, 11 (1989): 61–83. Reprinted with permission of Taylor & Francis, Inc., http://www.routledge-ny.com

Chapter 10: Stuart Cosgrove, "The Zoot-Suit and Style Warfare," *History Workshop Journal*, 18 (Autumn 1984): 77–91. Reprinted with permission of Oxford University Press.

Chapter 11: Matthew Frye Jacobson, "Looking Jewish, Seeing Jews," in Jacobson, *Whiteness of A Different Color: European Immigrants and the Alchemy of Race*. Cambridge, MA: Harvard University Press, 1998: 171–99. © 1998 by the President and Fellows of Harvard College. Reprinted with permission.

Chapter 12: Catherine A. Lutz and Jane L. Collins, "The Photograph as an Intersection of Gazes," in Lutz and Collins, *Reading National Geographic*. Chicago: University of Chicago Press, 1993: 187–216. © 1993 by the University of Chicago. Reprinted with permission.

Chapter 13: Ardis Cameron, "When Strangers Bring Cameras: The Poetics and Politics of Othered Places," *American Quarterly*, 54:3 (September 2002): 411–35. © 2002 by the American Studies Association. Reprinted with permission of the Johns Hopkins University Press.

Illustrations

Introduction: "Great Hall Number Three," Ellis Island. Reprinted courtesy of the Statue of Liberty National Monument.

2.1: Anonymous carte de visite. Reprinted courtesy of Historical Collections and Labor Archives, Pennsylvania State University Library.

2.2: Posing stand of Philadelphia photographer, March 1868.

2.3: Anonymous carte de visite. Reprinted courtesy of Historical Collections and Labor Archives, Pennsylvania State University Library.

3.1: Francis Galton, "The Jewish Type," composite portraits. Reproduced from Karl Person, *The Life, Letters and Labours of Francis Galton*, vol. 2: *Researches of Middle Life*. Cambridge: Cambridge University Press, 1924.

3.2: Frances Benjamin Johnston, *Saluting the Flag at the Whittier Primary School*, 1899. Reprinted courtesy of the Library of Congress.

3.3: Frances Benjamin Johnston, *Thanksgiving Day Lesson at the Whittier*, 1899. Reprinted courtesy of the Library of Congress.

3.4: Frances Benjamin Johnston, *Class in American History*, 1899. Reprinted courtesy of the Library of Congress.

3.5: From *Types of American Negroes, Georgia, U.S.A.*, compiled by W. E. B. Du Bois, 1900. Reprinted from the Daniel Murray Collection courtesy of the Library of Congress.

3.6: From *Types of American Negroes, Georgia, U.S.A.*, compiled by W. E. B. Du Bois, 1900. Reprinted from the Daniel Murray Collection courtesy of the Library of Congress.

4.1: Orson Lowell, *Untitled*, from *Life* magazine, 1908.

4.2: Gabriel Harrison, *Youth Adoring the Bust of George Washington*. Reprinted courtesy of the George Eastman House.

4.3: Gabriel Harrison, *Young America*. Reprinted courtesy of the George Eastman House.

4.4: Gabriel Harrison, *Infant Saviour*. Reprinted courtesy of the George Eastman House.

4.5: Albert Sands Southworth and Josiah Johnson Hawes, *Girl with Portrait of Washington*, c. 1850. The Metropolitan Museum of Art, gift of I. N. Phelps Stokes, Edward S. Hawes, Alice Mary Hawes, and Marion Augusta Hawes, 1937 (37.14.53). Reprinted with permission of the Metropolitan Museum of Art.

4.6: Jacob Riis, *Girl of the Tenements*, c. 1898. Reprinted with permission of the Museum of the City of New York.

4.7: Photograph of Yuk Kwun's family (mother, two siblings, wife, and four children) received while he worked in Pacific Grove, California, early 1950s. From Ruthanne Lum McCunn, *Chinese American Portraits*. Seattle: University of Washington Press, 1996. Reprinted by permission of Ruthanne Lum McCunn and Betty Woon Jung.

4.8: The photograph as the only space in which the complete family can exist. From Arthur Dong's film *Sewing Woman*, 1982. Reprinted by permission of Deep Focus Productions and Arthur Dong.

5.1: H. N. Mullinax (left), the secretary (not the president) of Local 886. To his left are UTW organizers Charles Miles and O. Delight Smith. Photograph by Duane A. Russell, a local professional photographer. Reprinted courtesy of the George Meany Memorial Archives, Washington, DC.

5.2: Made into a postcard, this photograph of Milton Nunnally, a 10-year-old boy who worked briefly at Fulton Mills, became the most widely circulated image of the strike. Elsas countered by arguing that Nunnally was hired at the insistence of his mother, who swore that the boy's father had deserted him and he had to work. The mill owner also asserted that Nunnally had been discharged for idleness and that his mother ran a house of assignation. Reprinted courtesy of the George Meany Memorial Archives, Washington, DC.

7.1: *Life* magazine cover, January 5, 1953. Nina Leen, Life Magazine/Getty Images.

7.2: The Manji family. Carl Mydans, Life Magazine/Getty Images.

7.3: Navy officers and their families share an apartment. Tony Linck, Life Magazine/Getty Images.

7.4: The Hemekes visit a model house. Al Fenn, Life Magazine/Getty Images.

8.1: Renewing labor traditions: Delegates at Steelworkers Organizing Committee Roseland–Harvey Subdistrict Convention, Harvey, Illinois, October 20, 1940. Chicago Historical Society ICHi 35893.

8.2: Challenging welfare capitalism: United Steelworkers of America District 31 Softball Team, Harvey, Illinois, 1950s, Chicago Historical Society ICHi 35894.

8.3: Complementing the working-class community: United Steelworkers of America District 31 Scholarship Test, Thornton Township High School, Harvey, Illinois, May 1955. Chicago Historical Society ICHi 35892.

10.1: Clyde Duncan, a bus-boy from Gainesville, Georgia, who appeared on the front page of the *New York Times* at the height of the zoot-suit riots. Reprinted courtesy of Stuart Cosgrove and Oxford University Press.

10.2: A Los Angeles police officer pretends to clip the "Argentine" hairstyle of a young *pachuco* zoot-suiter. Reprinted courtesy of Stuart Cosgrove and Oxford University Press.

12.1: The gaze of the camera is not always exactly the same as the gaze of the viewer, but in most *Geographic* photographs the former structures the latter in powerful ways. In this August 1976 photograph of a Venezuelan diamond transaction, the viewer is strongly encouraged to share the photographer's interest in the miner rather than in the broker. Photograph by Robert Madden. © by National Geographic Society. Reprinted courtesy of National Geographic Society.

12.2: Photographs in which Western travelers are present encode complete messages about intercultural relations. The nonreciprocal gazes in this February 1960 picture encode distinctly colonial social relations. Photograph by Lowell Thomas, Jr. Reprinted courtesy of National Geographic Society.

12.3: A surprising number of *Geographic* photographs feature mirrors and cameras, with Westerners offering third-world peoples glimpses of themselves. In this August 1956 picture, a staff artist in what was then French Equatorial Africa shows a woman "her look-alike." Photograph by Volkmar Kurt Wentzel. © by National Geographic Society. Reprinted courtesy of National Geographic Society.

12.4: This February 1925 photograph is captioned "His first mirror: Porter's boy seeing himself as others see him," suggesting that self-awareness comes with Western contact and technology. Photography by Felix Shay. © by National Geographic Society. Reprinted courtesy of National Geographic Society.

12.5: A rare picture from August 1982 draws attention to the presence of the camera by photographing people being photographed for pay. Photography by O. Louis Mazzatenta. © by National Geographic Society. Reprinted courtesy of National Geographic Society.

13.1: Deer kill, the fundamental referent of rural authenticity. From *Belfast, Maine*.

13.2: "*Belfast, ME*, The Movie," cartoon by Darryl Smith. Reprinted with permission.

Appendix A: Advertisement for Matson Line cruises, *Vogue*, November 1, 1941, inside cover. Edward Steichen, photographer; Lloyd B. Meyers, art director.

Every effort has been made to trace copyright holders and to obtain their permission for the use of copyright material. The publisher apologizes for any errors or omissions in the above list and would be grateful to be notified of any corrections that should be incorporated in future reprints or editions of this book.

Laughing on the bus, playing games with the faces
She said the man in the gabardine suit was a spy.
I said "Be careful his bowtie is really a camera." . . .

Counting the cars on the New Jersey turnpike
They've all come to look for America
Simon and Garfunkel

Introduction

ARDIS CAMERON

The true mystery of the world is the visible, not the invisible
Oscar Wilde

In the fall of 1967, the filmmaker Hugh O'Connor stopped by the side of a Kentucky road to shoot some footage for his film about poverty in America. Like many journalists and photographers, he and his crew had turned their lenses on Letcher County, Kentucky, where images of barefooted children, gritty miners, toothless women, and rickety old shacks were both in abundance and in demand as supporting evidence for America's "war on poverty." But in the time between O'Connor's request to film a tenant miner with his family and his crew's ability to do so, word had spread around the county of O'Connor's presence. Soon, Hobart Ison, whose family had owned land in eastern Kentucky for generations and who now owned the property O'Connor was filming, drove up, looked at the cameramen, and fired a round of gunshot. Two bullets lodged in the camera. A third made a gaping hole in O'Connor's chest killing him almost instantly.

In many ways the confrontation between O'Connor and Ison embodies the complex relationship between image-makers and their subjects: it forces those who represent "others" to acknowledge in new ways those who take on the representative burden of authenticity and become the visual emblems of social and cultural difference. But the incident also reminds us that looking is always a mediated act capable of arousing intense emotions and desires as it simultaneously calls forth narratives of difference – of us and others, of home and away, of the citizen and the alien, of the normal and the deviant – and communities of belonging.

Building upon the work of theorists such as M. M. Bakhtin, Walter Benjamin, and Michel Foucault, scholars in a number of fields have shown the degree to which image-making and the kinds of looking relations they exercise, entered into the formation of new types of power – those located not at the level of economics or government but at the more general level of social perception and conceptualization. Like the notorious *flâneur*, whose power in the nineteenth century derived less from his links to institutional power than from his unfettered ability as a bourgeois male "at home in the city" to observe without being noticed himself, modern relations of looking appear on the surface of things as both unremarkable and unremarked. Indeed, it is the very ordinariness of looking that gives to everyday habits of seeing both their constitutive power and their historical invisibility.

Not surprisingly, looking relations came to the center of historical analysis as a way to understand covert forms of resistance among populations where open insubordination and overt acts of rebellion were futile, if not altogether suicidal. Historians of American slavery, for example, have long noted the importance of eye contact and the visual management of imaginary spaces in maintaining the symbolic order of plantation life, while a nod, a wink, an upturned finger, a stare, or a glare was always an effective, if risky, "weapon of the weak."[1] So too have looking relations been important, if under-studied, strategies of female resistance, evasion, and defense. "In order to survive," noted the feminist poet Audre Lorde, "those of us for whom oppression is as American as apple pie have always had to be watchers." By closely watching the oppressor, African American women learned the "look" of social deception in order to nurture and protect "a self-defined standpoint from the prying eyes of dominant groups."[2]

More recently however, historians have turned to the broad terrain of looking as a way to explore the kinds of visual skirmishes unloosed by modern technologies and the visual practices and performances they structure and shape. This has been especially true among feminist scholars and historians of gender, ethnicity, sexuality, and "race," where representation, image-making, appearance, spectatorship, and bodily display have provided critical insights into the codification, maintenance, and disassembling of identities. In his prize-winning book on American immigration and ethnicity, *Whiteness of a Different Color*, historian Matthew Frye Jacobson effectively argues that "race is not just a conception; it is also a perception. The problem is not merely how races are comprehended, but how they are seen." And, one might add, how people are *seen* goes a long way in determining who "they" are and how they take on meaning as citizens and as Americans.

This book introduces readers to the historical operations of looking as image-making and image-reading became, in Martha Banta's words, "a major cultural activity" in the modern era.[3] By "looking," we mean to define visual culture broadly, including both practices of representation, such as photography, documentary filmmaking, self-fashioning, spectacle, and display, as well as the kinds of relationships and imaginary topographies

2

such practices composed. As the title suggests, the collection is especially concerned with the ways in which visual culture became, in the last century, a primary means through which differences were imagined and notions of "Americanness" produced, resisted, defamiliarized, and reframed. The essays collected here show that in many ways the visual economy of American culture has been as powerful a determinant of social place and position as modes of production. Neither benign nor neutral, looking is always an exercise in power.

Consider, for example, the image in Figure 1. If we proceed from the premise articulated by Catherine Lutz and Jane Collins that "all photographs tell stories of looking," how do we read this image for what it can tell us about the signifying practices of the modern eye and the kinds of narratives that image-making and image-reading authorize? The photograph is entitled "Great Hall Number Three," and it shows Ellis Island sometime in the first decade of the twentieth century. It shows the vast waiting room where, under a large American flag, new arrivals, mostly from southern and eastern Europe, wait to be processed by US immigration officials who sit at their desks immediately under the flag and at the end of each row. Note too the inspectors standing mid-picture watching the crowds

Figure 1. "Great Hall Number Three," Ellis Island. Reprinted courtesy of the Statue of Liberty National Monument

before them: they gaze out above the seated rows, their bodies poised to look this way and that as the clerks in front of them conduct their interviews. The slight blurring in the bottom half of the picture conveys something of the famously described "teeming masses" as shawls and hats anxiously shift about. They are waiting to be examined – to pass the physical inspections that are the worry of every alien who ever passed through Ellis Island. To fail means to be deported, to be sent back perhaps alone without their families to places where many no longer have homes. But as they wait, the examination has already begun.

The inspectors look out over the seated crowds with eyes alert. Many of them have been trained in "visual detection" at the University of Virginia, or perhaps at the Vineland School for the Feeble-Minded in southern New Jersey. Earlier in the day, as the immigrants passed through the many receiving lines, or now, as they simply wait, officials adept in the "art of snapshot diagnosis" scrutinize their bodies for any signs of physical, mental, or moral "defection."[4] Sheer numbers no doubt helped elevate this ability to sleuth out the "defective" for, when this picture was taken, inspectors had to examine between 2,000 and 5,000 arrivals each day. But as the articles in this collection make clear, the visual markers of bodily difference have always taken on shape and meaning within historically specific moments of social formation and the discursive topographies of belonging they enact.

This collection begins, then, with two essays that help situate the modern body by exploring everyday habits of seeing as they congealed and operated in the wake of the Civil War as new visual technologies reflected and helped shape emerging class and national identities. Both Ardis Cameron and Andrea Volpe demonstrate the constitutive role of visual culture in stabilizing, even inventing, "racial," class, and national identities and making them visible within a hierarchy of typologies. Cameron provides a general introduction to this process as it took shape in nineteenth-century discourses of physiognomy as visions of bodily difference insinuated themselves into racialized and class-bound habits of seeing. Volpe shows how the mass production and consumption of commercial portrait photographs, known as cartes de visite, was especially instrumental in the processes of class and nation formation. Her essay details how the form and pose of the portrait sitter helped produce a standardized body around which middle-class consciousness was visually "made real" as the rituals and performance of national identity intensified in the decades that followed the Civil War.

In many ways, then, the inspectors shown here at Ellis Island were only marginally better trained than ordinary Americans in the visual codes they used to sort out, categorize, and interpret physical differences. The "defectives" they watched out for had long been associated with particular bodily features that by 1900 had sedimented into a canon of national types whose outward appearance was read as a sign of inward character traits that varied only by gender and marital status. Single women from southern and eastern Europe, for example, were especially suspect as possible carriers of venereal disease or as prostitutes fleeing host countries. Looking out for these women involved watching for "shifting eyes" or, in the case of women between the ages of 25 and 45, scrutinizing the facial hair of those not married. "A fine hairy growth on the face," wrote one expert, "is at least evidence that they do not indulge in sexual congress with any degree of regularity or frequency." A smooth face, on the other hand, suggested "physiological stimulus" thus marking the unmarried woman as a possible prostitute. Similarly, the facial inspection of men could lead investigators to discover "unusual sexual proclivities" among those whose erotic abdominal tattooing might otherwise go undetected.[5] To understand this photograph, then, we need to recognize its participation in a distinct visual genealogy that gave shape and meaning to the art of "visual detection" and the kinds of looking it engendered.

Look at the photograph again. While the bottom half depicts discrete moments of visual indexing and detection, the picture viewed as a whole is more representative of looking relations as a general mode of social legibility and interpretation. If we step back and view the full image, we find ourselves gazing not only at multiple scenes of surveillance and observation, but at the new kinds of looking relations forged in tandem with global capitalist expansion and the disparate kinds of "travel" it produced. We see in this picture not only the spectacle of Ellis Island but also the phantasmagoria of mass human migration, displacement, homelessness, and exile. But note too the balcony that supports the American flag. Observe the couples that seem to lounge about along the railing. Just to the left of the flag a man casually crosses his legs and leans over while his escort in stylish hat and cloak stiffly gazes below. The men to the right bend their upper bodies to get a closer look. The spacious perch of these men and women, well above the crowded rows of immigrants below, signals their privileged position as "watchers" and mirrors the national preoccupation with working-class and immigrant life that was captured, as Paula Rabinowitz notes, in 1930s films and songs as a form of class "slumming." In the spacious eyrie above the Great Hall, middle-class men and women watch in fascination, but cross-class looking was always, as Rabinowitz shows, a complicated mixture of pleasure, thrill-seeking, fear, social concern, and, at times, sheer voyeurism. The artist John Sloan "peeped," at his neighbors on Manhattan's 23rd Street because, as he put it, "I am in the habit of watching every bit of human life I can see about my window." "I peep," he explained, "through real interest, not being observed myself."[6] Others, like Progressive reformers, new dealers, radicals, intellectuals, and photojournalists such as Margaret Bourke-White, whose poverty pictures for *Life* magazine made her one of the highest-paid women in 1930s

America, cloaked their "peeping" in the garb of social science: participant observation and social documentation. In her self-reflexive article, Rabino-witz explores various forms of Depression-era boundary-crossing as revealed in moments of visual encounter between those who were privileged observers with the power to regulate and represent others and their subjects, usually the poor. When a middle-class woman looks across her class privilege at another woman what, asks Rabinowitz, does she see?

The genteel tourists shown above most likely see the spectacle of "Other-ness" as they scan the faces of those whom they too have learned to recognize through mass-circulation magazines, where images of the "new" immigrant circulate within, and in relation to, an archive of "primitive" types collected both from around the world and along the hidden byways and remote "pockets" of America. This Sunday, they have come to see for themselves. Yet as they look down at the exotic shawls and felt hats, the long beards and strange clothes, the stooped postures and weary faces, they enter what Shawn Michelle Smith describes as a "visual terrain" already mapped in terms of both "race" and "nation." As they looked they encountered the historical legacy of physiognomical surveillance that gave to the bodies of private immigrants a knowing "public" recognition and, to those who watched from above, the cultural tools to ascribe meaning and value to what they saw below. They had, after all, seen these faces before and, as the essays in this collection show, the mass reproduction and representation of "physical types" and bodily differences conjoined specific historical formations of class, ethnic, race, gender, and national identities. Like Sloan and other fascinated cross-class observers, the Ellis Island tourists peeped through real interest, but the world they saw reflected and reproduced essentialized types that simultan-eously ascribed social value and meaning to physical differences and gave to them as well the power of social authorship. "This is not to say," writes Jacobson, "that people all 'really' look alike; rather, it is to argue that those physical differences which register in the consciousness as 'difference' are keyed to particular social and historical circumstances." In the history of looking, bodies have been ubiquitous storytellers whose fictions have helped fix the face of America and the changing look of those conceived as alien to it.

For many reformers and journalists, the camera provided a powerful means to gather evidence and so "document" the nation's social ills. And, as Maren Stange notes, it offered as well a way to articulate class differences and buttress middle-class claims to social and moral guardianship. "Throughout the century," writes Stange, "the documentary mode testified both to the exist-ence of painful social facts and to reformers' special expertise in ameliorating them, thus reassuring a liberal middle class that social oversight was both its duty and its right."[7] But images like these circulated amidst a wide terrain of representation, especially after 1890 as the cheaper half-tone process made illustrations available to a national market and to readers of every class. Part II therefore picks up on Laura Wexler's important observation that this "burst of photographic invention corresponds quite closely with the era of national self-creation." What is often missing in discussions of Progressive documentary is how these images worked in tandem with other forms of turn-of-the-century photography and in relation to assimilationist rituals and performances, such as "saluting the flag," re-enacting the Pilgrim landing, and memorizing the words of "illustrious Americans," whose mass-produced faces were increasingly offered up as the embodiment of Americanness. Both Shawn Michelle Smith and Laura Wexler use the expansion of print capitalism and illustrated newspapers and magazines as a way to explore these connections, especially as they affected white women and the "American Negro," a term that, as Smith points out, "would have registered as a kind of oxymoron" for many turn-of-the-century whites who "attempted to define 'American' as an exclusively Anglo-Saxon purview." Both Wexler and Smith utilize Benedict Anderson's influential study *Imagined Communities* as a point of entry into the gendered and racially codified topographies of American identity as they took shape in the highly charged atmosphere of imperial expansion and middle-class concerns about racial and class reproduction. Both bring into discussions of nationalism not only the central role of photography but also the critical role of domestic visions and racial self-fashioning as central elements in the formation and construction of Americanness.

Like Volpe's, these articles bring into play as well everyday forms of photography, including the family photograph album and the ubiquitous "snapshot." If we look once more at the Great Hall, for example, we can appreciate the importance of the hand-held camera as it became more accessible and thus more involved in the visual operation of everyday life. Consider the "eyes" which take us into the Great Hall and turn us into "peepers" too. While we don't know much about the photographer, Augustus F. Sherman, except that he was a customs official stationed at Ellis Island, we know from his photograph collection that he belonged to a new class of amateur picture-takers collectively known as "Kodakers" and, more derisively, as "camera fiends." Labels like this attest not only to the popularity of the hand-held camera and new possibilities it afforded the amateur, but also to the public suspicion and anxiety that accompanied it. With their ability to snap an unguarded face and "capture reality" with the click of the shutter, owners of these "deadly little boxes" presented an array of troubling questions, especially as the newspaper and magazine industries expanded the uses of photographic images. What, if any, were the moral and ethical responsibilities of the ubiquitous snapshooter? Who owned an image? Could images of private persons "captured" without their permission or knowledge be made public? Did the snapping of a photo constitute an invasion of privacy? Should the so-called "detective" camera, popular among amateurs and professionals alike, be regulated or outlawed altogether? So disturbing was the popularity of the camera that the Cleveland administration banned amateur Kodakers from the grounds of the White House in 1887.[8]

For Sherman, camerawork seems to have been a source of recreation and pleasure. Unlike the progressive sleuths who used photographs to document social ills and the painful realities of industrial life, Sherman did not plan to display his collection, nor did he elect to use it as evidence to advocate reform. But, by clicking his shutter to record the events before him, he put himself firmly within the Progressive tradition, using his camera to freeze the present and the photograph to establish what it could never become: an unmediated record of the world around him. Unlike Sherman, however, many other amateurs turned to the camera not only as a way to document historic events, but as a way to shape them. Labor organizers and strikers saw the camera as a way to present to the public their side of industrial struggles. During the great uprisings at Lawrence, Massachusetts, Paterson, New Jersey, and the Lower East Side of New York City, the Industrial Workers of the World gave cameras to strikers, who used them to snap images of scabs who crossed the picket line. Union leaders also used them to bolster support for a strike and gain sympathy from allies. But, as Jacquelyn Dowd Hall demonstrates, union leaders did more than simply "appropriate established forms"; they used their cameras "to show strikers to themselves." The camera becomes autobiography. Focusing on the 1914 strike at the Fulton Mills in Atlanta, Georgia, Hall shows how one leader in particular, O. Delight Smith, scurried about town taking hundreds of photos. She then captioned them and displayed them in the city's store windows. Seeing themselves "in action and in captivity" workers saw themselves in solidarity and in relation to a radically reconfigured social landscape. They saw as well a dramatically reimagined America. In newspapers and magazines, as well as in local shops, strikers presented themselves carrying and at times wearing large American flags, turning their strikes into ritualized performances that situated national character and Americanness firmly within the turbulent industrial struggles that characterized the era.

Like Sherman's photo, Hall's article alerts us to the complexity of looking relations and the multiplicity of gazes as marginalized groups turned clothes, cosmetics, gestures, tattoos, hair, and American flags into a distinctive personal and collective sense of self that was potentially challenging to normative habits of seeing and seemingly fixed visions of national identity. Note, for example, in the Great Hall, the many wide-brimmed hats worn by the female arrivals. Those who wear the traditional shawls are actually a minority, and, while the hats are not as grand as the one displayed by the lady observer

8

above, they demonstrate a cultural style that was far more complex than genteel observers recognized. As Kathy Peiss has shown, "putting on style" was for working-class women a "particularly potent way to display and play with notions of respectability, allure, independence, and status."[9] It was also a way to distance oneself from the old world and embrace the new. Paying attention to how people present themselves points to the kinds of sartorial politics and visual skirmishes embedded in acts of "dressing up" as well as going "undercover" – of public looks, as well as "private eyes." Essays by Hall and Stuart Cosgrove make the purposeful use of clothing and style a locus for examining the political agency of bodily display and the emblems of visibility – a spectacular way in which oppressed groups and self-defined subcultures could negotiate alternative identities, refused subservience, or "pass" in complex and, at times, contradictory ways. This was made clear not only in Atlanta, but in the complex history of the zoot-suit riots that erupted across the country in the 1940s. Worn by young black and Mexican Americans, the zoot-suit was unmistakable in its flamboyant style, but for those who wore them they were more than merely gaudy outerwear. "The zoot-suit," Cosgrove writes, "was more than the drape-shape of the 1940's fashion, more than a colorful stage-prop hanging from the shoulders of Cab Calloway, it was, in the most direct and obvious ways, an emblem of ethnicity and a way of negotiating an identity. The zoot-suit was a refusal."

It is no coincidence that the zoot-suit riots broke out during a period of war, when tensions over what and who constituted an American citizen were at their greatest. For minorities and subcultures whose status as Americans was probationary at best, appearance provided an immediate "in-your-face" way to assert a community of difference and to resist narratives of subservience. The end of the war, however, did not end the clash over national identity. Always a contested site, Americanness grew even more narrowly defined in the postwar years as images of nationhood serviced competing emotional and political claims. Nowhere is this more revealing, perhaps, than in the warring images over what constituted the "all-American family" during the Cold War. Wendy Kozol, Larry Peterson, and Mary Beth Haralovich show that "ordinary American families" were not born; they were created in the pages of popular magazines like *Life*, and in the new technologies of television and the sit-coms it promoted. Unlike the images taken in the 1930s by *Life* magazine photographer Margaret Bourke-White, those of Nina Leen put white, middle-class domesticity at the heart of *Life*'s portrait of the postwar nation. As Kozol argues, "In the hegemonic struggle to define and assert a national identity... *Life* vigorously promoted a vision of the American nation through pictures of nuclear families surrounded by consumer products in suburban homes." Television programming reinforced these images with popular shows like *Father Knows Best* and *Leave it to Beaver*, two sit-coms that stressed the centrality of women's place in the home at the very moment that more women than ever were entering the paid labor force. As Haralovich notes, "*Father Knows Best* was applauded for realigning family gender roles" at a time when "an ideal white and middle class home life was a primary means of reconstituting and resocializing the American family after World War II."

Less widely known, however, was the visual response to these images on the part of the American labor movement which, as Larry Peterson shows, began to contest corporate domination of the photographically illustrated press by publishing its own picture format magazine *Steel Labor*, one of many vividly illustrated newspapers that served millions of American workers. Countering corporate images that sought to link workers' real families with the company's paternalistic "imagined community," *Steel Labor* depicted union members at the local hall, attending meetings, and with friends, purposefully including as well portraits of black workers along with whites. As an alternative to dominant images of the era, it challenged the monopoly of corporate-sponsored representations that associated white, middle-class suburbia with the face of postwar America.

Let me use Sherman's evocative photograph one last time as a way to call attention to one final concern these essays collectively raise: our own position as spectators in what Benjamin described as "the age of mechanical reproduction." Always a meaningful form of exchange, looking became, in the expanding market economy of the late nineteenth and twentieth centuries, a profitable one as well. Images, these essays remind us, were viewed with historically and culturally tutored eyes, but as commodities, they circulated as well in a system of commodity exchange and aesthetic value. The poverty pictures taken in the 1930s and 1960s, the images of non-Western peoples published by *National Geographic*, the documentary films of the socially marginal are re-examined here for what they can tell us about the visual encounters between those who stand in front of and those who stand behind the camera, and between those who consume these images and those who market and value them as "art." What are the politics and poetics of cross-class looking? How can feminist academics and social historians committed to writing history "from the bottom up" theorize, as Paula Rabinowitz suggests, "a politics that acknowledges women's class and generational differences as 'an exchange between these moments of female humanity, between the woman who wants and the woman who knows'?" The essays by Rabinowitz, Cameron, and Lutz and Collins especially challenge us to think about the cultural operation of cross-class looking as a historic and political act.

Consider then, where, and how do "we" as readers of books like this locate ourselves as consumers and producers of visual culture and the kinds of narratives our "peeping" helps produce? What are the competing views elicited by camera work? How is our gaze shaping the nation and the world into something it is not for those we imagine to be "Other"? What do we see when we look at images different from our own and how do these visual representations work to shape, as Lutz and Collins put it, "who Americans are and who others might be"? Exploring "Otherness" Catherine Lutz, Jane Collins, and Ardis Cameron make questions like these central as the former analyze photographs from *National Geographic* as an intersection of gazes, and as Cameron scrutinizes the politics and poetics of socially concerned filmmaking as represented in two recent documentary films, *Strangers With a Camera*, by Elizabeth Barret, and *Belfast, Maine*, by Frederick Wiseman.

If, as Benedict Anderson has argued, "communities are to be distinguished, not by their falsity/genuineness, but by the style in which they are imagined," then we need to pay attention to the critical role of visual culture in historically shaping notions of who and what constitutes this thing we call "Americanness." The essays collected here provide a beginning to such a project, asking not just how images reflected a nation, but rather how, in specific moments and under certain circumstances, the American nation was conceptually forged; its identity envisioned in and through physically encoded discourses of difference and hierarchies of belonging. Like Sherman's photograph, these essays provide a spectacular reminder that looking is always a constitutive practice. But they demonstrate, as well, that visual culture is also and always a reflection of power-infused, unequal situations. Whether as amateur Kodakers, documentary filmmakers, photojournalists, family snapshooters, reformers "botanizing the asphalt," company spies, or scientific observers for *National Geographic*, image-makers and the looking relations they exercise have occupied a privileged place in shaping and reshaping narratives of citizenship and the inequalities they enacted. By looking at this history, perhaps we too can begin to see the look of a more just society and the face of a more equitable America.

Notes

1 James C. Scott, *Weapons of the Weak: Everyday Forms of Peasant Resistance* (New Haven: Yale University Press, 1985), 28–41.

2 Audre Lorde, *Sister Outsider* (1984), 114.

3 Martha Banta, *Imaging American Women: Ideas and Ideals in Cultural History* (New York: Columbia University Press, 1987), p. xxviii.

4 L. E. Cofer, quoted in Anne Emanuelle Birn, "Snapshot Diagnosis: The Medical Inspection of Immigrants at Ellis Island, 1900–1914" (BA thesis: Harvard University, 1986), 40.

5 Howard A. Knox, MD, "A Diagnostic Study of the Face," *New York Medical Journal* (June 14, 1913), 1227–8.

6 John Sloan, quoted in Patricia Hills, "John Sloan's Images of Working-Class Women: A Case Study of the Roles and Interrelationships of Politics, Personality, and Patrons in the Development of Sloan's Art, 1905–16," *Prospects*, 5 (1980), 157–96: 178. My thanks to Donna Cassidy for this citation.

7 Maren Stange, *Symbols of Ideal Life: Social Documentary Photography in America, 1890–1950* (New York: Cambridge University Press, 1989), p. xiii.

8 See especially Robert E. Mensel, "Kodakers Lying in Wait: Amateur Photography and the Right of Privacy in New York, 1885–1915," *American Quarterly*, 43 (Mar. 1991), 24–45.

9 Kathy Peiss, *Cheap Amusements: Working Women and Leisure in Turn-of-the-Century New York* (Philadelphia: Temple University Press, 1986), 63.

Introduction:
Suggested Readings

As Nicholas Mirzoeff recently noted, visual culture "is not just a part of your everyday life, it is *your* everyday life." Yet understanding the visual – how it works and how we might better interpret visual experience, both in the present and in the past – is only just emerging as an essential part of the historian's craft. This book pays close attention to the historical operations of the visual as they affect national identities and a collective sense of belonging. Readers, however, will find the following useful sources for a general exploration of visual culture.

Marita Sturken and Lisa Cartwright, *Practices of Looking: An Introduction to Visual Culture* (2001).

Judith Fryer Davidov, *Women's Camera Work: Self/Body/Other in American Visual Culture* (1998).

Nicholas Mirzoeff (ed.), *The Visual Culture Reader* (1998).

Norman Bryson, Michael Ann Holly, and Keith Moxey (eds.), *Visual Culture: Images and Interpretations* (1994).

Ivan Karp and Steven D. Lavine, *Exhibiting Cultures: The Poetics and Politics of Museum Display* (1991).

Richard Bolton, *The Contest of Meaning: Critical Histories of Photography* (1989).

John Tagg, *The Burden of Representation: Essays on Photographies and Histories* (1988).

John Collier, Jr. and Malcolm Collier, *Visual Anthropology: Photography as a Research Method* (1986).

PART ONE

1860 – 1900

Modern Types

Modern Types

1

Sleuthing Towards America: Visual Detection in Everyday Life

ARDIS CAMERON

In the early 1960s special investigator Tom Scarborough was sent to Granada, Mississippi, to investigate rumors that the out-of-wedlock child recently born to a local white woman was fathered by a black man. Employed by the Mississippi State Sovereignty Commission, Scarborough's task was to see if the birth was in fact part of what many Southern politicians called the "mongrolization" of the races. As reported in the *New Yorker Magazine* by Calvin Trillin, Scarborough's report details the critical role that visual evidence and the physical body played in such investigations. "I was looking at the child's finger nails," wrote Scarborough, "and the end of its fingers very closely." Apparently searching for noticeably developed half-moons at the cuticles, Scarborough hoped to establish the African ancestry of the child, and hence its complicity in undermining the "sovereignty" of the State of Mississippi. He went on to report however, that the exam had been inconclusive. "We both agreed we were not qualified to say it was a part Negro child, but we could say it was not 100 percent Caucasian." As an indicator of mixed blood, the fingernail inspection proved effective, but without other physical clues that would only come with age, the infant body proved disappointing. Whether sensing their doubt as Trillin suggests, or simply describing the child's father, the mother shrewdly carved out a position of in-betweenness: the baby's father, she told investigators, was Italian.[1]

State concern over "race mixing" kept the Sovereignty Commission (the commission had files on about 10,000 people) unusually busy throughout its career tracking down suspected cases in order to both verify events and prevent what the commission believed to be the soft underbelly of white sovereignty: miscegenation. Trillin writes, for example, that in 1964 Governor

Paul Johnson received a letter from a couple in Biloxi. "Dear Governor Johnson," it began, "We regret to say that for the first time in our lives we need your help very badly. We are native Mississippians and are presently living in Biloxi. Our only daughter is a freshman at the University of Southern Mississippi. She has never before given us any worry. However, she is in love with a Biloxi boy who looks and is said to be part Negro..."[2] Johnson quickly wrote back to assure the couple that he would have the matter investigated and, in a 3,000-word report, Scarborough says once again that, while the boy in question cannot be verified as a Negro, he is clearly not Caucasian. According to his investigations, the boy came from a group of people living in Vancleave, Mississippi, who were known as "red bones" or "Vancleave Indians," a population long rumored by neighbors to be black despite their attendance in the town's white schools and churches. How this story ends is unclear (Trillin suggests there were plans to draft the boy and send him to Vietnam but he was under-age), but like the tale of the "Italian" child born out of wedlock to a "white" mother, Scarborough's lengthy narrative of the "red bones" suggests the degree to which "race" as a measure of human difference, depended upon popular, if inexact, modes of visual indexing – the pseudo-scientific practice, that is, of simultaneously looking at, ordering, and ranking the body according to culturally shaped codes of taste and meaning. In the cartography of the modern body, "Race" took place.

As Scarborough discovered, however, bodies are difficult maps to read. Consider, for example, the case of John Svan. Born in Finland, Svan came to the United States sometime before 1882. As the new century began he and sixteen of his countrymen decided to remain in Minnesota and become US citizens. Their applications, however, were rejected. According to the US Department of Justice, Svan was not "white" because as a Finn he carried within him the blood of his "Mongolian" ancestors. Indeed, according to federal laws at the time, American citizenship was reserved only for "aliens being free white persons and to aliens of African nativity and to persons of African descent." Had Svan been black or white he would have been eligible, but as a Mongolian he fell into a newly emerging categorization that racialized immigrants from China, Japan, India, and the Philippines as different from both of these designations. Through a sequence of laws enacted by Congress in 1882, 1917, 1924, and 1934, Asians, Orientals, and Filipinos were configured as a particular type of non-white persons, as "yellow" and declared ineligible for naturalization. Furthermore, because the Chinese had been barred from legal entry to the United States under the Chinese Exclusion Acts, Svan and his group were also threatened with deportation.[3]

Just as the state of Mississippi struggled to define whiteness, the Minnesota courts wrestled to delineate the parameters of "the yellow race." Was Svan, born in Finland and calling himself white, really a Mongolian and hence Chinese? Were Finns actually white despite ethnological claims to a Mongol origin "in very remote times?" To the former, the lower courts answered in the affirmative, thus denying Finnish immigrants the right to citizenship and opening the path to their deportation as "illegal" immigrants. The issue, however, was far from settled, although Judge William A. Cant, deciding in Svan's favor, overturned the lower court's ruling, declaring in 1908 that "the Finnish people are not members of the yellow race."

Cant came to his conclusions in two ways, both of which are worth a little exploration. His first line of reasoning took on the issue of origins, and here he agreed with ethnologists that Finns were of Mongol origin. But Cant argued that such ancestries radically changed over time so that a number of groups said to be of Mongolian extraction were now "among the purest and best types of the Caucasian race." Furthermore, noted the judge, "the various groupings of the human race into families is arbitrary, and, as respects any particular people, is not permanent but subject to change and modification..." Having noted the mutability of human classifications and the apparent impermanence of racial "stock," Cant turned to what he believed was the only reliable measure of racial difference: the body, writing that:

> The chief physical characteristics of the Mongolians are as follows: They are short of stature, with little hair on the body or face: they have yellow-brown skins, black eyes, black hair, short flat noses, and oblique eyes. In actual experience we sometimes, though rarely, see natives of Finland whose eyes are slightly oblique. We sometimes see them with sparse beards and sometimes with flat noses; but Finns with a yellow or brown or yellow-brown skin or with black eyes or black hair would be an unusual sight. They are almost universally of light skin, blue or gray eyes, and light hair.

Indeed, in Cant's opinion they had the lightest skin of any foreign-born person "applying for the full rights of citizenship" in the region. Svan won his case, then, because the judge believed Finns to be white even though they had once been "yellow." "The question," declared the judge, "is not whether a person had or had not such an ancestry, but whether he is now a 'white person' *within the meaning of that term as generally understood*" (emphasis added). Race, in other words, existed only to the extent that people "generally understood" it, and social value accrued in relation to the body's proximity to whiteness. What Svan understood was that his looks had the power to make him citizen or pariah, an American or an "illegal," depending upon the particular social meanings afforded at any given time. As Matthew Frye Jacobson argues, "social and political meanings... generate a kind of physiognomical surveillance" that renders racial difference into a particular set of physical traits. "The visible markers may then be interpreted as outer signs of an essential, immutable, inner moral-intellectual character; and that character, in turn – attested to by physical 'difference' – is summoned up to explain the social value attached...in the first place."[4] Had the Finns *looked* like Mongolians, the official eye would have seen "yellow" and defined them as "undesirable aliens."

What becomes difficult to fully appreciate in the racially and ethnically inflected world of today is the degree to which categories like race and ethnicity, as well as gender and even sex, emerge in power-charged, unequal situations. As a measure of difference and as a marker of some "body" – the "colored" infant, the "mulatto" boy, the "yellow" Finn, even the "white" parents – race became part of a modern regulatory force spawned in the service of white supremacy.[5]

Like all modern categories then, race is "unreal"; more a regulatory ideal than a stable identity. It exists, that is not in the body but rather as part of a complex discourse about bodily difference that depended upon and helped shape modern habits of seeing. To simultaneously look, order, and rank the body of others according to culturally shaped codes of taste and meaning was not new to Mississippi. As we shall see, the modern body was a coded site. The modern body had tales to tell.

But how did these codes develop? Why did they take on such importance in modern life? When did physical appearance, bodily shape, and skin color become central modes of classification, hierarchy, and differentiation? By what alchemy does a Finn become a Mongolian, a Mongolian "yellow," "the white man" a colorless figure, "a Negroid" a specific percentage of blackness, an Italian something in between? Where did state officials like Tom Scarborough or Judge Cant learn that a half-moon on a child's cuticles was a sign of African or "mixed" parentage? Or that Mongolians were "yellow-brown"? More intriguing still is how an untrained mother in Mississippi could beat state officials at their own game by employing visual codes of heredity only to turn them on their head. Her shrewdness warns us as well that the state was not alone in its fascination with the social meanings of the body and its telltale parts. Indeed, as Trillin tells it, the physical inspections of Scarborough brought back memories of his own youth in Missouri where popular wisdom held it that Japanese people had yellow blood. Like much of the South's obsession with what Trillin aptly calls "yard-sale anthropology," such physical differences became popular indices of mental and moral character. "Any number of white people," recalled Trillin, "would explain to me...that the brains of black people were capable of processing specific statements but not general or abstract statements." As in Minnesota fifty years earlier, the characteristics of the body signified a "race," a "race" marked a body, the marked body then rose or fell according to the anthropological codes of the street, the yard, the country store, the university, the courthouse. Visual indexing was never benign or neutral.

The City as Theater

Because narratives of identity take shape and derive meaning in and through a system of differences, the physical minutiae of bodies take on heightened importance in modern societies where, as the German philosopher Martin Heidegger observed, "the world becomes picture."[6] Visual detection and physical differentiation become a constant, if unrecognized, practice of everyday life. Indeed, both Scarborough and Judge Cant were following a long tradition of scientific convention that sought to measure (and thus rank) racial differences through anatomical characteristics. Enlarged half-moons at the cuticles of a child's fingers conformed to nineteenth-century racial taxonomies that suggested an affinity to "non-Aryan" populations. In some ways, of course, the MSSC was unique in the annals of American history, but if Mississippi state officials were unusual in their diligence in tracking down and rooting out racial mixing and preserving the purity of white Caucasians, they were certainly not alone in their attempt to link political sovereignty, social stability, and cultural identity with notions of racial purity and sexual restraint. Indeed, by conflating the body politic with "white" bodies, and by representing the social body with images of the physical body (the head of state, the arm of the law, etc.) state officials in Mississippi were speaking a symbolic language that many nineteenth-century Americans would have understood. The very "minutiae" that fascinated investigators – a person's cuticles, the contours of a nose, the texture of hair, and even the lilt of a voice – obsessed the Victorian middle classes, who suffered from what some scholars refer to as a "semiotic breakdown," a confusion of signs. As historian John Kasson points out, urban Americans needed to decode the city by learning how to "read" it. "Of all the voluminous texts produced in the nineteenth century," writes Kasson, "among the most massive and challenging were the new metropolises themselves. They were recognized by writers of all sorts as the great signifying structures of the age: vast, intricate repositories, dense with meaning, out of which more specific texts might be created."[7]

To read such a text, however, was not an easy task. By the late nineteenth century urban populations were rapidly increasing, with rates as high as 50 percent in some decades. The growth of very large cities such as Chicago, New York, and San Francisco was by any measure spectacular. New York City increased its population fourfold between 1860 and 1910, while Chicago, "the wonder of the West," was home to just over 2 million by 1910. Even smaller towns like Omaha, Kansas City, Wichita, and Minneapolis

21

experienced rapid demographic change and striking growth. It was the large metropolitan areas, however, that reflected the magnitude of change that became the hallmark of modernism. Self-supporting women, wealthy moguls, struggling artisans, prostitutes, factory workers, Anglo-American business-men, middle-class shoppers, African American seamen, and newly arrived immigrants shared city streets, trolley cars, workplaces, neighborhoods, and places of leisure. As face-to-face patterns of deference weakened and finally collapsed, new public spaces emerged where social identities could be masked, and/or created.

As urban populations increased and diversified, new social arrangements and possibilities emerged, as did a wide range of confusing and, at times, beguiling social "types." By 1900, "mashers," "dandies," "flirts," "snoozers," "flim-flam men," "swells," and "bowery gals" comprised only a few of the new types to walk down metropolitan sidewalks and onto the social imagination of modern American.[8] Far more troubling to the respectable classes, however, was the urban imposter who found in the anonymity of the city the means to conceal his or her "real" identity and character. In stories such as Edgar Allan Poe's "The Man of the Crowd" or Herman Melville's *The Confidence Man*, social deception and detection became highly charged themes that resonated with a public besieged by tabloid exposés of men and women living "double lives," of daring masquerades, and countless stories of forgeries and counter-feits. "The line that separated a shopper from a shoplifter, a gentleman from a confidence man, and respectability from criminality," Kasson notes, "could be disturbingly thin" in the modern city.[9] Simply by adopting the codes, mannerisms, and postures of the genteel, urban imposters – male and female – could shield themselves and their villainy from the eyes of both the authorities and their victims. "Perhaps the real crime of the confidence man," notes the sociologist Erving Goffman, "is not that he takes money from his victims but that he robs all of us of the belief that middle-class manners and appearance can be sustained only by middle-class people."[10] To enter the modern city was to negotiate a landscape of subterfuge and charade.

The fantastic nature of the modern metropolis put new pressure on one's ability to read a face, to interpret correctly the character, even the emotion, underneath the clothing, or behind the manner and, especially, the facial expression. In the new and fashionable "department stores" where even "ladies went a-thieving," managers valued store clerks and detectives for their skills in the popular art and "science" of physiognomy and phrenology, the belief that character, behavior, and even intelligence could be *seen* in, and thus determined by, the shape and/or position of a person's head, nose, ears, or brow. As historian Elaine Abelson points out, in the ambiguous and often chaotic environment of the department store, shoplifting, especially among the seemingly well coifed and well to do, posed new problems in criminal detection, shoring up the belief among dry-goods management that "the best clerk is a reader of human nature."[11]

But for others the modern metropolis seemed thoroughly unreadable, a nefarious landscape where deception and trickery, rudeness and chaos, greeted the respectable at every corner. Overwhelmed by the complexity and human diversity of Boston in 1900, writer Henry James found the modern city "illegible," a tangle of confusion, a riot of "multiplicity," and he joined a generation of Americans who both sought and helped to create a visual language with which to negotiate its landscape and understand its terrain. How to represent oneself in the midst of such multiplicity? How to read others? And, most importantly, how to make clear these differences and shore up the boundaries between the respectable and the vulgar and distinguish the "authentic" from the counterfeit, the civilized from the savage, the "man" from the "stuffed shirt" or the "sissified" – in short, between "us" and "them"?

The Art and Politics of Modern Detection

As early as 1850, technological inventions such as photography provided at least a partial solution for those who sought to "tame" urban life by exposing its dangerous classes. In Boston, police had developed a weekly "show-up of rogues" whereby petty thieves, known troublemakers, and other suspicious persons were paraded before department operatives who wrote down their physical descriptions and memorized their features in hopes of "getting a spot" of the criminal as he or she walked the streets or mingled among unsuspecting crowds.[12] But "spotting" was at best an imprecise and tedious affair in a city of several thousands and it had the disadvantage of exposing the face of the policeman to the suspect. The photograph, on the other hand, allowed operatives to see without being seen. Hanging the portraits of suspected felons on department walls in a "rogues' gallery," police could study the criminal face undetected. Rogues' galleries also provided victims with a means of identifying their assailants without having to "spot" and round up the "usual suspects." But perhaps the most powerful result of the police photo was its ability to shore up and popularize the "scientific" links between anatomy and character.

As early as the 1830s, American proponents of phrenology and physiognomy found a large audience for the claim that the outward appearance of the body, especially the head and face, bore the clues to inner character. Based on what was actually an ancient belief, phrenology took on new importance in the 1770s when the Swiss theologian Johann Casper Lavater systematized visual precepts of physiognomy by isolating the skull in order to map the mental faculties hidden in the brain but revealed in the contours, shape, and size of the head and face.[13] Both "sciences" depended on an interpretive process whereby physical characteristics such as the size and shape of ears, brow, chin, eyes, nose, etc., conformed to specific types. Encouraged by many self-styled "professors" whose lucrative "How To" books and lecture tours brought widespread prestige to phrenology and physiognomy, an enthusiastic public set out to master these interpretive codes. To be sure, phrenology had its critics, including a highly skeptical Mark Twain. When Huck Finn's companion, the fast-talking Duke of Bridgewater, promotes himself up and down the Mississippi as the "celebrated Dr. Armand de Montalban of Paris who would lecture on the Science of Phrenology at ten cents admission, and furnish charts of character at twenty-five cents apiece," readers no doubt recognized a scoundrel at work. But in its desire to map the "inner" man or woman with the outward compass of the body phrenology discovered its own enduring appeal. Long after it had been discredited as a pseudo-science in the late nineteenth century it continued to play a significant role in popular culture as a kind of "yardsale" or "commonsense" anthropology through which one could casually decipher in the bodies of strangers the supposedly hidden terrain of temperament, character, and morality. Indeed, as the childhood memories of Calvin Trillin attest, the lessons of Dr. Armand de Montalban continued to flow up and over the Mississippi well into the 1960s.

It was the police photograph, however, that helped keep physiognomy in the public eye long after the "How To" books faded from view. A product of both new methodologies and technologies, the "mug" shot systematized topologies of the body, bringing emblematic images of "the criminal" into focus and into the social imagination. The rogues' gallery generated as well a new logic of seeing: the art of the "public look," what historian Allan Sekula describes as "a look up at one's 'betters' and a look down at one's 'inferiors.'" The specimen-like photograph ascribes value to particular images by both quantifying the body and its characteristics and placing them in a circulating system that continually measures their worth and value by emphasizing their similarity to, or difference from, other sorts or categories. In the case of the gallery, the look of the vicious is observed in relation to that of the virtuous. Embedded within the visual empiricism that supposedly served "to distinguish the stigmata of vice from the shinning marks of virtue," was a social and moral hierarchy that implicitly framed every private look and marked each individual body. The portraits of criminals were viewed not with innocent eyes of objectivity, but with eyes already practiced in the art of the "public look." The continually comparative and relational act of looking thus shadowed the modern photographic experience, turning what on the surface appears a simple response to technological innovation into a profoundly complex and powerful cultural practice of image-making and social meaning. "We can speak then," writes Sekula, "of a generalized, inclusive *archive*, a *shadow archive* that encompasses an entire social terrain while positioning individuals within that terrain."[14] The private moments of looking were always and also social moments of public spectatorship.

Here we would do well to remember that the terms "daguerreotype" and "stereotype" came into popular discourse together.[15] The former recognized the French inventor Louis Jacques Daguerre's 1839 method for fixing an image onto a silver plate, but over time it came to connote the type of precision and detail representative of this type of photographic picture-making.[16] Stereotype, on the other hand, was a method of duplication introduced in the early nineteenth century to standardize plates cast from a printing surface or mold. By mid-century it was widely used to indicate a generalized kind of reproduction. The archive described by Sekula drew its logic from the slippage between these two realms: the details of the daguerreotype and the generalized form of the stereotype. By holding up to public scrutiny the bodily characteristics and faces of criminals and rogues who were then arranged and ordered in relation to each other, the complex relationship between the specifics of the daguerreotype and the generic codes of the stereotype collapsed. In their place emerged the banal image of "the type."[17] Because both physiognomy and phrenology were built around comparative, taxonomic classifications that sought to both quantify and display the entire range of human diversity, Sekula implicates them in the hierarchical construction of the very archive they claim to interpret. These disciplines, in other words, did not simply sort out and arrange bodily types, but, in very real ways, they worked to invent them.

To be sure, "the type" could be read in a multitude of ways, but because the criminal archive was constructed and organized as a means to identify deviations from a "norm," it simultaneously reflected and produced a standard or non-criminal body against which the "criminal type" was measured. This new logic of seeing received additional support from emerging theories of heredity which argued that criminality was in fact innate, a product less of poverty and environment than of evolution run amuck. Loosely formulated around the theories of the Italian physician Cesare Lombroso, *l'uomo delinquente*, or "the criminal man," was believed to reside in some unfortunate individuals whose savage ancestral past, normally dormant, comes suddenly alive.[18] Thrown back in evolutionary time, these born criminals act as "normal" savages or apes might, but because such acts are committed in civilized time they are deemed abnormal. Lombroso came to his conclusions in the 1870s after studying the anatomical differences between criminals and insane men and discovering a set of atavistic features on the skull of one notorious rogue. "This was not merely an idea," Lombroso tells us, "but a flash of inspiration":

> At the sight of that skull, I seemed to see all of a sudden, lighted up as a vast plain under a flaming sky, the problem of the nature of the criminal – an atavistic being who reproduces in his person the ferocious instincts of primitive humanity and the inferior animals. Thus were explained anatomically the enormous jaws, high cheek bones, prominent superciliary arches, solitary lines in the palms, extreme size of the orbits, handle-shaped ears found in criminals, savages and apes, insensibility to pain, extremely acute sight, tattooing, excessive idleness, love of orgies, and the irresponsible craving of evil for its own sake, the desire not only to extinguish life in the victim, but to mutilate the corpse, tear its flesh and drink its blood.[19]

As biologist Stephen Jay Gould points out in his study of biological determinism, aptly entitled *The Mismeasurement of Man*, Lombroso's theory gave specificity to otherwise vague notions that claimed crime to be hereditary. "Such claims," notes Gould, "were common enough at the time – but a specific *evolutionary* theory based upon anthropometric data" promoted the belief that criminal behavior was inherent, a product of evolutionary biology. "The Criminal" was thus categorized not only as a social type but as a biological "throwback" whose atavism, while both mental and physical, could be read from decisive "stigmata" that marked the physical body.[20] A formidable buttress to the belief that anatomy was destiny, Lombroso's theories invited observers of all sorts to identify and define both the marks of atavism and those "types" marked by them.

Reading Lombroso's "flash of inspiration" we can readily see the importance of appearance and the visual field in the construction and detection of modern types. Both store clerks and good detectives could literally "read a face." Brilliant detectives, it seemed, could also read thoughts. "Do you mean to say that you read my train of thoughts from my features?" asks an astounded Dr. Watson upon hearing Sherlock Holmes do just that. "The features are given to man as the means by which he shall express his emotions," explains a somewhat bored Holmes, "and yours are faithful servants."[21] For Lombroso and his followers, however, physical appearance expressed not simply emotions, but an aesthetic and moral standard based upon romanticized ideals of both classical beauty and "democratic" civilizations. The former was typically represented in the nineteenth century by the neoclassical arts, whose reinvented Greek bodies took on a highly sentimentalized and statuesque ideal of beauty: straight, chiseled noses, strong chins, and high foreheads. Reinscribed by art critics into a Caucasian, Anglo-Saxon type, this idealized body quickly became a popular standard against which derogatory images of non-Western (popularly termed non-Aryan) peoples were measured and judged.[22] At times, artist and anthropologist appeared to be in collusion as hundreds of so-called scientific monographs illustrated the physical similarities between the profiles of the "superior" Caucasian types and those of Apollo-like faces and skulls. "Non-Aryans" – such as the Irish, French, and Africans – on the other hand, were sketched in relation to living specimens deemed closer to their "type" and character. In one highly regarded book on comparative physiognomy, for example, the Irishman is paired with a "scrounging, yapping, terrier dog," a Frenchman with a series of frogs, and the "Creole Negro" with a young chimpanzee.[23] The pictorial criterion for the culturally superior and civilized was, on the other hand, a highly idealized "Greek" type. If not all moderns looked like Apollo in their person, they did when compared to, and remodeled as, their own "best" type. Art becomes life.

Indeed, so popular was this reinvented ideal of classical beauty that hundreds of cities in nineteenth-century America commissioned sculptors to commemorate revolutionary heroes by carving their images with the Apollo-like features of Greek statuary. George Washington, the most popular subject for classical representation, was thus repeatedly chiseled from pure white marble, one arm typically held tightly over a draping toga while the other gestured as if in debate at the public forum. But it was the French sculptor Bartholdi who no doubt did more than most to enshrine the classical body into the American imagination when he presented the Statue of Liberty to New York City in 1886. Deeply influenced by the ideal of classic female beauty, he designed his "daughter Liberty" to look the part of a classical goddess, and even today her visage embodies the visual power of this invented type. It is easy to forget, for instance, that this "bearer of a million dreams" once competed with another powerful and popular type of female figure, Miss Columbia, who was widely depicted not as a Greek or Roman, but as a more ambiguous figure who frequently wore an American Indian headdress.[24] By 1900, however, Bartholdi's visual ideal had become the measure of the "best" type: what popular commentators soon regarded as "the American face."[25]

We can begin to appreciate some of the visual complexity that marked modern practices of everyday detection by briefly recalling older forms of sleuthing. During the eighteenth century, for example, the identification and classification of criminals and rogues grew out of their own specialized forms of subterfuge, such as the sham deaf-mute, the fake shipwrecked sailor, or the sighted "blind beggars" whose tin cups rattled the conscience of the bourgeois urbanite.[26] Both Lombroso's theories and the modern archive, however, significantly shifted attention away from types of crime to types of criminals. As in phrenology, crime was believed to be a kind of disease, but whereas phrenology treated crime as a moral disease that could be corrected with proper treatment, the American followers of Lombroso, many of them physicians, adopted a more biological model. If crime was a disease with physiological roots, they argued, then the criminal was not simply a different kind of person; he was "a separate species – the criminal type."[27]

Such arguments emerged in tandem with specific longings among many Americans to see Africans and Indians as a separate and distinct type of humanity. The theory of polygenesis, the belief that certain races of mankind are in fact a separate species, received wide currency and fueled arguments that claimed blacks to be nonhuman, that is a mere sub-species of *Homo sapiens*. Formulated on the eve of the American Civil War, such arguments held great appeal to slaveholders who sought to justify slavery and defend their right to own Africans. But to theorists like Harvard professor Louis Agassiz and Dr. Samuel Morton, whose work on "separate creation" became the basis of the American School of Ethnology, polygenesis was the product of science, not politics. "We disclaim," declared Agassiz in 1850, "all connection with any question involving political matters."[28] Here, of course, the problem of fact and fiction, of real things and things made up, confronts us once again. As Galileo found out, science can profoundly alter and destabilize the social order by challenging the very conceptual systems that gave it birth. It can and has brought down regimes of oppressive dogma, and it can also illuminate a factual reality, as Gould points out: the earth is not flat.[29] But science is also embedded in the culture that surrounds it and is thus never free of politics. Despite disclaimers to the contrary, the topological systems that sought to "scientifically" analyze physical differences between European whites and African blacks could not escape the cultural constraints that nurtured them.

The problem, in other words, is not that Agassiz manufactured data to support his views about the superiority of the white "race," but rather that his data were already a manufactured product of modern habits of seeing. Based upon photos that compared the physical bodies of individual slaves from Southern plantations, his study simultaneously depended upon and helped establish two central "truths": that "science is disinterested empiricism," and that photography is transparently real. The proof, in other words, was to be found in the data and not in the narrative traditions that gave them meaning – in this case, in the seemingly unblemished topological photograph whose claims to objectivity and reality were held to be both obvious and self-evident.

The idea, initially formulated in European scientific journals, was to create a global photographic archive (not unlike that of the rogues' gallery) that would represent all human specimens. Agassiz hoped to contribute to such an archive by arranging to have black male and female slaves captured from various African regions photographed to determine their differences from other races and types. Agassiz's ethnographic research thus mirrored the physiognomic practices employed by criminologists and others who saw in the photograph a tool enabling an impartial methodology. Photographs, after all, don't lie. But as recent scholars have made clear, neither do they tell the truth, nor show "reality." Indeed, it is the "seeming transparency of photographic realism" that critics see as implicating them even more thoroughly in the production of illusion and distortion.[30] They might produce what Roland Barthes calls a "reality effect," but this is not the same thing as reality. This is because topological photos, like Lombroso's classificatory project, were highly comparative in that they depended upon relational images and the cumulative effects of measurement and ordering. Like the "mug shot" they demanded the creation of a norm or a standard against which to evaluate or judge the "evidence." The body, displayed in photographic sequence and held up next to different types, thus played a critical role in formulating the "look" of physiognomical "difference" and of the racialized other. It also signaled the normal and abnormal, the standard and the deviant, the "best" or "right" type and the "wrong" type. Like the image they purported to capture, photographs were hardly the unmediated truth of the natural body.

Such methodologies, in other words, could not be objective because, while science could record body shape, posture, and proportion without reference to a standard, it could not *compare* or interpret the images of whites and blacks without reference to a pictorial hierarchy that enforced and created a set of divisions and rankings between an imaginary "us" and "them." Again, Allan Sekula argues that, "Since physiognomy and phrenology were comparative, taxonomic disciplines, they sought to encompass an entire range of human diversity. In this respect, these disciplines were instrumental in constructing the very archive they claimed to interpret."

But objectivity is further complicated by the narrative traditions that give trajectory and meaning to so-called raw data. To read a photograph in the archive of human topology around the turn of the twentieth century was, in other words, to read a tale of progress and civilization, of white supremacy and black inferiority, of male energy and female stasis. "Inspired" at the height of both European and American imperialism, signs of atavism – hairy brows, full lips, large jaws, high cheekbones, a low and receding forehead, but also tattooing, idleness, and "insensitivity to pain" – both mirrored and shaped anthropological observations and reports of whites working in Africa as well as in America. Viewed as signs of savage or primitive types, such features helped as well to justify in the minds of white Europeans and Americans the colonizing policies of imperialism. The physical characteristics of non-Anglo Europeans quickly became marks of inferior "savage" types; their customs, rituals, food ways, and traditions proof of their low, "animal-like" status on the evolutionary scale.

Perhaps the best way to appreciate the essential links between practices of racialization and economic expansion, and modernist narratives of civilization, progress, and advancement, is to look briefly at the curious business in Western societies of human display and the touring of "exotic" peoples for profit, entertainment, and education. The display of American "Indians" in London and Paris, of course, had thrilled Europeans as early as the sixteenth century, but by 1870 the practice took on new entrepreneurial zeal as paid agents combed remote regions of the globe for the sole purpose of procuring primitive types for public exhibition. Typically, these tours contained some claims to ethnographic authenticity, although showmen like Phineas T. Barnum appreciated as well the commercial value of including in his sideshow of oddities and freaks both the Wild Man of Borneo and Fijian man-eaters.[31] By the second half of the nineteenth century, however, the display of "primitives" took place as an essential part of industrial expositions, or "world's fairs." These were enormous undertakings that brought together government officials, industrialists, and capitalists to promote and celebrate the marvel of Western development, especially technology and industrial innovation. The expositions entailed building temporary exhibit halls, such as London's Crystal Palace in 1851, as well as restaurants, midways, or as in the case of the 1893 World's Columbian Exposition in Chicago, an entire "White City" comprised of dazzling bright marble and palatial reflecting pools.

Organizers, however, did more than just display machines. By incorporating "primitive peoples" into the exposition, they hoped to create for fairgoers an understandable narrative of Western triumph over darkness, of civilization over savagery, of progress over stasis. In New York, Philadelphia, St. Louis, San Francisco, and numerous other American cities, world fairs thus touted the nation's progress by putting on display technological innovations in juxtaposition with exhibits of non-white populations. Cast as the human remnants of a primitive past, the indigenous peoples of Africa, America, Asia, the Middle East, and the Pacific Rim became the yardstick by which fairgoers could measure and understand both progress and "the future." As one organizer put it, "The fair...would illustrate 'the steps of progress of civilization and its arts in successive centuries, and in all lands up to the present time.' It would become, 'in fact, an illustrated encyclopedia of humanity.'"[32] In the narrative structure of the industrial exposition, "primitive" people were essential because they helped define and give meaning to the "modern."

Indeed, without indigenous peoples to embody the "primitive" how could one recognize the civilized? It was exactly this problem of defining and identifying "our race" that worried Frederick Ward Putnam, director and curator of the Peabody Museum at Harvard, and head of the Ethnology and Archaeology Department, for the Chicago fair:

> But what will all this amount to without the means of comparison in the great object lesson? What, then, is more appropriate, more essential, than to show in their natural conditions of life the different types of peoples who were here when Columbus was crossing the Atlantic Ocean and leading the way for the great wave of humanity that was soon spread over the continent and forced

those unsuspecting peoples to give way before a mighty power, to resign their inherited rights, and take their chances for existence under the laws governing a strange people? The great object lesson then will not be completed without their being present. Without them, the Exposition will have no base.

Strolling down the midway and into the anthropological building, fairgoers could thus marvel at the distance that separated them not only from the donkey-boys of Cairo and the Samoan natives in their re-enacted villages, but also from the paddles of Greenland Eskimos, the tepees of the Crow Indians, and the canoes of the Micmacs. Here was the baseline with which to both measure progress and formulate the Modern. By definition, indigenous peoples had no future.

For most Americans, however, their first and usually only look at "exotic" populations was enabled by pictorial representations in the new mass-circulation publications such as newspapers and magazines, and, increasingly, through the illustrated encyclopedias aimed at middlebrow readers and their families. By the 1890s entire populations were envisioned along an axis of civilization and savagery. Organized, categorized, and ranked in an ascending order based upon the optical measures of physiology, images of generic racial "types" flooded mass publications. In popular encyclopedias like *The Book of Knowledge*, hundreds of topological images accentuated head shape, facial hair, skin color, and the kinds of physical characteristics believed to characterize their "race." As art historians have pointed out, these kinds of topological photos differed significantly from conventions of portraiture in which the artist sought to express the individuality of the subject. Here, style and composition are a fundamental concern. The type, however, whether displayed in the rogues' gallery or in the *Book of Knowledge*, works to obscure the individual by emphasizing the body as a representational form of many others. What are subjective distortions and composite images are made to appear as objective facts by presenting the type in a straightforward and non-stylistic manner. The portrait, for example, seeks to convey abstract meaning by showing the subject "in thought" or with particular items and adornments that signify individuality. By contrast, the "type" simply embodies a subject by using a minimum of external information. As art historian Brian Wallis notes, "The emphasis on body occurs at the expense of speech; the subject as already positioned, known, owned, represented, spoken for, or constructed as silent; in short, it is ignored." In the "type" the complexities of diversity and individual difference diminish and grow mute.

Because "types" took on form and meaning during a period of intense economic expansion and global competition, they entered into modern habits of seeing as a form of "representational colonialism."[33] Behind every photographic type or representational model, in other words, stood the shadow of whiteness, now a trope for civilization and modern progress against which the typologies of non-Westerners would be measured and evaluated. At the top of the scale stood civilization and progress, while at the bottom lingered the primitive and savage. At times, rankings would be subtly refined, as when Madison Grant in his enormously popular book, *The Passing of the Great Race* (1916), moved Indians a step up from the bottom by placing them with Mongoloids and Nordics instead of with "the Negro," whom white supremacists typically placed at the bottom of their charts.

Despite such fine-tuning, representations of savagery seldom varied. In the highly charged atmosphere of turn-of-the-century America, where Jim Crow laws and white lynch mobs were deepening racial divisions in both the north and south, black men were frequently burdened by tropes of savagery, their claims to both manhood and civilization denied by their supposedly "natural" tendency to vice, violence, and brutality, the traits of "normal" savages. As Gail Bederman argues, it was only by constructing "the Negro" as "unmanly and outside civilization" that notions of "the white man" could be made meaningful as the mark of civilization. Indeed, by 1890 and continuing well into the twentieth century, the term "the white man" became virtually synonymous with the term "civilization." As Bederman points out, "The trope was meaningless unless it was juxtaposed to a reference to non-white races." Rudyard Kipling defined "The White Man's burden" as the mission to civilize savage races, while the editors of the Arena entitled a symposium on several nonwhite ethnic groups, "The White Man's Problem."[34] Conversely, the Negro, like the Indian, was represented in opposition to the "whiteness" of civilized manhood. Take, for example, the remarks of two popular journalists of the Progressive era describing the problem of lynching: "The Negro," writes Edward C. Gordon, "is especially prone to certain crimes of violence which are particularly obnoxious to the white man... The Negro must, like the Indian, go down and out before the white man..." And here's the muckraker Ray Standard Baker calling for an end to lynching:

> Nothing more surely tends to bring the white man down to the lowest level of the criminal Negro than yielding to those blind instincts of savagery which find expression in the mob. The man who joins a mob, by his very acts, puts himself on a level with the Negro criminal: both have given way to brute passion. For if civilization means anything, it means self-restraint; casting away self-restraint the white man becomes as savage as the Negro.[35]

By avoiding, as Bederman points out, the logical use of a parallel construction which would have situated the "the Negro man" (or "the Indian man") in tandem with "the white man," popular discourses like these "linked white supremacy, male dominance, and evolutionary advancement in one powerful figure. He ["The white man"] embodied the notion that non-white men were neither manly nor civilized."[36] But popular discourses like these reinforced as well an almost blanket criminalization of the Negro, a term increasingly indistinguishable from those repeatedly paired with it, such as: "brute passion," "savagery," "animal," and "baseness."

It should come as no surprise then, that as a new generation of social scientists and reformers turned their gaze on the nation's increasingly diverse and heterogeneous population, they found a world of both difference and danger. In the images they used, the stereotypes they produced, and the metaphors they deployed, writers, politicians, journalists, reformers, and artists charted an American underworld as strange and alien as the "Dark Continent." Inhabited by "the dangerous classes" or, as Lombroso preferred, "the under-class," the geography of the down-and-out emerged in the minds of armchair explorers and vicarious adventurers, a disturbingly foreign country: an urban "underbrush" that teamed with strange beings, "savage brutes," and "primitives" of all types. These included not only the waves of "new" immigrants that began to flood American cities between 1890 and 1924, but also many of the children of "old" immigrants – Irish men and women, Native Americans, Finns, and poor children of all sorts who eked out a living as unskilled workers and migrants in factories, shops, boarding-houses, canneries, fields, and mills. It included as well those populations excluded by law from citizenship: the descendants of African men and women, and immigrants from Asia and the Pacific Rim.

But the world of the "dangerous classes" was more than simply a racialized or class-inflected trope used by middle-class Americans to describe others. It also worked to create them. The figure of the domestic "Dark Continent" emerged out of deep-seated fears and anxieties on the part of many ordinary Americans over the increasing fluidity and instability of modern life. All that seemed fixed and certain in the decades of Victorian America now seemed to fall apart as the new century approached. The imagined existence of an "underclass" allowed the respectable classes to both distance themselves from those who had indeed fallen, not only apart, but also "down and out," and to contain those elements in the modern world that seemed most capable of disrupting the codes of "civilization." Unlike radicals and revolutionaries however, who frightened the established order because of what they said and hoped to do, those within the "dangerous classes" troubled authority because they operated below the level of official scrutiny. Like the remote peoples of Africa or Asia, they seemed to live hidden lives in queer places maintaining their own rules, values, and secret codes. They were, wrote social gospel leader Walter Rauschenbusch, an "unknown race." Their very bodies – the hue of their skin, their "shifty" eyes, their "frightful looks," even the clothes they wore, or, more infuriating still, "mis-wore," became the modern embodiment of social devolution and moral anarchy. Together with the immigrant, the poor, and the non-white, the growing ranks of other liminal types – the feeble-minded, the homeless tramp, the sexually non-conforming, the trans-gendered, even the adolescent – provided in modern society a kind of phantasmagoric "Other" against which "normality" and "Americanness" itself came to be defined and discursively fixed in the social imagination. Seeing was believing.

By 1900, millions of Americans thus entered America's streets and the social imagination less as individuals with rights to personhood than as representative types dramatically at odds with the civilized world. Stamped by an overwhelming sense of pernicious otherness, their foreignness appeared both strange and illicit. Indeed, as Lombroso's followers argued, criminality itself appeared as normal behavior among the shadowy denizens of the underclass. Yet, whether figured as savages, primitives, an "unknown race," inverts, or feeble-minded, the "dangerous classes" provided the conceptual glue with which anxious middle classes hoped to shore up and piece together the flimsy fabric of their own nationhood. By defining who and what they were not, they simultaneously imagined and invented who they were. Like the criminals whose portraits hung in the rogues' gallery, the nineteenth-century underclass was thus twice framed: once by the material practices that displayed their bodies to the public gaze, and again by the stereotypical images of essentialized difference that visually fixed and summoned up identities of otherness. The traditional cry of the falsely accused – "I've been framed" – was perhaps far truer than even the modern rogue suspected.

Botanizing the Asphalt

By 1900 the art of looking became both a powerful and prosaic practice of modern life which frequently blurred the distinctions between social types and biological traits. Readers of the increasingly popular genre of social-scientific writing learned, for example, of a new type, "The Tramp," whose exploits and dangers filled the pages of both the tabloid press and the middlebrow magazine. The careful reader learned as well that the tendency among certain types of the poor to wander about the countryside in search of food and a job resulted in a "gipsylike" character that would require gener-ations to "breed out of their progeny." What had for centuries in Europe been a problem of poverty and homelessness – of social inequality and the unequal distribution of wealth – became, in the minds of modern Americans, a problem less of history and power than of heredity and "bad stock." The tramp, it appeared, was both a modern type and a biological possibility: it (rather than poverty and inequality) could reproduce itself.

This is not to say, however, that writers of the "underclass" agreed with Lombroso who so named them. Often, in fact, the reverse was true. In a very popular 1901 exposé, *Tramping with Tramps*, Josiah Flynt took his clues not from the hereditarian school of criminal anthropology, but from Progressive ideas that emphasized the influence of environment and history over racial formalism and biological determinism. Yet, as one student of "down-and-out" literature points out, Flynt's portrayal of the tramp was a contradictory combination of explicit rejection and implicit emulation of hereditarian thinking. Like an "entomologist poring over his specimens," Flynt collated his tramps into "classes," "species," and "subspecies" according to apparently physiognomically expressed and inherited traits even as he denied their essential difference from members of other social classes.[37] In effect, argues Mark Pittenger, Flynt's text did as much to construct as to describe a world where the working poor and the home itinerant lived a shadowy existence that was "fundamentally different – a strange breed in classless America."[38] "Botanizing the asphalt" – to use Walter Benjamin's phrase – the urban explorer and social investigator simultaneously protested and graphically depicted a topography of difference that gave to unstable identities and social problems a narrative structure of visual strangeness and immutable otherness.

As with explorers to the Dark Continent, the way into the American underclass was through fieldwork and observation. The domestic trek was both "down and out" and it was marked by a combination of reform, education, admiration, and voyeurism. "I went to Paterson," wrote the young journalist John Reed, "to watch it." Stirred by what he saw in the silk city during the strike of 1913, Reed returned to New York City, quit his job, and dedicated himself to bringing the story of industrial workers – "the wretchedness of their lives and the glory of their revolt" – into the imaginative repertoire of genteel readers, As he "watched" Paterson, the artist John Sloan "peeped" at his rear-window neighbors on Manhattan's 23rd Street. "I am in the habit of *watching every bit* of human life I can see about my windows," wrote Sloan in his diary. I peep," he explained, "through real interest, not being watched myself."[39] Others, like reformers Marie Van Vorst and her sister-in-law Mrs. John Van Vorst, joined Flynt by cloaking their peeping in the new garb of social science: participant observation and social documentation. They watched by going undercover. Like Flynt they dressed for the part, exchanging their sealskin coats and kid gloves for the gray serge and wool of a working woman's budget. Disguised as workers, these two "gentlewomen" entered the ranks of the working class as Bell Ballard and Esther Kelly, names they believed would reflect the dull simplicity of the common worker. Many others, however, simply strolled into the working-class districts of nearby industrial towns or, on special occasions, took the ferry to Ellis Island to promenade along the upper balconies and to see for themselves America's exotic new arrivals from eastern and southern Europe. In the decades that bridged the nineteenth and twentieth centuries, explains Martha Banta, "image-making and image-reading had become a major cultural activity."[40]

Because immigrants and the poor seemed as alien and remote to the middle classes as did the populations of the non-Western world, it is not surprising that image-makers deployed a similar set of metaphors and images to recount their experiences among the denizens of the "underbrush." Tenements in New York City thus became both exotic and dangerous places, "a jungle abounding in treacherous quicksand," or at times, "a swamp in which any misstep may plunge you into the choking depths of a quagmire or the coils of a slimy reptile." Here too was a whiff of imperial anthropology as middle-class observers longingly noted a pre-modern sense of spontaneity and simplicity among the poor. The Van Vorsts waxed poetic over the "primitive love of ornament" which New York's knitting-mill girls displayed, while undercover explorer Francis Donovan marveled at the "vulgarity and robustness of primitive life everywhere" along her travels into the world of the waitress.[41] To the popular author Jack London they were both a "new race," and a "People of the Abyss." The Dark Continent had moved to America.

As image-making and image-reading became major cultural activities in America, so too did they become a primary means for understanding and interpreting social difference and economic inequality. Those who became (either because of their poverty, their skin color, or simply their looks) the "Other" increasingly figured as a species apart: a people who appeared, as one social investigator wrote in 1898, "widely severed from all things human."[42] From this perspective poverty and race could be seen as the product, not of politics and history, but of culture and biology, a position recently reintro-duced with little modification by anthropologist Oscar Lewis, whose classic work *The Culture of Poverty* has had just this effect on policy-makers today. In newspapers, encyclopedias, magazines, museums, novels, plays, and, by 1914, feature films, Americans learned both the visual codes that marked modern "types" and a way to ensure their segregated position on the margins of modern life.

Yet as looking relations took on new importance for modern Americans at the turn of the century, appearance and physical typologies grew increasingly problematic in the scientific community. Franz Boas, who had served as Frederick Ward Putnam's chief assistant at the World's Columbian Exposition in 1893, launched a series of attacks on racial formalism and argued that biological determinism was more the result of politics and national chauvinism than of thoughtful study. America's imperialist activities in the 1898 Spanish–American War, along with the rising tide of both racist and anti-immigrant sentiment in the first decades of the century, convinced him and many other academics that anthropology in general, and museum display in particular, could be easily manipulated and exploited by those who hoped to profit in either cash or cultural capital. "The American who is cognizant only of his own standpoint," wrote Boas on the eve of World War I, "sets himself up as arbiter of the world."[43] After two decades of jingoist rhetoric and global expansion, Boas retreated from public anthropology and turned to the study of ritual as a source of wisdom and history in human cultures. Boas's ideas, especially those concerning cultural relativism, gained popularity and widespread credibility in the 1930s and 1940s, through works by Margaret Mead, Ruth Benedict, and Gunnar Myrdal among others.

Academics were not only critics of visual detection. Criminology itself underwent new scrutiny as the amateur sleuth and genteel reader of character became replaced by a professional corps of detectives, floorwalkers, and police. All agreed: the modern criminal was simply too well versed in the habits and haberdashery of the respectable to depend on the untrained eye of the amateur. Cross-class passing could, at least in the mind's eye, go both ways. To the professional detective, the science of phrenology seemed to lack the precision now required to detect "the criminal man," or, in some cases, "the criminal woman." Recalling the career of Catherine Bloch, who successfully shoplifted at New York's finest department stores for over thirty years, a former New York City detective who began his career in 1899, explained the problems of depending on ordinary visual empiricism:

> Catherine had the manner that makes department store managers bow on sight. Hard-boiled store detectives would give her a glance of respect whenever she appeared. She looked to be exactly what she represented herself to be, the wife of a rich and distinguished citizen ... her expensive clothing, her cultivated voice, her treatment of department store staff were just what might be expected from a matron of the "400".[44]

Because the modern criminal was capable of great deception in the manner of his or her dress, posture, and speech, detection was thought most effective when it depended upon the expert scrutiny of physical characteristics *combined with* a studied knowledge of criminal behavior. The ability to read human nature from physical evidence thus assumed heightened importance among a new class of professional detectives, including the controversial Allan Pinkerton, whose private detective agency recruited and trained the vast majority of undercover agents and company spies employed by the nation's manufacturers to break strikes and prevent union organizing.

But the modern detective also faced the problem of a congested and increasingly chaotic police archive of criminal images. The visual empiricism that marked modern modes of detection sagged under the weight of over-exposure. There were simply too many photos of too many faces to watch and observe. By 1890 the Pinkerton National Detective Agency, whose motto was "the eye that never sleeps," had amassed one of the largest criminal archives in the world. But the problem of identification persisted as the specificity of individual images overwhelmed the physiognomic standards of the day. By 1900, few departments of police maintained any faith in the practice of visual detection. Fingerprinting turned professional detection away from the representative type and towards the invisible mark of individual difference.

Nevertheless, racial and social topologies did not disappear, nor did popular reliance upon them. Between 1890 and 1930 popular interest accelerated as readers of magazines, newspapers, encyclopedias, and popular novels learned to decode the bodies of modern types. Some, as Banta notes, "trundled ashore, loaded down by the baggage of unfamiliar languages, customs, religions, and genes, under the watchful eye of the colossal American Girl set on her pedestal since 1886 in New York's harbor."[45] They would be joined by sharecroppers who trekked into southern and then into northern cities from rural farms and delta towns, by migrant farm workers who moved north and south, up and down the two coasts or between the borders of Mexico and Canada, by migrant cannery workers, and by an army of others whose social distinctions registered in the national mind's eye a physicality of Otherness that in turn confirmed and fixed their social difference. Half-moons at the cuticles, dark skin, "shifty eyes," low brows were clues to social value and national belonging. Scientifically discredited, the pseudo-science of physiognomy nevertheless continued to influence and shape modern habits of seeing. It was no accident, after all, that Agatha Christie, whose mystery novels would outsell all other books in the twentieth century, created as her first sleuth the amateur detective Anne Beddingfield, whose father "was one of England's greatest living authorities on Primitive Man." Puzzled over the disappearance of "The Man in the Brown Suit," a key witness to murder, police turn to Anne, who has caught a brief but telling glimpse of the poorly dressed suspect. The key to solving Christie's mystery rests on just one question: "What," Anne asks the authorities, "do you know of brachycephalic heads?" Like her readers, they knew a great deal indeed.

Notes

1 Calvin Trillin, "State Secrets," *New Yorker Magazine* (May 29, 1995), 54.
2 Ibid. 56.
3 The case was based on Section 2169, United States Revised Statutes. For a discussion of the process of Asian racialization, see Lisa Lowe, *Immigrant Acts: On Asian*

American Cultural Politics (Durham: Duke University Press, 1996), especially pp. 16–36.

4 Matthew Frye Jacobson, *Whiteness of a Different Color: European Immigrants and the Alchemy of Race* (Cambridge, MA: Harvard University Press, 1998), 174.

5 Judith Butler, *Bodies That Matter: On the Discursive Limits of "Sex"* (London: Routledge, 1993), 123.

6 Martin Heidegger, quoted in Nicholas Mirzoeff (ed.), *The Visual Culture Reader* (London and New York: Routledge, 1998), 6.

7 John F. Kasson, *Rudeness and Civility: Manners in Nineteenth-Century Urban America* (New York: Hill & Wang, 1990), 70.

8 See especially Guy Szuberla, "Ladies, Gentlemen, Flirts, Mashers, Snoozers, and the Breaking of Etiquette's Code," *Prospects*, 15 (1990), 169–95.

9 Kasson, *Rudeness and Civility*, 109.

10 Erving Goffman, *The Presentation of Self in Everyday Life* (Garden City, NY: Doubleday, 1959), 18 n.

11 Elaine S. Abelson, *When Ladies Go A-Thieving: Middle-Class Shoplifters in the Victorian Department Store* (Oxford: Oxford University Press, 1989), 136.

12 For a discussion of these and other nineteenth-century police practices see Roger Lane, *Policing the City: Boston, 1822–1885* (New York: Athenaeum, 1975), 66; Larry K. Hartsfield, *The American Response to Professional Crime, 1870–1917* (Westport, CT: Greenwood Press, 1985); David Ray Papke, *Framing the Criminal: Crime, Criminal Work and the Loss of Critical Perspective, 1830–1900* (Hamden, CT: Archon Books, 1987).

13 Johann Casper Lavater, *Essays on Physiognomy, for the Promotion of the Knowledge and the Love of Mankind*, 2nd edn. (London: Thomas Holcroft, 1804). Ironically, Lavater's aim was to classify racial types in order to know and therefore love the world's diversity. See Martha Banta, *Imaging American Women: Idea and Ideals in Cultural History* (New York: Columbia University Press, 1987), 104.

14 Allan Sekula, "The Body and the Archive," in Richard Bolton (ed.), *The Contest of Meaning: Critical Histories of Photography* (Cambridge, MA: MIT Press, 1992), 347.

15 Sander L. Gilman, *Difference and Pathology: Stereotypes of Sexuality, Race, and Madness* (Ithaca, NY: Cornell University Press, 1989), 1–35. See also Alan Trachtenberg, *Reading American Photographs: Images as History, Matthew Brady to Walker Evans* (New York: Hill & Wang: 1989), 67. Brian Wallis makes this point and elaborates on the important connection between the two in "Black Bodies, White Science: Louis Agassiz's Slave Daguerreotypes," *American Art*, 9:2 (Summer 1995), 48.

16 See Peter B. Hales, *Silver Cities: The Photography of American Urbanization, 1839–1915* (Philadelphia: Temple University Press, 1984), 11–12.

17 For a discussion on the various uses of the term daguerreotype see Alan Trachtenberg, "Photography: The Emergence of a Keyword," in Martha A. Sandweiss (ed.), *Photography in Nineteenth-Century America* (Fort Worth: Amon Carter Museum, 1991), 13–47; Wallis, "Black Bodies, White Science," 48. See also Elizabeth

Edwards, "Photographic 'Types': The Pursuit of Method," *Visual Anthropology,* 3 (1990), 5–58: 23.

18 Stephen Jay Gould, *The Mismeasurement of Man* (New York: W. W. Norton, 1981), 122–45; Hartsfield, *American Response,* 62–165.

19 Quoted in Gould, *The Mismeasurement of Man,* 124.

20 Ibid.

21 Sir Arthur Conan Doyle, "The Adventure of the Cardboard Box," in *Sherlock Holmes: The Complete Novels and Stories,* vol. 2 (New York: Bantam Books, 1986), 322.

22 Brian Wallis, "Black Bodies, White Science," 52. See also Peter Stallybrass and Allon White, *The Politics and Poetics of Transgression* (Ithaca, NY: Cornell University Press, 1986), 1–27.

23 Mary Cowling, *The Artist as Anthropologist: The Representation of Type and Character in Victorian Art* (Cambridge: Cambridge University Press, 1989), 35, 37, 61.

24 Christian Blanchet, "The Universal Appeal of the Statue of Liberty," in Wilton S. Dillon and Neil G. Kotler (eds.), *The Statue of Liberty Revisited* (Washington and London: Smithsonian Institution Press, 1994), 32–3. See also Barbara A. Babcock and John J. Macaloon, "Everybody's Gal: Women, Boundaries, and Monuments," in Dillon and Kotler (eds.), *The Statue of Liberty Revisited,* 79–100.

25 Banta, *Imaging American Women,* 116.

26 See especially Jean-Christophe Agnew, *Worlds Apart: The Market and the Theater in Anglo-American Thought, 1550–1750* (Cambridge: Cambridge University Press, 1986), 63–7.

27 Hartsfield, *American Response,* 163; see also pp. 160–5.

28 Wallis, "Black Bodies, White Science," 44.

29 This point is nicely made by Gould, *The Mismeasurement of Man,* 22.

30 Wallis, "Black Bodies, White Science," 47; Maren Stange, *Symbols of Ideal Life: Social Documentary Photography in America, 1890–1950* (New York: Cambridge University Press, 1989); and John Tagg, *The Burden of Representation: Essays on Photographies and Histories* (Minneapolis: University of Minnesota Press, 1988).

31 See especially, Curtis M. Hinsley, "The World as Marketplace: Commodification of the Exotic at the World's Columbian Exposition, Chicago, 1893," in Ivan Karp and Steven D. Lavine (eds.), *Exhibiting Cultures: The Poetics and Politics of Museum Display* (Washington, DC: Smithsonian Institution Press, 1991), 344–65.

32 Quoted in Hinsley, "The World as Marketplace," 346.

33 Wallis, "Black Bodies, White Science," 54.

34 Madison Grant, *The Passing of the Great Race.* See also Frederick E. Hoxie, *A Final Promise: The Campaign to Assimilate the Indians, 1880–1920* (Cambridge: Cambridge University Press, 1984), 115–46; Gail Bederman, *Manliness and Civilization: A Cultural History of Gender and Race in the United States, 1880–1917* (Chicago and London: University of Chicago Press, 1995), 49.

35 Edward C. Gordon, quoted in Bederman, *Manliness and Civilization,* 50. Ray Standard Baker, "What Is a Lynching? A Study of Mob Justice, South and North," *McClure's Magazine,* 24 (Feb. 1905), 429.

36   Bederman, *Manliness and Civilization*, 50.
37   Mark Pittenger, "A World of Difference: Constructing the 'Underclass' in Progressive America," *American Quarterly*, 49:1 (Mar. 1997), 51.
38   Ibid. 27.
39   John Reed, "Almost Thirty," *The New Republic* (Apr. 29, 1936), 335; John Sloan in Patricia Hills, "John Sloan's Images of Working-Class Women: A Case Study of the Roles and Interrelationships of Politics, Personality, and Patrons in the Development of Sloan's Art, 1905–16," *Prospects*, 5 (1980), 157–96: 178.
40   Banta, *Imaging American Women*, p. xviii.
41   *Four Years in the Underbrush: Adventures as a Working Woman in New York* (New York: Charles Scribner's Sons, 1921); Francis Donovan, *Woman Who Waits* (1920; New York: Arno Press, 1974), 224.
42   Walter Wyckoff, *The Workers: An Experiment in Reality*, 2 vols., vol. 2: *The West* (New York, 1898), 321.
43   *The Shaping of American Anthropology, 1883–1911: A Franz Boas Reader*, ed. George W. Stocking, Jr. (New York: Basic Books, 1974), 332.
44   Quoted in Abelson, *When Ladies Go A-Thieving*, 138.
45   Banta, *Imaging American Women*, 113.

2

Cartes de Visite Portrait Photographs and the Culture of Class Formation

ANDREA L. VOLPE

In his 1852 novel, *Pierre, or the Ambiguities*, Herman Melville's Pierre offered this commentary on daguerreotype portraits and the standardization of identity and image production suggested by photography at midcentury:

> Whereas in former times a faithful portrait was only within the power of the moneyed, or mental aristocrats of the earth. How natural then, the inference, that instead of, as in old times, immortalizing a genius, a portrait now only dayalizes a dunce. Beside, when everyone has his portrait published, true distinction lies in not having yours published at all. For if you are published along with Tom, Dick and Harry, and wear a coat of their cut, how then are you distinct from Tom, Dick or Harry?[1]

By contrasting the ability of the painted portrait to memorialize a subject with the daguerreotype's ability to momentarily represent the ordinary, Pierre sees that photography could multiply the visual marks of distinction to the point of formula, and in the process visually transform distinction into its opposite. His observation can also be read as marking the emergence of a standardized, conventional social and visual identity that came to distinguish the respectable, middle-class body in the middle decades of the nineteenth century.

Andrea L. Volpe, "Cartes de Visite Portrait Photographs and the Culture of Class Formation," in Burton J. Bledstein and Robert D. Johnston (eds.), *The Middling Sorts: Explorations in the History of the American Middle Class*. New York: Routledge, 2001: 157–69. © 2001 by Routledge. Reprinted with permission of Routledge/Taylor & Francis Books, Inc.

Pierre's insight foreshadowed the rise of a new form of photographic portraiture, cartes de visite, that by 1860 would replace the daguerreotypes of which he spoke. Just two and a half by four inches in size, cartes de visite were the first form of commercial portrait photographs made as multiple paper prints. Cartes were invented in Paris in 1854 by A.A.E. Disdéri, and capitalized on the bourgeoisie's interest in self-representation. They first gained notice in the United States in 1859 and had become the preeminent form of portrait photography by 1861. "Cartes de visite" translates as "visiting card," although there is little evidence that the little portraits were used literally as visiting cards. They were, however, incorporated into rituals of social exchange, display, and collecting, all of which locate them in the culture of a coalescing American middle class. The genre, as one account in the photograph trade papers described it, formed a "deluge," and the sheer volume of images prompted the first photograph albums.[2] Cartes sold for a dollar a dozen, or for as little as a dime each, and their economy, both for photographers and sitters, sustained their popularity through the end of the 1860s.[3] Detractors criticized urban, high-volume portrait studios as "picture factories," implying that the mass production of conventional portrait photographs yielded correspondingly indistinct social identities.[4]

Cartes are viewed traditionally as a conventional and derivative genre unworthy of scholarly consideration because they were made in such great number, by far too many now-nameless, or minimally skilled, photographers to be of significance. But conventionality, rather than serving as evidence of aesthetic shortcoming, provides historians with evidence of collective forms of expression with wide appeal. The ubiquity of cartes points to what Jane Tompkins calls "cultural work": popular and conventional texts should be read "as attempts to redefine the social order" and for the ways they "[tap] into a storehouse of commonly held assumptions, reproducing what is already there in typical and familiar form."[5] Cartes are conventional, in other words, not because they are the product of ill-trained photographers, but because the genre's visual formula offered a template for individual and collective identity that resonated with the social and economic lives of nineteenth-century Americans.

The rising demand for photographic portraits was grounded by the portrait's place in American cultural history and galvanized by the expanding market economy of antebellum America. Portraiture had appealed to Americans as a representation of economic and cultural status since the early Republic, when finely painted portraits were embraced by the urban gentry to visualize their position in the social order. In the antebellum Northeast, self-trained itinerant limners traveled through the countryside, "creating countless images from stark black-and-white silhouettes to colorful full-length-oils" for a growing circle of farmers and craftsmen seeking visual representations "to consolidate their position in a new bourgeoisie," explains David Jaffee.[6] By the 1840s, traveling portraitists were trafficking in the new technology of photography, offering first daguerreotypes and then ambrotypes (both techniques yielded single, unique images) as cheaper and more accurate portraits for the growing ranks of the middling sort. Historians often view this effect as evidence of photography's "democratization" of visual culture from the 1840s onward, as if the dispersion of photographic portraits merely expanded, but did not change, the essential cultural work of portrait images. The ability of cartes de visite to be printed even more cheaply and as multiple copies could be read as further evidence of such a democratizing impulse. But in the 1860s, the mass production of cartes did more than simply make the portrait more accessible: the expanded availability of portrait photographs quickly reduced a portrait sitter to conventional pose and formulaic form, and by so doing helped produce a collective middle-class body. So rather than consider visual culture as simply a progressive mirror onto social formation in this period, this essay considers the constitutive role of cartes de visite portrait photography in the culture of class formation.

"There is little question," Michel Foucault writes in volume one of the *History of Sexuality*, "that one of the primordial forms of class consciousness is the body."[7] Foucault identifies the body as a form and product of class consciousness because of its central position in modern forms of power. Social, political, or economic power is not exercised through prohibition, but through discipline, and its component techniques of observation, administration, correction, improvement, normalization, examination, and surveillance. Bodies, in this account, become both the subject and object of knowledge and are themselves deployed actively as agents of power in social formation. Foucault's conceptions of power and the body are, as Patricia O'Brien writes, "an alternative model for writing the history of culture," because rather than reducing "culture to the product of social and economic transformations" or reading cultural forms that transparently convey the events of the past, his method proposes that the visual and textual rhetorics, deployments and strategies of culture must themselves be the central subject of historical inquiry.[8]

This emphasis on the agency of cultural formation is crucial to my reading of cartes de visite in the cultural work of nineteenth-century American class formation. As the literary historians Wai Chee Dimock and Michael Gilmore formulate:

> Our sense [is] that the boundaries of class are unstable, that the experience of it is uneven, that it is necessary but not sufficient for the constitution of human identities.... Our desire [is] to build on these limitations, to use the analytical inadequacy of "class" as a rallying point, a significant juncture from which to

rethink the concepts such as "identity," "explanation" and "determination." We are interested . . . in the category of class less as an instance of "reality" than as an instance of the "made-real," less as an empirical description of social groups than as a theoretical enterprise, an attempt to attach a cause and give a name to "something which in fact happens (and can be shown to have happened) in human relationships."[9]

In this conceptualization, class is a fundamentally unstable category that is "fixed" and stabilized by representational practices, such as literature or visual culture. It is through representations, in other words, that social formation is visible. Because photographs employ what Foucault calls "the view point of the objective," they are particularly powerful in making class seem an unquestionable fact.[10] Against this framework, cartes de visite photographs can show us how middle-class identity was made more visible and, as a result, "made real" in the 1860s. The carte de visite photograph combined the traditional associations of portraiture with the visual authority of mechanical realism, which allowed the portrait photograph to be read as "proof" of social position, when in actuality the carte is evidence of the cultural production of such claims.

In the United States at midcentury, the American middle class embraced a wide range of cultural forms – education, religion, moral reform, and child rearing among them – that created a distinct physical body associated with economic and social position. Bodily pedagogies, directed by school books, hygiene, and self-culture manuals as well as phrenological magazines, instructed readers on how to manage the individual body and read the social body. Social and cultural historians argue that these preoccupations with appearance, manners, and bodily discipline offered ways to cope with the rapidly changing political economy of nineteenth-century America and ultimately came to be seen as the signature forms of middle-class culture. Control over the body was not only the focus of lessons in self-improvement, it was also a crucial element for establishing social and cultural authority: the shape and behavior of the physical body itself enacted class formation. Contemporary concern with bodies as expressions – indeed embodiments of class – suggests that cartes de visite can and should be read for the ways in which the popular photographic genre helped to visually invent a respectable body. This approach suggests the contribution of cultural history to the study of social formation.

The primary mechanism for producing the body as it appeared in cartes de visite were the posing stands used by photographers to hold the body in place during long exposure times. Stands shared a common design, in which a waist-high metal rod was anchored to a broad wooden or metal base. Two adjustable clamps extended from the spine of the stand, one to rest against the small of the back, and one to hold the neck. Ideally, the posing stand was hidden from sight, behind a woman's billowing skirts or a man's carefully crossed legs, but was often left visible. The limited-light sensitivity of glass plate negatives and cameras put real constraints on photographic practices, but these mechanisms did not single-handedly determine the poses in which sitters were put before the camera. To notice the legs of the stand peeping out from behind a sitter's legs is to be reminded that posing stands were an exoskeleton for the aspiring middle class: an exterior, visible mechanism by which bodies were held and molded. These stands were both brace and caliper. As instruments, they suggest the correcting of individual bodies and the comparison and measurement among them championed by comparative anatomy. If we consider the posing stand not as a simple technical tool, but as an instrument of culture – the most palpable mechanism for imposing ideas of respectability onto the body – then it becomes possible to trace the visual construction of a respectable *type*. The repeated application of the

Figure 2.1. Anonymous carte de visite. Reprinted courtesy of Historical Collections and Labor Archives, Pennsylvania State University Library

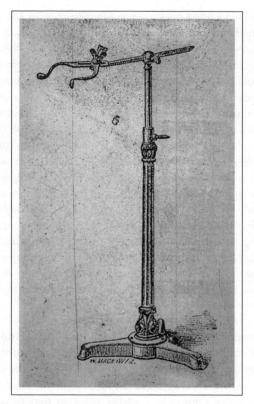

Figure 2.2. Posing stand of Philadelphia photographer, March 1868

stand imposed a standardized bodily form on the individual body, and by doing so, visualized a generalized form associated with upstanding social position.

Together posing stands and cartes de visite exemplify what Foucault called a "positive mechanics" for producing a sort of body and type of social identity through visual and textual representations that naturalized and empowered the respectable body by subjecting it to heightened visibility.[11] This positive means of disciplining, and thus producing, the middle-class body is evident in directions from the photographic trade press on how to best pose sitters, as well as in commentaries on and evaluations of the visual formulas that emerged among commercial photographers as cartes de visite portraiture took shape as a genre. The posing advice of trade journals published in New York and Philadelphia worked as a "literature of correction," in which posing advice instructed photographers to use the posing stand as an instrument of correcting and controlling improvement.

The trade press depicted operators as eager to control and eager to please, caught between their desires for an efficient pose and a satisfied sitter. The problem of posing was most immediately a practical one for photographers: how to get a sitter to sit still?[12] Photographers came to rely on the stand to enforce their hold over the body, all the while working to distract sitters from the control implied by its cold embrace. To let a sitter take a pose without the stand threatened disaster for the photographer and subject alike. The photographer would fail to obtain a satisfying pose and would lose time and money to an unhappy customer. At the same time, overuse of the stand would immobilize sitters so completely that they could not move, drawing too much attention to the instrumental authority of the procedure. Posing often began with the photographer arranging the sitter "in an attitude entirely devoid of ease," only to "delude him, or her, into sickly contortions of countenance they facetiously denominate 'looking pleasant.'" Editors and advisers pointed to stiff poses as evidence of the "tyrannical officiousness" of the photographer and pleaded with them to emphasize comfort over control.[13] *Tyrannical officiousness* shows contemporary awareness of the power dynamics and the particular form of bodily discipline embedded in the production of cartes de visite, as photographers were instructed to walk the fine line between flattering and restraining their sitters.

In the hands of a capable operator, the cold arms of the posing stand were felt not as instrumental coercion but as comforting control during a procedure that was compared to the anticipation of sitting in the dentist's chair.[14] Photographers were instructed to use the stand to secure "complete rigidity so as to afford complete immobility" of the sitter so that their efforts yielded a "natural, graceful and harmonious pose."[15] The tension between control and comfort evident in directions to photographers reveals how management of the body depended on authoritative use of the stand that would also conceal its interventions.[16] Photographers coerced their sitters into the embrace of the posing stand by complimenting and composing them. Photographers were advised to use the posing stand to find a position "perfectly free from all constraint," even as instructions for using head rests and posing stands emphasized a tight hold on the sitter's body: "First, raise the main rod the proper height and tighten the screw; let it remain; then put your back-rest to the sitter, crowding him forward as much as you please, and tighten the screw. This holds him firm," advised one manual.[17]

The literature of correction, intended to aid photographers and ease the problems of posing, helped produce a respectable body by standardizing poses. "The majority of photographers have two or three different positions in which they submit all their models, whether tall or short, long or small," concluded *Humphrey's* in 1863.[18] Standardized compositions prevailed to such an extent that, by 1865, the journal complained that "the conventional pillar and curtain" used in so many cartes de visite had become "untoler-able."[19] Standard posing was bemoaned as a shortcoming of the profession; "Is it absolutely necessary that every member of the family should lean on the same pedestal or stand staring over the same balustrade?" asked one critic, noting hopefully that diversity of pose would not be a bad thing.[20] If a photographer relied too heavily on the posing stand, John Towler feared that portraits would reveal the sameness produced by the "silly clinging to uniformity in the position of the sitter."[21] Edward Wilson, editor of *The Philadelphia Photographer*, chastened his readers: "None of you are so ignor-ant as to be told that it is not well to choose a stereotype set of positions, and make all your sitters assume one or the other."[22] But photographers did not resort to predictable poses out of ignorance. Just the opposite – formulaic poses were the product of careful study and the literature of correction offered in the trade press.

When photographers used the stand to fit their customers' bodies into prescribed poses, they were imposing on each body common ideas of what a particular type of body should look like. The practical concerns of commer-cial photography joined with the positive motivations of photographers to naturalize the way posing stands were used to enforce bodily attitudes. Directions for shaping the body that informed the iconography of cartes had thus become indispensable and seemed the only possible and productive way to pose a sitter. Ultimately both the rhetorical formula of photographic advice and the visual composition of cartes de visite became so familiar as to be accepted as fact. The posing stand standardized and multiplied the respect-able body through an aesthetic defined by comforting control; the resulting portrait photograph was an enactment of, and representation of, what Foucault refers to as "membership in a homogeneous social body" and what historians call the middle class.

Cartes de visite visualized the respectable body in a social climate in which the signification of the body and assumptions of its transparency weighed heavily on the national consciousness. The popular sciences of phrenology and physiognomy, alongside the new sciences of comparative anatomy and phys-ical anthropology, provided the visual and intellectual framework for reading a sitter's body and for deploying the posing stand. Posing stands were the most explicit instrument used to gauge a sitter; they enacted a visual and intellectual vocabulary for reading and producing the body based upon ideas of physical essentialism, visual transparency, and social classification. Scientists from Samuel Morton to Louis Agassiz based their work on visual inspection and the self-evident authority of physical bodies, where "a glance might suffice to read an individual's character and destiny," explains Cynthia Eagle Russett.[23] The result was a social and physiological determinism that used the shape of head and the proportions of limbs to chart the progress of human society from the primitive to the civilized, from the slouched to the upright. Together sight and body were the basis for an essentialism that found meaning in typologies and comparisons, rooted in the assumption that the respectable body could be distinguished on sight from the primitive or criminal body.

The trade press endorsed the terms of comparison, hierarchical social organization, and visual evaluation of the human figure articulated by these popular and scientific theories of the body.[24] Photographers agreed that physical and visual generalization was the key to evaluating and posing their sitters.[25] The doctors, scientists, and physiologists who dispensed directions for managing the body inhabited the same intellectual universe as the journal editors and manuals authors who directed photographers on questions of pose.[26] Photographers shared with physicians the belief that the entire human frame represented a more accurate index of inner qualities than the head and face alone. "The whole body manifests the character, or comparative strength of a man's intellectual faculties," wrote reformer Dr. John Ellis. Photographers expressed similar views. The directive from *Humphrey's* was that "the entire figure, from head to toe," was "the most suitable of any to express the complete resemblance of the individual, from expression of the physiognomy down to fine attitude and proportion."[27] Belief in the natural transparency of the body, and photography's visual realism, figured heavily in the poses that photographic writers recommended to their readers. Titles from the trade press such as "Anatomy, Phrenology, and Physiognomy and Their Relation to Photography," "A Hint for Posing Your Sitter," and "Defects in Our Sitters," suggested that the visual vocabulary of physiognomy was the key to reading the body.[28] "Attitudes, dresses, features, hands, feet, betray the social grade of candidates for portraiture. The picture tells no lie about them," penned Oliver Wendell Holmes in his 1863 discussion of the card photograph in *Atlantic Monthly*.[29] Praised as "photographic aids to physiognomy," the visual authority of cartes were at once shaped by these assumptions about bodily transparency and used to verify the accuracy of the theories they represented.

The Philadelphia photographer M. A. Root advised that bodily position should conform to the sitter's social position.[30] The traffic in sitters made quick study of the human form a necessity, so that the transparency of the body was naturalized as a visual truth that would be self-evident to a photographer. A visual reading of physical form started with running "your eye over the subject, regarding the dress, its color, style and trimmings...all the time studying the face and expression."[31] Once the photographer had sized up the face and dress of a sitter, he should then turn his eye to the body, turning it this way and that, in order to find the best view, just as a sculptor modeled

50

clay or a painter rendered a figure.[32] This practice was one of constant measuring and comparison, with the result that the photographer's judgment reflected "just how we would have the world estimate and rank us, and how we rank ourselves," as one sitter put it.[33] The repetition of this comparing, gauging, and ranking process, combined with ideas of bodily form institutionalized by the posing stand, visually produced the respectable body. Notably, social position determined bodily position, even as bodily carriage was read as evidence of social position.

Bodily difference was considered self-evident, so that Root, for example, recommended poses and settings that mirrored natural gender difference: "the whole and every part of the male form, taken generally, indicates an aptness and propensity to action, vigorous exertion and power," he wrote in *The Camera and the Pencil*. The female form, in contrast, "gives the idea of something rather passive than active . . . created not so much for the purpose of laborious utility as for the exercise of all the softer, milder qualities."[34] Yet, by using photographs to reflect well-established white, middle-class gender roles, the photograph helped to produce them as social reality. The *American Journal of Photography* suggested that cartes de visite were best suited for portraits of sitters engaged in appropriately gendered activities. A woman, for example, might be positioned "examining a bouquet, arranging a vase of flowers, buttoning a glove, examining a picture, reading a letter."[35] *Humphrey's Journal* explicitly directed that a "mother be represented playing with her children," and cartes de visite albums are filled with images of maternal tenderness.[36] All these labors emphasized a woman's natural capacity for moral influence, tenderness, and gentleness, captured by moments of thoughtful reflection or delicate tasks, such as turning the pages of a photograph album. The sentimental emotions attached to cartes emphasized feminine feeling, deference, and dependence as natural qualities that could be depicted in portraiture.

Posing conventions for men, in contrast, reinforced the cultural authority of patriarchal individualism. Photographers were coached to pose male subjects as upstanding and self-controlled figures. Photographer H. J. Rodgers instructed his readers that temperance, self-control, and constraint were the most worthy qualities a man could display in a portrait.[37] Self-control was the preeminent value of middle-class masculinity, which in part may explain men's willingness to endure the posing stand: amidst directions for physical and pecuniary restraint, the arms of the posing stand assured that they would display the physical marks of their social position. Poses such as the "contra posto" standing pose were reproduced on such a wide scale that the viewer sees an individual portrait that is also, simultaneously, a social role and identity into which the portrait sitter has been fitted.

51

Figure 2.3. Anonymous carte de visite. Reprinted courtesy of Historical Collections and Labor Archives, Pennsylvania State University Library

Both popular and scientific understandings of bodies in the nineteenth century turned around the concept of *type*, in which differentiations from standard forms were understood as distinctions of varying degrees from norms of physique, behavior, and biology. Typological photographs rely on comparative categories, finding meaning not in an individual image, but in the organization of a group of images in relationship to each other. Stylistically these images emphasize generalization, clinical observation, and classification of generic examples. The typological photograph both generalizes about and visually constructs a category of identity and a region of the social body, such as "the criminal."[38] The appearance of any one body in typological photographs is besides the point, because one photograph of a thief stands for the appearance of all thieves: the viewer does not see an individual but a type. The most instrumental of nineteenth-century photographs, those in which the circumstances of production deny agency to the point of coercion (such as the daguerreotypes Louis Agassiz commissioned to prove his theory of the separate creation of the white and black races), visualizes the taxonomic qualities of typological images. Yet nineteenth-century preoccupations with classification, physiognomy, and the reading of exterior physicality as the mirror onto interior substance were not limited to the visual construction of "the insane" or "the criminal" but also extended to the "respectable" bodies visualized in cartes de visite. Cartes de visite were representations of "the normal," in opposition to which other images, such as those produced under the eye of science or reform, were understood. Standardized representations of visibly respectable bodies staked out the upper ranks of a social hierarchy that was as dependent on representations of respectability as it was on visual depiction of otherness. But like the asylum inmate or the criminal, the respectable body became recognizable not by marks of individual distinction, but for its reference to a particular segment of American society.

Cartes made visible the defining physical features of the individual middle-class body and positioned the middle class as part of a larger social body. The carte was both proof and artifact of status and position, naturalized by the cultural authority of photographic realism that located status in the body itself. The respectable body became recognizable and powerful, not by marks of individuality, but for its reference to a particular segment of American society, identified by posture and props. Through repeated representation of the upright and the upstanding, cartes de visite linked a particular *kind* of visual body with essential physical distinctions, so that the appearance of restrained bodies in these images both reinforced and constructed the importance of bodily control as an element of respectability.

Not only did the cartes de visite help produce the physical form of the middle-class body, the purchase and exchange of such images further enacted and verified class position. Cartes visually constituted the changing meaning of culture and its implications for representations of the body. In these decades the concept of culture was "becoming a form of consumption necessary to the maintenance of one's class standing," as Mary Kupiec Cayton observes.[39] Culture, as Cayton defines it, was a familiarity with a particular body of knowledge as a measure of status and position, not the embrace of transcendent values. The commercial photographer's studio and the legions of cartes de visite produced in the 1860s helped negotiate this redefinition of culture as an object of consumption. Cartes de visite photographs made it possible to mass produce and mass market a bodily form increasingly associated with middle-class position. In the process, they helped consolidate middle-class social authority and solidify the changing meaning of culture.

From the late 1850s to the early 1870s, the posing stand mobilized a social body in the culture of class formation by immobilizing individual bodies before the camera. Cartes de visite were made possible by the perfecting accuracy of photography, the corrective embrace of the posing stand, and the desire for self-discipline and increased visibility among the emerging middle class. Together, these elements constitute what Foucault called "the gentle way in punishment."[40] Posing for a photograph was not an explicit punishment of the body; it was, ideally and often in practice, a partial and indirect form of control, veiled by the attentive impatience of the photographer. The dynamics of obliging regulation voiced in the trade press echo what Richard Brodhead has called "disciplinary intimacy, or simply, discipline through love." This tender control, visible in cultural institutions and practices such as schools, child rearing, and sentimental fiction, was distinct to the "thinking of the American middle class as it "redefine[d] itself in the antebellum decades."[41] Directions for posing the sitter were not simply a matter of technical instruction, nor were the images produced in the photographer's studio mirrors onto nineteenth-century social formation. The literature of correction used to direct posing should be viewed as a commercial variation on the sentimentalized discourses of corporeal control, that, like the circulation and reproduction of cartes de visite photographs themselves, helped to produce a particular kind of body and identity associated with the consolidation of middle-class social authority.

Cartes de visite did not cause middle-class consolidation, nor do they simply reflect its composition. But causation, in this instance, is productively explored and probed by considering the role of visual images in representing middle-class identity and social formation for its nineteenth-century participants. Just as important, cartes de visite complicate and enrich historians' accounts of the mid-nineteenth century by suggesting that middle-class formation ought to be as much a question of representation as of narration. For it is only by exploring the interior workings of cultural forms and bodies of thought that we will begin to see how a middle-class identity was "made real."

Notes

1 Herman Melville, *Pierre, or the Ambiguities*, quoted in Robert Sobieszek and Odette M. Appel, *The Spirit of Fact: The Daguerreotypes of Southworth and Haws* (Rochester and Boston: D. R. Godine, 1976), xxi.
2 "Photographic Eminence," *Humphrey's Journal*, July 15, 1864, 93–4.

3   "The Photographic Art a Blessing to the World – Cartes de Visite," *American Journal of Photography*, August 15, 1862, 77.

4   On nineteenth-century photography, see William Darrah, *Cartes de Visite in Nin[e]teenth-Century Photography* (Gettysburg, PA: W. C. Darrah, 1981); Elizabeth Edwards, ed., *Anthropology and Photography and the American Scene* (New York and Ft. Worth: Harry N. Abrams, 1991), 17–47; Laura Wexler, "Tender Violence: Literary Eavesdropping, Domestic Fiction and Educational Reform," in Shirley Samuels, ed., *The Culture of Sentiment: Race, Gender and Sentimentality in Nineteenth-Century America* (New York: Oxford University Press, 1992), 9–38; Susan S. Williams, *Confounding Images: Photography and Portraiture in Antebellum American Fiction* (Philadelphia: University of Pennsylvania Press, 1997).

5   Jane Tompkins, *Sensational Designs: The Cultural Work of American Fiction, 1790–1860* (New York: Oxford University Press, 1985), xi and xvi.

6   David Jaffee, "'One of the Primitive Sort': Portrait Makers of the Rural North, 1790–1860," in Steven Hahn and Jonathan Prude, eds., *The Countryside in the Age of Capitalist Transformation* (Chapel Hill: University of North Carolina Press, 1985), 130 and 104, respectively.

7   Michel Foucault, *The History of Sexuality*, vol. 1, trans. Robert Hurley (New York: Pantheon Books, 1978), 126.

8   Patricia O'Brien, "Michel Foucault's History of Culture," in Lynn Hunt, ed., *The New Cultural History* (Berkeley: University of California Press, 1989), 25.

9   Wai Chee Dimock and Michael Gilmore, eds., *Rethinking Class: Literary Studies of Social Formation* (New York: Columbia University Press, 1994), 2.

10 Foucault, *History of Sexuality*, 102.

11 Michel Foucault, *Discipline and Punish*, trans. Alan Sheridan (New York: Pantheon Books, 1979), 112.

12 Edward L. Wilson, "Trouble in the Studio," *Photographic Mosaics* (Philadelphia, 1869), 131.

13 "Sitting for a Picture," *American Journal of Photography*, February 15, 1863, 367.

14 "Having Your Photograph Taken," *American Journal of Photography*, January 1, 1853, 292.

15 M. de Valincourt, "Photographic Portraiture, Continued: On Likeness in Photographic Portraits," *Humphrey's Journal*, March 15, 1862.

16 H. Garbanati, "The Influence of the Operator on the Sitter," *American Journal of Photography*, October 1, 1858, 134–6; F. Welch, "A Few Hints on the Best Means of Obtaining Good Cartes de Visite," *Humphrey's Journal*, June 15, 1865, 59–60.

17 A. K. P. Trask, *Trask's Practical Ferrotyper* (Philadelphia, 1872), repr. in Robert A. Sobieszek, *The Collodion Process and the Ferrotype, Three Accounts, 1854–1872* (New York: Benerman and Wilson, 1973), 49–50.

18 Disderi, "The Aesthetics of Photography, Continued," *Humphrey's Journal*, September 15, 1863, 155.

19 "Troubles of a Photographer," *Humphrey's Journal*, January 1, 1865, 265.

20 Morton, "Photography Indoors," *Philadelphia Photographer*, July 1864, 105.

21 John Towler, *The Silver Sunbeam* (New York: J. H. Ladd, 1864; repr. Hastings-on-Hudson, NY: Morgan & Morgan), 31.

22 Edward L. Wilson, "Trouble in the Studio," *Photographic Mosaics* (Philadelphia, 1869), 131.

23 Cynthia Eagle Russett, *Sexual Science: The Victorian Construction of Womanhood* (Cambridge, MA: Harvard University Press, 1989), 7.

24 For the pervasive and general influence of phrenology and physiognomy on nineteenth-century life, see Allan Sekula, "The Body and the Archive," *October*, 39 (Winter 1986), 3–64; John Davies, *Phrenology, Fad and Science: A 19th-Century American Crusade* (New Haven, CT: Yale University Press, 1955); Madeleine B. Stern, *Heads and Headlines: The Phrenological Fowlers* (Norman: University of Oklahoma Press, 1971), 214; John F. Kasson, *Rudeness and Civility: Manners in Nineteenth-Century Urban America* (New York: Hill & Wang, 1990), 96–7.

25 "Photography and Truth," *Philadelphia Photographer*, November 1876, 323.

26 The editor of *Humphrey's Journal*, Dr. John Towler, was professor of mathematics, natural philosophy, and modem languages at Hobart College, as well as professor of chemistry and pharmacy and dean of the medical faculty at the Geneva Medical College in New York State. Towler published his photographic manual, *The Silver Sunbeam*, in 1864; the book went through four editions within the next ten months. "Important Editorial Change," *Humphrey's Journal*, July 1, 1862, 17. Beaumont Newhall, introduction to *The Silver Sunbeam*; and Stanley H. Bums, "Early Medical Photographs in America, 1839–1883, Part II," *New York State Journal of Medicine*, 79 (May 1979), 943–4. Charles A. Seely, founder of the *American Journal of Photography* in 1855, was a chemist by training and had worked at *Scientific American* and served as professor of chemistry at New York Medical College. While working as a chemist, book dealer, and publisher of photographic titles, Seely edited the photography journal until 1867.

27 Disderi, "The Aesthetics of Photography, Continued," *Humphrey's Journal*, August 15, 1863, 127.

28 "Anatomy, Phrenology, and Physiognomy, and their Relation to Photography, No. 2," *Philadelphia Photographer*, April 1876, 103; E. D. Ormsby, "Defects in Our Sitters," *Photographic Mosaics*, 1875, 31; "A Hint for Posing the Sitter," *Photographic Mosaics*, 1866, 59–60; W. H. Lipton, "Anatomy, Phrenology and Physiognomy, and their Relation to Photography, No. 1," *Philadelphia Photographer*, February 1876, 53–4; "How to Sit for a Photograph," *Photographic Mosaics*, 1866, 46–50.

29 Oliver Wendell Holmes, "Doings of the Sunbeam," *Atlantic Monthly*, July 1863, 9.

30 See Root, "Some Items, Relating to the Process of Sitting for a Heliographic Portrait," *Photographic and Fine Arts Journal*, September 1858, 263.

31 "The Treatment of the Sitter," *Anthony's Photographic Bulletin*, December 1873, 377.

32 "Position and Composition," *Photographic World*, June 1871, 25.

33 Revd A. A. E. Taylor, "The Photographer's Study of Character," *Philadelphia Photographer*, October 1864, 151.

34 *The Camera and the Pencil, or the Heliographic Art* (Philadelphia: J. B. Lippincott & Co., 1864), 253.

35 "A Few Words on Portraiture," *American Journal of Photography*, August 1, 1863, 50.

36 "The Aesthetics of Photography," *Humphrey's Journal*, September 15, 1863, 154.

37 H. J. Rodgers, *Twenty-Three Years Under a Skylight, or Life and Experiences of a Photographer* (Hartford, CT: H. J. Rogers, 1872; repr., New York: Hill & Wang, 1973), 148–57.

38 Sekula, "The Body and the Archive"; Brian Wallis, "White Science, Black Bodies: Louis Agassiz's Slave Daguerreotypes," *American Art*, 9 (Summer 1995), 39–61.

39 Mary Kupiec Cayton, "The Making of an American Prophet: Emerson, his Audiences and the Rise of Cultural Industry in Nineteenth-Century America," *American Historical Review*, 92 (1987), 615.

40 Foucault, *Discipline and Punish*, 104.

41 Richard Brodhead, "Sparing the Rod: Discipline and Fiction in Antebellum America," *Representations*, 21 (Winter 1988), 144.

Part I, 1860–1900:
Suggested Readings

The emergence of new-looking relations in the nineteenth century joined with technological innovations to help reframe the social imaginary in a number of important ways. The readings below help unpack the relationship between these changes in the visual landscape, class formation, hierarchies of difference, and constructions of national identity in the critical decades following the Civil War.

Joshua Brown, *Beyond the Lines: Pictorial Reporting, Everyday Life, and the Crisis of Gilded Age America* (2002).

Jennifer Green-Lewis, *Framing the Victorians: Photography and the Culture of Realism* (1996).

Deborah Poole and Vincente Rafael, *Vision, Race, and Modernity: A Visual Economy of the Andean Image World* (1997).

Julie Brown, *Contesting Images: Photography and the World's Columbian Exposition* (1994).

Angela Miller, *The Empire of the Eye: Landscape, Representation, and American Cultural Politics, 1825–1875* (1993).

Jonathan Cary, *Techniques of the Observer: On Vision and Modernity in the Nineteenth Century* (1990).

Elaine Abelson, *When Ladies Go A-Thieving: Middle-Class Shoplifters in the Victorian Department Store* (1989), especially chapter 5, "The Dilemmas of Detection."

M. C. Cowling, *The Artist as Anthropologist: The Representation of Type and Character in Victorian Art* (1989).

Alan Trachtenberg, *Reading American Photographs: Images as History, Mathew Brady to Walker Evans* (1989).

Peter Bacon Hales, *Silver Cities: The Photography of American Urbanization, 1839–1915* (1984).

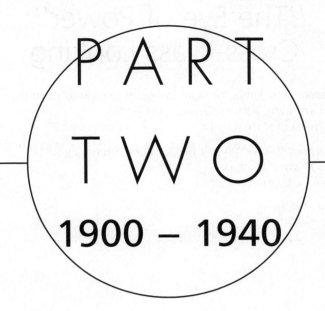

PART TWO
1900 – 1940

The Embodied Nation: Race, Gender, and the Politics of the Camera

"The Eye of Power":
Cross-Class Looking

The Embodied Nation: Race, Gender, and the Politics of the Camera

3

Photographing the "American Negro": Nation, Race, and Photography at the Paris Exposition of 1900

SHAWN MICHELLE SMITH

In "The Conservation of Races," published in 1897, W. E. B. Du Bois asks, "What, after all, am I? Am I an American or am I a Negro? Can I be both? Or is it my duty to cease to be a Negro as soon as possible and be an American?"[1] As Du Bois attempts to plot a course through the "doubleness" of racial and national identities facing African Americans at the turn of the century, he asserts that distinct racial cultures must be maintained, even as different groups come to coexist as citizens of the same nation.[2] His essay is entitled, after all, "The *Conservation* of Races," and Du Bois asserts that African Americans must resist the ethnic erasure that assimilation into a dominant white culture would entail, while simultaneously fighting for political, economic, and social equality in Jim Crow America.

Du Bois affirms that the African American must struggle to be both an "American" and a "Negro" in his essay of 1897, and he helps to define the position of the African American further with his prominent participation in

Shawn Michelle Smith, "Photographing the 'American Negro': Nation, Race, and Photography at the Paris Exposition of 1900," in Smith, *American Archives: Gender, Race, and Class in Visual Culture*. Princeton, NJ: Princeton University Press, 1999: 157–86. © 1999 by Princeton University Press. Reprinted with permission of Princeton University Press.

the "American Negro" exhibit at the Paris Exposition of 1900. Du Bois assisted in preparing many of the displays for the American Negro exhibit, and he also assembled hundreds of photographs of African Americans into a series of three albums (four volumes) for the presentation. Frances Benjamin Johnston, a professional white woman photographer, provided another collection of photographs for the exhibit, a series of images of the Hampton Institute commissioned expressly for the Paris Exposition. Reading Du Bois's photograph albums against Johnston's images of the Hampton Institute, this chapter investigates how racial and national identities were posed and negotiated in the terrain of visual culture at the Paris Exposition of 1900. Proposing that the American Negro exhibit itself was deeply invested in defining the place of the "Negro" in the United States, I examine how such positions were established in the visual codes of turn-of-the-century photography.

While most studies of the nation and of national identity have focused on the printed word as the medium through which a national community could be imagined in the nineteenth century, I demonstrate the role photography, another medium of mass reproduction, played in envisioning a racially codified American identity.[3] In order to understand fully the ways in which the photographs displayed in the American Negro exhibit participated in the formulation of visual codes of national belonging, one must locate the images within the historical legacy of representations which they both draw upon and significantly challenge. Johnston's and Du Bois's photographs of the "American Negro" entered a visual terrain already mapped in terms of both "race" and "nation" over the course of the nineteenth century. The American Negro exhibit itself, the frame in which Johnston's and Du Bois's photographs were presented, signified at the nexus of scientific discourses defining both race and national character at the turn of the century. Further, the images Johnston produced and those that Du Bois assembled circulated within a redefined field of photographic representation. Situating Johnston's and Du Bois's images within a changing historical context, I examine photographs not simply as signs that represent "real-world" referents but as signs with distinct visual genealogies – signs that enter into conversation and contest with other photographs. My argument proposes that visual culture is not a mere reflection of a national community but one of the sites through which narratives of national belonging are imagined. In other words, I suggest that photographic images not only represent but also produce the nation.[4]

Johnston's photographs and Du Bois's photograph albums initiated new visual strategies for representing both race and national character at the turn of the century. Both sets of images challenged the essentialized discourses of race and national identity dominant during this period, although they did so to varying degrees. While Johnston's photographs forwarded the American identity of Hampton students over their racial identities, Du Bois's albums suggested that the African American could indeed be both an "American" and a "Negro." This chapter illustrates how the photographs displayed in the American Negro exhibit marked a new and internally contested moment in the history of American visual culture.

Racialized Bodies, National Character, and Photographic Documentation

The American Negro exhibit itself participated in a new era in the history of race representation, both for the United States and for international expositions in general. Following a trend initiated with the "Negro Building" at the Cotton States and International Exposition of Atlanta in 1895,[5] Paris Exposition organizers invited African Americans to present their history, cultural achievements, and social advances to the world in their "own terms" at the Paris Exposition of 1900. A very few years after African Americans were denied official participation in the Columbian World Exposition of 1893,[6] they were invited to contribute as self-defining agents to the Atlanta Exposition of 1895, the Nashville Centennial Exposition of 1897, and the Paris Exposition of 1900. As W. E. B. Du Bois describes the American Negro exhibit at the Paris Exposition, it was "planned and executed by Negroes, and collected and installed under the direction of a Negro special agent, Mr. Thomas J. Calloway."[7] Unlike the exoticized displays of African villages that reinforced white European estimations of their own "civilized" superiority in relation to "Negro savages," the American Negro exhibit of the Paris Exposition represented African Americans as thoroughly modern members of the Western world. Through a series of maps, charts, models, photographs, and detailed descriptions of work in African American education, as well as hundreds of examples of African American literary production, the American Negro exhibit presented the progress made by African Americans in the terms of white Western culture. The exhibit was considered one of the most impressive in the Palace of Social Economy, and was honored with an exposition grand prize.[8]

While it is important to underscore the unique nature of the American Negro exhibit, it is also important to note that this was by no means a utopian moment. Housed in the United States section of the Palace of Social Economy, the American Negro exhibit was framed by international notions of social progress. According to Du Bois, the exhibits in the Palace of Social Economy did not portray sociology, the "'science of society'" per se, but instead various systems of social reform. Included in national exhibits were the "mutual aid societies of France," "the state insurance of Germany," as well as "the Red Cross Society."[9] The United States section presented models of tenement houses, maps of industrial plants, and the work of factory inspectors. Within the Palace of Social Economy, amid displays expounding treatments for social ailments, the American Negro exhibit provided a social success story, but it was compelled to deliver that story within the implicit context of solutions to national problems, in this case, no doubt, the ubiquitous white-coined American "Negro problem." Thus, while the American Negro exhibit provided an opportunity for African Americans to visualize complex racial and national identifications, it remained confined within a white-dominated system of social surveillance.

The very term "American Negro" would have registered as a kind of oxymoron to particularly strident Anglo-Saxon American nationalists at the turn of the century. [. . .] by the turn of the century, many whites attempted to define "American" as an exclusively Anglo-Saxon purview, and their white supremacist nationalism was backed by the scientific discourse of eugenics.[10] Eugenicists and biological racialists in the United States were intent on establishing much less permeable national borders than those configured through the reading practices enabled by the expansion of print capitalism, and they sought to delineate the borders of an "imagined community"[11] through discourses of essentialized racial characteristics. As we have seen, Francis Galton claimed that national character was an effect of race, a kind of racial attribute. Further, Galton believed that the racialized properties of national character could be enhanced and controlled through monitored breeding. Conversely, Galton claimed that national character might be enfeebled both through unmonitored procreation of the "weak" and through interracial reproduction. In Galton's universe races were measured according to a hierarchical scale, in which the ancient Greeks represented a lost ideal, nineteenth-century Anglo-Saxons claimed the modern pinnacle, and "Negroes" occupied the lowest link. According to Galton, improvement might be bred within a race, but crossbreeding between the races would always result in tragically weakened stock. Further, while Galton argued explicitly against amalgamation, his work also implicitly buttressed anti-assimilationist policies. Cultural equality among the races – a sharing of "essential" national character – was inconceivable according to Galton's notion of biological difference. In Galton's terms, nations of races were by definition separate and not equal.[12]

Galton's eugenics provided a scientific basis for the arrangement of racialized "others" commonly presented at international expositions by the turn of the century. Even as African Americans were represented as successful participants in white Western "progress" in the American Negro exhibit at the Paris Exposition, other "Negroes" were hired to people the living displays that represented an exoticized "sliding scale of humanity" popular at international expositions since their introduction at the 1889 Paris fair.[13] As Thomas J. Schlereth describes the racialized spatial logics of such exhibits on the Midway Plaisance at Chicago's Columbian Exposition of 1893, "ethnic" displays were arranged along the periphery of the fairgrounds, around the center of the exposition, which celebrated western European triumphs in science, industry, and art. At the Chicago Columbian Exposition, the imagined Western whiteness of the exposition center was dramatically represented by architect Frederick Law Olmsted's literally white stuccoed buildings, modeled after ancient Greek and Roman architecture. Outside this Greek and Roman-inspired Anglo-Saxon "White City," ethnic displays in the Midway Plaisance were arranged according to their imagined proximity to Anglo-Saxon culture. The Teutonic and Celtic races, represented by German and Irish exhibits, occupied the Midway territory closest to the "White City" center of the exposition, while the Muhammadan and Asian worlds stood farther away, and the "savage races," including Africans and North American Indians, remained at the farthest reaches of the Midway.[14] A similar structure, in which a city center celebrating Western industrial, social, and artistic achievements, replete with educational exhibits, was surrounded by a relatively "chaotic" zone filled with new forms of entertainment and "exotic" displays of non-Western peoples, many the "trophies" of Western imperialism, dominated international expositions throughout the early twentieth century. It is within this context that one notes the most radical, and indeed perhaps the most contained, critique of turn-of-the-century notions of race and culture forwarded by the American Negro exhibit at the Paris Exposition of 1900. Contesting the colonialist and imperialist logics forwarded by living racial and ethnic displays, the American Negro exhibit disrupted the essentialized narratives that depicted people of color as the uncivilized infants of human evolution. The American Negro exhibit dissociated "race" from a single set of cultural practices and progressive potentialities.

While the space in which Johnston's photographs and Du Bois's albums were presented was the already unique and contested domain of the American Negro exhibit, the photographs themselves were also imbedded in changing conceptions of photographic documentation. Unlike Mathew Brady's daguerreotype portraits of "Illustrious Americans," which received the most prestigious awards at the London Crystal Palace Exposition of 1851,[15] Johnston's and Du Bois's photographs were not presented as art objects in a separate photographic salon. Instead, the images were meant to *document* and *illustrate* the "progress and present conditions" of the "American Negro." Johnston's and Du Bois's photographs signified in photographic registers developed outside the auratic domains of both the sentimental portrait keepsake and the photographic work of art.[16] Displayed in the Palace of Social Economy, alongside model tenement houses and the reports of factory inspectors, the photographs included in the American Negro exhibit functioned as evidence, just as the many charts and graphs included in exhibits served as scientific documentations of progress. Unlike the photographic portraits that dominated popular and professional photography in the United States throughout the nineteenth century, Johnston's photographs aimed not to emulate an individual but to capture the imagined essence of an entire group, namely, the "American Negro." Johnston rarely photographed solitary individuals, and the majority of her Hampton photographs depict entire classes concentrating on lessons staged for the camera. The students in Johnston's photographs are not named, nor in any other way identified as individuals. They are not memorialized as relatives, lovers, or glamorous stars; in short, they are not sentimentalized. In Johnston's images, Hampton students become examples, samples of the disciplined, successful "American Negro." Even Du Bois's photographs, the large majority of which are portraits, do not name or identify individuals but instead present portrait photographs as the unnamed evidence of African American individuality.

Presented within the context of both sociology and reform, Johnston's and Du Bois's images may have resonated with the contemporary sensationalist images Jacob Riis produced of the "other half," even as they foreshadowed the social documentary photography of Lewis Hine.[17] However, unlike Riis's dramatic images of tenement squalor and Hine's detailed images of child laborers, the photographs Johnston and Du Bois brought to the American Negro exhibit aimed not to document social problems but to record the progress made by African Americans at the turn of the century. Johnston's photographs, in particular, do not attempt to illustrate a need for social reform but, instead, to demonstrate the success of a social reform already in place, namely, the Hampton Institute's program of manual training.[18] Rather than attempting to incite public furor at social ills, the American Negro exhibit, as a whole, proclaimed to present the work of "a small nation of people, picturing their life and development without apology or gloss."[19] While the celebratory tone of the exhibit certainly marked a well-deserved source of African American pride, it also may have communicated a much more problematic message to Anglo-American viewers. The congratulatory nature of the exhibit may have demonstrated to white viewers that they no longer needed "to be afraid of black people or [to feel] guilty at what had happened to them after Reconstruction."[20] To white American viewers schooled in the rhetoric of the "Negro problem," the American Negro exhibit may have indicated that segregation, disfranchisement, and poverty were not debilitating social forces, and that in fact, the "Negro problem" itself could be socially segregated.

Functioning as a kind of visual testimony or evidence, Johnston's and Du Bois's images dovetailed not only with the photographs of social science but also with the photographs that circulated in the registers of biological science. By the turn of the century, photographs were being used in the United States to map "deviant" bodies in prisons, medical treatises, and scientific explorations into the nature of both gender and race.[21] Within eugenics itself, photographs were used to illustrate the biological roots of social structures. As we have seen in previous chapters, Francis Galton devised two photographic techniques for recording what he believed to be the physical indices of essential biological difference, both "composite portraiture" and a standardized system of family photography. I would like briefly to review both of these photographic forms here because they exemplify the scientific representations of racialized bodies that Johnston's and Du Bois's photographs implicitly contest.

Readers will recall that Galton believed his system of composite photographic portraiture would enable one to document the common physical features of a predetermined group. Further, as Galton maintained that physical features indexed the intellectual and creative potential of races, he felt corporeal signs could legitimately be said to demarcate an individual's appropriate position in a hierarchical society. Faithful to the purported objectivity of the photographic image, Galton held that the abstract, "perfected" signs of common physical characteristics could be determined by overlaying a series of standardized frontal and profile "mug shots" of any given group. Galton imagined his composite photographic records would serve as a kind of key for (presumably white) viewers, as a map of the racialized body, allowing one to study abstract, "pure" racial characteristics, and later to discern the racial identity of individuals according to that model, to assess their corresponding intellectual attributes and to situate them "appropriately" along a sliding social scale stratified by biological difference.

While Galton aimed to identify the salient characteristics of predetermined biological groups with his composite portraiture, he hoped to monitor the reproduction of racial attributes with his scientific "family albums." Once again, in 1884 Galton designed both the *Record of Family Faculties* and *The Life History Album*.[22] The *Record* served as a chronicle of one's ancestry (a kind of detailed family tree) and was intended to aid individuals in predicting their own, and their children's, future abilities and ailments. Galton suggested that photographic portraits would provide important illustrations of family members in the *Record*, enhancing verbal descriptions and medical histories. The photograph played a more central role in *The Life History Album*, as Galton proposed a system of thorough, standardized photographic documentation for that album. *The Life History Album* was designed to record the growth and maturation of an individual child (functioning as a precursor to the modern "baby book"), and Galton called upon parent contributors to make a standardized set of photographs of the child, "an exact full-face and a profile,"[23] every five years. In each of his records, Galton treated the

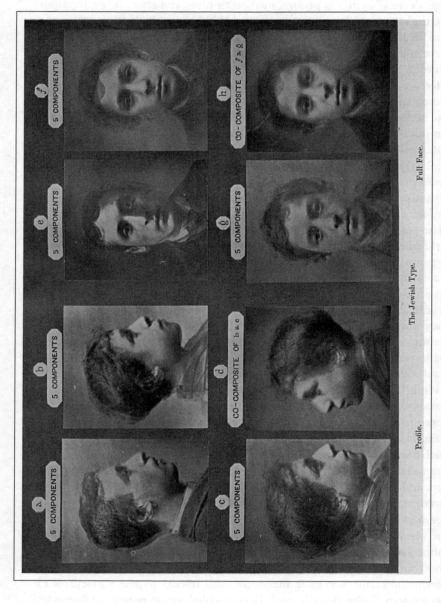

Figure 3.1. Francis Galton, "The Jewish Type," composite portraits. Reproduced from Karl Person, *The Life, Letters and Labours of Francis Galton*, vol. 2: *Researches of Middle Life*. Cambridge: Cambridge University Press, 1924

photograph as a transparent document of the body, which was in turn regarded as the physical record of an essential racial character transmitted through the blood. By standardizing family photograph albums, Galton hoped to open the sentimental family archive to scientific scrutiny.

While systems of photographic documentation were being designed to record and codify the body as the ultimate sign of racial essence at the turn of the century, representing the more elusive national character that supposedly corresponded to racialized physical features (the very core of racial identity in Galton's terms) proved a more difficult task. It is at this juncture, between the photographic documentation of "race" and of "nation," that Johnston's and Du Bois's photographs for the American Negro exhibit enter public visual culture. While the photographic work of Frances Benjamin Johnston and W. E. B. Du Bois represents an important moment in the history of building national photographic archives, Johnston and Du Bois themselves were not the first to attempt to portray "American character" in photographs. Mathew Brady, a famous forerunner in the history of visualizing American identity, sought to emblematize national character in his portraits of "Illustrious Americans," which he made throughout the 1850s and 1860s.[24] Brady was one of the first, and one of the most famous photographers in the nineteenth-century United States, making a name for himself and his portraits in the early days of daguerreotype, the first photographic process. Adhering to a long-standing aesthetic tradition that positioned the eminent individual of the formal portrait after the larger-than-life posture of Roman busts, in three-quarter profile, looking loftily up and away from viewers, Brady photographed an extraordinary number of famous American politicians, artists, and authors.[25] Brady showcased his portraits of "Illustrious Americans" in his popular New York galleries, intending, no doubt, to heighten his own public renown and also, as he himself explicitly contended, to provide salient examples of the American character for the praise and emulation of others. Hoping to increase the circulation of his portraits, in order to provide both a national historical record and an exemplary model of national character for Americans at large, Brady selected twelve of his many portraits to be reproduced and circulated in a printed *Gallery of Illustrious Americans*. Each of Brady's daguerreotype portraits, reproduced as a lithograph for printed form, was accompanied by a written biographical text that expounded the particularly American character of each representative individual. Brady's "Illustrious Americans" were not "typical," but model Americans, the embodiment of abstract ideals, and their biographies attested to the specific achievements that could not be read in their faces. Unlike Galton, who attempted to represent in abstract form the "typical" physical features of a "national race" with his composite photographs, Brady aimed to depict the equally abstract spiritual and moral characteristics of individuals who emblematized "national ideals" in his daguerreotype portraits. While Galton looked to the lowest common physical denominator as the definitive sign of a racialized national identity, Brady heralded the highest spiritual denominator as the signal of "true" American character.

While his aim was quite distinct from Francis Galton's later "scientific" attempts to document a racialized national identity, Mathew Brady's portraits of "Illustrious Americans" also, if only implicitly, forwarded a distinctly racialized notion of national character. As Alan Trachtenberg has argued, Mathew Brady's printed *Gallery of Illustrious Americans*, produced in 1850, placed "national heroes" from opposing sides of a dissolving nation upon the same patriotic landscape.[26] A portrait of Zachary Taylor, the Whig president, joins a portrait of John Calhoun, outspoken Democrat, on the patriotic horizon of Brady's *Gallery*.[27] In this way, Brady's images of "Illustrious Americans" extricate national character from the tense political conflicts developing over slavery and racial difference in the pre-Civil War era, reproducing (white, male) Americanness as an exalted quality removed from and unmarred by divisive politics rooted in racial conflicts. Half a century later, Johnston's and Du Bois's photographs delineate national character after the Civil War, and decades after Reconstruction, in a period of heightened racial tension, continuing debate over the so-called Negro question, Jim Crow segregation, African American disfranchisement, and increased lynching. By representing the American character of people excluded from many levels of legal and cultural American privilege, namely, African and Native Americans at the turn of the century, Johnston and Du Bois situate national identity within the terrain of racial identity and racial conflict. In this later period, as evidenced by Galton's eugenics, racial divisions actually fueled the definition of national character, as this once ephemeral, interiorized quality was harnessed to a racially inflected biology. Indeed, reading Brady's earlier images of "Illustrious Americans" from this turn-of-the-century vantage point, the implicit, albeit unmarked, signs of a racialized white national identity become (if not already) apparent in Brady's portraits.

While not the first photographs to attempt to portray "American character," Johnston's and Du Bois's images represent new visual strategies for representing an explicitly racialized version of national identity (unlike Brady's implicitly racialized "Illustrious Americans"). Responding to new notions of national and racial identities, Johnston and Du Bois present new means of visually codifying American identity. At the time of the Paris Exposition, Galton's theories of racial difference were gaining wide acceptance among physical and social scientists in the United States, and it is against an increasingly dominant discourse of racialized national essentialism that one must read Johnston's and Du Bois's efforts to visualize competing versions of the "American Negro" at the turn of the century. As I will demonstrate, Frances Benjamin

Johnston's Hampton photographs and W. E. B. Du Bois's photograph albums both contest the racialist biological determinism of Galton's particular national paradigm, even as the two projects work toward different ends.

Making Americans

Frances Benjamin Johnston's views of the Hampton Institute may have been slightly anomalous in what Du Bois described as an exhibit produced and executed exclusively by African Americans. Indeed, in his review of the exhibit, Du Bois praises Johnston's work, which won a gold medal at the exposition, but as he evaluates the images, he completely effaces Johnston herself as photographer. Du Bois states: "From Hampton there is an especially excellent series of photographs illustrating the Hampton ideas of 'teaching by doing.'"[28] In Du Bois's account, Johnston's images are important because they "illustrate" Hampton ideas, and the photographs themselves come "from Hampton," not from Johnston. Du Bois emphasizes the discursive formulation of Johnston's subject matter, the pedagogical philosophy of the Hampton Institute, but he fails to comment on the codified construction of the photographs themselves. In his review, Du Bois draws upon discourses of documentary and scientific photography that erase the ideological underpinnings that inform photographic images and styles. Putting Johnston back into a reading of the Hampton photographs, one can begin to tease out her ambiguous position as photographer, if only, finally, to heighten the conundrum of her role as white woman photographer for an African American exhibit. It is important to underscore the ways in which the American Negro exhibit was implicitly tied to a complexly gendered and racialized system of white social surveillance at the turn of the century, in order to explain some of the tensions and conflicting racial ideologies apparent in Johnston's photographs themselves.

The Hampton Institute was an industrial arts and teachers' training school founded in 1868 by Colonel Samuel Chapman Armstrong and originally designed to educate former slaves after the Civil War. Toward the latter part of the nineteenth century, the institute began to admit Native American as well as African American students. In 1899, the second president of Hampton, Hollis Burke Frissell, invited Frances Benjamin Johnston to photograph the school specifically for the Paris Exposition of 1900.[29] Johnston produced dozens of images at Hampton, including landscapes, group portraits of bands, teams, and graduating classes, and a couple of family portraits taken in homes. By far her most common views, however, were those made in classrooms, depicting students "in action" working on a project or paying exaggerated attention to the day's lesson. All of Johnston's classroom images are marked by a certain stiffness, the result of long camera exposures combined with a staginess aimed at illustrating a particular skill, idea, or theme for later viewers. Messages written on the board and visual spaces constructed to privilege the camera's point of view mark the intended presence of a later viewing audience. However, this future audience (and, indeed, the photographer herself) is not acknowledged directly by the student subjects in Johnston's images. In Johnston's photographs, Hampton students never meet the camera with curious, approving, or challenging eyes; instead they are depicted as the objects of a scrutinizing gaze, one that has been invited to evaluate their "progress and present conditions." The omission of any recorded interaction between Hampton students and Johnston, photographer standing in for later viewers, the absence of even a documented glance in the direction of the camera, poses Hampton students as the willing objects of an outside investigation, the test subjects of an external study.

Johnston's unquestioned role as observer, as practitioner of a dominating, unreturned gaze at the Hampton Institute, may at first surprise contemporary viewers schooled in a tradition of psychoanalytic feminist film theory. After Laura Mulvey's groundbreaking analysis of the "male gaze" posed and propelled by the film industry, how can one explain a white woman's visual mastery over African American and Native American students at the turn of the century?[30] Does Johnston adopt a masculine position from which to represent her subjects as the feminine objects of a "male gaze"? Must Johnston perform a kind of "transvestism" in order to visually represent her desire in these images?[31] And what is the nature of the desire Johnston's photographs project? The answers to these questions are not readily available within a field that poses the visual representation of desire as strictly sexual, hegemonically heterosexual, and invisibly white. Scholars such as bell hooks, Jacqueline Bobo, Jane Gaines, Richard Dyer, Manthia Diawara, Isaac Julien, Kobena Mercer, and Mary Ann Doane, who are revising Mulvey's influential work, addressing "race" and "ethnicity" as discourses central to the development of modern visual culture, have problematized understandings of desire and of the gaze that have been dominated by gender categories, reading the history of visual culture (and specifically the history of Hollywood film) as a trajectory bound by white Western ethnocentrism.[32] In addition, artists and scholars such as Coco Fusco and Trinh T. Minh-ha, and cultural critics such as Timothy Mitchell, Deborah Poole, Mary Louise Pratt, Fatimah Tobing Rony, and Deborah Willis are beginning to identify what bell hooks has called a "white supremacist gaze"[33] as a key constituent of Western colonial and imperial power.[34] Bound to a mythology of scientific "objectivity" and a system of increasing social surveillance, an invisible "white gaze" functioned as the arbiter of biological and cultural difference in Jim Crow U.S.A. While one cannot discard the terms of gender in assessing Johnston's gaze, it is important to rearticulate Johnston's visual practice according to the *racialized* discourses of gender and sexuality dominant at the turn of the century.[35]

In the post-Reconstruction South, "the gaze" functioned as a powerful threat within the racist discourse of sexual assault. According to one cultural historian who assesses the spread of lynching at the turn of the century, "If a black man so much as looked a white woman in the eye he risked being accused of lechery or insolence, and in some cases this was as good as committing an actual assault."[36] Given this racist dynamic, Johnston's inability to photograph students looking at the camera, looking at her, takes on profoundly disturbing connotations. Photographing the Hampton Institute during the height of racial terrorism in the South, at a time when African American men were lynched in the name of protecting the sexual (and racial) purity of white womanhood, Frances Benjamin Johnston herself may have posed a dangerous threat to her Hampton subjects.[37] Indeed, while Johnston was pursuing another photographic project six years later, one of her African American male hosts was attacked for his audacity in accompanying a white woman alone at night. In this cultural context, eyes buried in tasks in Johnston's photographs signify doubly the charged power dynamics out of which her images were produced. As a white woman, Johnston represented both a threat and a potentially powerful advocate for young African Americans. African American feminist scholars and activists, like Ida B. Wells and Anna Julia Cooper, recognized the white woman's singular power to dismantle the mythology of rape that fueled post-Reconstruction lynching.[38] However, Johnston's photographs do not forward the radical defense of African American virtue heralded by Wells but instead ambiguously skirt the "challenging" gaze, thereby subtly reproducing a legacy of racial hierarchy in the turn-of-the-century South.

Johnston's position as photographer was embedded within a particularly troubling sexual discourse, a cultural logic sexualized primarily according to a paradigm of white supremacism. As a white woman, Johnston was able to scrutinize African American bodies because, according to white supremacist lynching logics, a white woman's sexual desire for a black man (or woman) was posed as unimaginable. While the white woman's sexual desire itself was marked as a disruptive perversion of "natural" white womanhood in turn-of-the-century U.S. culture, her willing alliance with an African American man could be attributed only to the perversity and moral depravity of her doubly "unnatural" white womanhood. Indeed, as we have seen, a patriarchal white discourse of lynching erased this potential "anomaly" by representing a white woman's alliance with an African American man as the result of a single destructive force, namely, black male aggression.[39] Given these racist mythologies specific to the turn-of-the-century United States, the potentially gendered or sexualized nature of Johnston's gaze cannot be separated from her racialized position as a white woman in an increasingly white supremacist nation. Johnston's role as subject, gazing upon nameless African American bodies, is not, first and foremost, a position privileged in terms of gender but in those of race. As an Anglo-Saxon woman, Johnston represented the very lifeblood, the potential reproduction, not only of the Anglo-Saxon race but also of the "American character" delineated by white supremacists and eugenicists in the United States. Her inability to represent an exchange of looks or glances between herself and Hampton students not only construes her images as the "natural" documents of an unobtrusive assessment but also points to the social distance maintained between Johnston and her photographic subjects. As photographer, and as white woman, Johnston has not "mixed" with her subjects; her photographs remain "objective," and her (white, female) person remains "pure."[40]

Frances Benjamin Johnston's Hampton photographs attest to the social progress of African Americans in several different registers. A set of six family portraits comprise a "before and after" series that demonstrates the upward class mobility of Hampton graduates. Run-down shacks turn into sparkling white mansions through the Hampton metamorphosis depicted by Johnston. Representing the middle-class "success" of Hampton's graduates, these photographs ideologically frame Johnston's images of classroom activities, setting the terms – modern, mechanical, and economic – in which the achievements of the Hampton Institute's program of rigorous discipline and manual training are to be measured. Inside this frame of upward economic mobility, photographs of classroom activities, by far the most numerous in Johnston's portfolio of Hampton images, depict students' rapt attention and willing participation in the day's lesson. The students in Johnston's photographs are shown mastering geography, arithmetic, sewing, welding, agriculture, and a remarkable focus and self-discipline, as well as the explicit codes of an American identity. I am particularly interested here in the images that illustrate Hampton students engaging in American rituals because these images begin to formulate one version of the "American Negro" at the turn of the century. Taken as a whole, Johnston's photographs for the American Negro exhibit would seem to propose that much of the progress made by African Americans after the Civil War was rooted in the process of Americanization itself.

Unlike Mathew Brady's portraits of "Illustrious Americans," Frances Benjamin Johnston's photographs of African American Hampton students do not single out famous individuals but instead depict anonymous groups of schoolchildren and young adult students simply *as* Americans.[41] Further, Johnston does not necessarily assume the American identity of her subjects, as Brady does, and she is at pains to *demonstrate* the American character of

Hampton students to the later viewers of her photographs. While Brady may have been eager to specify the exemplary characteristics of his model Americans, Johnston worked hard simply to delineate the American character of Hampton students. In a political climate increasingly dominated by eugenicist white nationalists, Johnston had to establish the American identity of her African American subjects for the resistant portion of her white audience.

In several of her most salient photographs, Johnston represents African American students, even the very young, as preeminently patriotic. The image entitled *Saluting the Flag at the Whittier Primary School* is almost impossible to read as anything other than a performance of national pride.[42] In this photograph the young students are packed so tightly into a square formation that it is very difficult to distinguish their individual characteristics – they are presented as one entity, performing one act – and thus, the image appears to be less about Whittier students than it is about the act they are performing, namely, "saluting the flag." A guiding adult presence is difficult to discern in the photograph, making the image read as the documentation of a self-compelled performance on the part of these African American children. With its visual emphasis on a patriotic performance that appears to be self-directed, this photograph subtly forwards a vision of assimilation that contests scientific definitions of racial difference and national character at the turn of the century. If eugenicists believed in biologically distinct races, and in national characteristics specific, and exclusive, to each race, then Johnston's image of Whittier students saluting the flag presents American patriotism as one of the natural dispositions of young African American students. In other words, Johnston's image naturalizes the *performance* of national identity. It highlights performance in order to demonstrate the "nature" of an essentialized *national character*, if not of an essentialized racial identity.[43] With this image Johnston would seem to cleave American national character from an essentialized Anglo-Saxon identity, countering eugenicists' coterminous delineation of nation and race with a potentially multiracial nation.

In another image taken at the primary school, *Thanksgiving Day lesson at the Whittier,* several young students construct a miniature log cabin as their classmates watch conscientiously. Despite the rather exaggerated attention of the seated classmates, it is clear that the set for this photograph has been constructed to privilege exclusively the gaze of the viewer of this image. The ring of students around the table opens up on the side closest to the photographic plane, allowing the photographer and later viewers to observe the activity with ease. The view of the children on the far side of the room (farthest away from the camera) is almost surely blocked by this group of students and teachers. The center stage has been shifted away from the students for the benefit of outside viewers. Nevertheless, most of the seated students pretend to watch the scheduled activity with great attention. Their poses are utterly rigid; they sit with hands folded on top of their desks, disciplined into postures of gratitude, as in prayer. The obedient manner of these students in the background, not watched by the teachers in the room, is, perhaps, a "reassuring" performance conducted for the (white) viewer of the photograph. The official, explicit classroom activity is contextualized by words written on the blackboard: "The Landing of the Pilgrim Fathers." These words literally frame the young builders; further, they point to the ideological framework that is being formulated around the performers. These young black children are taught new American histories, and they are given (symbolically) new "fathers." Whittier students become heirs to a patriarchal national lineage, learning where to anchor an official American identity. Their *national heredity*, if not their *racial origin*, is reinvented as they are taught to forget the boats that brought many of their forebears to North American in chains, and to relocate their roots on the Pilgrim ships.[44] They are being symbolically reborn, as it were, as Americans of an Anglo-Saxon tradition.

One of the most profoundly disturbing and revealing of Johnston's Hampton photographs is her image entitled *Class in American History*. In this photograph, an American Indian, in fully codified ethnic regalia, including feather headdress, beaded leather, and braided hair, joins the stuffed

Figure 3.2. Frances Benjamin Johnston, *Saluting the Flag at the Whittier Primary School*, 1899. Reprinted courtesy of the Library of Congress

American bald eagle behind him as a symbol of the American nation. The photograph functions as a "before meets after" image, in which Native and African American Hampton students observe a Native American from the past. The Native American most explicitly on display is studied as part of American history – as an object, an ancient relic, but not as a subject of that history. The other Native Americans, also on display for the viewer in Johnston's image, are to look on him as part of their American, but not their ancestral, past; they are to substitute a national narrative, one now shared with their African American colleagues, for a racialized hereditary bloodline. The Native American students in this image bear no apparent relation to the historic display; like their African American colleagues, they stand in military uniforms and Victorian dresses, with hair worn short or pulled back in a single knot. In this photograph, racially specific ethnic identities have been erased in a narrative of national belonging. The image constructs a lesson in which "Americans" learn about the past of "Indians."[45]

Circulating in a period of vast immigration in the United States, Johnston's assimilationist images do not anchor national identity in the land of one's ancestors, but instead in a specific set of cultural codes. Indeed, if the photographs did root American identity in ancestral land, there would be no need to Americanize Hampton students, whose ancestors had resided in

Figure 3.3. Frances Benjamin Johnston, *Thanksgiving Day Lesson at the Whittier*, 1899. Reprinted courtesy of the Library of Congress

Figure 3.4. Frances Benjamin Johnston, *Class in American History*, 1899. Reprinted courtesy of the Library of Congress

the territories of the twentieth-century United States for hundreds (in the case of African Americans) and thousands (in the case of Native Americans) of years. If land occupation were the measure of national inclusion in Johnston's photographs, Johnston's own American identity might prove more tenuous than that of her subjects. Instead, Johnston's Hampton photographs forward a narrative of assimilation in which national identity is first untangled from and then reintegrated into the visual codes of racial identity.[46] Johnston's Hampton photographs show students actively engaged in the process of learning national histories and performing national rites. The photographs would seem to separate national character from a racially encoded discourse of blood, marking American identity as a set of performative rituals. However, despite this seeming rupture between an essential and a performative national identity, the rituals of turn-of-the-century Americanness posed in Johnston's photographs are rooted, ultimately, in a history delineated by Anglo-Saxon bloodlines – the blood of the "founding" "Pilgrim fathers." Thus, while Johnston's photographs first de-essentialize the markers of American identity, they then re-essentialize those performances by anchoring them in a distinctly Anglo-Saxon lineage. Johnston's images forward the beginnings of Anglo-Saxon heritage on North American soil, celebrating the ethnically specific national identity that was founded with the "landing of the Pilgrim fathers." The unmarked signs of whiteness are visualized through patriotic perform-ances in Johnston's images; Anglo-Saxon identity is consolidated in a specific discourse of national American identity. In Johnston's photographs the "American character" of African American students is measured by the success with which those students can adopt and perform Anglo-Saxon-inspired national rituals. At "best," then, this seeming erasure of racial identity in favor of a common national character is tenuous and readily recuperated in the terms of racial essentialism. Johnston's Americans are easily reinterpreted in the "separate but equal" terms of turn-of-the-century segregation.

Conserving Race in the Nation

While Frances Benjamin Johnston's photographs of the Hampton Institute forward a narrative of assimilation, tenuously erasing racial difference under the signs of a national identity, W. E. B. Du Bois's photograph albums recuperate a sense of racial autonomy and self-determination. The three photograph albums (four volumes) that I discuss here constitute one of three displays supervised by W. E. B. Du Bois for the American Negro exhibit at the Paris Exposition of 1900. In addition to the albums, other exhibits included a series of charts and graphs documenting the social and economic progress of African Americans, and a three-volume set containing the com-plete legal history of African Americans in Georgia.[47] As the photographers who produced the images for Du Bois's albums remain unidentified, the focus of authorship is transferred to Du Bois himself, the person most conspicu-ously associated with the albums, as collector, organizer, and presenter of the images. Thus, while Du Bois may not have produced the photographs for his albums, I pose Du Bois as the archivist who framed the images both materially and ideologically.

Du Bois's photograph albums, entitled *Types of American Negroes, Georgia, U.S.A.* (volumes 1–3) and *Negro Life in Georgia, U.S.A.*, include formal studio portraits of African Americans, as well as informal snapshots of groups outdoors, children playing, and people working, images of homes and busi-ness establishments, and interior views of elaborately decorated middle-class parlors. Unlike Johnston's formal photographs of students at the Hampton Institute, Du Bois's snapshots convey a sense of spontaneity and immediacy. The subjects and scenes of these images are diverse, and many of the photo-graphs suggest an interaction between unnamed photographers and subjects, through the variously questioning, surprised, laughing and smiling faces that greet later viewers. Signifying in the context of Johnston's professional group portraits, the snapshots collected in Du Bois's albums may have functioned in ways similar to those images preserved in African American family archives throughout the twentieth century, as described by bell hooks. According to hooks:

> Photographs taken in everyday life, snapshots in particular, rebelled against all of those photographic practices that reinscribed colonial ways of looking and capturing the images of the black "other." Shot spontaneously, without any notion of remaking black bodies in the image of whiteness, snapshots posed a challenge to black viewers. Unlike photographs constructed so that black images would appear as the embodiment of colonizing fantasies, these snapshots gave us a way to see ourselves, a sense of how we looked when we were not "wearing the mask," when we were not attempting to perfect the image for a white supremacist gaze.[48]

hooks's sense of snapshots "rebelling" against institutionalized racist representations is important to bring to a reading of the images collected in Du Bois's albums, as Du Bois himself proposed that many of his images of "typical Negro faces...hardly square with conventional American ideas."[49] However, while the spontaneity of the snapshot may have enabled a form of African American self-imaging outside the dominant domain of racist representation, it is also important to remember that Du Bois's snapshots were viewed not only privately but also publicly, by a racially and ethnically mixed international audience. Read against Johnston's photographs, and in the context of the American Negro exhibit, Du Bois's images pose a challenge to both black and white viewers. They are offered up explicitly and self-consciously as images that contest racist "American ideas" and representations, as photographs that ask white viewers to rethink dominant American "conventions."

While the presumed spontaneity and informality of the snapshots Du Bois gathered for his albums may have posed them somehow at odds with dominant racist imagery, the more profoundly contestatory images in Du Bois's albums are those that both adopt and subvert turn-of-the-century imaging conventions. The photographs that most powerfully differentiate Du Bois's collection from Johnston's work are the formal, individual portraits that introduce each volume of *Types of American Negroes*. The portrait series presents individuals posed for two photographs each, one a frontal image, the other a profile or semiprofile image. Each pair of photographs is presented on a separate page, and the first two volumes of *Types of American Negroes* consist almost entirely of such portraits (there are well over two hundred). Unlike Johnston's group photographs, constructed uncannily around the "unnoticed" presence of the camera, these images mark their subjects' intentional interaction with the camera, and as the viewer progresses through the albums, she is met with the gaze and the likeness of one individual after another. The subjects of these formal portraits engage the gaze of photographer and later viewer, forcing white viewers to recognize what bell hooks has called a resistant, "oppositional gaze,"[50] a gaze that confronts and challenges the privileged position of the white viewer, a gaze that makes that position apparent.

While Johnston's Hampton photographs, framed by "before and after" images, mark the Hampton Institute's notion of advancement, Du Bois's series of portraits does not produce a narrative of teleological development. In Du Bois's albums there is no explicit activity performed to demonstrate a particular ideology of race progress for later viewers. Further, signs of Americanness, such as those performed in Johnston's photographs, are utterly absent from Du Bois's albums. Du Bois assumes the Americanness of his subjects and indicates no need to demonstrate the "American character" of the "Negroes" of "Georgia, U.S.A." Articulating such a position in "The Conservation of Races," Du Bois delineates the collateral boundaries of "Negro" and "American" identity as follows: "We are Americans, not only by birth and by citizenship, but by our political ideals, our language, our religion. Farther than that, our Americanism does not go. At that point, we are Negroes, members of a vast historic race."[51] The African Americans in Du Bois's albums need not prove their right to be included in an American Negro exhibit; because they are Americans by birth, they need not assimilate. Further, while Du Bois defines the national ties of Americanism in the cultural terms of "political ideals," "language," and "religion," he also defines racial identity primarily in cultural terms that transcend theories of physical difference founded in blood. Rejecting "the grosser physical differences of color, hair and bone" as the definitive determinants of racial identity, Du Bois identifies "subtle, delicate and elusive" forces as the foundation on which distinct races develop. According to Du Bois, "While these subtle forces have generally followed the natural cleavage of common blood, descent and physical peculiarities, they have at other times swept across and ignored these."[52] In other words, for Du Bois, "race," like "national character," is not an essential property, and it does not always follow the reproduction of a single bloodline.

Given Du Bois's assertions regarding the inessential "nature" of racial identity, it is disturbing how the title of his albums – *"Types" of American Negroes* – echoes the terms of turn-of-the-century scientific "race" taxonomies.[53] Even the repetition of poses and props evident in Du Bois's collection of portraits marks a consistency in formal representation roughly congruent with the mathematical evenness of scientific photographic archives that sought to map codified bodies of racial "others." Further, the very style in which Du Bois's portraits are made and presented, the combination of frontal and semiprofile poses, marks a striking formal parallel to the photographs

Galton hoped parents would collect of their children in *The Life History Album* – "An exact full-face and a profile should be obtained" (5). As noted previously, Galton's *Life History Album* was designed to document the maturation of a single child by creating a standardized archive of images of the child. The archive allowed a reader to compare later documents to earlier documents, and to measure change, valued in terms of "growth" or "progress," via apparent physical alteration over time. While Galton's albums set up a comparison of various representations of a single individual, Du Bois's albums structurally invite a comparison of one individual to another. Like Galton, Du Bois keeps the terms of his archive consistent – Du Bois's images adhere to a singular format that limits the factors of difference to the individuals photographed. Assembled as they are, individuals posed in parallel, Du Bois's photographic portraits encourage viewers to read one image against the next, comparing the aspect of one individual to another. What one finds after a comparative scrutiny of the individuals represented in Du Bois's albums is a vast diversity in the physical characteristics generally held to determine racial identity at the turn of the century. In Du Bois's albums, blond and blue-eyed "Negroes" take their place beside brunette and brown-eyed "Negroes."

Reproducing the variations of "color, hair and bone" that were legally encompassed by "one drop" of blood identity laws at the turn of the century,[54] Du Bois's albums confront white America's obsession with the color line in two ways. First, they dismantle the stereotyped and caricatured images of African Americans reproduced in American popular culture. To that end, Du Bois's portraits construct a kind of composite image in reverse. Instead of blending individual portraits or likenesses into a single, abstract "type," Du Bois's albums dismantle the notion of a unifying image, filtering difference back into the picture, decomposing the singular "American Negro" into diverse, multiple "Negro *Types.*"[55] Second, the albums point toward the dual nature of "colonial desire," the white supremacist's simultaneous repulsion from and fascination with interracial reproduction.[56] Du Bois's albums of "types" represent the biracial subjects of the unions so powerfully repressed by lynching at the turn of the century, challenging the very social dictates that forbade Frances Benjamin Johnston's black male subjects to return her gaze.[57] The portraits dispute the notion of racial purity upheld by eugenicists and white supremacists, and the anti-miscegenation laws that prohibited legal, mutually desired unions between whites and blacks, but not the rape of African American women by white men.[58] Looking back at the images of African American men, women, and children procured by Du Bois at the turn of the century, I hope to participate in Du Bois's antiracist project by transforming the trajectory laid out for the white woman scholar, namely, the position culturally delimited for Frances Benjamin Johnston at the turn of

Figure 3.5. From *Types of American Negroes, Georgia, U.S.A.*, compiled by W. E. B. Du Bois, 1900. Reprinted from the Daniel Murray Collection courtesy of the Library of Congress

the century. To that end, I suggest that Du Bois's images do not purport to represent "real" blackness, to invite white (or black) viewers of the early or late twentieth century to gaze upon blackness "revealed." Du Bois's images do not lift "the Veil" that distorts images of African Americans by projecting them through a lens of colonial desire.[59] Instead, the photographs begin to enable white viewers to see the Veil itself, to see the cultural logics and privileged practices that reproduce racism. Consequently, it is toward an investigation of the visual structures of white supremacy, and of resistance to those forms, that I have directed my reading of Du Bois's images, situating the photographs in the context of the visual legacies produced by the converging discourses of eugenics and white supremacist nationalism at the turn of the century.

Du Bois's photographs signify somewhere between the images collected in scientific archives of "race" at the turn of the century and Mathew Brady's earlier portraits of "Illustrious Americans." Formally similar to Galton's frontal and profile portraits standardized to meet the needs of scientists, Du Bois's albums of "types" present a kind of evidence, but not proof of the essential, physical racial identity sought by eugenicists and white supremacists.[60] If in style and even title Du Bois's albums evoke a history of racist photographic

Figure 3.6. From *Types of American Negroes, Georgia, U.S.A.*, compiled by W. E. B. Du Bois, 1900. Reprinted from the Daniel Murray Collection courtesy of the Library of Congress

documentation, they do so only to undercut that scientific register of dehumanized bodies with formal portraits of African Americans elegantly dressed in middle-class trappings. Further, Du Bois's profile and semiprofile portraits formally approximate not only Galton's scientific photographs but also Brady's "illustrious" images. Many of Du Bois's near-profile portraits represent individuals posed not at exact right angles, but instead positioned like Brady's "Illustrious Americans," in a three-quarter turn, with eyes directed slightly upward, out of the photographic frame, perhaps focused on political ideals. Unlike Brady's "model" portraits, however, Du Bois's pairs of portraits enact both the visual tropes of "illustriousness" and those of engagement and recognition. Within the codes of late-nineteenth-century U.S. visual culture, Du Bois's portraits represent African Americans both as "Illustrious Americans" contemplating shared ideals and as distinct individuals. Du Bois's frontal portraits meet and engage the eyes of later viewers, individualizing and particularizing American identity, placing a lofty American character squarely back on the terrain of negotiation, conflict, and "race."[61]

While Du Bois's "American Negroes" are Americans both legally and philosophically, their fundamental identity remains racial within the nation. Du Bois's photograph albums contest a program of assimilation by portraying not the "American Negro" but instead the "Negroes" of "America." In his albums, Du Bois subtly challenges the exclusive authority of white Americans, assimilationists and eugenicists alike, to represent and to signify, to embody, the boundaries of national identity. Unlike Galton's racially essentialized notion of American character, Du Bois's sense of national identity is cultural, philosophical, and legal. However, while Du Bois's version of American character corresponds to a set of ideals, his vision of national identity, unlike Brady's, does not erase or conceal racial identity. Unlike Johnston's assimilationist images, Du Bois's photographs do not harness patriotic performance to a single racialized bloodline. In the power-laden struggles to define "nation," "race," and "American" at the turn of the century, W. E. B. Du Bois envisions a nation of multiracial Americans.

Notes

1   W. E. B. Du Bois, "The Conservation of Races" (1897), in *A W. E. B. Du Bois Reader*, ed. Andrew G. Paschal, introd. Arna Bontemps (New York: Macmillan, 1971), 25.

2   In *The Souls of Black Folk*, published in 1903, Du Bois asserts that "double consciousness, "the "twoness" of living as both a "Negro" and an "American" (8), is central to "the strange meaning of being black" (3) in the United States at the dawn of the twentieth century. W. E. B. Du Bois, *The Souls of Black Folk* (1903; New York: Vintage, 1990).

3   Studies of the "nation" that focus on the printed word generally follow the influential work of Benedict Anderson. See Anderson, *Imagined Communities: Reflections on the Origin and Spread of Nationalism* (London: Verso, 1983).

4   Deborah Poole and Vicente Rafael have begun the important task of investigating the role photography played in nation-building. See Poole, *Vision, Race, and Modernity: A Visual Economy of the Andean Image World* (Princeton, NJ: Princeton University Press, 1997); Rafael, "Nationalism, Imagery and the Filipino Intelligentsia in the Nineteenth Century," *Critical Inquiry*, 16:3 (Spring 1990), 591–611; id., "White Love: Surveillance and Nationalist Resistance in the US Colonization of the Philippines," in Amy Kaplan and Donald Pease (eds.), *Cultures of United States Imperialism* (Durham, NC: Duke University Press 1993), 185–218.

5   See the section entitled "The Negro Building" in the *Report of the Board of Commissioners Representing the State of New York at the Cotton States and International Exposition Held at Atlanta, Georgia, 1895* (Albany, NY: Wynkoop Hallenbeck Crawford, 1896), 197–9. This text also reproduces Booker T. Washington's famous "Atlanta Compromise" speech delivered at the opening ceremonies of the Cotton States and International Exposition in Atlanta, 1895.

6   For discussions of racism at the Chicago World's Columbian Exposition of 1893, see Hazel V. Carby, " 'Woman's Era': Rethinking Black Feminist Theory," in *Reconstructing Womanhood: The Emergence of the Afro-American Woman Novelist* (New York: Oxford University Press, 1987), 3–19, and Robert W. Rydell, "The Chicago

World's Columbian Exposition of 1893: 'And Was Jerusalem Builded Here?'" in *All the World's a Fair: Visions of Empire at American International Expositions, 1876–1916* (Chicago: University of Chicago Press, 1984), 38–71.

The exclusion of African Americans from official participation in the Chicago World's Columbian Exposition was protested by both Ida B. Wells and Frederick Douglass. See Wells, *The Reason Why the Colored American Is Not in the World's Columbian Exposition* (1893), in *Selected Works of Ida B. Wells-Barnett*, introd. Trudier Harris (New York: Oxford University Press, 1991), 46–137.

7   W. E. B. Du Bois, "The American Negro at Paris," *American Monthly Review of Reviews*, 22:5 (Nov. 1900), 576.

8   The success of the exhibit is reported by Morris Lewis in "Paris and the International Exposition," *Colored American Magazine*, 1:5 (Oct. 1900), 295.

9   Du Bois, "The American Negro at Paris," 575.

10   [...] See Richard Hofstadter, *Social Darwinism in American Thought*, rev. edn. (Boston: Beacon Press, 1944), esp. 161–7; Daniel J. Kevles, *In the Name of Eugenics: Genetics and the Uses of Human Heredity* (New York: Knopf, 1985); and Donald K. Pickens, *Eugenics and the Progressives* (Nashville, TN: Vanderbilt University Press, 1968).

11   Anderson, *Imagined Communities*.

12   Francis Galton, *Hereditary Genius: An Inquiry into Its Laws and Consequences* (London: Macmillan, 1892); id., *Inquiries into Human Faculty and Its Development*, 2nd edn. (London: J. M. Dent & Sons, 1907); id., *Memories of My Life* (London: Methuen, 1908); and id., *Natural Inheritance* (London: Macmillan, 1889).

13   Fatimah Tobing Rony describes such exhibits in her fascinating essay on anthropology and early ethnographic film entitled "Those Who Squat and Those Who Sit: The Iconography of Race in the 1895 Films of Felix-Louis Regnault," *Camera Obscura*, 28 (Jan. 1992), 262–89.

Robert W. Rydell uses the image of a "sliding scale of humanity" to describe the racialized spatial logics that organized "ethnic" displays at the World's Columbian Exposition of 1893. See Rydell, "The Chicago World's Columbian Exposition of 1893: 'And Was Jerusalem Builded Here?'" esp. 64 and 65.

14   Thomas J. Schlereth, "The Material Universe of the American World Expositions, 1876–1915," in *Cultural History and Material Culture: Everyday Life, Landscapes, Museums* (Ann Arbor, University of Michigan Press, 1990), 284–5. See also Rydell, "The Chicago World's Columbian Exposition of 1893."

15   Alan Trachtenberg, "Illustrious Americans," in *Reading American Photographs: Images as History, Mathew Brady to Walker Evans* (New York: Hill & Wang, 1989), 38.

16   [...] See Walter Benjamin, "The Work of Art in the Age of Mechanical Reproduction," in Hannah Arendt (ed.), *Illuminations*, trans. Harry Zohn (New York: Schocken Books, 1969), 217–52. I do not mean to claim that Johnston's or Du Bois's images were more "objective" than any others, but simply to underscore that these images were imbedded in new discursive contexts, new institutional

paradigms that sought to claim the photograph as objective evidence for social science.

17 For an analysis of the ways in which Lewis Hine and Jacob Riis were posed as the "fathers" of documentary photography in the United States by photography historians working in the 1940s, see Sally Stein's essay "Making Connections with the Camera: Photography and Social Mobility in the Career of Jacob Riis," *Afterimage*, 10:10 (May 1983), 9–16. After first outlining how many historians have conflated the work of Hine and Riis, Stein goes on to analyze important political and aesthetic differences in the work of these two men. For more on the invention of "documentary" photography, see Alan Trachtenberg, "Camera Work/Social Work," in *Reading American Photographs*, 164–230. For more on the work of Lewis Hine and Jacob Riis see Verna Posever Curtis and Stanley Mallach, *Photography and Reform: Lewis Hine and the National Child Labor Committee* (Milwaukee, Wis.: Milwaukee Art Museum, 1984); Judith Mara Gutman, *Lewis W. Hine and the American Social Conscience* (New York: Walker, 1967); and Jacob Riis, *How the Other Half Lives* (1890; reprint, New York: Dover, 1971).

18 Booker T. Washington, Hampton's most famous graduate and founder of the Tuskegee Institute, has come to be regarded as one of the most important advocates of manual training for African Americans at the turn of the century. Washington argued that manual training and strict self-discipline would provide economic independence for African Americans, a resource Washington viewed as more immediately important than political power. Washington advocated slow, gradual economic and social advancement for African Americans, arguing that manual, as opposed to professional, white-collar labor, was a necessary first stage in "the natural law of evolution" for any race. Washington claimed: "In a word, we have got to pay the price for everything we get, the price that every civilized race or nation has paid for its position, that of beginning naturally, gradually, at the bottom and working up towards the highest civilization." See Booker T. Washington, "The Storm before the Calm," *Colored American Magazine*, 1:4 (Sept. 1900), 202. See also the following works by Washington: "Industrial Education: Will It Solve the Negro Problem?" *Colored American Magazine*, 7:2 (Feb. 1904), 87–92; *The Successful Training of the Negro* (New York: Doubleday, 1903); and *Up from Slavery* (1901; reprint, New York: Penguin, 1986).

For counterarguments to an educational system focused exclusively on manual labor, see W. E. B. Du Bois, *The Souls of Black Folk*, and "The Training of Negroes for Social Power," *Colored American Magazine*, 7:5 (May 1904), 333–9.

19 Du Bois, "The American Negro at Paris," 577.

20 This is how James Guimond describes Frances Benjamin Johnston's photographs of the Hampton Institute, displayed at the Paris Exposition of 1900. I am suggesting that the entire American Negro exhibit may have communicated this sense of moral and political reprieve or reconciliation to white viewers. James Guimond, "Frances Johnston's *Hampton Album*: A White Dream for Black People," in *American Photography and the American Dream* (Chapel Hill: University of North Carolina Press, 1991), 39.

21 See Allan Sekula's fascinating study of the body as constituted by its imagined place within (or outside of) the photographic archive in "The Body and the Archive," *October*, 39 (Winter 1986), 3–64.

22 Francis Galton, *Record of Family Faculties* (London: Macmillan, 1884); id., *The Life History Album* (London: Macmillan, 1884).

23 Galton, *The Life History Album*, 5.

24 For more on Brady's "Illustrious Americans," as well as a history of the "celebrity" photographic portrait in nineteenth-century U.S. culture, see Barbara McCandless, The Portrait Studio and the Celebrity: Promoting the Art," in Martha A. Sandweiss (ed.), *Photography in Nineteenth-Century America* (Fort Worth, TX: Amon Carter Museum, 1991), 48–75.

25 Alan Trachtenberg describes the formal style of Brady's daguerreotype portraits in relation to a tradition of Roman sculpture in "Illustrious Americans," in *Reading American Photographs*, 46.

26 Ibid., 50–1.

27 Ibid., 50.

28 Du Bois, "The American Negro at Paris," 577.

29 Frances Benjamin Johnston, *The Hampton Album*, ed. Lincoln Kirstein (New York: Museum of Modern Art, 1966). For more background information see also James Guimond, "Frances Johnston's *Hampton Album*: A White Dream for Black People," in *American Photography and the American Dream* (Chapel Hill: University of North Carolina Press, 1991), 21–53, and Laura Wexler, "Black and White and Color: American Photographs at the Turn of the Century," *Prospects*, 13 (Winter 1988), 341–90.

30 Laura Mulvey, "Visual Pleasure and Narrative Cinema," in Brian Wallis (ed.), *Art after Modernism* (New York: Museum of Contemporary Art, 1984), 360–74.

31 In a piece entitled "Afterthoughts on 'Visual Pleasure and Narrative Cinema' Inspired by *Duel in the Sun*," Laura Mulvey explains a woman's pleasure in the scopophilic process of film viewing as the result of a kind of "transvestism" through which the female viewer adopts a masculine viewing position. The film Mulvey reads in order to come to this conclusion, namely *Duel in the Sun*, follows the life course of a "mixed-blood" female protagonist who is exoticized, feared, and desired primarily in terms of her racialized identity. Mulvey's analysis of "transvestism" does not account for the power of racialized identities and racialized identifications in this film, and it is into this interpretive space that my own reading of Frances Benjamin Johnston's photographs enters a history of visual theory. I read Johnston's work, and her position as photographer, not only through the terms of gender but also through the terms of race posed at the turn of the century in the United States. Mulvey, "Afterthoughts on 'Visual Pleasure and Narrative Cinema' Inspired by *Duel in the Sun*," 69–79.

32 bell hooks, "The Oppositional Gaze: Black Female Spectators," in *Black Looks: Race and Representation* (Boston: South End Press, 1992), 115–31; Jacqueline Bobo, *Black Women as Cultural Readers* (New York: Columbia University Press, 1995); Jane M. Gaines, "White Privilege and Looking Relations: Race and Gender in Feminist Film Theory," *Screen*, 29:4 (Autumn 1988), 12–27; Richard Dyer,

"White," *Screen*, 29:4 (Autumn 1988), 44–64; Manthia Diawara, "Black Spectator-ship: Problems of Identification and Resistance," in *Black American Cinema*, ed. Manthia Diawara (New York: Routledge, 1993), 211–20; Isaac Julien and Kobena Mercer, "Introduction: De Margin and De Centre," *Screen*, 29:4 (Autumn 1988), 2–10; Mary Ann Doane, "Dark Continents: Epistemologies of Racial and Sexual Difference in Psychoanalysis and the Cinema," in *Femmes Fatales: Feminism, Film Theory, Psychoanalysis* (New York: Routledge, 1991), 209–48.

Discussing the "characteristic aesthetic and political problems of postmodern-ism," Isaac Julien and Kobena Mercer note: "It is ironic that while some of the loudest voices offering commentary have announced nothing less than the 'end of representation' or the 'end of history,' the political possibility of the *end of ethnocentrism* has not been seized upon as a suitably exciting topic for description or inquiry" (2). Julien and Mercer call for critical theorists of visual culture to "recognize and reckon with the kinds of complexity inherent in the culturally constructed nature of ethnic identities," and to assess the "implications" such complexity "has for the analysis of representational practices" (3). Julien and Mercer, "Introduction: De Margin and De Centre," 2–10.

33 bell hooks, "In Our Glory: Photography and Black Life," in Deborah Willis (ed.), *Picturing Us: African American Identity in Photography* (New York: New Press, 1994), 42–53.

34 Coco Fusco, *English Is Broken Here: Notes on Cultural Fusion in the Americas* (New York: New Press, 1995); Trinh T. Minh-ha, *Woman, Native, Other: Writing Postcoloniality and Feminism* (Bloomington: Indiana University Press, 1989); Timothy Mitchell, *Colonizing Egypt* (Berkeley: University of California Press, 1988); Poole, *Vision, Race, and Modernity*; Mary Louise Pratt, *Imperial Eyes: Travel Writing and Transculturation* (New York: Routledge, 1992); Rony, *The Third Eye*; Willis, "Introduction: Picturing Us," in Willis (ed.), *Picturing Us*, 3–26.

I find hooks's "white supremacist gaze" useful as a means of making explicit the ways in which the cultural privilege of looking has been racially coded in the United States. Playing upon Richard Dyer's notion that "white" generally func-tions as an invisible cultural category, while, as Julien and Mercer note, the "colored" is made all too visible, I would suggest that "white" is rarely the object of the Western gaze because it is almost always behind (not in front of) that gaze, imbedded in the viewing position, structuring the reception and the evaluation of Other bodies represented. hooks, "In Our Glory," 50; Dyer, "White"; Julien and Mercer, "Introduction: De Margin and De Centre," 6.

35 In my analysis of Frances Benjamin Johnston's racially encoded viewing privilege, I have tried to follow the lines of analysis suggested by Mary Ann Doane in her individual response for the "Spectatrix" special issue of *Camera Obscura*. According to Doane, "Consideration of race ought to transform the entire framework of the questions posed to the media rather than simply initiating an extension of existing feminist categories (such as the female spectator) to include other, neglected differences. Racial difference and sexual difference are not parallel modes of differentiation that are equally accessible to the same theoretical appar-atus. Neither are they totally unrelated: there is a densely intricate history of

relations between the two which requires analysis. What is needed is a theorization of the relation between racial and sexual differences, particularly with respect to questions of visibility and invisibility, power and sexuality." Mary Ann Doane, "Introduction," *Camera Obscura*, 20–1 (May–Sept. 1989), 146.

According to bell hooks, such a space is opened up by the critical black female spectator. "Black female spectators, who refused to identify with white womanhood, who would not take on the phallocentric gaze of desire and possession, created a critical space where the binary opposition Mulvey posits of 'woman as image, man as bearer of the look' was continually deconstructed." hooks, "The Oppositional Gaze," 122–3.

In my reading of Johnston's position as photographer/viewer I am trying to tease out the "densely intricate" relations posed between "race" and "gender" at the turn of the century in the United States. I am trying to read Johnston's position as one inscribed not only by a heterosexual, binary gender hierarchy but also by a racial hierarchy of access to the gaze.

36 Vron Ware, *Beyond the Pale: White Women, Racism, and History* (London: Verso, 1992), 182. bell hooks also discusses this powerful cultural prohibition against the African American gaze in her analysis of an "oppositional gaze," specifically the critical gaze of the African American female spectator who interrogates filmic representation in order to protest the negation of African American women in Hollywood films ("The Oppositional Gaze"). Jane Gaines also notes that there is a need for work that analyzes "the social prohibitions against the black man's sexual glance" (21), in order to demonstrate the ways in which "racial difference structures a hierarchy of access to the female image" ("White Privilege and Looking Relations," 17).

37 Lynching, legally defined as murder committed by a mob of three or more persons, increased dramatically in the 1890s. See George M. Fredrickson, *The Black Image in the White Mind: The Debate on Afro-American Character and Destiny, 1817–1914* (New York: Harper & Row, 1971), and Paula Giddings, *When and Where I Enter: The Impact of Black Women on Race and Sex in America* (New York: William Morrow, 1984), 18.

38 Wells, *Southern Horrors: Lynch Law in All its Phases* (1892), in *Selected Works of Ida B. Wells-Barnett*, introd. Trudier Harris (New York: Oxford University Press, 1991), 14–45; Cooper, *A Voice from the South*.

39 See Karen Sanchez-Eppler, "Bodily Bonds: The Intersecting Rhetorics of Feminism and Abolition," *Representations*, 24 (Fall 1988), 28–59.

40 My discussion of Johnston's relative social privilege in relation to African American students at Hampton is not meant to suggest that Johnston's own visual mastery of African American bodies was not itself subject to a more comprehensive white male social prerogative. Indeed, the discourse and the practice of lynching worked to protect the interests of the white male body and the reproduction of a patriarchal white bloodline. See especially Sanchez-Eppler, "Bodily Bonds," and Ware, *Beyond the Pale*.

41 I wish to distinguish both the aim and the signifying context of Johnston's Hampton photographs from Brady's earlier portraits of "Illustrious Americans."

However, the terms of these distinctions might become much more subtle if one were to compare Johnston's own presidential portraits to those of Brady's. In addition to her extensive work photographing Hampton and Tuskegee Institutes, Johnston ran a successful portrait business, and she established herself as a kind of court photographer for several presidents, including Theodore Roosevelt.

For biographical information on Johnston, see Pete Daniel and Raymond Smock, *A Talent for Detail: The Photographs of Miss Frances Benjamin Johnston, 1889–1910* (New York: Harmony, 1974); Olaf Hansen, "Frances Benjamin Johnston," in *Notable American Women: A Biographical Dictionary*, vol. 4, ed. Barbara Sicherman and Carol Hurd Green (Cambridge: Belknap Press, of Harvard University Press, 1980), 381–3.

42 Whittier was the primary school affiliated with the Hampton Institute. According to Eric Hobsbawm, "The educational system was transformed into a machine for political socialization by such devices as the worship of the American flag, which as a daily ritual in the country's schools, spread from the 1880s onward." Eric Hobsbawm, "Mass-Producing Traditions: Europe, 1870–1914," in Eric Hobsbawm and Terence Ranger (eds.), *The Invention of Tradition* (Cambridge: Cambridge University Press, 1983), 280.

43 My reading of the way patriotic performance establishes an essentialized "Americanism" for Hampton students in Johnston's images is informed by Judith Butler's innovative work on gender. Butler reads gender as an endlessly repeated performance that fabricates an interiorized, "essentialized," sexual identity. Judith Butler, *Gender Trouble: Feminism and the Subversion of Identity* (New York: Routledge, 1990), esp. "Subversive Bodily Acts" (79–141), and "Conclusion: From Parody to Politics" (142–9).

While I find Butler's work particularly useful because her analysis denaturalizes the notion of "essence," I do not mean to suggest that gender identities and national identities (or racial identities) are culturally coextensive, or even parallel. I am chiefly interested here in noting the ways in which "essences" of various kinds are inscribed on the body through ritualized and repeated performances.

44 According to Laura Wexler, "The students she [Johnston] photographs are the sons and daughters of 'freedom's first generation,' but nothing about their appearance reveals this fact. Instead, the invisibility of the marks of slavery seems to be part of the point." Wexler, "Black and White and Color," 369.

45 My reading of this image is inspired by Laura Wexler's insightful interpretation of this image and other of Johnston's Hampton photographs in "Black and White and Color," esp. 381–3. For another important reading of this image, see Guimond, "Frances Johnston's *Hampton Album*," 35.

46 In a lecture he delivered at the University of California, San Diego, on March 4, 1992, entitled "Nationalism and Ethnicity," Benedict Anderson argued that ethnic identities were maintained in the modern age of international migrations through the family photograph album. According to Anderson, before modern mass migrations, ethnic and national identities were considered almost coextensive, subsumed under the single category "nationality." In premodern days, one "knew

who [and what] one was" because his or her ancestors were buried in the local graveyard, in the earth, where one would someday join them. Families and identities were tied to the local, to the land of one's "patria." After the mass migrations of the nineteenth and twentieth centuries, ethnic identities ceased to be isomorphic with national identities. In the new social context of the late twentieth century, Anderson claims that the photograph album replaces the graveyard as the site of ethnic identifications. Grandmother and grandfather are no longer buried in one's local graveyard – they are buried in the family photo album. Thus, the photograph album enables one to formulate and maintain an ethnic identity distinct from one's national identity.

In this chapter, I examine the intersection of racial (Anglo-Saxon) and national identifications in the construction of "American" identities at the turn of the century, and explore photographs as sites of racially inflected *national* identities.

47   This collection of Du Bois's papers is housed in the Prints and Photographs Division of the Library of Congress.

48   hooks, "In Our Glory," 50.

49   Du Bois, "The American Negro at Paris," 577.

50   hooks, "The Oppositional Gaze."

51   Du Bois, "The Conservation of Races," 26.

52   Ibid., 21.

53   For a detailed analysis of how nineteenth-century white supremacists came to use the category of "type" to describe what they considered permanent racial differences, see Robert J. C. Young, *Colonial Desire: Hybridity in Theory, Culture and Race* (New York: Routledge, 1995), esp. 13–18 and 129–33.

54   In her fascinating study of how the law was employed to perpetuate a "broad-reaching ideology of white supremacy" at the turn of the century, Susan Gillman demonstrates how "for purposes of racial identification, the color line was more stringently and narrowly defined" in legal terms in the early twentieth century. Gillman also notes that "the legal fraction defining blackness was still one thirty-second 'Negro blood'" in Louisiana, as late as 1970. Susan Gillman, "'Sure Identifiers': Race, Science, and the Law in Twain's *Puddn'head Wilson*," *South Atlantic Quarterly*, 87:2 (Spring 1988), 205.

55   In his reading of the latter portion of *The Souls of Black Folk*, Paul Gilroy suggests that W. E. B. Du Bois makes "a bid to escape not just from the South or even from America but from the closed codes of *any* constricting or absolutist understanding of ethnicity." Paul Gilroy, *The Black Atlantic: Modernity and Double Consciousness* (Cambridge: Harvard University Press, 1993), 138.

56   See Young, *Colonial Desire*, chapter 6, "White Power, White Desire: The Political Economy of Miscegenation."

57   Du Bois's biracial "types" problematize the notion that "race" is visible in physical characteristics by demonstrating that "Negroes," legally defined as such by "one drop" of African American blood, may nevertheless bear the stereotypical features of "whiteness" (blond hair, blue eyes, and pale skin). Du Bois's photographs of "types of Negroes" thus function in ways similar to the typecasting of white actresses to play mulatta characters in mid-twentieth-century Hollywood films

that Mary Ann Doane describes in "Dark Continents." According to Doane, the practice of employing white actresses to represent mulatta characters "tends to demonstrate inadvertently the quiescent discordance between ideologies of racial identity (defined by blood) and cinematic ideologies of the real (as defined by the visible)" (235).

58　Ida B. Wells makes this critique in *Southern Horrors*, 26–8.

59　I am drawing on Du Bois's well-known image of "the Veil," which he employs to introduce *The Souls of Black Folk*. Du Bois, *The Souls of Black Folk*, 3. I am also borrowing the notion of "colonial desire" from Young's *Colonial Desire*.

60　Adapting Henry Louis Gates, Jr.'s theory of Signifyin(g) to the domain of visual culture, we might say that Du Bois's photographs of "Types of American Negroes" Signify upon Francis Galton's eugenicist photographs and albums, reproducing those images with a difference. Henry Louis Gates, Jr., *The Signifying Monkey: A Theory of African-American Literary Criticism* (New York: Oxford University Press, 1988). Coco Fusco has utilized Gates's theory of Signifyin(g) in her analysis of Lorna Simpson's photographic art. Fusco, *English Is Broken Here*, esp. 100.

61　Fatimah Tobing Rony describes the Other's resistant "look back" as a "third eye" in her fascinating study of ethnographic film, *The Third Eye*.

4

Techniques of the Imaginary Nation:
Engendering Family Photography

LAURA WEXLER

A s a professor of American Studies, I find I can no longer stand in the early morning queue in the coffee shops that seem to be New Haven's only current growth industry, or sit down to drink my coffee and read the paper at a small table in such a place, without thinking that we are literally the same group of people described by Benedict Anderson as the vital communicants of the quasi-religious mystery of the productivity of print capitalism. In the glancing recognition of one another simultaneously engrossed in absorbing the daily newspaper, we perform a ritual transubstantiation of ourselves from disparate anonymous individuals into a modern nation. "The obsolescence of the newspaper on the morrow of its printing," writes Anderson, in a justly famous passage of *Imagined Communities*,

> creates this extraordinary mass ceremony: the almost precisely simultaneous consumption ("imagining") of the newspaper-as-fiction. We know that particular morning and evening editions will overwhelmingly be consumed between this hour and that, only on this day, not that.... The significance of this mass ceremony – Hegel observed that newspapers serve modern man as a substitute for morning prayers – is paradoxical. It is performed in silent privacy, in the lair of the skull. Yet each communicant is well aware that the ceremony he performs is being replicated simultaneously by thousands (or millions) of others of whose existence he is confident, yet of whose identity he has not the slightest notion.

Laura Wexler, "Techniques of the Imaginary Nation: Engendering Family Photography," in Reynolds J. Scott-Childress (ed.), *Race and the Production of Modern American Nationalism*. New York: Garland, 1999: 359–81. Reprinted with permission of Routledge/Taylor & Francis Books, Inc.

Furthermore, this ceremony is incessantly repeated at daily or half-daily inter-vals throughout the calendar. What more vivid figure for the secular, historically clocked, imagined community can be envisioned? At the same time, the news-paper reader, observing exact replicas of his own paper being consumed by his subway, barbershop, or residential neighbours, is continually reassured that the imagined world is visibly rooted in everyday life. As with [the Filipino nation-alist novel] *Noli Me Tangere*, fiction seeps quietly and continuously into reality, creating that remarkable confidence of community in anonymity which is the hallmark of modern nations.[1]

Bleary-eyed we may be. Nonetheless, *l'état, c'est nous*. In conjuring up the mutuality of persons who are transfixed simultaneously by the spatial and temporal juxtapositions on a page of newsprint as an image of the common-ality of the nation, Anderson has constructed a powerful metaphor of the nation as a community of readers. We are to take the ceremony of reading the newspaper, he writes, as the best "figure . . . that can be envisioned for the secular, historically clocked, imagined community." Apparently, American artists, such as mid-nineteenth-century photographer Gabriel Harrison, have also had a similar insight at critical points in our national formation.

However, as a *woman* professor of American Studies, I have come to realize that Anderson's figure of the origin of national consciousness as mediated through print capitalism manages its persuasion through two absolutely crucial, and structuring, absences, both of which are contradicted in my own experience in the coffee shop. The two intricately related absences are gender and photography, both of which, if accepted uncritically, portend badly for the capacity of scholars in American Studies to develop a theory of national formation that will adequately address its embeddedness in what Amy Kaplan and Donald Pease have called the "cultures of U.S. imperialism." It was not only printed texts but also accompanying images that formed the print culture that served preeminently from the mid-nineteenth century on to consolidate the institutions through which shone the "remarkable confidence of community in anonymity" that is the national faith. And women, along with the domesticity for which they are the sign, were the vehicle for the exploitation of gender as a mechanism of the racial distinctions by which and through which the imperial formations of the nineteenth century daily pic-tured their national community. If either women or the photomechanical reproductions of images are absent from an analysis, the history of modern nationalism cannot be fully understood.

Not to say that the absence or marginalization of women in accounts of nationalism is unusual. Stories of the nation often portray its origin as a *gender-inverted* birth, tending to incorporate its genesis in a narrative of masculine priority and privilege. The story told in *Imagined Communities* is not an exception. Indeed, the account in *Imagined Communities* of the coming into being through print capitalism of a modern national consciousness describes the birth of national consciousness solely as an act of masculine self-creation that erases the presence, the subjectivity, and the labor of women: "The newspaper reader, observing exact replicas of *his* own paper, being consumed by *his* subway, barbershop, or residential neighbours, is continually *reassured* that the imagined world is visibly rooted in *everyday life.*" Since this "everyday life," no doubt, is also "visibly rooted," pervaded, staffed, and perhaps made anxious by the presence of women, it suggests that the vision of an "imagined world" of "the newspaper reader" establishes communal bonds between men as an act that are preceded by the abjection of women.

Or, to put it another way, the parable of the newspaper suggests that whereas the emotion of nationalism draws a line between men, ambiguously demarcating both a border (us *or* them), and an avenue of communication (us *and* them), nationalism draws a line *around* women, a *cordon sanitaire* that variously encloses and extrudes them, constructs them as a fictive threat of difference that is a consequence of gender, and submits the actual differences between women themselves to erasure within the field of vision of the masculine gaze. One result is women's exclusion from representation either as actors or as instruments in the birth of the nation. In the coffee shop I like to attend, at least half of the newspaper readers, as well as the service personnel who are too busy in the morning crush to read the newspaper, are women. They are sure to harbor vibrant imaginings of this community in time and space, and perceptions formed through conflicts behind the counter *within* gender, race, and class as well as confrontations across the line of service. To these observations behind the *cordon sanitaire*, however, "the newspaper reader" seems studiously, even rather willfully, indifferent.

This erasure is not inevitable. Indeed, Orson Lowell's 1908 illustration for *Life* magazine takes the gender differences between the community of newspaper readers on the subway as its subject, interrogating both commonality *and* conflict in the varying political perspectives of their individual newspapers (Figure 4.1). From a more explicitly political point of view, a photo-collage made by the brilliant illustrator John Heartfield for the German Communist publication *AIZ* during the rise of the Nazis in the early 1930s expresses not only the existence but the meaning of different perspectives on, and in, newspapers that are the product of a culture defined not by the gracious coexistence of readers, as implied in Lowell's image, but by violence and domination.

Heartfield pictures a man wearing what looks to be a coarse shirt and heavy leather harness. The man's entire head is wrapped round with pages of a newspaper called *Varmaerz* ("Before March"), a title that refers to the time

Figure 4.1. Orson Lowell, *Untitled*, from *Life* magazine, 1908

previous to the March 1848 revolution in Germany. A text written in the lower right-hand corner of the collage is an acid nursery rhyme which reads, "I'm a head of cabbage, do you know my leaves? / Don't know up from down of my cares, / Yet quiet I keep and in a saviour believe. / I want to be a black-red-golden cabbage head: / Don't want to see or hear, don't want to rock the state's affairs. / And even if I'm to my underwear shed, / The red press won't come into my good lair." The "head of cabbage" is both a visual and a verbal pun that plays upon the fact that the German word for leaf, *Blatt*, also refers to a sheet of paper or a newspaper.

At the bottom of the collage, Heartfield has signed off with an impassioned plea to connect the refusal of "the newspaper reader" prior to the 1848 revolution to inquire into the authentic source and solution of his problems with the same ominous denial of "the newspaper reader" of the present. Declaring that it is vital to think about what nation one is imagining when one reads what newspapers, Heartfield writes: "He who reads bourgeois [news-]papers turns blind and deaf. Away with those deadening bandages!"[2]

In other words, different newspapers interpolate subjects differently into the national imaginary. The *substance* that transubstantiates from newsprint into nation during the "extraordinary mass ritual" of "consuming the 'news-paper-as-fiction'" matters crucially. And any description of reading the newspaper that allows us to forget that newspapers and readers differ by race, class, gender, and history is deceptive as well as irresponsible. If Anderson's gendered account of communal consciousness captures a real dynamic of the imagined community – and numerous jokes from American popular culture evince a similar awareness of a subtext of gender and of the compelling need to erase evidence of difference in power in the ritual of reading the newspaper – it also suggests that as national subjects, female readers would be better off to use our *own* newspapers, when we are at leisure to read them, to imagine how we have been represented as *outside* the boundaries of national community.

The absence or marginalization of photographic images, on the other hand, *is* usual in accounts of the birth of nationalism. It is striking to me, as I study the relation of photography to American nationalism, that photography is so repeatedly given such a minor role to play in the development of national consciousness, even though the activity of looking at photographs has been infinitely valuable since the early nineteenth century in the production of exactly that sense of "community in anonymity" that is the hallmark of the modern nation.

The notion of print capitalism spotlighted in *Imagined Communities* does not remark upon the existence of pictures in the newspapers and novels it considers. Even though Anderson writes explicitly and insightfully about photography in his discussion of "census, map, museum," these cultural forms are supplemental to his original figure of the newspaper and have not been permitted to affect it. Visuality does not infiltrate the newspapers he conjures up, nor are his newspapers imagined as serialized and mobile imperial (or anti-imperial) museums. Instead, *Imagined Communities* presents newspapers only as "one-day-best-sellers" that conform to the history of the book. From Anderson's vantage point, the newspaper is merely an 'extreme form' of the book…a book sold on a colossal scale, but of ephemeral popularity."[3] And as his discussion of the novel also makes clear, the book he has in mind is a purely textual form.

However, pictures have long been integral to the consumption of the newspaper-as-fiction. And after the invention of a practical photography in 1839, the astonishingly rapid series of technical inventions that supported increasingly cost-efficient methods to mass produce camera-made images challenged that form of the book profoundly. The nineteenth century's thrust into visuality culminated at the turn of the century in the discovery first of a photomechanical printing method that was able to translate actual photographs and then of the halftone process that was able to reproduce them along with text in both books and newspapers. The implications of these inventions were social as well as technological, philosophical as well as political. They remapped the spectatorial stance in a position of mass consumption and supported what critical theorist Jonathan Crary calls "the remaking of the individual as observer into something calculable and regularizable and of human vision into something measurable and thus exchangeable."[4] By so widely distributing the structural elements of a commodified gaze, photography both focused "the desire of contemporary masses to bring things 'closer' spatially and humanly," as Walter Benjamin described the political meaning of the "decay of the aura," and intensified the capacity of fascist or imperial governments to keep them at a distance. Mass photography changed the newspaper by "rendering [politics] aesthetic."[5]

Printed images in newspapers and magazines existed, of course, prior to photography. Before the halftone era, wood engraving and lithography were the only ways to mass produce printed images, and they were very expensive. Because of this, it was the elite publications, like *Century* and *Harper's* in the United States, that were illustrated and the penny, nickel, and dime novels that were not. In fact, as photography historian David Phillips observes, "[I]t was precisely *because* of their lack of illustration that ordinary people could afford these publications."[6]

Once the halftone process was in place, newspaper and magazine publishing changed and their demographics shifted accordingly. Although "in the late 1880's, it cost about $300 to prepare a full-page, wood-engraved printing plate," writes Phillips,

> a few years later using the halftone process, a like-sized plate could be prepared for less than $20. As a result, it became possible for every publisher in the country to illustrate their books, magazines, and newspapers. With the turn of the American printing industry to halftone technology in the 1890s, the national market for illustrated publications, which had sustained itself through the 1880s almost exclusively on the patronage of middle-class readers, was suddenly opened up to the ranks of the American working-class.[7]

What is particularly important here is that this burst of photographic invention corresponds quite closely with the era of national self-creation that most concerns Anderson. When print capitalism entered the era of nationalism, illustration was the property of the propertied classes. But as modernity got fully underway, this changed. Students of nationalism need to be imagining not only a different scene of reading, but a different object of reading as well. The newspaper that instantiates the nation is an illustrated text, and one whose messages concerning class and race are as potent as its circulation is wide and its readership gendered.

With its class coding in flux, the late nineteenth-century illustrated newspaper gave rise to mixed associations that were intimately bound up with masculine anxieties about gender and social control. These worries referenced concerns over racial and class reproduction from the point of view of the bourgeois newspaper reader. They accompanied what Walter Benjamin identified as the "age of mechanical reproduction" and taken together with Anderson's parable, they register a fuller sense of the revolutionary force of nineteenth-century print capitalism than we have yet confronted.

For instance, according to photography historian Derek Price, the *Illustrated London News*, which sold 26,000 copies of its first edition in 1842, had a weekly print run of 310,000 by 1863, and "claimed for itself a civilizing mission rather than a concern for profit."[8] But such a mission, while gratifying to a particular class vanity, could also be surprisingly depleting to key reservoirs of hegemony. Witness one of William Wordsworth's last poems, a sonnet written in 1846 in response to the *Illustrated London News*, and entitled "Illustrated Books and Newspapers." In it, Wordsworth articulated quite clearly the dangers that such pictures posed to a masculine print culture used to owning the means of textual interpretation.

The poem reads, in part:

> Now prose and verse sunk into disrepute
> Must lacquey a dumb Art that best can suit
> The taste of this once-intellectual Land,
> A backward movement surely have we here,
> From manhood – back to childhood; for the age –
> Back towards caverned life's first rude career.
> Avaunt this vile abuse of pictured page!
> Must eyes be all in all, the tongue and ear
> Nothing? Heaven keep us from a lower stage!"[9]

With a gesture of revulsion against picturing the news rather than merely writing about it, Wordsworth equated pictures in newspapers with the regression of the nation, or "Land," from "manhood back to childhood." He also associated them with a reversal of the evolution of *human* childhood toward "a lower stage!" In a double formulation that expresses the two characteristic poles of racist imperial discourse, Wordsworth blamed a crisis in masculine authority ("prose and verse sunk into disrepute") on the defeat of manliness by women, who rule childhood and "life's first rude career." He also blamed it on the "vile" contamination of civilization by the colonized in whose image all that had been "reputable" was turned upside down, so that the men in the "Land" play "lacquey" to "a dumb Art." The pictures that showed up in the *Illustrated London News*, it seems, brought disturbing news about the empire – news that could be more easily controlled in words.

Wordsworth died in 1850, well before the "halftone revolution" of 1885, as Neil Harris called it, placed the illustrated newspaper within reach of the British underclass, yet the newspapers were still too much for him.[10] But had he lived even until the turn of the century he would have found, as photography historian Robert Taft reports, that in one single week of March 1899 the *Illustrated London News* carried no fewer than forty-seven illustrations, twenty-eight of them based on photographs, and the majority reproduced by halftone, not to mention forty-three in the United States' *Harper's Weekly*, and forty-seven in *Leslie's Weekly*.[11] Shortly thereafter, London's *Daily Illustrated Mirror* became the first newspaper to be entirely illustrated

100

by photographs. By the time the early twentieth-century newspaper reader was recognizing himself in the sight of other men on the subway, at the barber shop, or in the neighborhood, photography and print were fully integrated institutions, newspapers were all over the place, and photographs were all over his papers.

What we learn from Wordsworth is that photography, like tattoos and hieroglyphics, threatened to collapse the virility of the nation into femininity, or into even more primitive or degenerate racially or class-marked types of communication. What we learn from Anderson is that women, though central to its formation, are excluded from the imagined "deep, horizontal comradeship" of the nation. Taken together, the dual erasure of women readers *of* the newspaper and feminine-gendered pictures *in* the newspaper blindsides the labor of national birth in Anderson's parable of national origin. That is, among the many "rude" persons looking over the shoulder of "the newspaper reader," women, the working classes, the nonwhite, and the colonized other all had access to the visual commodity form in newsprint, and all had the power to shatter the imaginary mirror in which the nation took its daily form.

It is partly for this reason that the Imaginary Nation invested so heavily in mechanical reproduction as a means of social control. It was necessary to force difference among readers into invisibility, or at least to erase its traces. Crary writes that in the optical regime subtended by what Michel Foucault on the one hand identified as "surveillance" and Guy Debord on the other as "spectacle," photography was used to endow "objects of vision [with] a mystified and abstract identity, sundered from any relation to the observer's position within a cognitively united field."[12] If the observer could be trained to accept an alienated and abstracted position vis-à-vis concrete objects of vision, that observer could probably also be enticed to accept a mystified position in the social order. In this context, it was possible to develop news photography as a preeminent site of gender, race, and class interpellation. News photographs could suture actual viewers into mythical spaces such as "the nation" with more efficiency than print, because more thoroughly than any hand-drawn illustration or written text news photography in the daily newspapers represented "the real." This was managed by an entire armory of codes that governed what was to be shown and what was not to be seen, what point of view made for "legibility" and what did not. Photography excelled at making things in newspapers appear truly to *be* the way that things *appeared* to be, to a viewer located at the proper outlook.

However, once again race and gender are integral. That this investment in a daily regime of visuality worked so well as an ideological vehicle for national self-fashioning also has everything to do with another domestic ritual that Anderson does not mention – the family photograph. The family portrait was a social practice which helped to a great extent to shape what was considered to be "real" in the first place. It provided an excellent screen through which the news could be filtered.

"After 1859, and the advent of Social Darwinism," writes Anne McClintock in *Imperial Leather*, the family became a figure of social cohesion at least as powerful and productive as the press:

> The family trope is important for nationalism in at least two ways. First, it offers a "natural" figure for sanctioning national *hierarchy*, within a putative organic *unity* of interests. Second, it offers a "natural" trope for figuring national time.... The family offered an indispensable metaphoric figure by which national difference could be shaped into a single historical genesis narrative.[13]

McClintock identifies another *gender-inverted* birth – that of the Family of Man – at another point of origin – that of "a single genesis narrative of global history." The story of "the universal family," she argues, was a master narrative that entirely disregarded the multiple contradictions and counter-narratives of actual families, and erased their relation to the "commodity market," to "politics," and even to "history proper." But if by this means the family as institution "became void of history," McClintock would have us understand that the Family of Man "as metaphor" became instrumental. Through it, the world's people were increasingly expected to conform to a single public image. "The central technologies that emerged for the commodity display of progress and the universal family," McClintock notes, were "those quintessentially Victorian institutions of the museum, the exhibition, photography and imperial advertising."[14]

In other words, the opportunity for constructing imagined communities was organized through cultural practices of display of, and to, the family. What I would like to add is that because of its centrality to all of them, including the newspaper, and because of its overwhelming coincidence with domestic portraiture, photography was the collating mechanism that bound the disparate units into one sturdy, ordered archetype. Once the national community was reconfigured as the evolutionary family, the historical simultaneity which Anderson identifies preeminently with print culture and McClintock with Victorian spectacle was evoked and naturalized not only through the public media but through the way shared public ritual rhymed with the privately experienced stages of the domestic life cycle recorded in the family album.

Photography played a specific ideological role in naturalizing the creation of the nation in the figure of the family. It was a trick mirror that presumably only reflected what it was actually helping to create. Conversely, it was the family's role to inoculate masculinity against the threat of feminization, degeneration, or devolution by posing (literally) the narrow, raced, classed, and gendered image of patriarchy as a microcosm of the nation. The result was that at one and the same time photography was able to project – even virtually embody – a vision of nationhood into the news dailies, the museums, the exhibitions, the ads, the censuses, and the maps; and to disguise exactly how much family violence, racial domination, and class exclusion actually underpinned its formation.

In the nineteenth-century U.S., many photographers sought quite consciously to work with the manifold implications of this articulation of family, race, and nation. In the discussion that follows I have room to examine just some of this vast amount of work. What interests me here is the repetition of the figure of George Washington, the "father of his country." Washington died before photography was invented, but his image, as icon, haunted America's nationalist photographers.[15]

The pioneering photo-constructions of New York daguerreotypist Gabriel Harrison offered hopeful early examples of ways to conceptualize the nation as family. An ardent nationalist during the War of 1812, a Free Soil Democrat during the election campaign of 1848, and an abolitionist, Gabriel Harrison was an adventurous patriot who placed his evolving conceptions of the nation's good above his own commercial success and his family's financial security. As the photographer who made the daguerreotype of "Receiving the News from California," Harrison clearly was thinking about the role of the newspaper in the production of the nation. But just as much to the point, he also produced a series of daguerreotype images depicting the nation as his very own family.[16]

In the first example, his son, whom he had named George Washington Harrison, embraces a bust of George Washington (Figure 4.2). The boy and the general commune across the generations in a physical relation that reflects both the fact of their shared names and the appearance of similar facial expressions around the mouth and eyes. Pygmalion-like, the living, breathing boy brings the stone statue into a kind of life by giving its name a symbolic circulation through his own "blood," and the statue prefigures its immortality. That is, the real George Washington lives again through the confusion of sires and surnames. Himself the father of his country, he has produced a young countryman whose own father, also a rightful heir of this now nationalized family name, has bequeathed it to his own son who, presumably, will continue the line.

In the second image, George Washington Harrison posed for his father as "Young America," delighting one contemporary critic with what he called the "life-like rendition of the flesh in this daguerreotype, which should arrest the connoisseur's attention at a glance" (Figure 4.3).[17] That is to say, the commentator believed that whosoever can discriminate ("the connoisseur"), will see how true to life is his conceit. The anti-type of Young America that the

Figure 4.2. Gabriel Harrison, *Youth Adoring the Bust of George Washington.*
Reprinted courtesy of the George Eastman House

living type of young George Washington Harrison has made real is a sight to
"arrest attention at a glance" because it demonstrates the epiphany that the
nation is incarnate in one's own family.[18]

In a third daguerreotype, Harrison took this notion of reincarnation even
further. He posed his son George Washington as "The Infant Saviour," further
conflating George the Father, George the Son, and Young America, the Holy
Ghost. If the American nation is a family, it is not just any family, but an
image of the divine family, "well calculated," as Gabriel Harrison said, "to
excite the admiration and awe of those who love the ideal, and can appreciate
a work of excellence" (Figure 4.4).[19] In a brilliant ambiguity that renders it

Figure 4.3. Gabriel Harrison, *Young America*. Reprinted courtesy of the George Eastman House

unclear whether the "work of excellence" is the daguerreotype, the family, or the nation, Harrison's statement expresses a generative paradigm that combines the Holy Family, the Family of Nations, and the Family of Man.

Two other early daguerreotype practitioners, Boston's Albert Sands Southworth and Josiah Johnson Hawes, also were fascinated by an idea of the nation as filiation.[20] Here, it is the Gilbert Stuart portrait of George Washington instead of a marble bust that is the focus of a child's attention, and the child is a girl instead of a boy. But the physically tight juxtaposition of the images placed at eye level with one another rivets the viewer's attention on the

105

Figure 4.4. Gabriel Harrison, *Infant Saviour*. Reprinted courtesy of the George Eastman House

question of resemblances between George Washington and the girl. As they face off against one another *en abîme*, the viewer scans the expressions of the old and the new Americans and compares them as one does the generations in a family portrait. Not being a son, the girl does not inherit George Washington's name, but as an American citizen she stands on his level, and indeed is a reflection of him, nonetheless (Figure 4.5).

Figure 4.5. Albert Sands Southworth and Josiah Johnson Hawes, *Girl with Portrait of Washington, c.* 1850. Reprinted with permission of the Metropolitan Museum of Art

But whether the relationship in these early daguerreotypes is posed as the literal consanguinity of a family name and family relationship, or as the social kinship conferred by race and class, the conceit of all the images is that the progeny of American democracy share an intimate identity with the same universal and sainted ancestor, George Washington. And the intensity of the relation of these children to the father of their country shows that although the actual configuration of the early national family might be fluid and might manifest itself in different combinations, the paradigm itself was already set.

In the work of Jacob Riis half a century later, we can see a shift. The intimate connection envisioned by Harrison and by Southworth and Hawes is no longer so easy to find. The point of view toward national identity is more distant and estranged, even when the camera is physically placed in close range. In Riis's 1890 book, *How the Other Half Lives*, racial difference, coded as a flood of dysgenic families unfit to care for their sons and daughters, threatens to erode the well-being of the nation.[21] The children were not a problem in the images from the early national period, but now, as Riis wrote, "the problem of the children becomes, in these swarms, to the last degree perplexing."[22] Riis took care to remind his readers that "these children with the training they receive – or do not receive – with the instincts they inherit and absorb in their growing up are to be our future rulers, if our theory of government is worth anything. More than a working majority of our voters now register from the tenements."[23] Apparently, he was not sure if "our theory of government" *was* a good basis on which to rest the nation.

Contemplating this potential flaw in the national bloodline of American democracy, Riis's viewer is split between the expression of a common sympathy (the universal family) and fear of contagion and devolution (the Darwinian jungle). By addressing viewers about the responsibilities of citizenship, Riis constructs them as national subjects and thus places them in opposition to the troubling child who is not at one with the nation (Figure 4.6). The viewer is the nation's child well grown. The family configuration used by Harrison, and Southworth and Hawes is still salient. But in Riis's imagery, unlike in that of Harrison and Southworth and Hawes, the symbolic "father of our country" is no longer anywhere to be seen. Instead of the marble bust, or the Stuart portrait, there is an empty space and a blank wall. Given an absent father, consanguinity curdles and the image of the nation as George Washington's natural, loving family ceases to exist. Instead, the images in *How the Other Half Lives* show families who need desperately to be *remade* in the image of Americans.

In reconfiguring the nation as a dysfunctional family, Riis was simultaneously remapping the relation of each nation to the others. And in fact, this remapping was profoundly expressive. Increasingly as the United States moved into the twentieth century, immigration, imperial incorporation, and internal migration were transforming the figure of the nation as an intimate nuclear group into one of far-flung families who necessarily, unwillingly, and sometimes even desperately bear the imprint of the nation. Countless American family albums illustrate this process of mutual remaking. To grasp the existence of "the secular, historically clocked, imagined community" while reading an immigrant family album is a very different communion than

Figure 4.6. Jacob Riis, *Girl of the Tenements, c.* 1898. Reprinted with permission of the Museum of the City of New York

reading the newspaper. The imagined nation reflected in the immigrant family album takes a distinctly alternate, often fragmented, and sometimes frightening form. These collections of vernacular images, hardly touched by historians, are the negative imprint of the ideological state apparatus: they offer a vivid counter-narrative to the official news.

Indeed, they are often uncanny repetitions of the original idea of an American family that allowed Gabriel Harrison and Southworth and Hawes to present George Washington and the nation's children as mirror images of one another. But with a difference. While in the early images the physicality of George Washington seemed almost palpable though he was merely a statue or a painting, in *these* pictures any literal representation of George Washington is missing. He appears as a symbol only, and that at the end of a long train of increasingly abstract associations between race, class, gender, and power. Here the name George Washington is no longer a straightforward patronymic, but a convoluted metonymy for the faceless city of officials who have made it so difficult to get into the country, or the gatekeeping currency that is so difficult to gather, or the broken promise of the protection of the law despite race, religion, and national origin. In the American immigrant family album, the earlier intimate embrace between the father of the nation and the sons and daughters of the family has disappeared. Instead, in order to be *part* of the nation, the immigrant family must triumph *over* it. The struggle of the immigrant family to do just that makes visible a nation that is a very different entity from the first.

The family album of the Jung family that is featured in Ruthanne Lum McCunn's *Chinese American Portraits: Personal Histories, 1828–1988* is a good example.[24] It pictures four generations of a Chinese-American nuclear family who, except for brief visits, never lived together in one place. For almost one hundred years, the only place this family was together was in the pages of the photograph album. In other words, it is the album itself that constructs the family. But it is also the nation that constructs the album. "For families like Betty's that have been separated for several generations, little is known about the individual members," remarks McCunn. "They exchanged few letters; visits home were rare. But there were photographs, and with them, fragments of information. The skeletal history they reveal is typical of the many families separated by economic and political circumstances beyond their control."[25]

For the Jung family, those circumstances included poverty, famine, war, and revolution in their Chinese homeland, and poverty, war, racism, and legal restrictions on land ownership, marriage, and immigration in the United States. Stopgap measures, temporary solutions, and phases of hope and despair are all reflected in the many pictures that show different configurations of the generations of Jungs living in different places, in China and America, and even under different surnames.

Simultaneously legible are interpenetrating configurations of American national consciousness. The 1895 photograph of Jung Pui Lun shows a laborer who jumped ship in order to enter California illegally, while the photograph of another sojourner, Yuk Kwun, taken around 1942 shows an immigrant drafted into the U.S. air force, sent to China as an American serviceman, yet unable to reunite with his family. Another photograph shows Yuk Kwun as a successful restaurateur in Carmel, California, in 1952, still separated from his family. And the 1950s photograph of his wife, Fung Yung, and their four children shows them stymied at the brink of immigration (Figure 4.7). It was when Yuk Kwun and his father tried to get their wives to the United States in the late 1950s that "the lies of fifty years started to unravel."[26] In 1962, the whole family was finally reunited in San Francisco thanks to a lawyer who advised them to "take advantage of the State Department Confession Program" and regularize their papers.[27] On this occasion, a group portrait of the simultaneous family finally assembled in America was added to the album. But what the photograph represents is easily as much the image of a changed national immigration policy as it is that of the newly undivided Jungs.

Arthur Dong's 1982 film, *Sewing Woman*, explores another solution to the imperative to recreate the image of the family in, around, through, and despite the image of the nation.[28] Once again, the space of the photograph is the only space in which the family can exist as a complete unit. However, in

Figure 4.7. Photograph of Yuk Kwun's family (mother, two siblings, wife, and four children) received while he worked in Pacific Grove, California, early 1950s. From Ruthanne Lum McCunn, *Chinese American Portraits*. Seattle: University of Washington Press, 1996. Reprinted by permission of Ruthanne Lum McCunn and Betty Woon Jung

111

this instance a photomontage instead of a collection of consecutive images is what constitutes the imagined whole.

Dong's film tells the life story of Zem Ping Dong who was brought illegally to this country as a war bride by her Chinese husband after he had served in the United States Army during World War II. They were eager to immigrate. But in order to take advantage of this rare opportunity, Zem Ping Dong and her husband had to pretend to be newlyweds. This meant they had to disown the eight-year-old son they already had, leaving him behind in China in the care of Zem Ping Dong's parents. When they arrived in this country, Zem Ping Dong and her husband began to have "our family's first American" children. But Zem Ping Dong longed for her first son and missed him terribly. The separation was supposed to be brief, but it dragged on for ten years. "One day [in 1953]," she recalls in the film, "we had a family picture taken and sent it back to our son waiting in China. We loved our American children. But we never felt like a complete family. So, we had our first son's portrait plugged into the picture. And that was as close as we *could* get to being a whole family" (Figure 4.8).[29]

The film ostensibly simply celebrates the iron-willed tenacity of a brave Chinese village girl whose courage, canny exploitation of American laws, and flat-out hard work eventually enabled her entire extended family to immigrate to the United States. But the spliced photograph reveals the emotional patchwork that making it into an *American* family demanded of this "simple sewing woman." It exposes as well the bricolage of American naturalization policy, fiercely enforced on some fronts, haphazardly on others, according to the changing whims, and the labor and military demands, of a nation whose self-conception seems alternately harsh, gullible, and indifferent to Chinese immigrant families like the Dongs. As is so often the case, a photograph in the family album is the clue to a much larger and fuller picture.

And finally, in an essay entitled "Nationalism, Imagery, and the Filipino Intelligentsia in the Nineteenth Century," Vicente Rafael uncovers the photographic substrate of a very different kind of American nation-making.[30] This one arises not in a domesticated, familial template for conceptualizing issues of citizenship, but in an entire country's resistance to that particular narrative of inclusion. Jose Rizal, the subject of Rafael's analysis, wrote the Filipino national novel *Noli Me Tangere* (1887), which serves as Anderson's prime example of the way that the national "fiction seeps quietly and continuously into reality." But Rafael is interested not only in Rizal's text but in photographs of Rizal as well, particularly the way that the circulation of studio portrait photographs of Jose Rizal nourished the growth of Philippine nationalism. Rafael proposes that the mechanical reproduction and proliferation of text and photographs may work at cross purposes in an era of national formation: "[W]hereas one [the text] involves the setting forth and

Figure 4.8. The photograph as the only space in which the complete family can exist. From Arthur Dong's film *Sewing Woman*, 1982. Reprinted by permission of Deep Focus Productions and Arthur Dong

working through of the contradictions and divisions of national identity, the other [the photograph] entails rendering such contradictions obvious, that is, visible and therefore tangential to conceptualization" (603).

The evidence is "two large photo albums" and numerous photographic portraits of Rizal and others of his circle which were "regularly taken in Europe for the benefit of his family and acquaintances" (603–4; ellipses deleted). Apparently, Rizal and his friends were eager to document themselves photographically in complex anti-imperialist, antiracist scenarios in which they challenged the infantilizing stereotypes of Filipinos and pictured themselves as virile men, cosmopolitan intellectuals, and potential national heroes. An example of this resistant "self-fashioning" may be seen in a photograph of Rizal and two of his friends in fencing uniforms, taken in Paris in 1890. The photograph explicitly works to reformulate gender, and would have been understood in Rizal's private circle as having an antiracist subtext, for the men's friends and families would have known that the photograph, as Rafael writes, "coincided with their interest in fencing, gymnastics, martial arts, and weight lifting – ways of marking their bodies apart from colonial categories. Posing with their swords firmly between their legs, [they] display a masculine alternative to what they conceived to be the menacingly androgynous and corrupt regime of the Spanish friars" (606; ellipses deleted).

But with Rizal's execution and subsequent translation into a national martyr, the family photographs of Rizal were taken out of their original context and displayed on "everything from stamps to currency notes, matchboxes to amulets, book covers to postcards" (610). The particular, subtle, and *gendered* reasons why such photographs were originally made no longer mattered; they were an individual's portraits no longer. With the family album splayed open, Rizal's photographs were transformed instead into publicly adoptable icons, personal fetishes turned inside out, tokens of friendship and brotherhood that had lost their idiosyncratic foundation in the private moment to become a national force.

It was this very capacity for iconicity, with what Rafael terms its "tension between imagination and imagery," that offered the chance for all Filipinos to become as one united family in simultaneous rebellion (593). At the same time, however, removing the photographs from their private context led to the "flattening of [Rizal's] legacy" through the tendency to "abbreviate the work of memory and imagination," and especially the memory of the historical complexities of his social positioning through the interface of race and gender that Rizal himself used those very photographs to display (610).

The legacy of the photographs is equivocal. As vernacular, nation-making commodities, they deftly figure the Andersonian "community in anonymity." But they also consign it to a historical "anonymity that persistently even if mechanically, haunts community" (611). In the supposedly instant legibility, and community, of the decontextualized photographs, the nation was smoothly remade in the image of a revolutionary son. But recontextualized, the photographs also channeled continued colonialism, the antithesis of Rizal's self-refashioning. What eventually happened was that they "serve[d] as the basis of the Rizal monument built in Manila in 1912 under the auspices of the U.S. colonial state" (610). That is, by disseminating Rizal's heroic image in this way, American nation-making managed to raise the phantom of

George Washington as the father of his country once again. But Jose Rizal's particular struggle was adulterated, and confused with the story of another father and another domination.

In closing, I want to propose that it would be highly worthwhile for scholars of American nationalism to attempt to clarify a photographic history of the national gaze, just as feminist scholars have long worked to elucidate a history of the male gaze. We might begin to codify when and where such a gaze comes into focus in the family album, just how it functions, and what it has been used to further and to disguise.

But, as I have been arguing, to do this absolutely requires attention to the intersection of women and nationalism, and more particularly of non-white families and nationalism. The nativist rhetoric illustrated in Jacob Riis's text illuminates historian Anna Davin's observation that in the age of empire the family and the state became mirrors for one another. "Since the parents were bringing up the next generation of citizens," she points out, "the state had an interest in how they did it. Child rearing was becoming a national duty, not just a moral one."[31] The struggle to resurrect the family around the mother in the immigrant family albums supports Chandra Mohanty's observation, in *Third World Women and the Politics of Feminism*, that "the construction of immigration and nationality laws and those of appropriate racialized, gendered citizenship, illustrates the continuity between relationships of colonization and white, masculinist, capitalist state rule"; and it extends the reach of Anna Davin's conclusion that "in the context of racism and imperialism at one level, and of class exploitation and sex prejudice at another, we come back to the mothers."[32] And finally, in the history of the decontextualization and recontextualization of the studio portraits of Jose Rizal, images that were once the domestic property of a private circle but later became the pious proprieties of a colonial state, we see how the commodification of visuality not only distributes points of view but uses gender to help enforce "depreciation" and "racialization" as, in Etienne Balibar's words, a "*historical system of complementary exclusions and dominations which are mutually interconnected.* In other words, it is not in practice simply the case that an 'ethnic racism' and a 'sexual racism' exist in parallel; racism and sexism function together and in particular, *racism always presupposes sexism.*"[33]

There has been so far no American model for thinking about the role of domestic visions in the formation and maintenance of an ideology of the nation. In this way, family photographs have seemed distinct from politics and the history of sentiment has been kept separate from the history of armament. But what I suspect is that one key component of the history of the national gaze would be the story of photography's production of images for the family album.

Notes

1 Benedict Anderson, *Imagined Communities: Reflections on the Origins and Spread of Nationalism*, rev. edn. (New York: Verso, 1991), 35–6.

2 I would like to thank Chi–Hyung Tessa Lee for her translation of the German text.

3 Anderson, *Imagined Communities*, 34.

4 Jonathan Crary, *Techniques of the Observer: On Vision and Modernity in the Nineteenth Century* (Cambridge, MA: MIT Press, 1992), 17.

5 Walter Benjamin, "The Work of Art in the Age of Mechanical Reproduction," in *Illuminations*, ed. Hannah Arendt, trans. Harry Zohn (New York: Schocken, 1978), 223, 242.

6 David Phillips, "The Birth of Mass Photography: Halftone Technology, Illustrated Magazines, and the Social Transformation of American Print Culture, 1890–1950" (Paper delivered at the Annual Meeting of the Modern Language Association, San Diego, 1994), 2.

7 Ibid., 2–3.

8 Derek Price, "Surveyors and Surveyed: Photography Out and About," in *Photography: A Critical Introduction*, ed. Liz Wells (New York: Routledge, 1997), 75.

9 William Wordsworth, "Illustrated Books and Newspapers [1846]," in *Poetical Works of William Wordsworth*, ed. William Knight (Edinburgh, 1850; reprint, in Robert Taft, *Photography and the American Scene* [New York, Dover, 1964], 447). Taft cites C. K. Shorter (in *Contemporary Review*, 75 [1899], 481) as his source for the opinion that the *Illustrated News* "is said to have caused the outburst" (Taft, *Photography and the American Scene*, 515 n 475).

10 Neil Harris, "Iconography and Intellectual History: The Halftone Effect," in *Cultural Excursions: Marketing Appetites and Cultural Tastes in Modern America* (Chicago: University of Chicago Press, 1990), 316; Harris's article addresses this revolution in American magazines, but holds in its general argument for Britain as well.

11 Taft, *Photography and the American Scene*, 441.

12 Crary, *Techniques of the Observer*, 19.

13 Anne McClintock, *Imperial Leather* (New York, Routledge, 1995), 357.

14 Ibid., 44; see also passim.

15 See the illuminating discussion of photography as national iconography in Alan Trachtenberg, *Reading American Photographs: Images as History, Mathew Brady to Walker Evans* (New York: Hill and Wang, 1989), esp. ch. 1.

16 An excellent source of information on Harrison is Grant B. Romer, "Gabriel B. Harrison – The Poetic Daguerreotypist," *Image*, 22:4 (Sept. 1979).

17 "The Anthony Prize," *Photographic and Fine Art Journal*, 7:1 (Jan. 1854), 8; cited in Romer, "Gabriel Harrison," 15; ellipses deleted.

18 Ibid.

19 Ibid.

20 For an informative and broadly inclusive discussion of the work of these early daguerreotypists, see Robert A. Sobieszek and Odette M. Appel, *The Daguerreotypes of Southworth and Hawes* (New York: Dover, 1980).

21 Jacob Riis, *How the Other Half Lives: Studies Among the Tenements of New York* (1890; reprint, New York: Dover, 1971).

22 Ibid., 137.

23 Ibid.

24 Ruthanne Lum McCunn, *Chinese American Portraits: Personal Histories, 1828–1988* (1988; reprint, Seattle, Wash.: University of Washington Press, 1996).

25 Ibid., 99.

26 Ibid., 105.

27 Ibid.

28 Arthur Dong (Producer and Director) and Lorraine Dong (Writer), *Sewing Woman* (San Francisco: NAATA, 1982).

29 Voice of Zem Ping Dong, ibid.

30 Vicente Rafael, "Nationalism, Imagery, and the Filipino Intelligentsia in the Nineteenth Century," *Critical Inquiry*, 16 (Spring 1990), 591–611; page references hereafter will be cited in the text.

31 Chandra Talpade Mohanty, "Introduction," in *Third World Women and the Politics of Feminism*, ed. Chandra Talpade Mohanty, Ann Russo, and Lourdes Torres (Bloomington: Indiana University Press, 1991), 23; and Anna Davin, "Motherhood and Imperialism," *History Workshop*, 5 (Spring 1978), 13.

32 Ibid., 55.

33 Etienne Balibar, "Racism and Nationalism," in Etienne Balibar and Immanuel Wallerstein, *Nation, Race, Class: Ambiguous Identities* (New York: Verso, 1991), 49; emphasis in original.

"The Eye of Power": Cross-Class Looking

5

Private Eyes, Public Women:
Images of Class and Sex in the Urban South, Atlanta, Georgia, 1913–1915

JACQUELYN DOWD HALL

> Can women who have been looked at for too long ever master the art of looking back?
>
> Martha Banta, *Imaging American Women*

I n the fall of 1985, historians and archivists in Atlanta, Georgia, made a startling discovery. They found hundreds of labor spy reports, stored and forgotten in the basement of the Fulton Bag and Cotton Mills, once the city's largest textile factory.[1] Hired in 1914, shortly before a protracted strike, the detectives who filed these reports masqueraded as workers, lived in the mill village, and infiltrated the union. They remained after the conflict ended, acting as management's eyes and ears in the mill, serving the more generalized needs of local manufacturers, and tracking the sentiment surrounding the trial, conviction, and subsequent lynching of Leo Frank, a Jewish factory superintendent accused of murdering a thirteen-year-old girl.

The South's textile barons left few paper trails, so these accounts are bound to attract the attention of historians eager for intimate details of management policy and labor strife.[2] Obviously, such evidence calls for special caution. The

Jacquelyn Dowd Hall, "Private Eyes, Public Women: Images of Class and Sex in the Urban South, Atlanta, Georgia, 1913–1915," in Ava Baron (ed.), *Work Engendered: Toward a New History of American Labor*. Ithaca: Cornell University Press, 1991: 243–72. © 1991 by Cornell University. Reprinted with permission of the publisher, Cornell University Press.

spies were agents of domination, and they fashioned their stories for particular readers – the powerful men they hoped both to manipulate and to serve. Their writings inscribed visually based modes of surveillance and portrayal, what feminist film critics call the "male gaze." The spies saw without being seen, revealed secrets without themselves being revealed. Their portrayals, by definition, were not reciprocal.[3] They were also deeply gendered, for they sexualized women and denigrated the manliness of mill village men.

Yet the spy reports' self-interestedness is part of their value, for these documents tell us as much about their writers and the conventions that directed their pens as about the workers they profess to portray. This reflexivity has a further advantage. It alerts us to the assumptions and strategies of the spies' adversaries, the trade unionists and reformers who sought to intervene on the workers' behalf. The workers who appeared in the trade unionists' photographs and the reformers' broadsides, like those who animated the spy reports, bore little resemblance to the flesh-and-blood individuals who worked in the mill. Read together, however, and with an eye to relations of dialogue and dominance, these warring images may indeed reveal secrets – about how visions of workers are constructed and deployed; about the shifting meanings of labor conflict when class and gender issues are transposed; about the modernization of sex and the discursive face of power.[4] By showing us a society in ferment, they also challenge the notion that the New South remained an isolated, cohesive, and backward region.

C. Vann Woodward, the South's foremost historian, made his mark in the 1930s and 1940s by attacking the notion of consensus and continuity, long before the consensus school of American history came under assault from other quarters. Yet even Woodward, by deflating the pretensions of the New South's pro-industry and pro-northern-capital boosters, encouraged the impression that the defeat of Populism and the triumph of Jim Crow in the 1890s ushered in an era of suffocating stagnation, relieved only by the jolt of World War II. This assumption has been reinforced in recent years by a recrudescence of consensus theories among southern scholars of every political stripe.[5]

Neither Woodward nor his critics saw women as historical actors, nor did gender conflict figure in their debates. That neglect is not surprising; more puzzling are the regional lacunae in the burgeoning field of women's history. Historians of women have produced a copious literature on the impact of industrialization, urbanization, consumerism, and commercialized leisure on working-class women in the Northeast and Midwest. But these modern workers, pioneers of a new heterosocial subculture, disappear below the Mason-Dixon line. Here feminist historians find no Sister Carries, no "women adrift," no "charity girls," only the familiar figures of a reactionary sexual mythology: the promiscuous black woman and the passionless white lady.[6]

The interweaving stories of the Fulton Mills strike and the Leo Frank case, as revealed in the competing versions of pro- and antilabor sources, confound such flat and timeless generalizations. They indicate the depth of the anxiety generated by the growth of a permanent working class with its own forms of heterosociability and social crime. They allow us to glimpse a major source of this anxiety: women in action, creating a new sexual system and challenging an older, rural-based patriarchal order. Attention to these women suggests the inadequacy of interpretations that stress the white South's monolithic sexual conservatism, pointing instead to the region's entanglement in national developments, to women's sexual agency, and to the competing discourses that constituted the public's response.[7]

--------------------------------- I ---------------------------------

Jacob Elsas, a German Jewish immigrant, founded the Fulton Bag and Cotton Mills in 1889, building houses for his employees in an area known first as the Factory Lot and then as Cabbagetown. Atlanta tripled in size over the next thirty years, and Fulton Mills grew with the city. By 1914, when Jacob's son Oscar took over the presidency, Fulton Mills was producing sheeting, twine, and cotton and burlap bags at branch plants throughout the country. Approximately 2,000 people worked in its Atlanta headquarters alone. Thirty-five percent of these employees were women, and 12 percent were boys and girls under sixteen.[8]

Fulton Mills had a reputation as a "hobo mill." Its high turnover rate was seen as a telltale sign of poor working conditions and a shabbily maintained company town. In truth, the Factory Lot resembled other working-class communities in the urban South, and the owners had much in common with their peers. Mill village conditions varied widely, but the outdoor privies, unpaved roads, poverty, and disease that marked the Factory Lot were not at all unusual.[9]

Three things, however, set Elsas's firm apart. One was a labor contract that codified – and thus revealed – the unilateral nature of labor relations in the mills. Unlike most mill owners, who simply hired and fired at will, Elsas required each worker to sign a contract specifying that the company assumed no responsibility for work-related injuries and that it could discharge and evict employees without warning at any time. Workers, on the other hand, were obligated to pay for damage to equipment, fined for minor infractions, and compelled to forfeit a week's wages if they quit without giving notice. Fulton Mills' other distinctions were vagaries of fate: Elsas had the bad luck, first, to come under the intense scrutiny of federal investigators during the strike, and second, to leave behind, in the form of the labor spy reports, an extensive record of the offstage attitudes and behavior other self-proclaimed paternalists successfully concealed.[10]

The earliest sign of the labor trouble that would engulf the mill came in October 1913, when several hundred weavers and loom fixers staged a work stoppage in protest over the firing of a loom fixer and the company's decision to increase the amount of time required for giving notice, a ploy designed to curb workers' mobility and thus to squelch the most common form of everyday resistance in the southern mills. This walkout, conducted mainly by men, was self-initiated and short-lived, but in its wake the workers organized Local 886 of the United Textile Workers Union of America (UTW).[11]

Elsas responded by contracting with the Philadelphia-based Railway Audit and Inspection Company, as well as with several smaller southern firms, to plant undercover "operatives" in his mill.[12] He also began firing union members, and in May 1914, workers walked out again. Their initial demand for the reinstatement of the discharged employees gradually expanded to include appeals for higher wages, shorter hours, an end to child labor, and the abandonment of the "present vicious contract system." This time the unionists mobilized men, women, and children alike, precipitating what one UTW organizer called "the first big strike of organized workers in the cotton mills of the South."[13]

The Fulton Mills walkout was not in fact southern mill hands' "first big strike." But 1914 did mark the first time that the UTW and the American Federation of Labor (AFL) poured significant resources into the South. Reeling from the southward shift of the textile industry and pressed from the left by the Industrial Workers of the World (IWW), the UTW had recently announced a southern organizing drive. Meanwhile, the AFL, alarmed by the surge of women into the industrial work force, authorized a special assessment on the membership of its affiliated unions to organize women workers. The Fulton Mills strike provided a perfect opportunity to launch both ventures. Once the walkout began, both the UTW and the AFL focused their attention on Atlanta, sending a total of seven organizers to the city and maintaining a tent colony for evicted workers during the year-long conflict.[14]

The strike drew reinforcement from other quarters as well. Atlanta's craft unions enjoyed considerable political influence, and the Atlanta Federation of Trades tried to arbitrate and publicize the conflict.[15] The local affiliate of the Men and Religion Forward Movement, a militant evangelical organization, also came to the workers' defense. Both the Federal Conciliation Service and the United States Commission on Industrial Relations investigated the strike, and both issued reports sympathetic to the union.[16]

The UTW's chief representatives on the scene were Charles A. Miles, who had led the AFL's battles against the IWW in New York, and Sara Conboy, a Boston Women's Trade Union League activist who was secretary-treasurer of the union and who would soon become the UTW's highest-ranking female official. Miles in turn persuaded the union to hire a local woman, O. (Ola) Delight Smith, a telegrapher who had been blacklisted after a 1907 strike. Dubbed the "Mother Jones of Atlanta," Smith was a talented labor journalist and president of the national Ladies Auxiliary of the Order of Railroad Telegraphers.[17]

Smith had no experience in organizing textile workers, but she moved quickly to capitalize on her skills as a publicist, combining the pen with the camera in a campaign designed both to encourage collective self-confidence among the workers and to garner public support. Working closely with Miles, she recruited a moving picture company to film the picket line, then invited the workers to free screenings in a local theater. Sporting a hand-held camera and adapting the formulas pioneered by Jacob Riis and Lewis Hine, she darted about the mill village, snapping pictures of child laborers, evicted families, defiant workers, and company spies. She also hired local commercial photographers to help document the strike. She then captioned those images, mounted them on cardboard, and displayed them in store windows, in order to expose the sneering arrogance of the company's agents and underscore the strikers' poverty and respectability.[18]

Smith's use of photography placed her squarely within the Progressive tradition, for the camera furnished progressivism's preeminent mode of proof. Lewis Hine had traveled through Georgia for the National Child Labor Committee in 1913, and Smith was surely familiar with his work. Like him, she created ensembles of images and words.[19] Smith, however, did more than appropriate established forms. Hine and the child labor reformers used the camera to persuade an indifferent public to endorse legislative reforms. Smith's photographs had a similar purpose, insofar as they aimed at marshaling public backing for the union. But by showing the strikers to themselves, in action and as a collectivity, she sought to foster insurgency, not to heal class divisions.

The camera was not the unionists' only weapon. They made use of words and rituals as well. They organized parades that contradicted the mill owner's charge that the strikers' ranks were limited to a few malcontents. Smith wrote a column called "From the Strikers' Camp," in which she emphasized the workers' gallant domesticity. The *Journal of Labor* editorialized that these workers were not " 'floaters.' ... [T]hey were men who had worked for years in the mills...of the class which creates all the wealth of the state." Their strike was conducted along "dignified, conservative lines."[20]

Organizers also appealed to white racial solidarity in their attempt to overcome the image of textile workers as a pariah class. Union literature designed for a national as well as a local audience played on the theme of "white slavery" in the southern mills. Unionists circulated pictures of the black men hired by the company to evict workers from their homes, with captions such as "Put out by a Nigger." "Just imagine," wrote UTW president John Golden, "white southern Americans,... little white children... thrown into the streets by negroes... all because their parents dared to join a labor union."[21]

The spies' job was to counter this multifaceted campaign. Their reports, which the mill owners fed to reformers, government investigators, and national union officials, sought to contest photography's claim to unmediated truth. Where the unionists pictured a struggle waged by hard-working men and women, the spies conjured an urban underworld composed of hobos, whores, and street urchins. Their aim was to discredit the local leaders and contradict the union's self-representations, thus dividing the rank-and-file and undermining the strike's public support.[22]

The spies ran with the young men of the village, whiled away their time on street corners and in Decatur Street dives, and infiltrated what they portrayed as an interracial crime ring that traded in bootleg whiskey, cocaine, and prostitution. They acted as provocateurs, fostering and exaggerating the underworld they described.[23] They shaped their narratives for particular readers, and their pens, like the photographer's eye, were guided by social conventions.

In fact, the spy reports belonged to a century-old literary tradition that had been given new life by muckraking reformers: a secrets-of-the-city genre of urban reportage. Tours of urban lowlife, written by novelists, journalists, and reformers for middle-class audiences, depicted the city as a dark continent peopled by the degraded and vicious poor. Similarly, textile folk, as construed by the spy reports, inhabited a hidden city dominated by vice, immorality, and crime.[24]

The spies drew distinctions between the rough and the respectable, the dangerous and the dependable, employing a trope that had long been a staple of writings on working-class life.[25] In their rendition, floaters dominated the more innocent members of the union. Stable workers were illiterate, vulnerable, and easily deluded; they resented the "Rough Necks" but could not escape their influence.[26]

This split image of workers dated back to the beginnings of the Industrial Revolution, but the spy reports added a modern permutation: these rough workers did not steal to survive; they were perverse consumers, exploiting the greed and pleasures of the marketplace. The Magnolia Pharmacy allegedly sold cocaine as well as Coca-Cola; restaurants offered gathering places where customers could get a quick meal while laying plans to "holdup, burglarize, [and] blow safes." Strikers-turned-streetwalkers were said to pillage Decatur Street stores, using "umbrellas, muffs and cloaks to hide the loot."[27]

Constructions of gender shaped the spies' message. As depicted in their reports, mill village ringleaders lacked the manliness required by trade union-ism. Possessing neither self-control nor self-respect, they combined weakness and gullibility with criminal aggression. The spies ridiculed these men's claims to the role of "father of this movement." Rather, outside organizers were responsible. Male strikers appeared mainly as yeggs, highway robbers, and bootleggers, too busy dodging the cops to maintain a tent city or run a union.[28] Mill women were usually cast either as sexual predators or as prey. The spies charged that lewd women from the union gathered in a popular saloon on payday to "tempt those now at work in the Mill to drink with them and quit work."[29] They saw women in the tent city as a source of contagion, as the dangerous carriers of venereal disease.

Because they viewed the factory as sexualized space, the spies routinely used seduction as a means of infiltration. Operative 429, who passed himself off as an aspiring dance instructor, spent days trying to get a date with Lillie Priest, a mill worker with an inviting smile and a reputation as a "very gay girl." Finally she let him take her dancing and to a movie. "I have made a good impression with her," he reported, "and I am sure I will know everything on her mind shortly." The dance instructor also charmed (or said he charmed) Mary Kelleher, a UTW organizer. He wined and dined her and forwarded her letters to his boss in Philadelphia.[30]

Even O. Delight Smith was not exempt from the spies' translation of female activism into illicit sexuality. Indeed, they devoted particular effort to decod-ing her sexual character and using it to undermine her leadership position. Their tactics ranged from rumormongering to blackmail and entrapment. They staked out her house and peeped through the windows until the lights went off. They observed her drinking beer at the German Cafe until long past midnight. A man claimed that he saw her registering at a hotel with UTW organizer Charles Miles but promised to keep the secret if she would have "intercourse" with him. He said that Smith refused but procured another woman – from whom he promptly caught gonorrhea.[31]

This was not O. Delight Smith's first experience with attempts to use her private life to undermine her public role. She had worked as an organizer for the Order of Railroad Telegraphers, riding in cabooses and handcars, staying in hotels, and dodging efforts to " 'catch me' with a man in my room."[32] What set the Atlanta case apart was the apparent collusion of her husband, Edgar B. Smith, with those who sought to do her in.

In the midst of the strike, Edgar initiated divorce proceedings, represented by Fulton Mills's law firm. He alleged that he had found his wife, drunk and "about half dressed," at home with a drifter named Pat Callahan. But his main charge was that Delight had "mapped out a line of conduct for herself entirely at variance with the duties of a good wife" and that she wouldn't stay "at home where all good women ought to be." Delight, in turn, accused her husband of circulating rumors detrimental to her "reputation of chastity" and advising and abetting the men who were trying to force her out of her job.[33] In the end, the jury refused her request for a divorce with alimony and granted her husband a divorce instead. It went further, giving him but denying her the right to remarry.[34]

Smith's nemesis was a wily and ambitious Railway Audit and Inspection Company detective named Harry Preston, and the interaction between them is particularly revealing. Preston had disliked Smith from the first, with an intensity that did not extend to the other UTW organizers.[35] The reasons for his animus are not altogether clear, but they were certainly aggravated by frustration. Try as he might, Preston could not worm his way into Smith's confidence. Nor could he establish a stable link between her outward behavior and her inner substance; he could not read her character or fathom her meaning.

Preston's depictions of Smith's words and actions were wildly contradictory. On the one hand, she was a foul-mouthed rabble-rouser whose "usual tirade" consisted of calling the company and its minions "'Liars, Pimps, Thugs, etc.'" On the other hand, it was her job to counsel moderation. He watched her every move and expression, hoping for signs that his campaign was taking effect, predicting – prematurely, as it usually turned out – that she could not stand the strain. Early on, he reported that Smith had told him "that she was worn out... and was almost sick, and she could not keep it up much longer." Long before Smith actually fell from grace, Preston was reporting that "the 'cockey' walk... she used to have [is] all gone, and she goes around like a smacked 'a—' now, (excuse [the] expression, it fits so perfectly)."[36]

It was, above all, Smith's partnership with Charles Miles that played havoc with Preston's powers of deduction. When she failed to take a back seat to the national UTW organizer, Preston decided that the two were locked in a power struggle and that Smith was trying to seize control of the union. When they continued to work together harmoniously, he jumped to the conclusion that they were entirely "too friendly." Unable to turn up any evidence of adultery, he hypothesized that Miles was a weakling who hoped the strikers would return to work so that he could "retire gracefully" with the excuse that the strikers had deserted him. Preston changed course again when Miles did eventually retreat, leaving Smith in charge of the strike. Then he maintained that the two organizers had been planning to run away together until Pat Callahan "broke in to Miles's arrangements."[37]

Preston's peregrinations illustrate a phenomenon with a long historical pedigree: the tawdry mudslinging directed at female trespassers who disrupt the hierarchies of the public sphere. But the spy's confusion was also emblematic of social relations in an increasingly pluralistic, mobile society. How, after all, could one read appearances in a metropolis of strangers, a world where social identity was no longer taken for granted and the self could become "a series of dramatic effects"?[38]

Northern Victorians cherished character. They feared the impostor who undermined social confidence by passing for something he was not. In the antebellum South, white men were less concerned with probity than with appearances; for them a man's honor depended on public acceptance of the self he projected. In either case, an accusation of lying, of projecting a false self, was a grave insult. But by World War I, urban-dwelling southerners – along with other Americans – were coming to "accept the idea of a social system filled with liminal men in pursuit of the main chance." A new success ethic made the confidence man less an object of fear than a model for ambitious young men to emulate. Personality and corporate gamesmanship replaced character as the keys to mobility in a fluid social world.[39]

Preston, for instance, was no run-of-the-mill nineteenth-century strike-breaker. He was a more protean modern figure: the confidence man in a gray flannel suit. He had appeared on the stage under the name Henry Green-hough. He could sing, and he worked his way into the union and the Men and Religion Forward Movement by arranging the music for their meetings. He had nothing but scorn for ordinary workers and concentrated his attention mainly on the UTW organizers, whose company he much preferred. He was seated as a delegate and honored guest at the annual convention of the Massachusetts Federation of Labor, had a private meeting with the executive board of the UTW, dined with President Golden, and attended the UTW annual convention in Scranton. After the strike, he moved quickly up the corporate ladder. By 1920 he was back in Atlanta as the Railway Audit and Inspection Company's southern district manager.[40]

If Preston was a modern "liminal man," Smith was a boundary-crossing New Woman whose reflection in the spy reports was understandably fragmented and opaque. Luckily, Smith's writings and photographs permit us to supplement the spy's version with a highly literate woman's self-representations. That wider lens discloses a complex social identity. It also suggests that in O. Delight Smith Preston met an impressive adversary, a woman fighting on uneven ground, yet still managing quite often to give as good as she got.[41]

For one thing, as the private eyes were spying on Mrs. Smith, Mrs. Smith was spying on them. She had her own "inside man" in the mill, who kept her informed about the company's machinations. She prided herself on her physical courage: "These pictures were taken by myself," she boasted, "while thugs and spotters were ever around me." Several cameras were "knocked from my hand and smashed before I succeeded in collecting these."[42] Her candid shots of company spies reversed the usual power relations between the seer and the seen, alerting us to the problems with the metaphor of a "male gaze" – which implies that women are the Other, the more or less helpless targets of objectification.

Moreover, Smith's columns in the *Journal of Labor* provide a rare glimpse of a little-noticed phenomenon: working-class feminism in the urban South. For years before the textile strike, she offered a running commentary on everything from the need for labor unity to "the penalty of being a woman." Like Charlotte Perkins Gilman, she warned of the dire effects of dependency on women's characters. She gave short shrift to the institution of marriage, "which very seldom helped to compensate matters but on the other hand made matters worse." She argued that the chief threat to a woman's autonomy lay in her vulnerability to character assassination, a vulnerability that bred a nagging fear of "what others say." When the "tongues of loafing men go wagging," she argued, women must rely on a sense of inner worth, not on male protection.[43]

Yet there were chinks in Smith's armor, inconsistencies, if not in her thought, at least in her rhetorical strategies. She spent pages in defense of female ambition, then bowed to custom by arguing that if only men were unionized, a woman could stay at home where "she rightfully belongs." Independence, she assured her readers, "has not taken from the True Woman one iota of that sweet feminine quality." Aside from oblique references to "wagging tongues," she offered no brief for women's sexual autonomy.[44]

These, of course, were precisely the conventions that Smith's enemies eventually invoked. Harry Preston's vendetta had a personal edge: he went after Smith partly because she seemed to lack feminine sweetness, not just because she was on the wrong side of a labor–management dispute. The divorce court punished her for both her work and her sexuality.

The difficulty of Smith's position can be read not only in her columns but also in her gestures, as caught and framed by the camera's eye. Posing in front of the union commissary with Charles Miles and another union man, Smith looks resolute yet curiously askew (Figure 5.1). The body language of the men conveys energy and determination. Their shoulders are set; they gaze directly into the camera, their heads and bodies joined in straight axial lines. Miles raises his chin belligerently. Smith stands to the side, avoiding the symbolic position in the center of the group which often reflects tokenism rather than collegiality. She appears as tall as the men; like Miles, she raises her chin. Yet she turns away, tilting her head back and to the side in a customary feminine gesture. The axis of her pose is broken, suggesting inconsistency, especially in contrast to the determined set of her mouth. The women photographed in the strikers' camp take a different stance. They occupy the background, but they face the camera more directly. Pictured in the camp kitchen, they perform

Figure 5.1. H. N. Mullinax (left), the secretary (not the president) of Local 886. To his left are UTW organizers Charles Miles and O. Delight Smith. Photograph by Duane A. Russell, a local professional photographer. Reprinted courtesy of the George Meany Memorial Archives, Washington, DC

private tasks in a public setting. They are not creating a new public role but asserting their right to an established one, whose normal venue they have been denied. Smith's presence in front of the commissary announces her bid to occupy new public space. But her stance hints at the precariousness born of the distance between possibility and aspiration.[45]

Whether they were written by small-time criminals, proto-efficiency experts, or aspiring bourgeois, the spy reports exposed the complexities of social life in a world that drew a thin line between con men and social climbers and allowed elites to rely on criminals to maintain their power.[46] More important for our purposes, they unmasked the class and gender conflicts that accompanied urban-industrial transformations. How pervasive were those conflicts? What do they reveal about the New South's sexual culture? To address those questions, we must bring other perspectives and other layers of meaning into play. Let us turn, then, to the new social circumstances of working-class women and to the tensions those circumstances aroused, as they manifested themselves in the fatal drama of the Leo Frank case and reverberated in the Fulton Mills strike as well as in more quotidian debates.

II

The years preceding the Fulton Mills strike were marked by profound changes in urban life. Atlanta's population mushroomed, and its female labor force increased at an even dizzier rate. By 1920, 42 percent of all Atlanta women aged sixteen and over had joined the work force. Only the Massachusetts textile cities of Fall River, Lowell, and New Bedford and the white-collar city of Washington, DC, had higher rates of female employment.[47] Traditionally, a large black population accounted for the high levels of gainfully employed women in southern cities, and black women continued to work in much greater proportions than whites. But from 1900 to 1920, as the city's population expanded by 123 percent (from 89,872 to 200,616), the number of black women wage earners in Atlanta advanced by only 60 percent. Meanwhile, employment among white women jumped by 276 percent. This disparity was due in part to a leveling off of the laundry and household service jobs to which black women were confined and in part to the exclusion of blacks from the textile and clerical jobs that drew white women into paid labor. The result was a marked change in the racial composition of the city's female work force. In 1900 white women constituted only 28 percent of wage-earning women. By 1920 they accounted for 48 percent.[48]

Such developments might have caused consternation in any case. But the living situations of these new wage-earning women made their presence in the city more disturbing still. In 1900, Atlanta, like most southern locales, ranked far below cities such as Chicago in the percentage of wage-earning women living apart from their families. By 1920, however, approximately one-fifth of working women in both Atlanta and Chicago were living "adrift." Single white women, migrating to the city to work in department stores and offices, accounted for most of this change.[49]

Middle-class observers in Georgia, like their counterparts throughout the country, responded to the surge of white women into wage labor with pity, puzzlement, and disapproval. They assumed that black women should work and would probably be sexually active. The tendency of the mill village to breed immorality was also axiomatic. The behavior of the young women in the expanding service sector was harder to read. Free from parental supervision and prey to the temptations of the city, they were a new phenomenon, and their visibility on the urban landscape aroused more general concerns about the female working class. Working mothers, it seemed, were threatening family life; wage-earning daughters were prone to promiscuity or vulnerable to abuse; children were being warped by factory labor. These worries helped nourish an antiprostitution campaign and a debate over child labor.[50] At their most sensational, they also fed the vendetta against Leo Frank.

In July 1913, Frank, a pencil factory superintendent, was arrested and charged with assaulting and murdering a thirteen-year-old employee named Mary Phagan. A jury found Frank guilty and the judge sentenced him to death. The case became a cause célèbre in the spring of 1914, a few months before the Fulton Mills strike, when national Jewish organizations rallied to Frank's defense. Appeal followed appeal, until, in April 1915, the United States Supreme Court denied a plea by Frank's attorneys to reverse the death sentence on the grounds that a mob atmosphere had prevailed during the trial. On June 21, 1915, two months after the Fulton Mills strike ended, Governor John Slaton commuted Frank's sentence to life imprisonment. Three weeks later, a band of prominent citizens from Phagan's hometown, the nearby suburb of Marietta, took Frank from his prison cell and lynched him.[51]

The furor against Leo Frank turned on the vulnerability of factory girls, and the case provided a forum for the expression of intense racial, class, and religious antagonisms. Frank's attorneys, as well as the country's major newspapers, invoked virulent racist stereotypes in their effort to shift the blame for Phagan's murder to Jim Conley, a black janitor who was the prosecution's chief witness.[52] Frank's opponents, on the other hand, cast the superintendent as the embodiment of rapacious capitalism. The former Populist leader Tom Watson and the William Randolph Hearst-owned *Atlanta Georgian* helped whip that perception into murderous rage. Although the spies tried hard to furnish evidence to the contrary, there is no indication that the Fulton Mills walkout was sparked by anti-Semitism. But once the strike began, prejudice undoubtedly fueled popular antagonism toward the Jewish mill owner, and resentment against Elsas spilled over into the outcry against Leo Frank.[53]

As they probed the nature of Frank's alleged crime, southerners also confronted the emergence of a modern sexual system that acknowledged a wide range of human desires even as it hedged them about with new psychological constraints. Public outrage rested in part on the tenacious belief that Mary Phagan had been sexually molested, despite strong evidence that no rape had occurred. Yet at Frank's commutation hearings, his attorney conceded that Phagan may indeed have been raped, an act that he defined as "the carnal knowledge of a female, normally accomplished, forcibly and against her will." Rape, he maintained, was "one of the natural conditions of life . . . it takes all the law and the religion to keep it within reasonable bounds, and then [they] don't quite succeed." A natural expression of male sexuality, rape was particularly irresistible to black men, who were seen not as deviants but as criminals, though less bound than white men by civilization's restraints. If Phagan was raped, it stood to reason that she was raped by the janitor, Jim Conley; anyone who knows the Negro, Frank's lawyer explained, "knows that the prize above life itself to him is the privilege of debasing a white woman."

The prosecution agreed that the girl had been molested. But partly because the evidence of rape was so flimsy and partly to deflect attention from Conley, they charged Frank with perversion, implying that he had engaged in cunnilingus or some other form of nonprocreative sex. These rumors of "perversion" probably did more than anything else to damn Frank in the court of public opinion.[54] And the rumors portrayed him less as a rapist than as an unmanly practitioner of sodomy or pedophilia, forms of male sexual expression that became objects of intense concern as the Victorian fixation on the "hypersexual girl" gave way to fears of the "psychopathic man" (who was seen not as a rapist but as a homosexual or child molester).[55]

There has been a good deal of speculation about why so many white Georgians chose to blame Leo Frank rather than Jim Conley for Mary Phagan's murder. The reasons were tangled and contingent, rooted as much in the particular circumstances of the case as in underlying forces. Among them were the anxieties inspired by urbanization, industrialization, and the rise of a modern sexual order. At the turn of the century, the image of the black rapist, cut loose from the bonds of slavery and purportedly retrogressing into criminality, had signified for whites the most frightful possibilities of social change. Those fears had crested in the Atlanta riot of 1906, Georgia's worst conflagration in an era of extreme racial violence. Apologists for lynching continued to rely on the notion of white women as the passionless victims of sexual assault. But as the twentieth century wore on, it became increasingly difficult to ignore the possibility that women had sexual urges of their own. Disfranchisement and segregation eliminated blacks from electoral politics and pushed them out of sight, if not out of mind, while capitalist develop-ment brought new social tensions to the fore.[56] As a result, white women and children – in the guise of wage earners, prostitutes, and street children – joined recalcitrant blacks as emblems of a society out of whack. In that context, the charge that a factory supervisor had molested a woman in his employ acquired explosive cultural meaning.

But the fate of "Little Mary Phagan" meant different things to different people, for there was no agreement about how the figure of the working girl should be construed. Were women's identities – and thus their social needs – rooted in class or in sex? Was their sexuality a site of exploitation or of experimentation? Were they victims or agents of a sexual revolution?

The *Atlanta Georgian*, which used the Frank case to transform itself into one of the most widely read daily newspapers in the South, offered Mary Phagan as a symbol of the respectable working-class woman besieged, willing to die in defense of her chastity. Yet the *Georgian*'s typical daily reporting featured stories of female desire, not testimonials to female virtue. A poem to working girls published in 1914 turned on the temptations of the city:

131

Lonely girl, little lonely girl!
Below you gleam the city lights –
Could your throbbing feet whirl on in dance
Dare you toss your head and take your chance
With the beasts that prowl o 'nights?
An eddy of life, perhaps, might whirl
A comrade or joy your weary way.
The street you dream might yield delight –
You long for color and friends at night
Who work so hard by day.[57]

Young women who did take their chances became the central characters in the crime and scandal stories that were the *Georgian*'s stock in trade. And the heroines of these tales, who ran the gamut from society girls who decamped with bigamists to reformatory inmates who went over the wall, were pacesetters in a nationwide revolution in morals and manners, not figures in a regional morality play.[58]

This is not to say that the *Georgian* celebrated women's rebelliousness. Adhering to Progressive Era convention, the paper often suggested that its protagonists had been drugged or forced into "white slavery" and stressed the "weird and unnatural tragedy" that was their actions' inevitable result.[59] Yet such ritualistic punishments were glosses on the main theme: a fascination with women's sexual agency that the *Georgian* both reflected and helped to create.

The *Journal of Labor*, mouthpiece for the Atlanta Federation of Labor and for the city's labor elite, took a different approach. It refused to sexualize Mary Phagan's death, casting her more as a victim of capitalism in general than as a symbol of women's physical vulnerability. The *Journal* argued that Phagan differed little from "the girl who has her life sapped away slowly by occupational disease or is maimed or killed by machinery at her work." It editorialized against a plan to erect a statue of the "martyred child" on the grounds of the state capitol, suggesting the endowment of a hospital ward for working girls instead.[60]

The agitation triggered by the Leo Frank case fed into a broader questioning of the implications of new patterns of women's work, a questioning that, in turn, helped shape the response to the Fulton Mills strike. In 1908, for instance, the *Journal of Labor* featured a spirited discussion at the Universalist Church on the merits of wage work for women. One man said that "girls these days wanted to dress better than their daddy could afford. They expect to work until they get married, they like to be independent of their father, and this same independence continues after marriage, and makes life miserable for both parties." His remarks "got the ladies all on their feet about the same time." The group decided to conduct a survey of how many white women worked out of "stern necessity" and how their wages compared with men's. At the next meeting, the investigators reported that few Atlanta women worked for "pin money"; indeed, 90 percent of the city's department store clerks and 100 percent of its textile operatives had to work, and they did so at wages considerably lower than men's.[61]

Five years later the *Journal* warned that women's economic disadvantages had led to a feminization of poverty in the city. The city warden, who was in charge of doling out "the pittance allowed by the municipality for the poor," reported that he had had 5,000 calls for help in 1913, 1,000 more than in 1912 and four times more than in 1903, when his office had been established. These pleas were equally divided between blacks and whites, and most came from women who were the sole supporters of their families. Some could not find work, but many were employed at jobs that paid far less than a living wage. Charity, the *Journal* insisted, served as an economic makeshift that subsidized "face-grinding employers." The solution it proposed was the organization of women workers and equal pay for equal work.[62] The warden's report also provided ammunition for the *Journal*'s campaign on behalf of the striking textile workers, for many of the women who relied on charity for survival apparently worked at Fulton Mills.

Unfortunately, this focus on women, however well meaning, could go only so far in illuminating the issues raised by the Fulton Mills strike. Labor historians have often subsumed women and children under the category of "worker," writing about the working class as if it consisted only of adult men. Contemporary observers made the opposite mistake. Preoccupied with gender boundaries and confronted by an industry that relied on a family labor system that seemed to threaten the authority of male household heads, crusading journalists, reformers, and craft unionists alike increasingly made their appeals for public sympathy in terms that shifted attention away from the bid for workers' control reflected in the strikers' protest against the contract system and the firing of union members. Ignoring male workers, they highlighted the anomalous position of wage-earning women and children instead. In the process, strikers' interests as workers disappeared, as did their collective agency.

At first, as we have seen, the *Journal of Labor* and the UTW had construed the strikers as "intelligent, industrious men." But as the conflict unfolded, they increasingly stressed the number of women involved and described the strikers in general in female-coded terms.[63] The UTW's most widely circulated photograph featured a skinny, barefooted boy seated alone on a curb. The caption identified the child as Milton Nunnally, "Age 10 Years," a Fulton Mills worker who had "received for 2 weeks wages only 64 cents" (Figure 5.2). This picture was distributed as a postcard throughout the country and reprinted by numerous newspapers and journals. Child labor, suggested the

Figure 5.2. Made into a postcard, this photograph of Milton Nunnally, a 10-year-old boy who worked briefly at Fulton Mills, became the most widely circulated image of the strike. Elsas countered by arguing that Nunnally was hired at the insistence of his mother, who swore that the boy's father had deserted him and he had to work. The mill owner also asserted that Nunnally had been discharged for idleness and that his mother ran a house of assignation. Reprinted courtesy of the George Meany Memorial Archives, Washington, DC

unionists and the reformers, caught mill workers in a cycle of ignorance and poverty. Women started work too young, then gave birth to stunted children who in turn became "slaves of the mill." The remedy was state intervention in the form of child labor legislation and compulsory education laws. Such laws targeted lazy mill fathers and greedy manufacturers alike, both of whom bore responsibility for what the *Georgian* termed "The Coming De-Generation."[64]

This tendency of gender issues to override class issues reached its apogee in the Men and Religion Forward Movement, whose quarter-page bulletins in Atlanta's major papers brought the strike to citywide attention. Initially an evangelical movement aimed at masculinizing the churches by recruiting male members and adopting modern business methods and aggressive advertising, the group quickly became an effective proponent of the social gospel. The Atlanta chapter was among the nation's most outspoken and long-lived.[65]

Like the spies – and unlike the craft unionists – these evangelical reformers saw the working-class district as sexualized space. They believed that 75 percent of Atlanta's prostitutes came from the mill village. The prostitute, to their mind, was a passive victim, drawn "by forces she does not understand, lured by lies or driven by want." The solution they proposed was a "living wage" that would enable men to keep their wives and daughters at home – out of the mills and, by extension, out of the brothels. In 1912 these ministers and businessmen led a campaign to shut down the city's red-light district. When the strike broke out, they continued to focus on the exploitation of women and children or to represent mill workers in general in feminine terms: "weak mentally, spiritually, and bodily," neither the men nor the women could do much to help themselves.[66]

In the case of O. Delight Smith, we were able to counter such images of victimization with a writer/photographer's self-representations. Mill workers left behind less evidence of how they saw themselves. Yet even the hostile reports of the labor spies are shot through with evidence that belies the reformers' assumptions about women's passivity. Indeed, for glimpses of women's agency – of women acting up and looking back – we must turn from prolabor sources to the problematic documents with which we began.

What set the spies apart from other visitors to the Satanic mills was the ease with which they blended into the urban underworld. To be sure, they spotlighted the rough and neglected the respectable; their accounts reveal their prejudices (or their eagerness to confirm the prejudices of their employers). But at least they show us a community in motion. Their descriptions of street life are often more matter-of-fact, and in some ways more valuable, than those of the reformers and government investigators on whom historians traditionally rely.

The Men and Religion Forward Movement, for instance, purveyed an image of the mill village as a "graveyard...of the living" where lost souls huddled together in "row after row of houses... dreary, drab, monotonously the same."[67] In fact, the Factory Lot stood beside the Georgia Railroad only a mile from the city's center, it was traversed by two street-car lines, and its outskirts accommodated many families that did not work in the mill, along with shopkeepers who maintained a thriving commercial district.[68] The graveyard came to life in the spy reports, and women popped up everywhere in this lively public space.

In the world of the spy reports, women's roles were active, if often unsavory. Mill girls pursued men they liked and fended off those they didn't. They negotiated a city that provided many new sites and situations for sexual bartering and exchange. In one report, a spooler broke a board over the head of a married man who pinched her; in another, a woman tried to blackmail her boyfriend into marrying her by promising to "play shut mouth" about his crimes.[69] Lillie Priest, the "very gay girl" courted by Operative 429, proved more than a match for the charming dance instructor. He suspected her of being a double agent, employed as an informer by the company but also working for the union. He was certain that she was "stuck on" him. But every time he managed to make a date, she thwarted him by bringing a girlfriend along. "I was compelled through circumstances," he complained, "to entertain them both." He confronted Priest with his suspicions, but she put him off with "a plausible story (all lies)." In the end, the detective was ordered back to Philadelphia, probably at the behest of Elsas, who had decided that 429's reports were full of "hot air."[70] Lillie Priest disappeared from the record, apparently still working both sides of the street.

Three female figures illustrate the difference between the reformers' and the spies' representations. A typical Men and Religion Forward Movement bulletin invoked an image of a "little girl not over twelve, her pink dress fluttering against the grime, [running] through a forbidding door to work." The girls in the spy reports occupied a more ambiguous milieu. These accounts showed Big Annie Pharr and her sidekick May Parkman donning overalls and caps instead of fluttering pink dresses. Cross-dressing, the two women dodged the cops and "hobo[ed] out of town." Pharr and Parkman were adopting a strategy familiar to rebellious working-class girls of the time, who sometimes wore men's clothing in order to earn men's wages and enjoy men's mobility. Before the emergence of a homosexual subculture in the cities, cross-dressing also enabled women to live in same-sex relationships.[71]

In short, the women who frequented the assignation houses on Decatur Street may have been meeting their lovers, exchanging sex for treats, or using their bodies for political advantage rather than sinking helplessly into prostitution, as the reformers believed. For them, sex could mean pleasure or danger; it suffused the politics of everyday life. The spies tell us little about the economic disadvantages that led women to barter sex for support; nor do they acknowledge women's vulnerability to sexual violence. But their images of working-class women do subvert the old mythology that cast women's virtue in the literal polarities of black and white. In the process, they add a new figure to the New South stage: the white working-class woman who saw no contradiction between fighting the mill boss and charting new sexual terrain.

III

Despite the combined efforts of the textile workers, the reformers, and the craft unions, Fulton Mills prevailed, in part because of its sheer implacability. Asked by a federal investigator what he considered the best way to break a strike, Oscar Elsas responded, "I'd just as soon get guns and mow 'em down as not." He refused to submit to any form of mediation or even to meet with labor leaders. Taking refuge in the tent city, two to three hundred families held out through the winter, only to see themselves replaced by an endless pool of labor recruited from the city and the surrounding countryside. As this war of attrition continued, local and national support faded away. Finally, in May 1915, the UTW closed the camp and admitted defeat. By then most of the strikers had moved on to other mills, though some remained in Atlanta trying "secretly to continue the fight."[72]

At issue in the strike were the needs of men, women, and children who were among the nation's most exploited workers. Different observers interpreted those needs differently, and their interpretations depended on varying constructions of workers' identities. But in each version, assumptions about gender figured centrally. Neither the craft unionists' emphasis on wages nor the reformers' stress on domesticity nor the spies' preoccupation with sexuality tells us how textile workers imagined and invented themselves.[73] Yet words are actions; outsiders' labels help create the fund of interpretive possibilities from which identity can be drawn.[74] Observers' reports can be fruitfully interrogated for clues to the lives of both the seers and the seen. And the downfall of O. Delight Smith, like the murder of Leo Frank, reminds us that images help construct relationships of power.

Notes

1   Robert C. McMath, Jr., "History by a Graveyard: The Fulton Bag and Cotton Mills Records," *Labor's Heritage*, 1 (Apr. 1989), 4–9; Fulton Mills Collection, Price Gilbert Memorial Library, Georgia Institute of Technology, Atlanta. I owe a special debt to Bob McMath for inviting me to use these papers soon after they became available.

2   For historians' relatively uncritical reliance on informers' reports, see Paul Thompson, *The Voice of the Past: Oral History* (New York: Oxford University Press, 1988), 40, 101. The literature on labor espionage itself, however, is quite thin. See US Congress, Senate, *Violations of Free Speech and Assembly and Interference with Rights of Labor: Hearings before the Subcommittee of the Committee on Education and Labor on S. Res. 266*, 74th Cong., 2nd sess. (Washington, DC: US Government Printing Office, 1936); Darryl Holter, "Labor Spies and Union-Busting in Wisconsin, 1890–1940," *Wisconsin Magazine of History*, 68 (Summer 1985), 243–65; Charles K. Hyde, "Undercover and Underground: Labor Spies and Mine Management in the Early Twentieth Century," *Business History Review*, 60 (Spring 1986), 1–27; Gene Caesar, *The Incredible Detective: The Biography of William J. Burns* (Englewood Cliffs, NJ: Prentice-Hall, 1968); Frank Morn, *"The Eye That Never Sleeps": A History of the Pinkerton National Detective Agency* (Bloomington: Indiana University Press, 1982); Dirk Hoerder (ed.), *Plutocrats and Socialists: Reports by German Diplomats and Agents on the American Labor Movement, 1878–1917* (Munich: K. G. Saur, 1981); and William M. Reddy, "The Batteurs and the Informer's Eye: A Labour Dispute under the French Second Empire," *History Workshop*, 7 (Spring 1979), 30–44.

3   Laura Mulvey, "Visual Pleasure and Narrative Cinema," *Screen*, 16 (Autumn 1975), 6–18; Judith Mayne, "Feminist Film Theory and Criticism," *Signs: Journal of Women in Culture and Society*, 2 (Autumn 1985), 81–100.

4   James Clifford, "On Ethnographic Authority," in James Clifford, *The Predicament of Culture* (Cambridge: Harvard University Press, 1988), 14, 23.

5   C. Vann Woodward, *Thinking Back: The Perils of Writing History* (Baton Rouge: Louisiana State University Press, 1986), 59–79; Morgan Kousser and James M. McPherson (eds), *Region, Race, and Reconstruction* (New York: Oxford University Press, 1982), xvii. Among those Woodward calls the "New Continuarians" are Dwight B. Billings, Jr., *Planters and the Making of a "New South": Class, Politics, and Development in North Carolina, 1865–1900* (Chapel Hill: University of North Carolina Press, 1979); David Goldfield, *Cotton Fields and Skyscrapers: Southern City and Region, 1607–1980* (Baton Rouge: Louisiana State University Press, 1982); Jonathan M. Wiener, *Social Origins of the New South: Alabama, 1860–1885* (Baton Rouge: Louisiana State University Press, 1978); George B. Tindall, *The Persistent Tradition in New South Politics* (Baton Rouge: Louisiana State University Press, 1975). A number of recent studies, however, reinforce Woodward's emphasis on discontinuity. Edward L. Ayers, *A Newer South: Life at the End of the Nineteenth Century* (New York: Oxford University Press, forthcoming), for instance, argues that the New South was even newer than Woodward imagined. See also David L. Carlton, "The Revolution from Above: The National Market and the Beginnings of Industrialization in North Carolina," *Journal of American History*, 77 (Sept. 1990), 445–75; Don H. Doyle, *New Men, New Cities: Atlanta, Nashville, Charleston, Mobile, 1860–1910* (Chapel Hill: University of North Carolina Press, 1990); Glenda Gilmore, "Gender and Jim Crow: Black Women and Politics in North Carolina, 1890–1920" (Ph.D. diss. in progress, University of North Carolina at Chapel Hill); Steven Hahn, "Class and State in Postemancipation Societies: Southern Planters in

Comparative Perspective," *American Historical Review,* 95 (Feb. 1990), 75–98; Anne
Goodwyn Jones, *Faulkner's Daughters* (manuscript in progress); and James
L. Leloudis, "'A More Certain Means of Grace': Pedagogy, Self, and Society in
North Carolina, 1880–1920" (Ph.D. diss., University of North Carolina at Chapel
Hill, 1989).

6 Theodore Dreiser, *Sister Carrie* (New York: Doubleday, 1900); Kathy Peiss,
"'Charity Girls' and City Pleasures: Historical Notes on Working-Class Sexuality,
1880–1920," in *Powers of Desire: The Politics of Sexuality,* ed. Ann Snitow, Christine
Stansell, and Sharon Thompson, 74–87 (New York: Monthly Review Press, 1983);
Joanne J. Meyerowitz, *Women Adrift: Independent Wage Earners in Chicago,
1880–1930* (Chicago: University of Chicago Press, 1988), and "Sexual Geography
and Gender Economy: The Furnished Room Districts of Chicago, 1890–1930,"
Gender and History, 2 (Autumn 1990), 274–96; and Estelle Freedman and John
D'Emilio, *Intimate Matters: A History of Sexuality in America* (New York: Harper &
Row, 1988), 171–235. There is an extensive literature on the South's split image of
female sexuality, a subject that was the focus of my own earlier work: Jacquelyn
Dowd Hall, *Revolt against Chivalry: Jessie Daniel Ames and the Women's Campaign
against Lynching* (New York: Columbia University Press, 1979); and "'The Mind
That Burns in Each Body': Women, Rape, and Racial Violence," in Snitow et al.,
Powers of Desire, 328–49.

7 For other glimpses of the emergence of new patterns of sociability and sexual
behavior in the South, see Barbara Shaw Anderson, "Struggling with the Burdens
of Feminine Virtue: The Case of Ida Ball Warren in North Carolina, 1914–1916"
(master's thesis, University of North Carolina at Chapel Hill, 1988); Jacquelyn
Dowd Hall, "Disorderly Women: Gender and Labor Militancy in the Appalachian
South," *Journal of American History,* 73 (Sept. 1986), 354–82; Jacquelyn Dowd Hall,
James Leloudis, Robert Korstad, Mary Murphy, Lu Ann Jones, and Christopher B.
Daly, *Like a Family: The Making of a Southern Cotton Mill World* (Chapel Hill:
University of North Carolina Press, 1987), 225–36, 252–88; and Rebecca Lallier,
"A Place of Beginning Again: The North Carolina Industrial Farm Colony,
1929–1947" (master's thesis, University of North Carolina at Chapel Hill, 1990).

8 US Department of Commerce, Bureau of the Census, *Eleventh Census of the United
States* (Washington, DC: US Government Printing Office, 1895), 1:454, and
Donald B. Dodd and Wynell S. Dodd, *Historical Statistics of the South, 1790–1970*
(University: University of Alabama Press, 1973), 74; *Davison's Textile Blue Book,
1910–1911* (New York: Davison, 1910), 69; "100th Anniversary Fulton Cotton
Mills," *Textile Industries* (Dec. 1968), 63–4; Memorandum for Secretary Wilson,
by Robert M. McWade and John S. Colpoys, Aug. 18, 1915, in Fulton Bag
Company, Case File 33/41, Record Group 280, Federal Mediation and Conciliation
Service Records, Suitland Branch, National Archives (hereafter McWade and Col-
poys Memorandum); Inis Weed, "Preliminary Report," July 28, 1914, in Records of
the US Commission on Industrial Relations, US Department of Labor, box 10,
Record Group 174, National Archives, Washington, DC (hereafter RG 174). The
Records of the US Commission on Industrial Relations are also available on micro-
film: Melvyn Dubofsky, ed., *US Commission on Industrial Relations, 1912–1915,*

Unpublished Records of the Division of Research and Investigation: Reports, Staff Studies, and Background Materials (Frederick, Md.: University Publications of America, 1985).

9   In 1911 the US Bureau of Labor found little difference in the living standards of workers in three typical mill settings: Atlanta; Greensboro, NC; and Burlington, NC. Families in all three communities suffered from serious illnesses, dietary deficiencies, and decrepit surroundings. See US Congress, Senate, *Report on Condition of Woman and Child Wage-Earners in the United States*, vol. 16, *Family Budgets of Typical Cotton-Mill Workers*, prepared by Wood F. Worcester and Daisy Worthington Worcester, 61st Cong., 2nd sess. (Washington, DC: US Government Printing Office, 1911), 19–171. For mill owners' treatment of their employees during this period, see Edward H. Beardsley, *A History of Neglect: Health Care for Blacks and Mill Workers in the Twentieth-Century South* (Knoxville: University of Tennessee Press, 1987). For mill village life, see Hall et al., *Like a Family*; I. A. Newby, *Plain Folk in the New South* (Baton Rouge: Louisiana State University Press, 1989); and Allen Tullos, *Habits of Industry: White Culture and the Transformation of the Carolina Piedmont* (Chapel Hill: University of North Carolina Press, 1989).

10 *Journal of Labor*, May 29, 1914, 4; Operative 16, Mar. 11, 1915, box 3, file 37, Operative Reports, Fulton Mills Collection (hereafter Operative Reports); Alexander M. Daly to Dr. Charles McCarthy, July 31, 1914, RG 174. For the useful metaphor of "onstage" and "offstage" behavior, see James Scott, *Weapons of the Weak: Everyday Forms of Peasant Resistance* (New Haven: Yale University Press, 1985), 25.

11 For the best account of the tensions leading up to this first strike, see "In the Matter of Fulton Bag & Cotton Mills, Atlanta, Georgia, before the United States Commission on Industrial Relations; Testimony Taken in Atlanta, Georgia," vol. 1, "Testimony for the Complainants," 3–13, Strike Records, Fulton Mills Collection (hereafter Strike Records). These hearings are summarized in Alexander M. Daly, "Sworn Testimony Taken before William C. Massey, Notary Public, in and for the City of Atlanta, and State of Georgia, of about Forty Witnesses," n.d., RG 174 (hereafter Daly, "Sworn Testimony").

12 According to Gary M. Fink, "Labor Espionage: The Fulton Bag and Cotton Mills Strike of 1914–1915," *Labor's Heritage*, 1 (Apr. 1989), 13, 17, the Railway Audit and Inspection Agency, a large interstate business, had been involved in the coalfield wars in Colorado and had provided strikebreakers in textile disputes from Maine to Georgia. The mill also dealt with such firms as the Graham Agency of Knoxville, Tennessee; Day's Detective Agency of Augusta, Georgia; and Sherman Services of New York.

13 Inis Weed, "Final Report on Strike in Fulton Bag and Cotton Mills in Atlanta, Georgia, and Conditions in Nearby Mill Towns," Sept. 19, 1914, 2, RG 174 (hereafter Weed, "Final Report"); *Journal of Labor* (June 19, 1914), 4; *Report of Proceedings of the Thirty-fourth Annual Convention of the American Federation of Labor* (Philadelphia, Nov. 9–21, 1914), 341.

14 The Knights of Labor in the 1880s and the National Union of Textile Workers in the 1890s had led extensive organizing campaigns in Georgia. The AFL's one-cent

assessment was levied by the Executive Council on Feb. 28, 1914, in accordance with a resolution adopted at the AFL's 1913 convention. It yielded funds that amounted to perhaps one-ninth of the AFL's regular organizing budget (e.g., $2,088.58 as compared to $18,588.43 during the month of July 1914). The funds were used to pay portions of the salaries of eighteen organizers (four of whom were women). Of these people, three women and three men, in addition to UTW president Golden, were active in Atlanta. See *Report of Proceedings of the Thirty-fourth Annual Convention*, 20, 58, 331; *American Federationist* (Sept. 1914), 743. This campaign reflected a realization that women were in the work force to stay, but it did not signal a serious, long-term commitment to bring them into the AFL on an equal basis with men. For the AFL's historical hostility toward women workers, see Alice Kessler-Harris, *Out to Work: A History of Wage-Earning Women in the United States* (New York: Oxford University Press, 1982), 152–66. For the organization's limited shift in attitude, see Ann Schofield, "Rebel Girls and Union Maids: The Woman Question in the Journals of the AFL and the IWW, 1905–1920," *Feminist Studies*, 9 (Summer 1983), 335–58.

15   The literature on labor politics in Atlanta and in the South generally is quite thin. For the salience of class issues and the participation of skilled workers in city politics, see Eugene J. Watts, *The Social Bases of City Politics: Atlanta, 1865–1903* (Westport, Conn.: Greenwood, 1978), esp. 73–4; Mercer Griffin Evans, "The History of the Organized Labor Movement in Georgia" (Ph.D. diss., University of Chicago, 1929), 258–9; Thomas Mashburn Deaton, "Atlanta during the Progressive Era" (Ph.D. diss., University of Georgia, 1969), 143–4; and Thomas M. Deaton, "James G. Woodward: The Working Man's Mayor," *Atlanta History: A Journal of Georgia and the South*, 31 (Fall 1987), 11–23.

16   Harry G. Lefever, "The Involvement of the Men and Religion Forward Movement in the Cause of Labor Justice, Atlanta, Georgia, 1912–1916," *Labor History*, 14 (Fall 1973), 521–35; McWade and Colpoys Memorandum; Herman Robinson and W. W. Husband to Secretary of Labor William B. Wilson, July 24, 1914, Federal Mediation and Conciliation Service Records; Daly to McCarthy, July 31, 1914; Daly, "Sworn Testimony"; Weed, "Preliminary Report" and "Final Report."

17   On Miles and Conboy, see Robert E. Snyder, "Women, Wobblies, and Workers' Rights: The 1912 Textile Strike in Little Falls, New York," *New York History*, 60 (Jan. 1979), 51–2; Meredith Tax, *The Rising of the Women: Feminist Solidarity and Class Conflict, 1880–1917* (New York: Monthly Review Press, 1980), 266–7; Alice Henry, *Women and the Labor Movement* (New York: Macmillan, 1927), 95; *A Look at the Record* (n.p., n.d. [UTW, 1976]), 9–12, 14, pamphlet celebrating the 75th anniversary of the United Textile Workers of America, in the Robert F. Wagner Labor Archives, Tamiment Institute Library, New York University; Textile Workers of America, *Proceedings of the Nineteenth Annual Convention*, Baltimore, Oct. 20–25, 1919. On Smith, see *Journal of Labor*, June 12, 1914, 7 (quote), and Oct. 17, 1913, 5; and Jacquelyn Dowd Hall, "O. Delight Smith's Progressive Era: Labor, Feminism, and Reform in the Urban South," in *Visible Women: An Anthology*, ed. Nancy Hewitt and Suzanne Lebsock (Urbana: University of Illinois Press, 1993). Of the six people who were, at one time or another,

paid by the AFL campaign to organize women workers, only O. Delight Smith was assigned exclusively to Atlanta. She earned considerably less than the other organizers, and her entire salary of approximately $20 a week came from the AFL's special fund. See correspondence in Frank Morrison Letterbooks, Perkins Library, Duke University: Morrison to Charles A. Miles, June 13 and June 16, 1914, vol. 387; Morrison to Mrs. E. B. Smith, Dec. 1, 1914, vol. 401; Morrison to Miles, June 16, 1914, vol. 387.

18   Operative H. J. D., June 3, 1914, box 2, file 15; Operatives J. W. W. and A. E. W., June 6, 1914, box 1, file 2, Operative Reports. Smith compiled and annotated three albums of photographs, which she titled "Conditions," "Evictions," and "Tent City." Along with 16 additional prints, these photographs form a unique collection of 136 images. They can be found at the George Meany Memorial Archives in Washington, DC. Copies of the photographs are available at the Southern Labor Archives, Special Collections, Georgia State University, Atlanta. Some copies are also located in "Exhibits," Fulton Bag Company, Federal Mediation and Conciliation Service Records. For this photographic record, see Clifford M. Kuhn, "Images of Dissent: The Pictorial Record of the 1914–15 Strike at Atlanta's Fulton Bag and Cotton Mills," paper presented at the annual meeting of the Organization of American Historians, St. Louis, Mo., Apr. 6, 1989. It was Kuhn who first brought this material to my attention. For the documentary tradition on which Smith drew, see Peter B. Hales, *Silver Cities: The Photography of American Urbanization, 1839–1915* (Philadelphia: Temple University Press, 1984); and Alan Trachtenberg, *Reading American Photographs: Images as History, Mathew Brady to Walker Evans* (New York: Hill & Wang, 1989).

19   Hales, *Silver Cities*, 168. The National Child Labor Committee apparently supplied copies of Hine's Georgia photographs to the *Atlanta Georgian*, which published them without attribution during the 1914 child labor campaign. See photographs in *Child Labor Bulletin*, 2 (Aug. 1913), 24, and 3 (Feb. 1915), 35. They are reprinted in *Atlanta Georgian*, June 29, 1914, 1.

20   *Journal of Labor*, June 5, 1914, 5; Sept. 26, 1914, 3; Sept. 19, 1914, 2; Oct. 3, 1914, 3; and Oct. 31, 1913, 4 (quotes).

21   Ibid., July 24, 1914, 2.

22   Hales, *Silver Cities*, 163; [Oscar Elsas] to B. Z. Phillips, Jan. 22, 1915, box 1, file 1, Operative Reports (hereafter Report to B. Z. Phillips).

23   Report to B. Z. Phillips.

24   Kasson, *Rudeness and Civility*, 72–111; Morn, *Eye That Never Sleeps*, 87; Report to B. Z. Phillips; Operative 16, Dec. 23, 1914, box 3, file 31; Operative 16, Mar. 22, 1915, box 3, file 37; Operative 16, Oct. 8, 1915, box 3, file 44, Operative Reports.

25   For the political uses of various representations of the working class, see Joan Wallach Scott, "A Statistical Representation of Work: La Statistique de l'industrie à Paris, 1847–48," in Joan Wallach Scott, *Gender and the Politics of History* (New York: Columbia University Press, 1988), 113–38; Christine Stansell, *City of Women: Sex and Class in New York, 1789–1860* (New York: Knopf, 1986); and Meyerowitz, *Women Adrift*.

26   Operative 470, Aug. 1, 1914, box 2, file 20; Operative 16, Mar. 22, 1915, box 3, file
     37 (quote); Operative 16, Dec. 27, 1914, box 3, file 31; R. H. Wright to Harry
     G. Preston, Sept. 23, 1914, box 1, file 6; Wright to Preston, Oct. 14, 1914, box 1,
     file 10; Operative 16, n.d., box 3, file 33, Operative Reports.
27   Report to B. Z. Phillips.
28   Operative 16, n.d., box 3, file 37 (quote), and Report to B. Z. Phillips. A "yegg"
     was an itinerant burglar, especially a safecracker. The self-described yegg Jack
     Black defined the type as "highly secretive, wary; forever traveling, always a night
     'worker.' He shuns the bright lights, seldom straying far from his kind, never
     coming to the surface. Circulating through space with his always-ready automatic,
     the yegg rules the underworld of criminals": Black, *You Can't Win* (New York:
     Macmillan, 1926), 5. There is a good deal of evidence that rank-and-file leaders
     such as H. Newborn Mullinax were in fact the founders and the mainstays of the
     union. These men were skilled weavers and loom fixers and long-time employees,
     not the hobos the spies made them out to be. See Mullinax, "Personals from
     Textile Workers," *Journal of Labor*, Jan. 9, 1914, 5; and "In the Matter of Fulton
     Bag & Cotton Mills."
29   Report to B. Z. Phillips.
30   Operative 429, Sept. 7, 1916, box 4, file 48 (quote), and Sept. 17 (quote), Sept. 21,
     Oct. 6, and Oct. 7, 1916, box 4, file 49; "Operative 16 Reports on Mrs. Kellar
     Organizer," Nov. 6, 1915, box 3, file 44, Operative Reports.
31   Operative 12, July 25 and 26, 1914, box 2, file 16; Operative 39, July 25 and July
     26, 1914, box 2, file 17; Operative 15, Aug. 1, 1914, box 2, file 18; Operative 16,
     Dec. 27, 1914, box 3, file 31 (quote), and June 7, 1915, box 3, file 41, Operative
     Reports.
32   *Journal of Labor*, Apr. 7, 1950, 1–2.
33   Callahan appears in various sources as "Pat Calahan," "Pat Callahan," and
     "J. Callahan." See Mrs. O. L. Smith v. Edgar B. Smith, Libel for Divorce, Depos-
     itions of Defendant, Aug. 17, 1915; Petition of Mrs. O. L. Smith, Aug. 3, 1915; and
     Mrs. O. L. Smith v. Edgar B. Smith, Divorce Suit, Aug. 27, 1915, all in Superior
     Court of Fulton County, Fulton County Courthouse, Atlanta. By the time the case
     went to court, Edgar was no longer being represented by Rosser, Brandon, Salton,
     and Phillips. It is clear, however, that the company sought to exploit the Smiths'
     marital difficulties and that Edgar Smith's inquiries about his wife to UTW
     officials helped to undermine her position in the union. See E. B. Smith to
     American Federation of Labor, Nov. 29, 1914, vol. 401, Morrison Letterbooks;
     and undated, unsigned, handwritten note in box 3, folder 4, Strike Records.
34   *Atlanta Georgian*, Jan. 19, 1917, 8; Foreman's report, Mrs. Ola L. Smith v. Edgar B.
     Smith, Jan. 18, 1917; Mrs. O. L. Smith v. E. B. Smith, Petition for Divorce, and
     Cross-bill by deft. and second verdict for defendant upon his Cross-bill in Fulton
     Superior Court, June 7, 1917, Superior Court of Fulton County. According to
     state law, three terms of court were necessary in divorce actions. The court
     impaneled a special jury for each term of court. Absolute divorce was granted
     only on the verdict of two concurring juries; the second jury determined the rights
     of the parties and could impose "disability of remarriage on the guilty party."

Disabilities could be removed in subsequent proceedings. See Franklyn Hudgings, Ll.B., *What Everybody Should Know about the Law of Marriage and Divorce* (New York: New Century, 1935), 23.

35 Operative 115, Oct. 14, 1914, box 1, file 10; R. H. Wright to Harry G. Preston, Oct. 14, 1914, Operative Reports.

36 Operative 115, July 3, 1914, box 1, file 6 (quote); Operative 115, July 6 (quote), July 11, July 13 (quote), and July 25, 1914, box 1, file 7; Operative 115, Sept. 14, 1914, box 1, file 9 (quote), Operative Reports.

37 Operative 115, Aug. 28 and Sept. 1, 1914, box 1, file 8; Operative 457, Dec. 11, 1914, box 2, file 27, Operative Reports; Fink, "Labor Espionage," 21; Frank Morrison to Mrs. E. B. Smith, Oct. 20, 1914, vol. 397, and Morrison to Charles A. Miles, Oct. 24, 1914, vol. 398, Morrison Letterbooks.

38 Mary Ryan, *Women in Public: Between Banners and Ballots, 1823–1880* (Baltimore: Johns Hopkins University Press, 1990); Kasson, *Rudeness and Civility,* 94 (quote).

39 Bertram Wyatt-Brown, *Honor and Violence in the Old South* (New York: Oxford University Press, 1986); Edward L. Ayers, *Vengeance and Justice: Crime and Punishment in the 19th-Century South* (New York: Oxford University Press, 1984); Kenneth S. Greenberg, "The Nose, the Lie, and the Duel in the Antebellum South," *American Historical Review, 95* (February 1990), 57–74; Warren I. Susman, "'Personality' and the Making of Twentieth-Century Culture," in *New Directions in American Intellectual History,* ed. John Higham and Paul K. Conkin (Baltimore: Johns Hopkins University Press, 1979), 212–26; Karen Halttunen, *Confidence Men and Painted Women: A Study of Middle-Class Culture in America, 1830–1870* (New Haven: Yale University Press, 1982), xiii–xviii, 198–210 (quote, 198); Peter Filene, *Him/Her/Self: Sex Roles in Modern America* (Baltimore: Johns Hopkins University Press, 1986), 69–93.

40 Fink, "Labor Espionage," 13, 17, 24–28, 31; Operative 115, July 19 and July 26, 1914, box 1, file 7; Operative 115, Sept. 24, 1914, box 1, file 9; Harry Preston Reports, Jan. 18, 1920, box 7, file 120, Operative Reports.

41 Smith's costs, of course, should not be minimized. She lost her job and left Atlanta. But she also persuaded the divorce court to remove the restrictions on her right to remarry, married for love, and resurfaced in Oregon, where she eventually earned the sobriquet "first lady of the Oregon labor movement." See Hall, "O. Delight Smith's Progressive Era"; and *Oregon Labor Press,* Dec. 12, 1958.

42 Operative 115 to Oscar Elsas, July 7, 1914; Operative 115, July 9, 1914 (quote), box 1, file 7, Operative Reports; O. Delight Smith, inscription on second page of album titled "Conditions," Meany Archives (quote).

43 *Journal of Labor,* Feb. 26, 1909, 5; Aug. 20, 1909, 5.

44 Ibid., Feb. 26, 1909, 5; Feb. 19, 1909, 2; Aug. 20, 1909, 5.

45 See Martha Banta, *Imaging American Women: Idea and Ideals in Cultural History* (New York: Columbia University Press, 1989), for a perceptive analysis of how pictorial images create "social types" and of women's uses of those images in their self-representations. I am grateful to Pamela Dean and to Helen Langa, "Narratives of Women's Propriety and Protection in Some Documents Concerning the Fulton Bag and Cotton Mill Strike in Atlanta, 1914–1915," seminar paper,

University of North Carolina at Chapel Hill, 1988, for help in reading this visual evidence. More generally, I am indebted to Langa and to the other students in my fall 1988 women's history course for their insights and camaraderie. They helped clarify my thinking at many points.

46　For the efforts of detectives to adopt the trappings of modern advertising and represent themselves as "industrial harmonizers and conciliators," see Sidney Howard, *The Labor Spy* (New York: Republic, 1924), 17–19, 21. For the argument that Fulton Mills did in fact use spies as proto-efficiency experts, see Gary M. Fink, "Efficiency and Control: Labor Espionage in Southern Textiles," paper presented at the annual meeting of the Organization of American Historians, St. Louis, Mo., Apr. 6, 1989; and Deborah Kim Dawson, "The Origins of Scientific Management in the Textile Industry" (master's thesis, Georgia Institute of Technology, 1990).

47　Julia Blackwelder, "Mop and Typewriter: Women's Work in Early Twentieth-Century Atlanta," *Atlanta Historical Journal*, 27 (Fall 1983), 24; Joseph A. Hill, *Women in Gainful Occupations, 1870 to 1920*, Census Monographs, 9 (Washington, DC: US Government Printing Office, 1929), 11, 146.

48　Hill, *Women in Gainful Occupations*, 145–46; US Department of Commerce, Bureau of the Census, *Fourteenth Census of the United States, 1920* (Washington, DC: US Government Printing Office, 1922), 3:222. It should be emphasized that the rate of labor force participation among black women increased more slowly than that of whites because so many black women were *already* working. Moreover, the black population rose less quickly than the white (76% versus 154%). The changes in the structure of the female work force remain striking nevertheless, and they seem to have been due mainly to the forces that pushed white women off the farms, on the one hand, and the exclusion of black women from urban job opportunities, on the other.

49　The comparison with Chicago is based on Meyerowitz, *Women Adrift*, 4–5; and US Department of Commerce and Labor, Bureau of the Census, *Statistics of Women at Work* (Washington, DC: US Government Printing Office, 1907), 29. Information on the 1920 Bureau of the Census study and other figures are from Hill, *Women in Gainful Occupations*, 139, 143–5, 333–6. The eleven cities included in Hill's study were Fall River, Mass.; Providence, RI; Rochester, NY; Paterson, NJ; Cincinnati, Ohio; Indianapolis, Ind.; St. Paul, Minn.; Kansas City, Mo.; Louisville, Mo.; New Orleans, La.; and Atlanta.

50　For an excellent survey of urban middle-class concerns during this period, see Paul Boyer, *Urban Masses and Moral Order in America, 1820–1920* (Cambridge: Harvard University Press, 1978), 191–219.

51　The standard study of these events is Leonard Dinnerstein, *The Leo Frank Case* (New York: Columbia University Press, 1968).

52　*Journal of Labor*, May 2, 1913, 14; Steven Hertzberg, "Southern Jews and their Encounter with Blacks: Atlanta, 1850–1915," *Atlanta Historical Journal*, 23 (Fall 1979), 21; Eugene Levy, "'Is the Jew a White Man?': Press Reaction to the Leo Frank Case, 1913–1915," *Phylon*, 35 (June 1974), 212–22. The evidence indicates that Conley was probably guilty of the crime.

53 The Elsases contributed to Frank's defense. Oscar's son-in-law, Benjamin Z. Phillips, who sat on the company's board of directors and served as the firm's general counsel, helped oversee the spy network. Phillips was also a law partner of Governor Slaton's, and their firm defended Leo Frank. For the spies' accounts of anti-Semitism among the workers and UTW organizers, see Special Work, June 3, 1914, box 3, file 14, and July 3, 1914, box 1, file 6; and the following reports of Operative 16: Apr. 16, 1915, box 3, file 38; May 3, 1915, box 3, file 39; May 27, 1915, box 3, file 41; June 20, June 21, June 25, and June 28, 1915, box 3, file 42, all in Operative Reports.

54 "Transcript of hearing before Governor John M. Slaton on request for commutation of death sentence of Leo Frank" [1915], 144, 148–9, Leo Frank Collection, box 1, folders 1–8, Special Collections, Robert W. Woodruff Library, Emory University; Dinnerstein, Leo Frank Case, 19; Clark Jack Freshman, "Beyond Pontius Pilate and Judge Lynch: The Pardoning Power in Theory and Practice as Illustrated in the Leo Frank Case" (honors thesis, Harvard College, 1986), 52–3.

55 For this transition, see Elizabeth Lunbeck, "'A New Generation of Women': Progressive Psychiatrists and the Hypersexual Female," Feminist Studies, 13 (Fall 1987), 513–43; and Estelle Freedman, "'Uncontrolled Desires': The Response to the Sexual Psychopath, 1920–1960," Journal of American History, 74 (June 1987), 83–106, esp. 97–8, 100–1.

56 For the argument that racial extremism subsided as whites convinced themselves that the "Negro problem" had been solved, see Joel Williamson, A Rage for Order: Black–White Relations in the American South since Emancipation (New York: Oxford University Press, 1986), 42–3, 83–6, 117–51, 240–4. John Dittmer, Black Georgia in the Progressive Era, 1900–1920 (Urbana: University of Illinois Press, 1977), on the other hand, underscores the continued salience of racial issues during the Progressive Era. For an intriguing analysis of the gender dynamics of the Frank case, see Nancy McLean, "The Leo Frank Case Reconsidered: The Role of Family Change and Gender Ideology in the Development of Political Reaction, Georgia, 1890–1930," paper presented at the Berkshire Conference, Wellesley College, June 19, 1987. McLean argues that the denunciation of Leo Frank illustrates the South's sexual conservatism. My emphasis is on the conflicts aroused by the modernization of sex.

57 Atlanta Georgian, June 5, 1914, editorial page.

58 See ibid., July 6, 1914, 1; July 23, 1914, 1; June 25, 1914, 1.

59 Ibid., July 4, 1914, 1.

60 Journal of Labor, May 2, 1913, 4; Sept. 5, 1913, 4. This is not to say that the Journal ignored the sexual dimensions of the case altogether. Its coverage was generally restrained, but at one point it called on its male readers to accept responsibility for finding the "fiendish brute" who committed the murder: ibid., May 30, 1913, 4.

61 Ibid., Nov. 13, 1908, 6; Nov. 20, 1908, 7.

62 Ibid., Nov. 7, 1913, 4; Jan. 9, 1914, 4.

63 Ibid., Oct. 31, 1913, 4. For the prevalence of "control strikes" and an upsurge in rank-and-file militancy during this period, see David Montgomery, Workers'

Control in America: Studies in the History of Work, Technology, and Labor Struggles (Cambridge: Cambridge University Press, 1979), 91–112. For the feminized representation of textile workers, see Lawrence J. Boyette, "Gender, Working-Class Culture, and Unionization: A Test Case" (diss. prospectus, University of North Carolina at Chapel Hill, 1988).

64 Kuhn, "Images of Dissent," 4–5; *Atlanta Georgian*, June 24, 1914, editorial page (quote); June 21, 1914; June 28, 1914. For an earlier controversy in which reformers substituted a concern for the domestic situation of women and children for a confrontation with class exploitation, see LeeAnn Whites, "The De Graffenried Controversy: Class, Race, and Gender in the New South," *Journal of Southern History*, 54 (Aug. 1988), 449–78. It is important to note, however, that this was a characteristic of the American reform tradition, not a peculiarity of the South. By 1915, most reformers had turned from direct organization to protective legislation as the best means of solving the problems of women workers. Kathryn Kish Sklar argues that Progressive reformers pursued such gender-specific solutions in part because of the American tradition of limited government and the weakness of class as a vehicle for political action: Sklar, *Florence Kelley and the Nation's Work: The Rise of Women's Political Culture, 1830–1900* (New Haven: Yale University Press, 1995). For a provocative discussion of the tendency of male trade unionists to assume that women's gender, not their membership in a class, defined their primary identity, see Patricia J. Hilden, "Women and the Labour Movement in France, 1869–1914," *Historical Journal*, 29 (1986), 809–32. Sklar's and Hilden's work underscores the need to place southern history in a broad comparative perspective.

65 Lefever, "Involvement of the Men and Religion Forward Movement"; Gail Bederman, "'The Women Have Had Charge of the Church Work Long Enough': The Men and Religion Forward Movement of 1911–1912 and the Masculinization of Middle-Class Protestantism," *American Quarterly*, 41 (September 1989), 432–65.

66 "Digest of Two Interviews with the Rev. G. R. Buford," RG 174; Harry G. Lefever, "Prostitution, Politics, and Religion: The Crusade against Vice in Atlanta in 1912," *Atlanta Historical Journal*, 24 (Spring 1980), 13; *Atlanta Constitution*, June 13, 1914, 5. See also "Atlanta Vice Commission Reports" and "Atlanta's Segregated District Gone," *Vigilance*, Nov. 1912, 28–30.

67 *Atlanta Constitution*, June 6, 1914, 7. This image was echoed and elaborated by W. J. Cash, Frank Tannenbaum, and others. See Cash, *The Mind of the South* (New York: Knopf, 1941), 204, and Tannenbaum, "The South Buries Its Anglo-Saxons," *Century*, 106 (June 1923), 205, 210–11.

68 Only in the 1930s did Cabbagetown become a mill-dominated community rather than a working-class neighborhood. For these changing residential patterns, see Stephen W. Grable, "The Other Side of the Tracks: Cabbagetown – a Working-Class Neighborhood in Transition during the Early Twentieth Century," *Atlanta Historical Journal*, 26 (Summer/Fall 1982), 51–66; and Gretchen E. Maclachlan, "The Factory Lot in 1900: Urban or Rural," seminar paper, Emory University, 1986. Maclachlan found that households in which all employed members worked at the mill constituted fewer than half of the 155 households in the Factory Lot.

69 Operative 331, Aug. 15, 1922, box 6, file 106; Report to B. Z. Phillips, Operative Reports. See Kathy Peiss, *Cheap Amusements: Working Women and Leisure in Turn-of-the-Century New York* (Philadelphia: Temple University Press, 1986); Stansell, *City of Women;* and Meyerowitz, *Women Adrift,* for studies of similar milieus.

70 Operative 429, Sept. 21, Sept. 26, and Oct. 7, 1916, box 4, file 49, Operative Reports.

71 *Atlanta Constitution,* June 6, 1914, 6, 7; Report to B. Z. Phillips. For this phenomenon, see D'Emilio and Freedman, *Intimate Matters,* 124–5; Jonathan Katz, *Gay American History: Lesbians and Gay Men in the U.S.A.* (New York: Crowell, 1976), 209–79; and Box-Car Bertha, *Sister of the Road: The Autobiography of Box-Car Bertha,* as told to Dr. Ben L. Reitman (New York: Macauley, 1937).

72 Weed, "Final Report" (quote); *Journal of Labor,* Sept. 4, 1914, 6; McWade and Colpoys Memorandum, 7; Operative 16, May 12, 1915, box 3, file 40, Operative Reports (quote).

73 This study, of course, is concerned with observers' representations, not workers' identities. For the latter, we would have to draw on sources that are less hierarchical and more dialogic, sources that allow those who have usually been the objects of surveillance and reform a voice in the representational process that produces our understanding of the past. For this issue, see Clifford, "On Ethnographic Authority," 21–54. For a study of southern textile workers that relies heavily on oral history – a source that is, by its nature, created in dialogue – see Hall et al., *Like a Family;* and Jacquelyn D. Hall and Della Pollock, "History, Story, and Performance: The Making and Remaking of a Southern Cotton Mill World," in *Reconstructing American Literary and Historical Studies,* ed. Günter H. Lenz, Hartmut Keil, and Sabine Bröck-Sallah (Frankfurt am Main: Campus and New York: St. Martin's Press, 1990), 324–44. For studies that take the complexity of women workers' identities as a central concern, see Susan Porter Benson, *Counter Cultures: Saleswomen, Managers, and Customers in American Department Stores, 1890–1940* (Urbana: University of Illinois Press, 1988), 229 and passim; Alice Kessler-Harris, "Gender Ideology in Historical Reconstruction: A Case Study from the 1930s," *Gender and History,* 1 (Spring 1989), 31–49; Ardis Cameron, *Radicals of the Worst Sort: The Labouring Women of Lawrence, Massachusetts, 1880–1912* (Urbana: University of Illinois Press, 1993); and Carole Turbin, "Beyond Dichotomies: Interdependence in Mid-Nineteenth-Century Working-Class Families in the United States," *Gender and History,* 1 (Autumn 1989), 293–308.

74 Nancy Fraser, "The Uses and Abuses of French Discourse Theories for Feminist Politics," paper presented to the Program in Social Theory and Cross-Cultural Studies, University of North Carolina at Chapel Hill, Apr. 14, 1989.

6

Margaret Bourke-White's Red Coat; or, Slumming in the Thirties

PAULA RABINOWITZ

— I —

A popular Irving Berlin song from 1933 invited its financially strapped middle- and working-class listeners to 'go slumming on Park Avenue.' Written in the midst of the worst year of the Depression, when unemployment soared between 25 and 33 per cent, the song sarcastically played upon the (downward) class mobility caused by the 1929 Crash. This turning of the class tables was a common theme in Hollywood as well, where spunky golddiggers displayed their goods ('We're in the Money') to entice wealthy men who visited the seedy nightclubs in which they performed before they retreated to the safety of their men's clubs.

During the 1920s, 'when Harlem was in vogue,' wealthy whites had traveled uptown, to take in the atmosphere of jazz and high living offered in Harlem's famous night spots. A decade before, tour buses passed through the ghettoes of the Lower East Side and were assaulted with missiles of paving stones and garbage, according to Mike Gold's autobiographical novel *Jews Without Money*. The class and ethnic boundaries superintending America's cities were rigid; yet popular culture encouraged their permeability: for the wealthy WASP elite, black and Jewish ghettoes provided a voyeuristic thrill. But after the stock market crashed, popular culture unleashed a new pastime – working

Paula Rabinowitz, "Margaret Bourke-White's Red Coat; or, Slumming in the Thirties," in Rabinowitz, *They Must Be Represented: The Politics of Documentary*. London and New York: Verso, 1994: 56–74. © 1994 by Verso. Reprinted with permission of the publisher.

stiffs gleefully surveying the lives of the tragically rich whose means left them incapable of adapting to straitened times.

If we take Irving Berlin seriously, then we can begin to understand class as *both* a social practice and a representation, precisely in the ways that Joan Scott and Teresa de Lauretis argue gender operates in culture.[1] In his famous sentence describing the peasants and small landowners of post-revolutionary France, Marx asserted, 'They cannot represent themselves; they must be represented.'[2] His doubled sense of representation is a political practice; someone must speak for, stand in for, perform as, the inchoate and unformed group – not yet a class because it cannot represent itself, yet surely a class because it can be represented – to and for itself and others. If representation is crucial to class formation and expression, then class, like gender, is performative, divined in the exchanges among representatives of and for classes. These exchanges were themselves the subject of intense representation and theorizing during the 1930s, a decade when class, racial, and gender divisions were both more pronounced than today and more thoroughly contested.

My project of revisioning 1930s documentary is necessarily about revising myself as well. Each individual, as Antonio Gramsci reminds us, 'is the synthesis not only of existing relations but of the history of these relations. [S]he is a précis of the past.'[3] Those of us drawn to pursue our scholarship in and among the remnants of leftist culture of the 1930s do so in part as a search for ourselves: we look carefully for evidence of a past moment when radical intellectuals felt they warranted a place in history. My discovery of radical women writers and artists of the 1930s coincided with my own recognition of myself as a radical woman writer in my thirties. Only after completing two books on women's literary radicalism did I understand that I was searching for a model that could tell me that it was possible to be all those things – radical, woman, intellectual, activist, mother – I felt I was (or wanted to be). Those women stepped out of the confines of their class and gender to join striking truckers in struggle as Meridel LeSueur's narrator does when she claims 'I Was Marching.' Those who could forthrightly assert *I Change Worlds* with Anna Louise Strong who fought in the trenches of Spain and China during that decade clearly presented a model sorely lacking in my own experience. They were fearless, ecstatically declaring 'I Went to the Soviet Arctic,' as Ruth Gruber did, to 'find women.' They had a sense of solidarity and community as Ella Ford did when she announced in the *New Masses*: 'We Are Mill People'; and they challenged us to take a political position, demanding to know 'Which Side Are You On?' These women, whose biographies belie their declarations of authority – revealing how difficult it was to be the Amazons of their and my imagination – had something to say to another generation of women freed by feminist agitation and other social movements for political change.

In writing about their struggles, I now see I was desperately seeking our own. Perhaps all scholarship is primarily autobiographical, perhaps it is simply that the dilemmas they faced as women and radicals and intellectuals have not been solved, because the terms through which we know the women and their struggles are already embedded in cultural assumptions about gender and politics which have made the 1930s so troubling for Americans. The middle-class women who went slumming in the 1930s present me with a complicating image of myself as I, too, slum in the 1930s seeking pleasures, thrills, and answers of my own. Perhaps my story will enable another one to surface: that of the middle-class women intellectuals of the 1930s whose situation gives a unique view of the quandary middle-class intellectuals in America find themselves in today.

To analyze how class represents, I want to explore the politics and meaning of boundary crossings – of slumming, so to speak. These crossings occur tellingly at moments of *visual* encounters between those whose lives were privileged to observe and regulate and detail the behaviors of others – journalists, novelists, photographers, and social workers – and their subjects, usually, because this is the Depression decade, the poor. As vehicles of regulation, exposé, and reification, photography and fiction become central mechanisms of class representation. This chapter looks at the complicated relations of cross-class looking encoded in the lives, novels, and images of working-class and middle-class women during the 1930s. It seeks out the tensions at the borders of class and racial boundaries when women cross them. Fiction and reportage by radical women – both middle-class and working-class – describe one horn of the dilemma I am tracing. Margaret Bourke-White, one of the highest paid women of the 1930s whose photographs helped propel *Life* magazine's spectacular success, embodies another. When a middle-class woman looks across her class privilege at another woman, what does she see? And because she herself is always also an object under investigation, how is she seen in turn? Can a working-class woman see herself? And because she is already under surveillance, might she refuse to look at others?[4]

The history of middle-class inspection of the poor begins long before 1920s slumming, and its purpose was more likely the regulation of (working people's) desires than the expression of (middle-class) pleasures. Nancy Armstrong has detailed the ways in which the rise of the domestic woman figured in eighteenth-century British novels placed middle-class women in a position to regulate their own lives and the lives of their children. According to Denise Riley and Linda Gordon, the consolidation of feminism and social reform movements in nineteenth-century Britain and America ensured that middle-class women would also regulate and superintend the lives of poorer females who failed to live up to proper standards of housekeeping and femininity.

151

Oversight would keep all deviations firmly in view in order to ameliorate them.[5] Moreover, with the invention of the mercury flash in the 1890s one could not only see into the dark spaces of poverty but, like Jacob Riis, photograph the tenements of New York's Lower East Side. The projects of state and capitalist regulation, reportage and fiction, documentary photography and feminism are thus curiously interwoven; each mode overseeing itself, its objects, and its others. But in the 1930s, a radical critique of capitalism turned the lens through which middle-class women looked over (and after) their poorer sisters.[6]

In 1928, Virginia Woolf powerfully etched the intimate links between feminism and writing. She produced a new understanding of British literary history by acknowledging the history of women's oppression and of their achievements as writers. Her formula – that to be a writer a woman needed 'five hundred pounds a year and a room of one's own' – signaled that literature was the province of the middle class who could afford time and space to meditate and study and write: 'the poor poet has not in these days, nor has had for two hundred years, a dog's chance.'[7] In her perambulations traced in the lecture/essay, the narrator periodically finds herself alone in a room looking from her window at the absurd but everyday bustle below.

This image of the writer separated from the streets, surveyor and overseer of the lives of her subjects, links the project of literary production to those of bourgeois domestic maintenance. There, too, as Nancy Armstrong has demonstrated, the middle-class woman learned to display her skills by self-inspection and projection onto the objects surrounding her. She assumed authority as the supervisor of her domestic surroundings, her qualities of perception indicating her intrinsic value. Like the early bourgeois 'domestic woman' Armstrong analyzes, Woolf's writer is set apart in her own room because of class difference. Rebecca Harding Davis had portrayed this in her 1861 novella 'Life in the Iron Mills' which begins as another unnamed middle-class female narrator stands at her window watching the mill workers trudge along the path before her as they return from work. Like Davis, Woolf notes that it is unlikely that we will find many working-class artists – male or female. Nevertheless, in the pages of contemporaneous socialist journals, writers were calling for a new 'proletarian' poetics to replace that of a defeated high modernism. Woolf herself wrote an introductory essay for a book of working-class women's tales collected by the Cooperative Working Women's Guild a few years later, entitled *Life as We Have Known It*.

The idea that literary production resulted from the observations of life, rather than from what one has known of it, simply reinforced the sense that writing and looking were the privileges of the middle class. Michael Gold's novel *Jews Without Money*, an enactment of his calls for proletarian art – a writing which would dramatize the lives of those in the tenements – brought the narrator downstairs. Smashing the pane of glass separating writer from the street-life below, he insisted that stories and their telling were also activities of the poor and working class.

Usually, the poor represent an absence in literary discourse – the *non-dit*, in Pierre Macherey's term – of the worlds and works of both high realism and high modernism. But, with Gold's call for proletarian literature, a new arena opened up for middle-class writers as well. Still, their desire to know and transmit (if not transform) the lives of poor and working-class subjects maintained the conventional boundaries separating art from life, seeing from knowing. The form of reportage was, in some measure, an attempt to refigure these relations; yet, when these boundaries were violated, they confounded generic (and gender) conventions. For example, when journalist Martha Gellhorn traveled America to record *The Trouble I've Seen* and found 'Ruby,' the eponymous girl of the first part of her book, she was at a loss to account for Ruby's behavior. No convenient story emerged to trace either Ruby's defiant pride (as well as her outlandish clothes) prostitution offered her, nor her shame at her mother's ineffectual morality which consigned them to poverty. But Gellhorn was also ambivalent about the social worker who saved Ruby from her unfit mother and lodged her safely with a middle-class family. It is not clear just what is the 'trouble' here – poverty, childhood prostitution, inappropriate mothering, or straitlaced social workers – nor what the 'I' who has seen it has learned or intends to do about it. As a reporter, Gellhorn is troubled by what she has seen, but she maintains her 'traditional' distance.[8] Is she slumming, even if her travels across class boundaries never yield a thrill?

Writings by and about radical women intellectuals, whose metaphoric annihilation as actors in the historical movement of the proletariat was doubled through their class *and* gender differences, stressed that they were always 'foreigners' among the American people and within the American Left.[9] 'Ruby' presented a typical feature of much radical women's writing of the 1930s: the inevitable scene in which the white middle-class social worker – proper representative of the state – enters the home of the working-class mother to supervise her failed attempts at homemaking. The occasion for the state's interest in the home of the poor was usually the arrest of a wayward daughter for prostitution. The blame for her transgressive sexuality – the money from which did not always see its way back into the home, but was used selfishly to buy pretty things for the young girl – was securely lodged on the inept mother. As the social worker surveys the filthy apartment cluttered with laundry and rancid food, howling babies underfoot, she registers the distance between her classed understandings of proper femininity and maternity and offers a view into the slovenly housekeeping of the poor. However, despite being ground down, the mothers fight back, if only to comment on the impossibility of living up to the standards of bourgeois housekeeping on a few dollars a week from relief.[10] Their anguish – the pain registered on the face of Dorothea Lange's Migrant Mother or the blank stare of a share-cropper's wife caught by Margaret Bourke-White – was a shameful admission that middle-class culture had failed to make over the face of America in its own image.

Even when the heroine of a feminist proletarian novel like Fielding Burke's *Call Home the Heart* was an 'organic intellectual' like Ishma, the mountain-woman-turned-mill-worker and union activist rather than a well-to-do news-paper woman, the motives of the female intellectual were suspicious. In the penultimate scene of the novel, Ishma single-handedly saves a black union organizer, Butch Wells, from a lynching at the hands of her former husband and his friends. Shaming them with the threat that she will kill herself and leave them with the reputation of having attempted to rape her, Ishma uses her whiteness and femininity to save a fellow worker. Burke restages the highly charged gender, racial, class, and sexual dynamics of lynching and rape through a subversion of stereotypes. Inverting the historical myth that the rape of a white woman by a black man causes his lynching at the hands of white men, Ishma, the working-class white woman, prevents Butch being lynched by charging the white men with rape. Later, at Butch's home, she is confronted with her own racism, marring the heroism of her act when his wife, Gaffie, seizes Ishma in an embrace and kisses her:

> Her lips were heavy, and her teeth so large that one needed the sure avouch of eyes to believe in them. It was impossible to associate her with woe, though tears were racing down her cheeks. As her fat body moved she shook off an odor that an unwashed collie would have disowned. 'Bressed angel, bressed angel ob do Lawd,' she kept repeating, and with a great sweep enveloped Ishma, her fat arms encircling the white neck, her thick lips mumbling at the quivering white throat.... The fleshy embrace, the murky little room, the smoking ashes, the warm stench, the too eager faces shining greasily at the top of big, black bodies, filled Ishma with uncontrollable revulsion.[11]

This heady hint of interracial lesbianism so disturbs Ishma that she reinstates racial stereotypes of black womanhood – as an animal, a mammy, a sexual predator. Disgraced in the eyes of the community, especially Derry Unthank, a white doctor and party member who has overseen Ishma's political education, she flees back to the mountains and her first husband. As protagonist of the novel, Ishma holds center-stage in the drama unfolding around her during the mill workers' strike. Her sexuality, limited by lack of contraception to a series of heterosexual 'marriages' (she never actually marries anyone), sparks her political commitments. Her pursuit of sexual freedom *and* economic equality set her apart from the proper, white, middle-class women of the mill town and from the less assertive women of her class. She is exceptional, but she can never fully become a radical because of her racism. Here, the white female (organic) intellectual again is separated from other women, whose bodily excess – too much money, too many children, too much flesh, whatever – threatens her political identity.

In both cases, the authors, themselves middle-class women, could not overcome through their prose the racial or class differences dividing women. The ideal of fraternity, often figured in the image of the maternal collective engulfing disparate workers within its embrace, escaped their women characters, as if class and racial divisions, marked by tasteless clothing and expressive sexuality, on one hand, a well-cut suit and heroic behavior, on the other, were more extreme among women.[12] Writing produced by working-class authors during the 1930s also dramatized class and racial divisions through the awkward distances produced when one's body is on display; but they challenged the stances of either passive observation or flight from confrontation. 1930s women's radical fiction reversed a classic image from Dickens's novels through *Stella Dallas*: the poor waif (or elderly mother) looking in longingly at the opulent dining rooms of the wealthy. It often placed poor and working women inside and subject to the view of those passing by.

For instance, in Ramona Lowe's painful story, 'The Woman in the Window,' a wry revision of Fannie Hurst's 1933 melodramatic novel *Imitation of Life*, Mrs Jackson answers a help wanted advertisement for a cook, only to discover she must dress the part of Aunt Jemima and fry chicken in the window of Mammy's restaurant. Her children, shamed by the taunts of white children who see her, challenge her to quit her demeaning job. But she explains that her job is cooking and it puts food on their table and shoes on their feet and that '*when a body say nigger, You turn roun' 'n' give'm such a thrashin' they woan never forget.*'[13] Her self-possession, in spite of her public humiliation, her demand that her employers address her as Mrs Jackson and raise her pay, her insistence to her children that some work is dignified and some not 'but it all got t' be done,' inverts Woolf's use of the window. Here the window is for display not for observation. It provides a glimpse of the object at work, not a view for the writing subject. Mrs Jackson may be the spectacle, but she is also the theorist of her position; an object who speaks back by simply asserting the need that drives her to claim her objectification. 'She leaned against the table and looked out, and the world looked in curiously at the embodiment of a fiction it had created' (p. 82). This woman in the window challenges Woolf's observer to cross through the glass, like Alice, and enter another world, to think another set of relations than observer/observed, subject/object, inside/ outside.

But that project is terribly difficult, and the awkward and often tragic attempts to cross class divides highlight social exclusions among women. These divisions – marking those who belong from those outside – are central to social privileges learned and experienced in childhood. Two books from the mid-1980s, *Landscape for a Good Woman* and *The House on Mango Street*, begin their explorations of 1950s girlhoods lived without resources with an image remarkably resonant with those I have been tracking in 1930s texts. Carolyn Steedman remembers seeing her mother cry only once:

> We both watched the dumpy retreating figure of the health visitor through the curtainless windows. The woman had said: 'This house isn't fit for a baby.' And then she stopped crying, my mother, got by, the phrase that picks up after all difficulty (it says: it's like this; it shouldn't be like this; it's unfair; I'll manage): 'Hard lines, eh Kay?'. . . And I? I will do everything and anything until the end of my days to stop anyone ever talking to me like that woman talked to my mother. It is in this place, this bare, curtainless bedroom that lies my secret and shameful defiance. I read a woman's book, meet such a woman at a party (a woman now, like me) and think quite deliberately as we talk: we are divided: a hundred years ago I'd have been cleaning your shoes. I know this and you don't.[14]

Steedman's tale of women's differences in post-war London turns on the view offered into her deprivation by an official, a representative of the state, whose comments confirm Steedman's (and her mother's and sister's) illegitimacy. The three of them can only watch impassively from their bare, exposed window, shamed, yet knowing.

In a similar vein, Sandra Cisneros begins her novel with the story of a nun passing Esperanza, her young narrator, playing on the street:

> Where do you live? she asked.
> There, I said pointing up to the third floor.
> You live *there*?
> *There.* I had to look to where she pointed – the third floor, the paint peeling, wooden bars Papa had nailed on the windows so we wouldn't fall out. You live *there*? The way she said it made me feel like nothing. *There.* I lived *there.* I nodded.
> I knew then I had to have a house. A real house. One I could point to.[15]

Again, an official woman, representative of the church this time, instills shame in a young girl by marking the distance between herself and the windows from which Esperanza's family looks out. Neither the health visitor nor the nun inhabits the seats of power; they are representatives sent to supervise the lives of those outside the view of power, yet subject to it. They remain guardians of the street and the home, of decency, patrolling the lives of these young girls, reminding them of the things they lack, of their terrible needs which can barely be spoken, much less met. Both stories condemn the female representative's insensitivity; blind to the hurt produced by their distance from the lives of those they visit and instruct, they offer no hope of ever learning about them – or themselves.

However, in her epic 1934 short story 'I Was Marching,' Meridel LeSueur traced the clumsy awakening of a middle-class woman to the experiences of working-class solidarity. Written in part to assuage the condemnation she had suffered at the hands of *New Masses* editor Whittaker Chambers for her earlier piece of reportage, 'Women on the Breadlines,' the first-person narrator is wary: a woman, a middle-class woman, a middle-class woman writer, who watches herself as much as she watches others and for whom language, the representation of an event, is more profound than its experience. 'For two days,' she writes,

> I heard of the strike. I went by their headquarters, I walked by on the opposite side of the street and saw the dark old building that had been a garage and lean, dark young faces leaning from the upstairs windows. I had to go down there often. I looked in ... I stayed close to the door, watching. I was afraid they would put me out. After all, I could remain a spectator. A man wearing a polo hat kept going around with a large camera taking pictures.[16]

This introduction establishes the narrator as an outsider, the middle-class onlooker who, as Georg Lukács theorized in *History and Class Consciousness*, perceives social relations as a 'passive observer,' much as one might view a theatrical performance. But LeSueur's narrator is drawn into the union hall, the masses of bodies working together and suffering in unison claim her and after days on the picket line and pouring coffee she finds herself an insider. 'I was marching,' she declares finally,

> with a million hands, movements, faces, and my own movement was repeating again and again, making a new movement from these many gestures, the walking, falling back, the open mouth crying, the nostrils stretched apart, the raised hand, the blow falling, and the outstretched hand drawing me in. I felt my legs straighten, I felt my feet join in that strange shuffle of thousands of bodies moving with direction, of thousands of feet, and my own breath with the gigantic breath. As if an electric charge had passed through me, my hair stood on end, I was marching. (p. 171)

Where the narrator began her tale by emphasizing sight, her looking in and looking on, the concluding ecstatic push of humanity incorporates feet, hands, nostrils, mouths, hair, but refuses to name the eyes.

LeSueur clearly wants to ease the separation which vision, the observation of the working-class other, produces by erasing the presence of the eye. Her final cry, 'I was marching,' despite its individualism, subsumes her body into the masses, the 'we' which has begun its funeral march. In a gesture repeated endlessly in proletarian fiction, the collective engulfs its characters and reforms them into an earth-shuddering force. Still, the narrator reasserts her presence here, I believe, because it is so important to LeSueur that she indicate that the relationship between middle-class woman and worker could be other than one of merely onlooker. She needs to return to her embodied presence to alert us to the fact that she does not merely see, she also moves. She is not slumming; she has crossed the threshold.

As in Lowe's story, the workers are inside, their heads glimpsed from the street below on which collect 'artists, writers, professionals, even businessmen and women' who watch with 'longing' and 'fear' the dark and solemn faces within. Those on the street (and notice how women are joined with the representative types of the middle class) remain unnoticed and uncomprehending. Despite gathering before the union hall, they appear as fully cut off from history as Woolf's narrator or Steedman's woman author. They need to enter the space behind the workers' doors and windows to enter history. And they need to do so with their marching feet, not their watching eyes. It was by passing through the door that LeSueur's narrator could overcome her distance from the working class – a distance, she noted in 'The Fetish of Being Outside,' that was fundamental to bourgeois, particularly romantic, notions about artists and writers – and to transform fiction from a tool of (self-) exploration into a space where boundaries between self and other blurred. And so 'change worlds,' as Anna Louise Strong emphatically proclaimed.

II

If looking at the bodies of working-class women marks a separation between professionals and the poor, then surely photographers, particularly female photographers, presented the most troubling figure of reform during the 1930s. The Depression spawned the careers of some of America's most prominent women photographers: Dorothea Lange and Marion Post Wolcott who both worked for the FSA; Berenice Abbott who worked for the WPA; and Margaret Bourke-White who was the only *Life* photographer with photo credits. These women negotiated precarious positions for themselves as artists, documentarians, and commercial photographers by using the signs of middle-class femininity – their supervising eyes – to track the impact of the Depression and the New Deal on the lives and landscapes of America's poor.

Paradoxically, the Depression provided middle-class women with opportunities to move out of the previously restricted roles open to them. They could travel the world as journalists, photographers, organizers, and teachers.

In their desire to make this opportunity meaningful, to 'change worlds,' they found their poorer sisters a moving target for their work. Certainly, these women made their mark on the backs of the poor women who filled their accounts and peopled their photographs, but without the middle-class incursion into the private lives of the poor their stories and faces would barely be heard and seen at all. Moreover, the mobility open to middle-class women meant that poor and working women could get a close look at their more comfortable sisters. As Muriel Rukeyser noted in a poem, what they saw – 'more of a corpse than a woman' – was not always desirable. This doubled and contradictory interaction is mirrored in the curious status of the 1930s as a period in American literary and cultural history.

Nancy Armstrong argues that the modern bourgeois individual is most fully embodied in the woman, because she is the repository of feelings not information, the center of desire rather than wealth. But what are the consequences of recognizing the female worker whose body traverses the spaces of the domestic and the economic? If we agree that the engendering of knowledge is an attribute of bourgeois society, we might fruitfully describe one project of the radicals writing novels or taking pictures during the 1930s as discovering a working-class form of knowledge. But proletarian theorists described class divisions through gender differences: the effeminate bourgeoisie was bound to be replaced by the virile working class. Knowledge was still deeply gendered, and this formula excluded women as agents of history. A working-class woman could have no place, no knowledge, because in this configuration she is insufficiently gendered and inappropriately classed. Not fully feminine because she works, neither is she a worker, because she does women's work. Her body is a site of the dual labor of productivity and reproduction and so appears outside the divisions constituting knowledge. Understanding this reconfiguration of gender, class and knowledge might provide one means of revisioning the 1930s.

What fiction and photography from the 1930s establish is the contradictory relationship of the state, capitalism, the family, art, and sexuality within the bodies positioned in and among those institutions. 1930s literary and photographic works by committed intellectuals – male and female – attempted to refashion the domestic narratives of nineteenth-century realism by foregrounding the objects of labor – workers' bodies, spaces, and tools. This reconstruction of the bourgeois relations embodied in the fiction of domesticity deforms conventions separating words, pictures, classes, and genders by making connections between political action and aesthetic representation, interpellating (male, worker's) history in (female, bourgeois) fiction.[17]

For example, the final volume of Josephine Herbst's trilogy *Rope of Gold*, which brings the story of the Trexler family into the 1930s, cleverly refashions one plot of nineteenth-century domestic fiction – the family saga – through the interpolation of documentary intertexts. Herbst uses excerpts from some of her own reportage, blurring the line between fact and fiction. The novel further blurs the gender and class divisions separating intellectual and manual labor, the home and the workplace. The domestic space is brought into the workplace as the Flint auto workers set up house during the sit-down strike; political strategizing in Realengo 18, the Cuban sugar soviet, goes on over dinner and cards. Victoria Chance, the radical journalist, writes herself out of the narrative as she travels by bus north to participate in a strike; Steve Carson, the militant striker, begins to write his narrative on the shop floor.

Documentary reportage and photography embraced these confusions bringing the observing, (usually) bourgeois individual writer or photographer into the participating (usually) proletarian mass to show the horrors of capitalism at home or fascism abroad. However, the presumptions of political efficacy lodged in the documentary project are based in the same ideal of depth modeled by bourgeois forms of knowledge: the psychological reading of the image. The documentary desire to 'expose' the crimes of bourgeois culture constructs an other class known not through the penetration of the subject but through the display of objects. Paradoxically, that objectified class then assumes the function of the psychological subject; its surface masks another layer of meaning to be penetrated. In this sense, the Left's use of the documentary image to reveal classed relations of power is an attempt to let the objects speak – in much the same way that Marx allowed commodities a voice in *Capital* to speak of their lack of value – and so challenges the construction of bourgeois subjectivity. Yet this challenge to the workings of subjective realism with a contesting realism of the object falters at the precise moment that the image is read by its audience. To whom do the objects speak? Those bourgeois subjects slumming among them?

In the appendix to *Let Us Now Praise Famous Men*, James Agee includes a *New York Post* clipping about Margaret Bourke-White. Quoted in its entirety it stands as the only place where middle-class women enter the text. May Cameron's breezy article describes Bourke-White's presence as flamboyant and flashy; her entrance signaled by the 'reddest coat in the world' she sports. After the thousands of words Agee has used to detail the meager wardrobe hanging on the nails of the Gudgers' bedroom walls and his meditation on the impossibility of fulfilling desire when space is so cramped and the body so exhausted by daily chores, this flagrant display of wealth and female sexual allure is intended to stun and more to discredit the most popular and widely known female photographer of the decade. Bourke-White's career as a Luce photographer, for *Fortune* and for *Life*, parallels Agee's own history of employment for the Time/Life empire; but she was among the highest paid women in America while he eked out a meager salary there. It is perhaps his queasiness about this fact that gives his citation an extra bite. The column stands unremarked – it needs no comment – save a footnote indicating its source as 'a liberal newspaper.'[18] But why do we feel Bourke-White to be so brazen in her red coat? Clearly, it has something to do with the image of the coat juxtaposed with the threadbare denim and calico of the tenant farmers she photographed for the book, *You Have Seen Their Faces*, produced with her second husband, Erskine Caldwell.

Bourke-White's signature style, 'the caterpillar view,' which she achieved by 'literally crawl[ing] between the legs of my competitors and pop[ping] my head and camera up for part of a second,' was unseemly.[19] It displayed her arrogance toward her subject as she purposely imaged black preachers and white tenant farmers from unflattering low angles. Moreover, these images are captioned with quotations gleaned from the conversations Caldwell had as Bourke-White shot: 'The legends under the pictures are intended to express the authors' own conceptions of the sentiments of the individuals portrayed, they do not pretend to reproduce the actual sentiments of these persons.'[20] Agee himself had ventured into the minds of Emma and Annie Mae Gudger, inventing soliloquies for them, but the layout of *You Have Seen Their Faces* juxtaposed captions and image. Evans's photos in *Praise* stand as testaments on their own.[21]

Even more than FSA photographers, Bourke-White made her living as a voyeur, as a middle-class tourist among the neediest people, sending dispatches back to the comfortable living rooms of *Life* magazine's readers. Her first assignment for *Life*, which coincided with its inaugural issues for which she provided the cover story, traced the new boom-towns of the West growing up around the multi-million dollar water projects of the Columbia River Basin. Her assignment to send back pictures from the town of New Deal, Montana disarmed her editors, who expected the architectural shots characteristic of Bourke-White's early career. Instead, what they received, 'everything from fancy ladies to babies on the bar,' she wired the New York office, 'surprised' her editors.[22] They expected 'construction pictures as only Bourke-White can take them. What the Editors got was a human document of American frontier life, which to them at least, was a revelation.'[23]

Bourke-White's revelation about New Deal was that not only were there women living amidst the trailers and cement block cabins, but these fancy women might be mothers carting children along with them. This slice of life, the basic theme of all *Life* magazine articles, opened the lives of the poor and working class to public scrutiny. Bourke-White's invasion of the homes of the impoverished meant she was a

foreigner who acted like one. I remember one occasion when we went into a cabin to photograph a Negro woman who lived there. She had thick, glossy hair, and I had decided to take her picture as she combed it. She had a bureau made of a wooden box with a curtain tacked to it and lots of little homemade things. I rearranged everything. After we left, Erskine spoke to me about it. How neat her bureau had been. How she must have valued all her little possessions and how she had them tidily arranged *her* way, which was not my way. This was a new point of view to me. I felt I had done violence.[24]

We wonder at Bourke-White's naiveté and at her arrogance.

Touching and rearranging objects had been something that Agee and Evans agonized over as they perused the shacks of the three tenant families who became the subject of *Praise*. Bourke-White's breezy entrance into a poor black woman's private space clearly marked off class and racial positions: one was the photographer from the North; the other the sharecropper of the South. Letting '*you*,' her middle-class audience, 'see *their* faces,' preserved the distance between her self and audience and the photographic objects contained in the book.[25] Despite recounting this incident retrospectively, Bourke-White seems to have learned nothing. We still know nothing of the woman – not her name, her town, her occupation: she is a negro woman with thick, glossy hair. I, for one, feel ashamed for her and for Bourke-White and ultimately for myself. The 'violence' that Bourke-White performed is rather akin to slumming. Still, something instructive is going on in this encounter about disjunctures between women and the attempts to overcome them. Their failures need recognition; they are crucial to revisioning the 1930s as a lived moment in our histories.

Looking across classes, like all transgressive looking, makes public the spectacle of private desire. Because the poor live outside the realm of bourgeois privacy, their lives are open to the inspection and regulation or amelioration of both the state and its radical opponents. The New Deal projects to document both the effects of the Depression and the benefits of government intervention helped erase the divide between public and private. The photographs to come out of the New Deal (including those of New Deal) melded the two spheres by bringing 'their' faces to 'you.' However, no matter how 'surprised' the editors of *Life* magazine were at Bourke-White's photographs of New Deal, Montana, the folks there end up revealing a familiar story: the story of *Life*.

The abuse poured on Bourke-White by Agee was picked up by critic William Stott, who condemns Bourke-White's photographs as 'maudlin' and 'sensationalistic,' with their faked quotations for captions and their excessive craft.[26] His most telling condemnation comes because *You Have Seen Their Faces* was so successful; it made Bourke-White a great deal of money. This 'double outrage: propaganda for one thing and profit-making out of both propaganda and the plight of the tenant farmers...was morally shocking to Agee and me,' says Walker Evans,

[p]articularly so since it was publicly received as the *nice* thing to do, the *right* thing to do. Whereas we thought it was an evil and immoral thing to do. Not only to cheapen them, but to profit by them, to exploit them – who had already been so exploited. Not only that but to exploit them without even *knowing* that was what you were doing.[27]

Evans calls Agee's attack 'vicious,' but justified, and goes on to repeat it for another generation.

Their 'vicious' critiques of Bourke-White *were* fully justified. But there is more to it. And to my mind that has to do with the gendered terms by which 1930s radical intellectuals described themselves and their work. In an effort to divorce themselves from the doubly feminized realms of popular and bourgeois culture, radical intellectuals were fervently committed to a 'virile' poetics which would give voice to the new worker and ultimately a new world. Hugo Gellert's illustrated edition of *Capital*, published in 1934, presents the picture of a masculine proletariat – man, woman, and child – with muscles bulging and ready to walk triumphantly into the future once the shackles of wage slavery are overthrown. That Bourke-White imaged a defeated peasantry pandered to middle-class sympathy for this vanishing breed – the tenant farmer. Yet it also resisted the vision of the powerful masculine worker who fired the imagination of male intellectuals. In so doing, she clearly asserted her privileged position both as observer of the poor and as disseminator of their images, without even gesturing toward guilt, much less solidarity. She kept wearing her red coat despite the threadbare muslin rags shrouding the slender bodies of those she photographed. Surely this was part of her crime – she flaunted her difference.[28]

In *Sensational Designs*, Jane Tompkins discusses the vilification Harriet Beecher Stowe received for writing (and making money from) *Uncle Tom's Cabin*. Contemporary criticism, fearing the feminization of American culture, railed against the dangerous sentiment oozing from Stowe's book. In condemning the popularity of this work by aligning popularity with femininity, thus marking off the serious work of men as unsentimental, unpopular, and artful, the cultural work of middle-class women is rendered suspect. Their political interventions, if they rely on popular sentiments, and the gender divisions privileging certain kinds of cultural practices over others, ensures that their cultural work will go unrecognized. *You Have Seen Their Faces* is a direct heir to *Uncle Tom's Cabin*, complete with the same equation of blacks, the poor, and women with suffering.[29] So Margaret Bourke-White's 'superior red coat ... and such fun' made for her by Dietrich's designer Howard Greer, presumably paid for from the profits from her book (which she worked on by taking unpaid leave from her *Life* job), makes Agee's and Evans's project all the more morally superior. Evans eschewed sentimentality in the pictures; he claimed to have 'brought photographic style back around to the plain relent-less snapshot,'[30] 'against the gigantism and bathos of Margaret Bourke-White, against the lurid excitements of *Life.*'[31] Agee catalogued simple objects in his prose; he remarked obsessively on their roles as 'spy and counter-spy.' And they never made a dime from their book. Thus *Let Us Now Praise Famous Men* is a 'classic,' and we are left feeling embarrassed by Bourke-White's efforts.

Bourke-White's acknowledged 'violence' was represented in countless incidents recorded in radical women's writings of the 1930s. Their dilemma about giving voice to working-class women was foregrounded when the 'foreigners,' representatives of the state or the public realm – writers, organizers, social workers, photographers – encountered poor women walking picket lines, hustling drinks, fixing stews, or retreating into silence. Recognizing the uneasy differences between women was crucial to women's revisioning of class relations in 1930s America. For some, this led to radical action, to an attempt to cross the threshold separating women, through identification, even glorification; for others, it remained a kind of socially responsive slumming, moving through the lives of the poor not for pleasure or thrills, but out of a sense of largesse, which left both working-class and middle-class women trapped in their conditions, though perhaps offering a glimpse, for each, of the restraints limiting their lives and the possibilities of changing them.

The working-class female body was a vivid text in 1930s America, from Mae West strutting before Cary Grant or W. C. Fields, to Ruby Keeler dancing her heart out on top of a taxi, to Ginger Rogers hawking her goods in Pig Latin, Hollywood presented 'working girls' whose bodies were traded as showgirls or as prostitutes to keep off the dole. Their energy and voluptuousness contrasted with the image of the hollowed out, empty men on the breadlines. These Hollywood dream girls were a far cry from the Migrant Mother's gaunt cheekbones and sad eyes, from the tough, grim faces of the women in New Deal who were barely getting by and hanging on. Yet these contrasting images, coupled with the vital 'revolutionary girl' celebrated in poetry by Maxwell Bodenheim and sketched in cartoon by Hugo Gellert, the women who 'sure [we]re scrappers,'[32] as they fought police and scabs on picket, all indicate the varied space that a working woman could occupy in 1930s American culture. There was a gap between what a working-class woman could look like – and by extension accomplish – and what her middle-class sister could only imitate, imagine, or observe.

Looking at the bodies of working-class females was certainly not a new activity in the 1930s. When Henry Mayhew walked the streets of London in the 1840s and found 'the little watercress girl ... although only eight years of age had already lost all childish ways, was indeed, in thoughts and manner, a woman,' the curiosity she represented for him lay in her failure to express proper femininity.[33] But the 1930s in America opened up a particular kind of visualization of the working-class female body, one which was founded on a transaction between middle-class women's opportunities to write, to photograph, to organize, and to reform, and which faltered on the very inequities which made poorer women their objects of narrative, image, and action. For rarely could either escape their lot.

The 1930s provided an opening for middle-class women to enter the public sphere, often through the inspection of the private lives of women poorer and darker and less powerful than themselves. As ethnographic imperialists, as tourists amidst the other half, their motives were sometimes suspect, their projects often corrupted. Lacking a place within dominant or radical cultures, these women looked to the objects traditionally left to their care – poor women – for inspiration, guidance, knowledge, and use. Yet even in their most arrogant and sentimental appropriations, the silenced and invisible objects of capitalist and patriarchal oppression could be heard, their faces could be seen. Without Fielding Burke's attempt to unpack Southern racism and its corrosive effects on working-class solidarity, without Meridel LeSueur's push through the doorway of the union hall, without even Margaret Bourke-White's invasion of the homes and churches of black and white tenants, working-class and poor women's determination, struggles, and failures might remain unremarked and unremarkable. In this transaction, I am suggesting, we find an earlier incarnation of the 'politics of disparity' and 'entrustment' theorized by contemporary Italian feminists – a politics that acknowledges women's class and generational differences as 'an exchange between these to moments of female humanity, between the woman who wants and the woman who knows.' A politics based on recognition of a 'regime of exchange' that insists that 'women owe women.'[34]

The stories and images we do have are not simply transparent views of social reality. The working-class woman resists theorizing in the usual terms, but that does not mean we must assume that she is any less of a subject. To do so is surely to reproduce the terms which marginalize or romanticize the working class and women. Failed resistance is not the same thing as no resistance.[35] Still, we too need to be aware of our position as we revision the 1930s. Are we a new generation of committed female intellectuals overseeing and regulating the stories and pictures of that other time? What is it we expect to know about them? How is our gaze shaping the 1930s into something other than what they were for the women who lived through them? What do we want from the archives when we go slumming in the 1930s? These are open-ended questions meant to draw attention to our complicity in the representations of class, racial, and gender differences operating in our work, even when our work is committed to exposing and eradicating the inequities caused by those differences. An earlier generation of women was moved to represent those who 'must be represented.' Their attempts often resembled slumming, especially when they sported 'superior red coats' as they worked; still they left us with an array of images which speak to us across time about deprivation and struggle – and the importance of women's urge to step out of bounds.

Notes

1 See Joan Wallach Scott, 'Gender: A Useful Category of Historical Analysis,' in *Gender and the Politics of History* (New York: Columbia University Press 1988), 42: 'gender is a constitutive element of social relationships based on perceived differences between the sexes, and gender is a primary way of signifying relationships of power.' In 'The Technology of Gender,' de Lauretis asserts: 'The construction of gender is both the product and the process of its representation.' Teresa de Lauretis, *Technologies of Gender: Essays on Theory, Film, Fiction* (Bloomington: Indiana University Press 1988), 5. However Judith Butler, *Gender Trouble: Feminism and the Subversion of Identity* (New York: Routledge 1990), challenges these perspectives by suggesting that although they see gender as a signifying practice, they still rely on foundationalist assumptions about subjectivity. 'Gender,' she says, 'proves to be performative – that is, constituting the identity it is purported to be. In this sense, gender is always a doing, though not a doing by a subject who might be said to preexist the deed' (p. 25).

2 Karl Marx, *The Eighteenth Brumaire of Louis Bonaparte* (New York: International Publishers 1963), 124.

3 Antonio Gramsci, 'The Philosophy of Praxis,' in *Selections from the Prison Notebooks*, trans. Quentin Hoare (New York: International Publishers 1971), 324.

4 For a discussion of a contemporary encounter between working-class female poets and a middle-class female critic, see Maria Damon, ' "Tell Them about Us",' *Cultural Critique*, 14 (Winter 1989–90), 231–57, in which Damon introduces poetry by three young women living in south Boston during the 1970s busing crisis. Here is how one of the D Street writers describes their situation: 'We're watching ourselves watching you watching us, we look at ourselves *through* you' (p. 253, emphasis in original).

5 Denise Riley, *'Am I That Name?': The Category of 'Women' in History* (Minneapolis: University of Minnesota Press 1988); and Linda Gordon, 'Family Violence, Feminism and Social Control,' in *Women, The State and Welfare* (Madison: University of Wisconsin Press 1990), 178–98, argue that during the nineteenth century in both Britain and the United States the realm of the social was created by and for middle-class women's supervision. Nancy Armstrong, *Desire and Domestic Fiction: A Political History of the Novel* (New York: Oxford University Press 1987), explains how this supervisory role was encoded and produced through literary forms developed in eighteenth-century Britain.

6 I consider this a companion piece to the previous chapter [of *They Must Be Represented*], in which I theorize the implications of cross-gender and cross-class

looking. In 'Voyeurism and Class Consciousness,' I look in detail at *Let Us Now Praise Famous Men* for clues to the history of specular relations. These I take to be founded on a classed sexuality which empowers bourgeois men to regard poor women as embodiments of sex/knowledge.

7   Virginia Woolf, *A Room of One's Own* (New York: Harcourt, Brace & Co. 1929), 113, 107.

8   This is Gramsci's term for the intellectuals whose function it is to maintain order and hegemony for the ruling class, in contradistinction to 'organic intellectuals' who rise from within the subaltern classes to forge revolutionary movements. See Antonio Gramsci, 'The Intellectuals,' in *Selections from the Prison Notebooks*, 3–23.

9   Margaret Bourke-White described herself as a foreigner, as did journalist and Smith College graduate, Lauren Gilfillan, whose book-length account of her life among striking coal miners, *I Went to Pit College* (New York: Literary Guild 1934), outlined the limits of middle-class women's ability to enter the lives of the working class. See my discussion of this work in *Labor and Desire* (Chapel Hill, NC: University of North Carolina Press 1991).

10 This scene can be found in Caroline Slade's *Triumph of Willie Pond* (New York: Vanguard Press 1940), and in Ruth McKenney's *Industrial Valley* (New York: Harcourt, Brace & Co. 1939), as well as in Martha Gellhorn's *Trouble I've Seen* (New York: William Morrow 1936). Variations can be found in Marita Bonner's story, 'The Whipping,' of how a young black mother is jailed for murdering her son after relief fails to help her feed him; and Meridel LeSueur's story, 'Sequel to Love,' which reveals how the state invades the reproductive bodies of young women, in Charlotte Nekola and Paula Rabinowitz (eds.), *Writing Red: An Anthology of American Women Writers, 1930–1940* (New York: The Feminist Press 1987). Slade was a prominent social worker whose novels often criticized the welfare institutions for which she worked. *Willie Pond* damns the logic of ADC (Aid to Dependent Children, the precursor to AFDC), the result of which is that an unemployed father is more valuable to a family dead than alive. McKenney's account of Akron, Ohio during the Depression contrasts ineffectual social services with militant Unemployed Councils and industrial unions.

11 Fielding Burke [Olive Tilford Dargan], *Call Home the Heart* (1932; rpt. New York: The Feminist Press 1983), 383.

12 For a moving tale of the politics of refusal and envy animating one working-class woman (and as such defying the cultural criticism surrounding working-class identity), see Carolyn Steedman, *Landscape for a Good Woman: A Story of Two Lives* (New Brunswick, NJ: Rutgers University Press 1986).

13 Ramona Lowe, 'The Woman in the Window,' in Nekola and Rabinowitz (eds.), *Writing Red*, 83 (emphasis in original).

14 Steedman, *Landscape for a Good Woman*, 1–2.

15 Sandra Cisneros, *The House on Mango Street* (Houston: Arte Publico Press 1984), 8–9 (emphasis in original).

16 Meridel LeSueur, 'I Was Marching,' in *Salute to Spring* (New York: International Publishers 1940), 159–60. For more on the skewering LeSueur received from then CPUSA-heavy Whittaker Chambers, see my *Labor and Desire*.

17 In effect, this is Susan Suleiman's point in her marvelous study of French *romans-à-thèse*, *Authoritarian Fictions: The Ideological Novel as Genre* (New York: Columbia University Press 1983).

18 James Agee and Walker Evans, *Let Us Now Praise Famous Men* (1941; rpt. Boston: Houghton Mifflin 1980), 454.

19 Margaret Bourke-White, *Portrait of Myself* (New York: Simon & Schuster 1963), 147.

20 Margaret Bourke-White and Erskine Caldwell, *You Have Seen Their Faces* (1937; rpt. New York: Arno Press 1975), frontispiece.

21 Agee and Evans were extremely critical of Bourke-White's photographic style – their book was a self-conscious refusal of the choices Bourke-White and Caldwell made – nevertheless they also ranged through the minds and possessions of their subjects, albeit in secret. Even a purist like Dorothea Lange, whose phototextual book with text by her husband, Paul Schuster Taylor, is another correction to the overdramatized words and images in *You Have Seen Their Faces*, also shot from odd angles and quoted her informants out of context, altering the meaning of their words. At least Bourke-White and Caldwell were open about their arrogance.

22 Bourke-White, *Portrait*, 142.

23 Editor's Note, *Life*, 1:1 (Nov. 1936), 3.

24 Bourke-White, *Portrait*, 126–7.

25 Notice how this title foregrounds the difference between 'you' and 'their faces' and does so by emphasizing voyeurism – seeing. Contrast this with the D Street writer's exhortation to Damon to 'tell' 'Them' about 'Us.' The girls demand action from Damon as they claim their subjectivity – 'us' writers – over and against 'them,' academic critics.

26 William Stott, *Documentary Expression and Thirties America* (1973; rpt. Chicago: University of Chicago Press 1986), 222–3.

27 Walker Evans, quoted ibid. 222–3.

28 I should note that I wrote this chapter during the 'Nannygate' disclosures involving the nominations for Attorney General, first of Zoë Baird, who had hired illegal immigrants and failed to pay their social security taxes, and then of Kimba Wood, who had neglected to pay taxes for her legal housekeeper; the parallels were inescapable: when a woman makes a lot of money, it's scandalous. Glaring class differences among women ignite tremendous public fury, even as Baird struggled to play down her class privilege. She spoke at her confirmation hearings about her plight in terms of gender (she was acting as a mother) and ethnicity (she was concerned as a Jew about how babysitters would respond to her household), but failed to register the plight of her exploited employees.

29 Stott quotes a review of *You Have Seen Their Faces* by Norman Cousins which dares to assert that Bourke-White's photographs will do as much to ameliorate the plight of tenant farmers as Stowe's novel did to arouse anti-slavery sentiments (p. 220).

30 Walker Evans, *Walker Evans at Work* (New York: Harper & Row 1982), 136.

31 Stott, *Documentary Expression*, 267–8.

32   Vivian Dahl, '"Them Women Sure Are Scrappers",' in Nekola and Rabinowitz, *Writing Red*, 252.

33   Henry Mayhew, *London Labor and London Poor*, vol. 1 (London: George Woodfall 1851), 151.

34   Milan Women's Bookstore Collective, *Sexual Difference: A Theory of Social-Symbolic Practice*, trans. Teresa de Lauretis and Patricia Cicogna (Bloomington: Indiana University Press 1990), 123. The Collective details a history of the genealogy of women's freedom in the entrustment of one woman to another. Their theory is radically anti-Enlightenment, rejecting a rights-based analysis of liberation. However, its focus on disparity and the retrieval of the symbolic mother leaves it open to the critiques which Teresa de Lauretis launches in her introductory essay to the collection.

35   I am indebted to Asha Varadharajan's useful distinction between failed resistance and no resistance, which she offered in conversation with me.

Part II, 1900–1940:
Suggested Readings

Imaging American-ness is a ceaseless activity that works within a shifting set of conceptual differences, but it is never without contention and never complete. In the decades between 1900 and the start of World War II, multiple technologies moved in tandem with both new documentary practices and new social groups whose physical appearance, skin color, bodily display, and cultural style challenged the "normative" in profound ways. The following studies provide readers with recent investigations into a variety of visual skirmishes that brought photography, documentary filmmaking, the cinema, and cultural style into new realms of political struggle as slippery weapons of power and resistance.

Elspeth Brown, *The Corporate Eye: Photography and the Rationalization of America* (forthcoming 2005).

Gerald R. Butters Jr., *Black Manhood on the Silent Screen* (2002).

Melissa A. McEuen, *Seeing America: Women Photographers Between the Wars* (2000).

Laura Wexler, *Tender Violence: Domestic Visions in an Age of U.S. Imperialism* (2000).

Daniel Bernardi (ed.), *The Birth of Whiteness: Race and the Emergence of the U.S. Cinema* (1996).

Patricia Morton, *Disfigured Images: The Historical Assault on Afro-American Women* (1991).

James Curtis, *Mind's Eye, Mind's Truth: FSA Photography Reconsidered* (1989).

Carl Fleischhauer and Beverly W. Brannan (eds.), *Documenting America, 1935–1943* (1988).

Martha Banta, *Imaging American Women: Idea and Ideals in Cultural History* (1987).

Kathy Peiss, *Cheap Amusements: Working Women and Leisure in Turn-of-the-Century New York* (1986).

David Nye, *Image Worlds: Corporate Identities at General Electric, 1890–1930* (1985).

PART THREE
1940 – 2000

Home and Nation: Imagining the ''All-American'' Family

The Eye of Difference: The Politics of Appearance

Troubling Sights (Sites): Visual Maps and America's "Others"

Home and Nation: Imagining the "All-American" Family

7

"The Kind of People who Make Good Americans": Nationalism and *Life*'s Family Ideal

WENDY KOZOL

In fact, within the very narrow range of family products, more than gardening or cake-making...photography affirms the continuity and integration of the domestic group, and reaffirms it by giving it expression.
Pierre Bourdieu, *Photography: A Middle-Brow Art*, 1990

Nation-ness is assimilated to skin-colour, gender, parentage and birth-era – all those things one can not help. And in those "natural ties" one senses what one might call "the beauty of the gemeinschaft." To put it another way, precisely because such ties are not chosen, they have about them a halo of disinterestedness.
Benedict Anderson, *Imagined Communities*, 1991

ife's January 5, 1953, cover photograph (Figure 7.1) depicts a woman kneeling with her arms around two blond girls who are leaning on a window sill. Behind them, a man in a business suit holds a toddler seated on the crosspiece of the window frame. Looking out of a large window, this neatly groomed white family smiles at the camera. The frame connotes a

Wendy Kozol, "'The Kind of People Who Make Good Americans': Nationalism and *Life*'s Family Ideal," in Kozol, Life's *America: Family and Nation in Postwar Photojournalism*. Philadelphia: Temple University Press, 1994: 51–95. © 1994 by Temple University Press. Reprinted with permission of the publisher.

Figure 7.1

domestic setting, yet the building is clearly unfinished without any glass in the frame. By itself, this picture does not provide information about the specific type of house, but read alongside *Life*'s numerous photographs of suburbia in stories about news events, architectural designs, and the Modern Living section of the magazine, the frame easily suggests a middle-class domicile. Underneath the window frame, the caption states: "Family Buys 'Best $15,000 House.'" The cost of the house confirms a reading of the family as middle-class, and the unfinished building suggests progress, a future that appears bright for this family. On a yellow banner cutting diagonally across the page, the headline connects this vision of familial intimacy to the newsworthy concerns of postwar America as it announces the topic of this special issue: "The American and His Economy."

Domesticity lies at the heart of photographer Nina Leen's portrait of middle-class suburban living, and in that sense it serves as a representative artifact of its time. In the postwar years, middle-class Americans increasingly turned toward the privatized world of home and children. Direct federal spending on highway construction and innovative home loan and taxation policies supported business efforts to create unprecedented opportunities for these Americans to inhabit single-family, detached suburban houses. At the same time, an ascendant ideology of domesticity based on strictly divided gender roles pervaded American life, involving such areas as hiring decisions in industry and child-rearing practices. These policies and ideals reshaped the contours of domestic life, encouraging a privatism isolated from broader community activities. Appropriately enough, the cover photograph for "The American and His Economy" underscores that turn to privatization with a visual representation containing no references to the outside world. Moreover, the composition repeats the gender divisions basic to postwar domestic ideology through the man standing above his kneeling wife and children. *Life* makes these connections between middle-class status and patriarchy explicit in the title that labels the economy "his"; her role apparently is only one of support. News images like the one of this family privileged heterosexist ideals of domesticity through photographic realism, visually inscribing culturally assigned gender roles. The woman's supportive embrace encodes her maternal responsibilities; the man's looming protectiveness identifies him as the patriarchal breadwinner. In turning the camera's gaze to the family to represent the American economy, *Life* visualizes postwar prosperity as a white, middle-class familial experience.

This celebratory cover photograph, so reminiscent of advertisements, creates a visual mystery through the unfinished building that encourages the reader to turn to the interior essay to solve. The photograph introduces a story titled "$15,000 'Trade Secrets' House," about a collaborative project in which the building industry pooled its resources to produce a design for a "good looking, skillfully engineered $15,000 house." The article shows color plates of model homes, design plans, and the various stages of building this suburban three-bedroom house. Although they represented an ideal, labeled as such by the generic "The American," the people who posed for this picture were not actors. *Life* presents Dale and Gladys Welling, the "real" family who recently bought one of these dream houses, as evidence of actual families living the American Dream. In this way, the magazine legitimizes its association of the American economy with a particular social group by individualizing the representation.

Despite the economic prosperity celebrated in this portrait, the 1940s and 1950s were a time of instability and unease. A severe housing shortage, labor unrest, McCarthyism, and the Korean War confronted postwar Americans. In addition, major technological developments in transportation and communications systems altered Americans' perceptions of themselves and their worlds. People were on the move, migrating from east to west, south to north, rural to urban, and urban to suburban. Locating "The American" in a suburban home visually narrates a pattern of migration out of urban centers experienced by many white Americans after the war. During the 1950s, 64 percent of the nation's population growth occurred in the suburbs. As Steven Mintz and Susan Kellogg write, "Suburbanization reinforced the family orientation of postwar society."[1]

Migration, of course, took on different meanings for people of color moving from rural poverty into urban slums than for the seven million white Americans moving from inner cities to the outlying suburbs. Between 1950 and 1970, five million African Americans, largely from the South, moved into central cities.[2] In addition, millions of immigrants facing poverty and unemployment at home came to the United States during this period, often through recruitment programs designed to supply cheap labor for agriculture and other industries. For instance, more than four million Mexican workers immigrated through the *Braceros* program. New arrivals to urban areas frequently confronted racial discrimination, low wages, a lack of health care, and other social dislocations.[3] The extremely varied consequences of mobility during the postwar years created upheavals in people's economic, political, and social lives, further contributing to the anxieties and tensions of the period. The special issue addresses white mobility but ignores this other story of migration. By visually excluding people of color who were physically barred from moving into the suburbs, the issue reproduces a discourse of racism. Moreover, when *Life* depicted the city, it was portrayed either as a place of danger and crime, or as a boomtown that exemplified economic prosperity. Rarely did the magazine show families living in cities, except if they were impoverished or in crisis. In the special issue, the only pictures of cities depict urban skylines without people.

In pictures like "The American and His Economy," *Life*'s figuration of the family, including the absences, reinforced racial, class, and gender differences that in turn had profound consequences for the magazine's representation of the nation. David Halberstam argues that *Time* was the most political magazine of the Luce publishing empire. "*Life* was different, less political, more open; it was more dependent upon pictures and thus more tied to events themselves rather than to interpretation of events.... *Life*, by its dependence upon photography, made itself closer to the human heartbeat."[4] Halberstam narrowly conceptualizes political representation in terms that retain a faith in photographs' ability to represent events transparently, events that he conceives as sharing a single heartbeat. But photographs are mediated signs that contain politically significant messages. This is especially true because politics involves more than battles to control the government; it is also the exercise of power in symbolic and practical activities of everyday life. As John Hartley and Martin Montgomery note, "The news is active in the *politics* of sense-making, even when the stories concern matters not usually understood as political."[5] In structuring ways of understanding the world, *Life*'s family portraits played an important political role in establishing, promoting, and reproducing hegemonic social relations.

In the postwar years, *Life* solidified a photo-journalistic formula that relied on images of the middle-class family to represent a national culture. Nationalism, a powerful but contradictory cultural force that shapes social identities, can construct a popular or democratic arena of shared interests and objectives. The concept of nation, however, typically relies on historically determined geographical, cultural, and conceptual distinctions. These distinctions too often are based on exclusionary assumptions of ethnic or racial superiority.[6] In the service of the nation-state, nationalism can offer "a privileged narrative perspective on the nation ('the people') and thus justifies its own capacity to narrate its story."[7] This does not mean that nationalism is a form of false consciousness. Instead, as Benedict Anderson argues, "Communities are to be distinguished, not by their falsity/genuineness, but by the style in which they are imagined." Anderson further argues that the nation is imagined because "members of even the smallest nation will never know most of their fellow-members, meet them, or even hear them, yet in the minds of each lives the image of their communion." National ideals may be arbitrary, but their power lies in their appeal to human needs for identity, order, and immortality. In this regard, people imagine the nation as a *community* "because, regardless of the actual inequality and exploitation that may prevail in each, the nation is always conceived as a deep, horizontal comradeship."[8] Moreover, Anderson observes that the nation appears, like the family, as "the domain of disinterested love and solidarity."[9]

I find Anderson's formulation that communities are defined by "the style in which they are imagined" useful for interpreting the power of media like *Life* to envision nationhood. His term "style" refers to representation and, more particularly, to the politics of representations that construct national identity. Examining the origins of nationalism, Anderson argues that the advent of print capitalism, especially the novel and the newspaper, "provided the technical means for 're-presenting' the *kind* of imagined community that is the nation."[10] Through reading, people could "imagine" shared experiences with thousands of other readers they would never meet. Print literacy may have supported the emergence of the concept of nation, but visual mass media have even greater capacities to visualize social norms and differences that form national identities. The mass media have the power to break down geographical and cultural barriers to connect viewers to other individuals who appear to share their concerns. In so doing, as Eric Hobsbawm points out, the mass media have the ability to make "national symbols part of the life of every individual, and thus to break down the divisions between the private and local spheres in which most citizens normally lived, and the public and national one."[11]

Life, for instance, claims a transcendent nationhood by presenting Dale Welling as "The American" who loves his family. Yet, there is nothing disinterested or neutral in this portrait. Closer inspection reveals how racial, class, gender, and sexual differences encoded in photo-essays forge the boundaries of national identity. The concept of imagined communities provides a way of understanding how photojournalism encodes the multiple consciousnesses that coexist and contradict each other, for even as they depend on and reinforce traditions and conventions, photo-essays reveal the tensions and struggles to define the nation. As Stuart Hall points out, the nation is always at stake when culture is invoked because nationalism is one of the identities advanced or displaced in any cultural utterance.[12] In the hegemonic struggle to define and assert a national identity in the postwar years, *Life* vigorously promoted a vision of the American nation through pictures of nuclear families surrounded by consumer products in suburban homes. The association between family and nation formed the justification not only for the Cold War but for social relations in both intimate personal and national public arenas. *Life*'s nonfictional news status, especially its photographs, enhanced the cultural legitimacy of this narrative. In the midst of many social changes in American society, *Life*'s special gift was to make change seem traditional by locating the tensions of an unfamiliar world within the seemingly familiar and nonthreatening orbit of the "happy" nuclear family.

War and Domesticity

Prior to World War II, *Life* relied primarily on representative families in crisis or in need to articulate problems in society, elicit sympathy for state policies, or warn of dangers to the state. In response to the historical imperatives of World War II, *Life*'s news coverage expanded its iconographic reliance on representative families. Similar to the shift in media coverage that occurred during World War I, *Life*'s wartime reporting began to associate the middle-class family with ideals of patriotism and moral obligation.[13] The magazine continued throughout the postwar period to depict social problems through representative families, but beginning in the 1940s, the editors increasingly relied on images of the white, middle-class family to signify national ideals.

Although *Life* began publishing during the economic upheavals of the 1930s, the magazine acquired its impressive national audience during World War II, in large part because of the high-quality and extensive visual record offered to its readers. Many of the great war photographers, including Robert Capa, Carl Mydans, and W. Eugene Smith, published their photographs in the news section. The magazine ran an average of two to three in-depth war stories a week, making itself indispensable with the amount of information, pictures, and diagrams provided to its readers. Although occasionally critical of war production shortages, *Life* supported the Roosevelt administration's war efforts and willingly cooperated with government censorship and propaganda restrictions. Henry Luce wrote President Roosevelt ten days after Pearl Harbor offering *Life*'s services "in the days to come – far beyond strict compliance with whatever rules may be laid down for us by the necessities of war – we can think of no greater happiness than to be of service to any branch of our government and to its armed forces. For the dearest wish of all of us is to tell the story of absolute victory under your leadership."[14] The magazine played an important role in wartime appeals for family sacrifice, patriotism, and support for a variety of federal programs such as rationing, bond sales, and scrap drives.

News stories about military personnel also contributed to the war effort by showing courageous, yet ordinary, men fighting to preserve American values. A November 1942 war report contains a page of photographs of the Allied forces fighting in Africa.[15] On the opposite page, under pictures of men wounded at Guadalcanal, captions identify the soldiers by their home towns, and by the number of Japanese they had killed. The accompanying text states that "in any man's army, they were heroes. . . . Ordinary Americans all, they found all they needed of courage and killing instinct when they needed it most." In turning back to the blurry photographs of the African battles, one could read into them the same masculine courage and military prowess *Life* encourages the reader to perceive in the close-up shots of the wounded. The Office of War Information (OWI) prohibited the publication of any pictures of American dead until 1943, which reinforced the magazine's visual representation of American military power and masculine strength.[16]

Wartime reporting associated men not only with masculinity but also with domesticity. In this November 1942 story, *Life* printed a letter that the unit commander in action at Guadalcanal wrote to his son before he was killed. The writer combines an explanation of patriotic duty and honor with a longing for his family, expressing his desire through references to such masculine activities as hunting and fishing with his son. Similarly, *Life* often visualized men's military participation through pictures of farewells and reunions between soldiers and their families. The Picture of the Week for November 25, 1940, shows a soldier hugging a small boy in a sailor suit. The father kneels to hug the crying child but holds on to his rifle which stands straight up at his side, framing the left side of the picture. The rifle, a signifier of the military reasons for his departure, acts as visual reassurance that the father is not abandoning his son but leaving to protect him. The child's uniform also envisions male military obligation as an intergenerational commitment to service and patriotic sacrifice. Thus, the picture visualizes the disruption of family life for national duty as understood and accepted by all members of the family. At the same time, the rifle, a crucial element upholding this narrative, also ruptures it by signifying violence. This rupture indicates the shifting terrain of national ideals; even patriotic imagery of the soldier going off to war to defend his family cannot easily secure national ideals.

Anderson states that for most people the nation appears "interestless," which justifies calls for sacrifices, especially in times of war.[17] Discursive strategies, however, based their war appeals as much on domestic concerns as on abstract ideals of democracy or freedom. In a study of World War II pinups, Robert Westbrook argues that government propaganda urged Americans to participate in the war effort for private moral reasons.[18] Because liberalism conceives of the function of the state as protecting citizens from interference from other individuals or states, war signals a failure of the state. Lacking compelling political imperatives for war, the state must turn to private interests in urging men to enlist and risk death. Westbrook argues that pinups encouraged men to participate in order to fulfill private (gendered) obligations to their sisters, wives, or sweethearts. Pinups of Betty Grable and other Hollywood stars both represented women as the bounty for male soldiers and connoted gender expectations of men as moral protectors. These images functioned as surrogate objects of heterosexual desire but also as symbols of the reasons American men were fighting.

Government propaganda and the mass media also turned to the private obligation of domesticity to encourage Americans' participation in the war effort. News stories about weddings and the rising birth rate, along with lonely wives waiting for news of their absent husbands, appeared throughout the war. Representative families functioned to remind readers of their obligations to protect "the American way of life." The July 6, 1942, Independence Day celebration issue, for instance, combines family portraits with more conventional nationalistic symbols in its coverage of the American war effort. A color cover photograph features an American flag and a caption that reads: "United We Stand." The big news story for the week reports on the town of

Harrodsburg, Kentucky, which was waiting to hear news about sixty-six soldiers of Company D missing in action on Bataan.[19] The text quotes the national anthem and patriotic slogans to urge Americans to "fight through every hardship to preserve our freedom," while photographs visualize the United States as a small town, not as an urban industrialized society. Pictures of the July 4 celebrations include a parade with home guardsmen, the Harrodsburg belles, and a church service in which parishioners pray for the soldiers. This portrait of a patriotic Southern community and the four pages of pictures of soldiers with their parents or wives feature only white people. In general, the magazine's war coverage included no news stories on soldiers or their families from other social groups. *Life* depicts community and family as signifiers of patriotic values through signs that combine dominant race and gender ideals. In the Harrodsburg article, the text quotes from several soldiers' letters addressed to their mothers telling them not to worry. Mothers carry the emotional weight of concern while masculinity is associated with protection of the family and the nation. In addition, cultural ideals also position mothers as the ones responsible for instructing their sons in moral obligations. The concluding full-page photograph reinforces the varied meanings of family as the moral obligation for war seen throughout the July 6, 1942, photo-essay. A close-up photograph shows a smiling three-year-old white girl holding a child's watering can and standing in a light-dappled garden. This picture of the daughter of the commander of Harrodsburg's Company D enhances the sentimentality of the story by focusing on the innocence of childhood to represent the moral obligation that sent her father and all the other fathers to war.

Throughout the war, advertisements reiterated the private obligation of domesticity seen in the news stories.[20] A 1943 ad for Oneida Community Silverware shows a man in uniform marrying a blond bride. The ad's vision of femininity encodes racial and heterosexual ideals in the stereotypical depiction of a beautiful white woman dressed in a conventional wedding gown. The headline emphasizes the white woman's role as object of desire, literally the prize for participation in war, by noting, "These are the things we are fighting for... the right to love and marry and rear children in security and peace."[21] This patriotic address uses the first person plural, "we," to connote a community of both fighters and readers based on imagined collective goals and aspirations. These goals link domesticity to consumption, ignoring other reasons for engagement in war. Ads like this one connected women's roles, as both objects of desire and consumers, to patriotism, thus linking the female body to national objectives.

Like representations of families that provided the reasons for men to go to war, depictions of the home front similarly relied on domestic ideals. On September 25, 1944, *Life* published a special issue titled "A Letter from

Home," which provided soldiers overseas with a portrait of the nation. Extra copies were sent free of charge to the troops. Of the six published letters to the editor, all praising the issue, four were clearly from military personnel. Their comments lend credibility to the magazine's authority through comments such as: "You really told us about home and the good old USA" or "You have given 11,600,000 of us 'our America' past, present and future in this issue. It leaves no doubt that we certainly have something worth our sacrifices."[22] The special issue's depiction of "our America" includes expensive color photographs of pastoral harvests, cows grazing, and three boys in overalls walking down a country lane. Merging cultural signs, a color photograph of a tree-lined suburban street that looks like the country-lane picture associates suburbia with the rural idyll portrayed in the color photograph. At the same time, black-and-white photographs of city skylines and industrial production envision modern prosperity. Photographs reproduce two currents of national identity, the pastoral and the modern, yet the people in the stories are located only in nonindustrial settings. *Life* envisions the home front in nostalgic terms associated with a small-town ideal. The issue also devotes a six-page color spread to pinups of women, offering, as Westbrook suggests, an image of desire that awaits men at home. The backgrounds in these pictures are studio scenes, famous archaeological sites, or natural settings. None of the women is associated with urban settings, which often have more sexually ambiguous connotations. This layout also features only white women, an important consideration in a war dominated by racism. War propaganda about Japan in particular fueled racist sentiments through images that showed Asians as subhuman or animal-like.[23] Throughout the special issue, there are no pictures of people of color.

Instead, *Life* features representative white women – pinups, wives, and mothers – to signify the heterosexual promise awaiting men at home. One two-page spread, "War Wife: She and Her Baby Son Are Waiting," contains a full-page close-up of a blond woman writing to her absent husband while her baby son sits in a high chair.[24] In the center of the composition, on a table behind and between the two figures is a small picture of her husband in uniform. Throughout the war, in stories like this one, *Life*'s focus on war wives waiting patiently for their men envisioned the American home front as a domestic ideal. Although elsewhere the magazine discussed changing gender relations on the home front, in this special issue *Life* chose to limit its depictions of women's social roles to domesticity and made no references to women workers.

The special issue also hails domesticity through pictures of the loving family. A story about the family of a soldier named Bill Elder begins with a full-page shot of Bill's mother hanging up laundry in the backyard.[25] Under a headline "Home: It's the Same as Ever," a photograph shows a white family seated in a plain living room listening to the radio. Other pictures reveal a very small bathroom and neat but small bedrooms. Medium-distance shots that reveal the details of the house underscore the family's ordinary or representative status. In a final full-page photograph reminiscent of pinups featured elsewhere in the issue, the camera peers into the car to provide the viewer with a full-length view of a woman smiling invitingly toward the viewer and wearing shorts that display her legs. The caption states that the "family car will be waiting for Bill when he comes home. So will Lois Bardwell, one of the girls he used to date." Despite the artificial nature of this posed picture, it secures credibility through the "realistic" depiction of an actual girlfriend. As with the "War Wife," the photographic vision of the waiting woman connects heroic sacrifice to an ideal of white womanhood. Sacrifice for a woman waiting at home, or a child as in the Harrodsburg photo-essay, connects human mortality to sexual and emotional desires, justifying war through the promise that the nation will live on despite individual deaths. In addition, the presence of the car in this layout exemplifies the way in which commodities were promised as the fruits of victory. The car and the woman are the objects waiting at home for Bill Elder and the other soldiers. Both of them are presented as available for the male gaze. In this regard, the spectacle of the female in the car eroticizes consumption. As part of a special issue on the home front, photographs of women like Bardwell and the war wife visualize war obligations as the need to preserve family values and heterosexual romance as well as encourage the spectator's pleasure in looking.

Patriotic representations that envisioned the American home front through domestic and sexual ideals confronted social conditions that challenged *Life*'s nationalistic agenda. One of the most painful legacies of the war was the government's relocation policy for Japanese Americans. As part of the hysterical reaction to the attack on Pearl Harbor, the federal government issued Executive Order 9066, which denied Japanese Americans their civil liberties and property through forced imprisonment without trial in internment camps inland from the Pacific Coast. *Life* supported this policy in an April 1942 news story about prisoners being loaded on trucks and arriving at the Manzanar camp.[26] There are no photographs of families even though Japanese Americans struggled to maintain family unity in the camps, and Ansel Adams, Dorothea Lange, and resident photographers like Toyo Miyatake, among others, took many family portraits of the relocated Japanese Americans.

A March 20, 1944, news story about the Tule Lake internment camp, with photographs by Carl Mydans, again does not question the ethics or human-rights implications of the policy.[27] Instead, the writer describes the prisoners as disloyal because they asked to be repatriated to Japan, refused to take an oath of allegiance to the United States, or were suspected of being dangerous to national security. Despite this pro-government position, contradictions pervade the story as domesticity competes with claims of disloyalty. In the opening photograph, Mydans uses a low-angle shot to make a row of male prisoners appear to loom menacingly above the viewer. In contrast, he uses a frontal, medium-distance shot to depict the Manji family in its apartment (Figure 7.2). Mydans creates an illusion of spontaneity by posing the subjects so that they seem to ignore the camera, a device frequently used in *Life*'s family portraits. Four daughters seated at the table are laughing and talking with each other. The parents sit nearby reading while younger boys read comic books on the floor. Family pictures on a bookshelf in the background include a wedding portrait. Although the caption explains that the Manjis are "all classed as disloyal," it does not explain why. Instead, their comfortable intimacy and social activities, as well as the familiar composition, echo *Life*'s portraits of white families.

Other photographs containing ambiguous messages about the prisoners include a nurse holding a newborn baby and a picture of children in a class, described by the caption as being "like those in any U.S. town." Above the final page of text, the headline "They Have Everything except Liberty" captures the irony of the situation, reinforced by the photograph of high school drum

Figure 7.2

majorettes practicing in front of a barbed wire fence. By 1944, *Life* began, visually at least, to acknowledge some of the painful contradictions in the policy. The writer does not question the government's actions but does state that 70 percent of these people are American citizens with no accents. Textual slippages between identifying the prisoners as Japanese and acknowledging their citizenship, like the photographs, create an ambivalent and confusing portrait.

These two stories reveal the centrality of the family in *Life*'s coverage of the war. The Japanese families challenged war narratives because they revealed the diversity of American families rather than the one form typically celebrated in the magazine. Consciously or not, the absence of family pictures in the first story reinforces the assumption of Japanese Americans' differences. *Life*'s reporting fostered a racism based not only on physical differences but on the visual absence of the family values that dominated the rest of the magazine. The powerful role of family imagery is equally apparent in the ways in which images in the later story challenge racist constructions of difference. The enemy's families looked like other families readers saw in the magazine. This could undermine justifications for war by destabilizing a national ideology based on racial differences. The ambiguities in visual constructions of family and ethnicity indicate the unstable and shifting meanings in wartime representations of domesticity.

Life's reliance on family iconography to represent the home front also faced a major challenge from the competing need for women's labor. During the war, certain barriers broke down in industries under the pressures of military production demands. White women and people of color gained access to better jobs in the defense industry, which substantially raised their income levels. With this incentive, six million women entered the labor force.[28] When white women left service jobs for higher-paying defense work, African American women and Latinas who previously held domestic positions were able to advance. Even so, discrimination remained pervasive and insidious. Whereas white women found jobs plentiful, opportunities remained low for women of color.[29] The absence of ethnic and racial diversity in *Life*'s depictions of the war effort reinforced the invisibility of other social groups' contributions to the war.

As labor shortages became increasingly severe, recruitment strategies coordinated by the OWI used a variety of media to attempt to combat gender, although not racial, stereotypes and discrimination. The magazine industry developed a close relationship with the OWI's Magazine Bureau, which recommended story lines as well as ads and cover copy.[30] Magazines like *Life* urged women to leave their homes to participate in the defense industry, often in jobs traditionally assigned to men, such as riveting and welding.

Equally important in the mobilization effort, however, was the continuity of social values and the maintenance of traditional gender roles. Maureen Honey's study of wartime images of women examines how advertising, news stories, and employment campaigns consistently emphasized femininity. She notes that "the intertwining of decorative femininity with militarism arose from the identification of women as domestic freedom fighters and it simultaneously reflected their continued sexual objectification."[31] Life's news photographs as well as advertisements typically showed war workers with brightly painted fingernails, make-up, and well-coiffured hair. Tensions and contradictions surfaced as the campaigns tried to limit or regulate suggestions of female independence in the face of war work that challenged definitions of femininity.

Undermining threats to gender conventions posed by war work, Life represented working mothers and wives as part of the moral obligations on the home front. In a June 1942 photograph, a woman wearing safety glasses and head scarf drills rivet holes into a plane.[32] She does not look at the camera, suggesting that the photographer caught her in the middle of her work. In contrast to the seemingly radical depiction of a woman in overalls working as a riveter, the text emphasizes traditional gender roles. "A Pearl Harbor widow, Mrs. Evelyn J. W. Casola, takes her small but effective revenge on the enemy who killed her husband on December 7." The caption reminds us not of her financial needs or her independence but rather of her sacrifice, as a widow, for the nation. Attention to her marital status exhorts women to believe that war work was compatible with conventional femininity.

Although recruitment campaigns used patriotic rhetoric, there were few discussions about the purposes or goals of the war. The media instead told middle-class women that civilian defense work would hasten the war's end and return their loved ones. The slogan that repeatedly captured this theme was that women were "working for the duration."[33] Life often pictured women as temporary workers eager to return to domesticity. A September 1942 news story reports on a soldier's wife who took over her husband's business until his return.[34] A caption describes a photograph of Emily Harrison putting on a hat in sexist language that trivializes her efforts by claiming that she wore her prettiest hat to "wow" war contractors. Another picture shows her in a dress, typing, with a photograph of a man in uniform on the desk next to her. This composition connects her to male authority in a manner similar to the photograph of the war wife in the home-front issue. Other photographs, however, reveal a more ambiguous message because they depict her in a position of authority. In one large picture of the manufacturing plant, Harrison writes on a pad while talking to a man in work clothes at a machine. The caption explains that she is checking the speed and quality of each man's production. The text goes on to say that after wowing the local

War Production Board with her pretty hat, she "impressed them even more with her determination and her smart business sense." Assertions of Harrison's femininity compete with acknowledgments of her business acumen, which enabled her to expand production and hire more workers. News accounts like these offered a factual counterpart to war films like *Since You Went Away* (1944), in which the absent husband also functions as a reminder of heterosexual desire alongside images of women's self-sufficiency and independence. Messages about women's capabilities competed with demands for conventional femininity and a nationalistic rhetoric that urged women to work for patriotic reasons.

Despite strategies that emphasized women's impermanent commitment to work, surveys taken in 1944 revealed that between 75 and 80 percent of the women interviewed wanted to keep their jobs after the war.[35] The government, however, viewed them only as a temporary reserve force and instituted few legislative, social, or political changes to help women keep their jobs. The lack of commitment is evident in the dearth of such support services as child care or accessible transportation.[36] At the end of the war, the media and the government worked in conjunction with business efforts to provide returning veterans with jobs by removing women war workers from heavy industry. In 1945, women experienced layoffs at a rate 75 percent higher than men. The largest involuntary reduction for women came in durable heavy goods industries, traditionally dominated by men, where one out of four women lost factory jobs.[37]

The media in 1945 often reasserted traditional gender ideals through cultural representations of acceptable female behavior.[38] Rhetoric frequently reminded women that it was their patriotic duty to give their jobs to veterans. Slogans emphasizing temporary work and domestic obligations addressed audiences in terms of the future. From the outset of World War II, the media, politicians, and social critics discussed the postwar world and frequently used visions of the future to justify military participation. As early as 1941, Luce's famous "American Century" editorial predicted American hegemony in a postwar global political economy. In support of intervention, Luce argues that "we must undertake now to be the Good Samaritan of the entire world. It is the manifest duty of this country to undertake to feed all the people of the world who as a result of this worldwide collapse of civilization are hungry and destitute." After connecting American principles with freedom of trade around the world, Luce specifically articulates reasons for an interventionist policy in Asia. "We think of Asia as being worth only a few hundred millions a year to us. Actually, in the decades to come Asia will be worth to us exactly zero – or else it will be worth to us four, five, ten billions of dollars a year."[39]

Luce was not alone in equating the United States' military objectives with its role in postwar society, nor in trying to assess how the United States would control that world. During the 1940s, internationalist positions gained popularity as intellectuals, government officials, and social critics argued that the United States would have to assume major responsibility for shaping the postwar world. Roosevelt coined the rallying cry of internationalists in his Fireside Chat immediately after Pearl Harbor: "We are going to win the war and we are going to win the peace that follows."[40] Central to these arguments was a radical shift in concepts of democracy and capitalism. David Noble argues that, until the 1940s, both progressive and republican traditions advocated isolationism to protect the United States from the corruption of international capitalist systems. Intellectuals including consensus historians like Richard Hofstadter and theologians like Reinhold Niebuhr rejected this position as they adjusted to the dramatic challenges wrought by global war. They replaced this argument with a world view that saw capitalism as the key to the survival of democracy against totalitarian regimes.[41] Similarly, in "American Century," Luce argues that capitalism was the means to ensure democracy at home and around the world. Advertisements and photo-essays in *Life* aligned democratic rhetoric with capitalist objectives, frequently through families who were exhorted to consume as a patriotic duty. The magazine thus demonstrates one mechanism through which a historical bloc advanced its hegemony in the 1940s.

Advertisements began to envision a post-war world long before V-J Day. Unable to produce many consumer products during the war, advertisers worked hard to keep consumers interested through promises of the goods that would be available after the war.[42] These ads relied heavily on clichés of the American middle-class dream in which white women appear amid the consumer splendors of domestic life. Ads frequently showed soldiers returning home to young women and children eagerly greeting them in front of single-family houses. Such images turned an abstract concept of democracy that justified war into a visual consumer ideal. A lengthy ad campaign for Kelvinator refrigerators used the testimonial format in which women envisioned their happy lives when their husbands returned from the war. One ad titled "We'll Live in a Kingdom All Our Own" depicts a privatized vision of a nuclear family in a home with a picket fence and lovely kitchen.[43] A General Electric ad copied *Life*'s photo-journalistic format to give the postwar dream increased visual credibility.[44] A before-and-after layout features the Chisholm family of White Plains, New York. Next to a picture of the patriotic Chisholms all in uniform, a small picture labeled "Before" depicts their current old-fashioned kitchen. In contrast, the largest picture, in the center of the layout, "After," visualizes postwar abundance as a modern kitchen with all new appliances. Advertisements like these repeatedly promoted postwar society as a middle-class ideal located variously in small towns or suburbs. The GE ad depicts White Plains with icons of small-town

America, such as picket fences, tree-lined streets, and single-family houses. Advertisements during and after the war frequently recycled small-town iconography for suburban settings. These icons appear as well in photo-essays like the Harrodsburg article and the home front issue. Similarly, suburban developers adopted the iconography of the small town, gave streets names like Cherry Lane, and designed houses in colonial or Cape Cod styles.[45] The collapse of distinctions between suburbs and small towns served to validate the newer residential form.

News reporting during the war, however, could not so easily construct a vision of the future as advertisements since reportorial conventions necessitated a focus on current conditions in which delays in demobilization, housing shortages, employment crises, and the slow reconversion of factories intensified rather than alleviated home front problems. Nonetheless, *Life*'s reports on readjustments during 1945 promised prosperity after the war. For instance, a news story from September 1945, "Peace Brings Temporary Unemployment," shows photographs of a CIO picket, a family migrating in search of a job, and a long line of applicants outside of a US Employment Service office.[46] Despite visual depictions of social instabilities, the caption underneath the picture of the employment line states that there were plenty of jobs available "but not always the kind workers happened to want." [...] Here too the text contrasts negative conditions in the present with the promise of a stable future. The text blames the workers for their unemployment, aligning nationalistic rhetoric with class by shifting between statements crediting high employment for American prosperity and representations of discontented workers as outsiders disrupting the nation.

The layout on the following page visually tried to secure the textual claims that social problems were only "temporary." A headline announces "Most Peacetime Goods Are on Their Way Back," even though many of the products discussed were actually not available for several years. Photographs show a woman putting on stockings, another placing dishes in an automatic washer, a garbage disposal unit, and a rotary ironer. The later photographs in the story offer consumption as the solution to economic instability. The Depression had hurt the political and cultural status of capitalism, and fears of debts and doubts about materialism persisted into the 1940s. Thus, advertisers during and after the war had to displace popular suspicions about buying goods, just as the media and intellectuals challenged an earlier republican view of capitalism as the enemy of democracy. Similarly, news photographs of products for women to use in the home united traditional gender roles, domestic ideals, and consumption to construct a prophetic vision of postwar America. Class was also essential to this vision since these costly products promised to give women more leisure time and greater domestic competence. Visual claims that consumer goods offered women freedom of choice and happiness at home linked gender to nationalism by associating their consumer practices with economic recovery.

Despite cultural practices that envisioned postwar domesticity, women continued to work after the war. They were shunted out of lucrative positions but remained in the work force. Women moved from defense industries to clerical, service, and sales jobs with a concomitant reduction of income and loss of union protection. Nine out of ten women suffered a decrease in earnings as average weekly salaries dropped from fifty dollars to thirty-five.[47] *Life* ignored these statistics in stories that associated the ideal family with national trends, conditions, and objectives. Articles about veterans coping, women welcoming them home, and employers offering soldiers jobs dominated the magazine. News stories did not report on women's changed labor status or desires to remain employed. Instead, *Life* focused on reconversion in terms of male employment, economic stability, and domestic happiness when soldiers returned. In so doing, *Life* clearly expanded the representative family beyond images of neediness to images that relied on gender, class, and racial codes to envision a social ideal rooted in suburbanization, consumption ideology, and conventional gender roles.

[...]

A Nation of Families

Scholars of the postwar period invariably identify radical changes in family life as a crucial development within American society. In explaining the baby boom, they frequently argue that the cohort of adults who grew up during the Depression and World War II compensated for earlier deprivations by turning to the pleasures of domesticity.[48] Elaine Tyler May demonstrates, however, that prosperity is only a partial explanation for the baby boom because the postwar period cannot simply be read as a time of affluence and complacency. She observes that in the face of Cold War anxieties and fears, many Americans turned to the private space of their families for stability and security.[49] The powerful reach and scope of the media reinforced this process through recurrent depictions of the nuclear family as a safe and ideal haven. Rather than reflecting or recording reality, *Life*'s photo-essays created an imagined community through pictorial realism that naturalized a particular social form – the middle-class nuclear family – into a transhistorical ideal that symbolized the United States. In so doing, this imagined community also functioned to regulate social forms and deny diversity at a time when anti-Communist campaigns made differences politically dangerous. Domestic ideology, however, was not monolithic or unified but a complex cultural terrain that attempted to reconcile social and political issues, like the ones May points out, through family values. Ambiguities apparent in photo-essays that visually reproduced gender, class, and racial hierarchies, as well as struggled between community and individualism, indicate the tensions embedded in narratives that aligned domesticity with nationalism.

In this context, we need to interrogate the centrality of the family to *Life*'s ideological project of national consensus. Jürgen Habermas argues that advanced capitalism destroys personal motivations for work and connection to others by turning work into a kind of status competition tied to the accumulation of goods, rather than a calling or an opportunity to contribute to society. Traditional depictions of the family present it as a voluntary site of intimacy and warmth, but it also functions as a site of consumption. At the same time capitalism lauds the work ethic and the family as spheres of morality safe from the materialism of the outside world. These contradictions produce a "legitimation crisis," by which capitalist societies become ever more dependent for legitimacy on the very sociocultural motivations that capitalism undermines. As Habermas describes this process, capitalist societies "feed parasitically on the remains of tradition," such as religion and the patriarchal family. But legitimation is always incomplete because the families praised as the location of desire and purpose are ill equipped to fulfill this role since they exist contradictorily as units of consumption.[50]

Life's almost obsessive attention to the nuclear family in stories about social issues such as housing, labor crises, and the economy demonstrates how strategies of legitimation aligned national imperatives with domestic ideals. These strategies often relied on a rhetoric of democracy. Like the World War II appeals that borrowed heavily from a small-town ideal, *Life*'s postwar pictorial record borrowed from the rhetoric of wartime emergency by linking the family to moral obligations and patriotic behavior. Specifically, narratives about postwar social, political, and economic situations tried to legitimate consumption by making it a matter of obligation to the family and the state.

Life appealed to middle-class Americans by connecting a vision of nuclear families owning their own homes and experiencing upward mobility with national ideals. As illustrated by the presidential transfer of power and the photographic representations of the Barkleys' and the Nixons' domestic bliss, the home was a prominent symbol in *Life*'s portrait of America. In its Modern Living and Design sections, *Life* featured model suburban homes as the new architectural ideal. Merging editorial and advertising material in these sections, *Life* promoted a vision of the United States as a nation of middle-class homeowners. Luce wrote in 1946 that "it is the first job of Modern Living to show how the multiplicity of goods in an industrial age can be used with relatively better rather than relatively worse taste."[51] News stories supported this consumer aesthetic by reporting on developments in suburban living. The January 5, 1953, issue "The American and His Economy," for instance, begins with a news story on the latest developments in suburban housing design.[52] Color plates show landscaped exteriors and the interior decor of houses with three bedrooms, $1\frac{1}{2}$ baths, a fireplace, and an open floor plan. Photographic realism demonstrates the popularity of suburbia through representations of young married couples with small children standing outside their new homes in Ohio, Louisiana, Colorado, Pennsylvania, Texas, and Indiana. Pictures of real families represented middle-class Americans from different regions as participants in a shared American Dream.

Housing, however, was not just a symbol of prosperity and domestic bliss in postwar America, it was also a source of tension and conflict. According to the National Housing Agency, at least 3.5 million new houses were needed in 1946 just to provide veterans with decent housing, yet there was only enough material and labor to build 460,000 units. In addition, the influx of people of color from rural areas to industrial centers resulted in a severe housing crisis in inner cities. Poor people who were most in need of government intervention in the housing crisis faced the racially discriminatory policies of both private landlords and government agencies, as well as limited job prospects and inflated rents and grocery bills.[53] Although the National Housing Act of 1949 established "the goal of a decent home and a suitable living environment for every American family," little progress was made in alleviating this problem. By 1964, only 550,000 of the 810,000 low-cost dwelling units promised by the Act had been completed.[54]

Instead, the federal government supported suburbanization through such programs as the FHA and VA mortgage guarantees.[55] With these government guarantees, buyers could secure mortgages at low interest rates and with small down payments, making it cheaper to buy than to rent. As taxes went up, the homeowner deduction became more important, creating an added subsidy for homeownership and an added penalty for renters. In this way, the government subsidized the move into the suburbs of millions of white Americans. Starting in 1956, federal government investments in interstate highway construction projects encouraged the use of private automobiles over public transportation and furthered suburban growth. At the same time, redlining policies and the refusal to fund renovation projects on older houses in the cities precluded poor people and people of color from participating in these social developments.[56]

Throughout the postwar years, *Life*'s news coverage of housing rarely discussed apartment buildings or urban renovation as possible solutions. Photographs of Americans living in trailers and Quonset huts, and doubling up in apartments, visualized the housing shortage, but the only solution the magazine showed was the single-family house. Photographs supplied the visual evidence for the claim that all Americans demanded suburban housing, but only white nuclear families were shown in their new suburban homes or standing in long lines to purchase these houses.

Although social crises challenged *Life*'s claims of consensus, the magazine's representational strategies worked to contain such threats. Ideology played a part not only in the proposed solution to the problem, but in how the narrative represented the problem. In December 1945, as the United States faced potential crises in unemployment, inflation, and housing during reconversion, *Life* featured a big news story titled "The Great Housing Shortage."[57] Housing was a serious problem for a nation whose central myth of the American Dream included home ownership.

A prominent full-page photograph shows two navy officers and their families sharing an apartment (Figure 7.3). In the foreground, an officer sits on a couch reading a newspaper. At his feet, a young boy lies on the floor while next to the man a baby sleeps in a bassinet. In an armchair in the middle distance a woman sits holding another baby. The other officer and another woman stand in the background in front of drying laundry. The composition accentuates the cramped conditions of seven people in two rooms through tight framing that cuts off any view into the rest of the apartment. The adult figures line up in a diagonal that emphasizes the sharply receding perspective. This diagonal encourages the eye to move quickly from the foreground to the background, further underscoring the small dimensions of the apartment.

Life's focus on military personnel was significant first because the housing crisis intensified with demobilization. Moreover, *Life* depicts navy officers who fought a war for democracy living under such "un-American" conditions. *Life*'s readers knew this was un-American because they had been shown numerous images of what was American. The cramped conditions and the laundry recall photographs of working-class tenements where tenants hung laundry between the buildings. This association casts the housing problem and solution in class terms whereby apartments are part of the problem that deprives these officers of their "natural" right to own a single-family home. *Life* locates democracy and nationhood as the stakes involved in the housing crisis by focusing on the military who were equated with patriotism.

After visualizing the crisis through the officers' apartment, *Life* presents statistics and graphs to document the problem. Such graphs provide empirical evidence to legitimize *Life*'s claims; they also indicate change through time, thereby suggesting the temporary nature of the crisis and the potential for future progress. The photo-essay also features single-family model homes in different price ranges and ignores altogether the more economical apartment solution. *Life* negates class differences by featuring different types of houses as choices instead of examining the conditions and options for people at different economic levels. In its penchant for narrative closure, *Life* ends with a picture of a factory making parts for prefabricated houses. This was the

Figure 7.3

privileged solution offered by *Life* at the dawn of the housing boom. In a letter to the editor responding to this report, Congressman Wright Patman insisted on the government's responsibility to ensure "that our scarce supply of building materials is channeled to the most worthy type of projects."[58] Letters like this one, and others from business leaders, praised the article without specifying what constituted a worthy type of project. Such praise legitimated the building industry and *Life*'s favored solution, the single-family home.

Advertisements also reinforced the ideal of suburbia since they featured only white families in suburban dwellings. Two pages before the news story, a Plymouth ad depicts a single-family house on a snowy night. A family of four looks out of a bay window at a sign on their garage that reads "Reserved for Our New Plymouth." On the page opposite the opening page of the article, an ad for Prudential Life Insurance titled "Bless This House," shows a family of four admiring a Christmas tree. The text emphasizes the importance of the home for the family's financial security. Both advertisements and news reports make explicit associations between domesticity and class through an emphasis on single-family suburban homes.

Life's reporting on political and social problems emphasized middle-class concerns by encouraging readers to identify with an ideology that equated democracy with capitalism through ideals of suburban home ownership. The consequences of this strategy are most evident in news coverage of class conflict where *Life* repositioned workers' actions as threats to democracy, not critiques of capitalist inequalities. One of the greatest fears at the conclusion of World War II was that the country would return to the desperate conditions of the thirties. This fear seemed warranted when, along with inflation and unemployment, conflicts between labor and management escalated in the immediate postwar years. Unions and corporations attempted to rationalize labor relations in ways that often ignored or hurt workers' interests. Workers registered their anger and frustration in wildcat strikes, insisting not just on wage increases but on control over the work place.[59] Prior to World War II, *Life* had strongly opposed unionism. Although it remained an avowedly conservative journal, its editors now accepted the trend toward union involvement in corporate management, even praising successful contract negotiations. What it would not tolerate were disruptions of the economy. *Life* often represented strikes through photographs of empty warehouses and idled factories that surely must have resonated with middle-class readers' pictorial memories of the Depression. Rather than looking at the faces of workers, *Life*'s readers saw pictures of empty warehouses that illustrated how work stoppages affected the middle class. The crucial question became whether middle-class Americans would be deprived of consumer goods; rarely did writers analyze the causes of strikes. In this way, *Life*'s news coverage of labor conflicts often deflected the politics of class struggle by focusing on the bourgeois family as the location for the successful resolution of social discord.

The June 3, 1946, big news story, "The Great Train Strike," angrily denounces a nationwide work stoppage by railroad workers because it asked too much of Americans.[60] According to *Life*, although Americans accept that "workingmen had a constitutional right to organize, negotiate and, if necessary, strike, to improve their working conditions," when strikes threaten the quality of life, the "United States" loses its temper. The text establishes social boundaries here by distinguishing Americans who are patient, and the United

States that loses its temper, from the workers who test this patience. Such rhetorical moves exemplify how *Life* addressed its readers as an imagined community facing externalized problems. This clearly addresses *Life*'s middle-class audience as well as indicating those whom the magazine represents as the Other. Along with textual distinctions, *Life* visualizes class differences by representing an America inconvenienced. Pictures show well-dressed commuters and shoppers waiting in huge crowds and cramming into the last trains leaving the railroad station. The only photograph of labor shows two white male workers sitting on the steps of a train "waiting for the deadline." Their inactivity, along with pictures of empty trainyards and factories, identifies those responsible for the breakdown of economic life resulting from this transportation crisis. The workers turn their heads to the left (narratively looking for a signal) so that they look at the facing page where one photograph shows two stranded women travelers seated amid their luggage while their three children sprawl on the floor in front of them. In the space of the layout, the workers look at what they are inconveniencing: middle-class families dislocated by labor's idleness.

A letter written by a housewife from Connecticut forms the centerpiece of the story. Instead of placing it in the letters section, *Life* prominently displays it in the photo-essay, printed in large typewritten letters offset by a thick gray border. Betty Knowles Hunt, a housewife and mother, condemns strikers for paralyzing the country and "killing our prestige abroad." She also criticizes the government for jeopardizing democracy by placing the public welfare in the hands of pressure groups. Who, she asks, "will save Democracy for America and the World?" As Habermas argues, dominant ideology mobilizes traditional ideals to legitimize administrative demands. This letter invokes both democracy and domesticity to legitimize the hierarchical inequalities of capitalism.

> I should be scrubbing the kitchen, mending the stockings, weeding the flower beds, and planning the dinner. Much of my time and energy has been spent in trying to teach my three little minorities that their private interests will often conflict, but that they must learn to sacrifice in the larger interest of our family as a whole. For what am I preparing them? Is it of any value to teach them Democracy at home, while our government in Washington fails to teach its minorities to sacrifice and work together for the common American good?[61]

Hunt establishes an us–them relationship by comparing "our family" and "our government" with working-class "minorities." Moreover, she trivializes working-class people's political efforts by equating her children with workers when she refers to them both as minorities. Hunt patronizingly represents labor activists as children to be taught by their parent, the government.[62]

Hunt represents this social crisis in terms of the family, which aligns middle-class interests with the state in opposition to the working class, which threatens social stability. The prominence of the letter privileges a bourgeois ideal of the family that in turn regulates knowledge about the political society. The discursive frame controls how readers understand this crisis as well as casts the working class outside the bourgeois norm. When she condemns workers for stepping outside of normative boundaries, Hunt defines national identity in terms of social conventions of respectability.[63]

Hunt also defines democracy in familial terms as a matter of working together for the common good (of economic prosperity), just as children must put aside their "private interests" for the sake of the family. The letter legitimizes capitalist structures by displacing political critiques of the system in favor of family concerns. In addition, Hunt represents workers' demands for self-determination as private interests of lesser value than the needs of (dominant) America. Indeed, the text presents class struggle not merely as a threat to a generalized social welfare but more specifically as a threat to the home. Not all readers accepted Hunt's claims. One of two letters to the editor critical of her position appropriated the same rhetoric, arguing that "the people also include a tremendous amount of union families. They're American too, Mrs. Hunt."[64] This response demonstrates both that texts are open to various interpretations and that domestic iconography is available to alternative perspectives. *Life*'s decision to highlight Hunt's letter, however, like the four letters praising her position, indicates the power of editorial manipulation to impose an ideological direction on the news coverage.

Framing the train strike as both an economic and a family crisis conforms to *Life*'s larger discursive attempt to align the middle-class family with the capitalist economy. Here, photographs visualized the danger to capitalism through idled factories. Elsewhere, *Life* connected the health of the political economy with a particular social class through photographs of families enjoying the postwar economic boom. Far from being subtle, the magazine repeatedly stated both in editorials and in news coverage of economic issues that it was Americans' patriotic responsibility to consume in order to keep demand high and the economy prosperous. Popular media like *Life* played an important role in promoting the consumer spending and government economic policies that helped bring about the preconditions for an unprecedented rise in the American standard of living that lasted until the 1960s.

The American economy underwent radical changes after the war. Government and business leaders sought to control the instabilities endemic to capitalism by regulating the economic structure. The federal government implemented Keynesian theories of economic stimulation by pumping vast sums into the economy to ensure the relative stability of the postwar boom. The federal budget rose from $38 billion in 1947 to $77 billion in 1960, with the most significant increases in military spending: the Defense Department budget climbed from $14.3 billion to $49.3 billion between 1950 and 1953 but did not decline after the Korean War. Structural modifications to welfare, social security, and unemployment compensation policies further protected the economy from major upheavals. Increasing centralization of the state accompanied the centralization of private multinational corporations. These corporations developed foreign markets where raw materials, cheap labor, and new investment opportunities stimulated American economic hegemony while foreign countries still labored under reconstruction efforts.[65]

Consumer spending, stimulated by suburban growth and demands for housing, appliances, automobiles, and shopping malls, also fueled the postwar boom. After fifteen years of economic crisis and war, Americans in 1945 were ready to spend, urged on by consumption ideologies promoted by the mass media. Between 1946 and 1950, manufacturers sold 21.4 million automobiles and over 20 million refrigerators.[66] The boom continued throughout the 1950s, despite several recessions and inflation. In 1955, for instance, automobile dealers sold almost 8 million new cars, and the housing industry initiated 1.6 million new housing units.[67] The government subsidized these remarkable postwar consumer habits through federally financed loan programs like those offered by the FHA and the GI Bill, which enabled more than 7.6 million veterans to go to college and 1.3 million to secure home loans. Banks also extended credit to middle-class Americans for mortgages, cars, and other large purchases.[68]

The boom, however, was not without social and economic costs: the government never fully controlled inflation, and unemployment went up and down throughout the 1950s. Even more significant was the failure to change social hierarchies despite this general affluence. As Marty Jezer points out, income distribution remained static: "Whatever the method of computation, the evidence is clear that though everyone except the hardcore poor gained during this period, the rich tended to get richer, the middle class tended to stay in its place, and the poor, relative to everyone else, were left further and further behind."[69] *Life*, like the government and private corporations, did not so much ignore social differences as argue that productivity would raise everyone to a higher level of affluence.[70] This ideal of productivity pervaded the magazine's vision of social progress.

As part of a national corporation with its own direct political and economic interests, and as an institution with responsibilities to its investors and advertisers, *Life* supported government and business efforts to maintain a stable economy and political consensus. Toward that end, *Life* often cajoled its readers to be civic minded by spending more money. In a May 5, 1947, article entitled "US Tackles the Price Problem," *Life* linked the ideal suburban family to the state by making the family accountable for economic prosperity.[71] The article ends with a two-page spread on Ted and Jeanne Hemeke and their three children. The headline specifically associates consumption with civic responsibility: "Family Status Must Improve: It Should Buy More for Itself to Better the Living of Others." The editors use a popular photo-essay formula of a before-and-after narrative. The Hemekes appear first in their present home, an old frame house, then visiting a new suburban house. The text explains the latter as the vision of the future, "what life should be like in the US by 1960."

In the foreground of the first picture, Ted Hemeke, having just returned from work, stands with his back to the camera holding a child's hand. The photographer's perspective encourages the viewer to identify with Hemeke's vision by putting us in his shoes. Following his gaze, we look past the foreground figures toward the house, observing the weeds and the grassless lawn as well as the poorly maintained house next door. In the background, Jeanne Hemeke stands in the doorway holding one child while another child sits on a barrel next to her. The other picture on this page shows Jeanne Hemeke using a large shovel to scoop coal into a "dirty coal furnace next to [the] stove" while her baby daughter sits on the floor nearby. This shot emphasizes the antiquated facilities of the old house as well as the woman's hard work.

On the facing page, two photographs parallel the ones on the previous page in composition, size, and layout. The first picture again shows the Hemekes in front of a house (Figure 7.4). This time, however, the wife stands in the doorway of a modern ranch-style house. By repeating the action of Ted Hemeke walking into the scene from the street, the visual narrative suggests that once again he is arriving home from work. Although the text explains that the Hemekes are visiting a model house, repeating the composition encourages a reading of economic progress from the old house to the new one. The Hemekes' attire underscores this narrative of upward mobility. In the first scene, Ted Hemeke wears heavy boots and a work jacket. His daughter does not wear a coat or socks. Here, he wears a suit and his daughter has on a coat, hat, socks, and dress shoes. The daughter in the background no longer sits on a barrel but rides a tricycle.

The second photograph of the alternative vision shows Jeanne Hemeke again in the kitchen but this time in a modern kitchen with gingham curtains and shiny new appliances. She stands at a counter with her hands on an electric beater, as if she were baking; behind her a kettle gleams on a gas stove. The baby no longer sits on the floor dangerously close to the furnace but plays with a toy in a high chair that has a bottle of milk on the tray. Visually, if not in actuality, Jeanne Hemeke and her family have attained these middle-class accouterments. The realistic *mice en scène* (for this is a staged performance by two different photographers) reinforces a reading that this woman is cooking in her own new kitchen. Here, domesticity constructs conventional gender

Figure 7.4

roles by positioning the woman in the private space of the home. Moreover, placing her in a modern kitchen with new appliances, a composition frequently used in advertisements, objectifies her as an ideal consumer. Her husband, on the other hand, occupies space in the outside public world, signified by the sidewalk and the narrative journey from work. Visually and textually, *Life* presents a vision of America that characterizes people like the Hemekes through conventional gender identities and material possessions.

As with photo-essays on Romy Hammes and other representative families, here too *Life* locates the consumer ideal in the physical space of the suburbs, an isolated space in which no one else appears on the sidewalk. Thus, the magazine's vision of the nation integrates the ideals of social progress with ideologies of consumption and the private realm of domesticity. Indeed, the article claims that families have civic responsibilities based on their roles as consumers. At the conclusion of the story on the Hemekes, *Life* cites a Twentieth Century Fund projection study on the economy in 1960, stating that:

> To achieve a health and decency standard for everyone by 1960 each US family should acquire, in addition to a pleasant roof over its head, a vacuum cleaner, washing machine, stove, electric iron, refrigerator, telephone, electric toaster and such miscellaneous household supplies as matching dishes, silverware, cooking utensils, tools, cleaning materials, stationery and postage stamps.

This prescriptive message presents a list of consumer goods as the minimum that families have not only the right to expect but the duty to acquire in order that everyone attain a decent standard of living. Concluding a story on inflation at a time when many still worried about an economic collapse, *Life*'s visual mediation of these fears takes on great ideological significance. In linking the family to the political economy, *Life* creates a portrait of the nation that legitimizes the social order by connecting moral authority to familial consumption.

In stories about people like the Hemekes, *Life* denied class distinctions when it pointed to consumption as evidence of upward mobility. Instead, the uniform domesticity that pervades photo-essays like this one offered a portrait of a national community of families with shared concerns. The political consequences of this nationalism are especially apparent in stories that explicitly linked domesticity to anti-Communist rhetoric. *Life* often supported the political tensions of the Cold War by contrasting the oppressive Communist state with the opportunities and freedoms of American families. For example, the January 1957 photo-essay on the Hungarian Csillag family [...] recreates the deeply familiar story about progress through the layout. The narrative moves geographically and temporally from a "homeland," represented as a physical space of deprivation and fear (the refugees in a snowstorm), toward "America," the land of opportunity (pictures of consumer goods in a middle-class home).[72] This article is different from many news accounts of group immigration that raise the specter of invasion or violation of boundaries. The realistic pictures in this story of progress represent an assimilated nuclear family easily adjusting to its new surroundings.

Pictures of the Csillags settled in the United States combine domesticity and consumption to represent what the American nation offers these refugees. Three large photographs on a two-page spread offer evidence of that success by showing the Csillags standing in front of a table laden with food, having just arrived home from the grocery store.[73] The first photograph shows the Csillags with American relatives unpacking groceries. In the second photograph, a relative demonstrates how to use a tissue. In the third photograph, the adults are all laughing as Pal Csillag tries one. The Hungarians' awe at the consumer products destabilizes the norm of American consumption in order to foreground it as evidence of national ideals. The focus on consumption exemplifies the magazine's frequent Cold War strategy to contrast communism with American capitalism, assured that such comparisons easily demonstrated which culture was superior. The Csillags join an imagined community of families that defines social conventions in terms of gender divisions and political action in terms of Americans' consumer habits. The text underscores this position through unsubtle contrasts between the United States and the impoverished conditions of the Communist system the Csillags left behind.

This narrative of immigrant assimilation submerges ethnicity as the Csillags become, as in Nixon's comment, the "kind of people who make good Americans" through the products they consume. Perhaps more than any other national narrative, this narrative of the successful immigrant enjoying the riches of capitalism embodies the American Dream.

Within the context of other media representations of the family, *Life*'s images of domesticity must be read as participating in the ongoing constructions of national social and political ideals in postwar America. The family's importance lies not only in its economic value in reproducing and maintaining the labor force or as a channel for socializing children, but equally important, in its role in reproducing cultural values.[74] *Life*'s narrative promoted the reproduction of a particular set of values and norms that formed a national culture around the dominant middle class.

Creating *Life*'s Audience

Life's narrative about consensus America did not merely reflect the trends of the baby boom or middle-class affluence. Instead, *Life* actively constructed meanings for its readers. This has significance for a postwar American society that was more heterogeneous than is typically imagined by stereotypes of postwar suburbanites, who were in fact a mixed group including returning GIs, second-generation immigrants, and working-class people.[75] Although the majority of *Life*'s readers were middle-class professionals, the letters to the editor indicate a degree of diversity among the magazine's audience. For instance, in response to the article on the internment of Japanese Americans at Tule Lake, a Nisei man used patriotic rhetoric to condemn "American fascists and race-baiters."[76] Similarly, a woman responding to a news article on a strike at a Detroit GM plant in 1946 identified with the striker, explaining that her husband was also on strike and therefore they could no longer afford her subscription.[77] Many in this heterogeneous group may have felt insecure about their place in the American Dream. Even 1950s television demonstrated more social diversity; not all shows were middle-class family comedies, especially in the early days, with shows like "The Goldbergs," "The Honeymooners," and "Amos 'n' Andy." What united these shows, however, was a capitalist ethos that typically resolved problems of work, family, and politics through consumption.[78] Similarly, *Life*'s news reports worked to convince its readers just then moving into the suburbs that they too belonged to "America." An America, that is, that was upwardly mobile and consumer oriented.

Life's focus on the middle-class family occurred at a time when Americans were reorganizing social relations into nuclear families. Documentary photography, historically aligned with reform movements, had previously turned the camera's gaze on groups with lower status than the middle-class audiences viewing these images. *Life*'s contribution to photojournalism was to turn the camera's gaze on the middle class in an effort to mirror the readers' world. Readers saw in *Life* an optimistic vision of American society, which, they were told, was a reflection of their lives as homeowners. *Life*'s photo-essays invited viewers to make connections between a single family form and national interests through identification with signs of domesticity.[79] Realistic photographs of the family visualized socially constructed relationships, such as that between the breadwinner and housewife, in concrete and seemingly unmediated ways. Stories about individuals directed attention away from the political meanings embedded in representation by encouraging viewers to relate emotionally to the people in the news.[80] Like the letter writers who recognized their old sinks, readers frequently wrote in with pictures or stories that resembled the ones published in the magazine, fostering a climate that urged people to recognize the similarities.

Life addressed these readers through representational strategies in which seamless narratives present the working-class Hemekes, or even the Hungarian Csillags, as families just like other Americans. In this way, the photo-essay hails the reader into the signifying spaces of national identity, a space severely circumscribed by the patriarchal and racist ideals of domesticity. Underlying the clear anti-Communist message in the Csillag story, for instance, is a didacticism common in *Life*: both photographs and texts demonstrate "the kind of people who make good Americans." These immigrants are clearly not middle class. Rather, through a progressive narrative about characters who embody the American success myth, the story about the Csillags depicts, like the one about the Hemekes, the aspirations of Americans. Readers are urged to identify with the emotional efforts and achievements of an imagined community of like-minded families. Displacing class and ethnic differences, *Life* repeats a deeply familiar story of progress and achievement in stories as varied as Romy Hammes' auto dealership and the Csillags' escape from communism. In part, *Life* was so effective in this regard because realistic photographs promote a reading of images as transparent mirrors of social reality.

In studying news stories that constructed an ideal of nationhood, it is also crucial to acknowledge who is left out of that ideal. In stories about representative Americans, ethnic differences were typically limited to Europeans, like the Hungarian Csillags. In contrast, people of color, including Latinos and Native Americans, appeared as representative of social problems but never to signify the American Dream. Moreover, some social groups, like Asian Americans after the close of the internment camps, were rarely seen. The one major exception, and we see how *Life* depicted them in Chapter 5, was African Americans and their struggle for civil rights.

The elderly were also notably absent from *Life*'s narrative of postwar family life. Suburban dwellers, at least in the pages of *Life*, did not live with elderly parents, much less aunts, uncles, or friends. When *Life* represented elderly people, it was typically in association with specific problems or issues. A June 1950 article on pension programs represents the elderly since they are the major recipients of these programs.[81] Photographs from a retirement settlement in St. Petersburg, Florida, include a group playing shuffleboard and an elderly couple smiling outside their cottage. In contrast, the final full-page picture depicts an old man in a county poorhouse. Seated on a wrought-iron bed showing signs of rusting, the man's unshaven face looks at the camera. Strong light from the window highlights his clenched hands while leaving his face in shadow. The text reassuringly notes that the surge in retirement plans will mean an "increasing scarcity of pictures of pathetic misery like that on the opposite page," yet the painful and disturbing photograph undermines any comfortable solution claimed by the text. The article praises retirement towns because the elderly there "entertain themselves, are a burden to nobody and best of all maintain the independence so cherished by old folks." The "nobody" evidently refers to the family relations who are not discussed. This story, which contains no photographs of children or relatives, identifies both the problem and the solution as socially and politically distinct from the ideals of domesticity. *Life*'s first major treatment of aging, a July 1959 special series "Old Age," begins with an article titled "In a Dutiful Family Trials with Mother."[82] Unlike the earlier photo-essay, here the editors present aging as a problem for the family. Cornell Capa's photographs narrate the story of an elderly woman living with her son and his family. In one picture, Capa captures the situation through a grainy close-up shot of the daughter-in-law and a friend laughing at the kitchen table in a scene of intimacy and informality. The mother sits in profile in the background, spatially isolated and excluded from the conversation. Other pictures reveal cramped conditions, and two full-page pictures feature an emotional confrontation between the mother and her daughter-in-law. Most significant, in this first extensive report on the elderly, *Life* characterizes them as a problem that invades the family home.

Life's coverage of the elderly may have been limited, but homosexuality was beyond the representational limits of the magazine for most of the period. Postwar persecution of homosexuality and the homophobic currents in anti-Communist rhetoric are well documented, but in *Life* the denial of sexual difference, rather than an attempt to condemn it, was most prominent.[83] Homophobic rhetoric permeated the magazine, as did the heterosexual imperative that shaped its representation of social life. The limited visibility of different social and racial groups clearly shaped the news discourse to produce an extremely narrow portrait of "the kind of people who make good Americans."

For *Life* magazine, the task of constructing a unified nation out of a diverse polity depended on news presentations that advanced the twin ideologies of consumption and domesticity not just as goals of the nation-state but as the fulfillment of the democratic aspirations of the people in the nation. The family was a primary site through which *Life* hailed its audience as part of that unified nation. It is incorrect to assume, however, that there was a priori an audience of nuclear families for the magazine to address. Audiences are not typically unified but, rather, disorganized and disparate communities. Media producers, however, need to imagine an audience because communication is a dialogic process oriented "toward an addressee."[84] In other words, a text has to address a reader, however that reader is imagined. *Life* envisioned its readers to be midwestern, middle class, not very sophisticated, and definitely not intellectual. It is clear, moreover, from the forms of address in the photo-essays that *Life* conceptualized its readers as family members and as consumers. Seeking empirical evidence for these assumptions about its readers, the magazine's demographic studies determined the composition of its audience through extensive questionnaires on the age, gender, number in the family, and income level of its readers.[85] *Life* used demographic information to attract advertisers, as well as to shape its own discourse for a perceived audience. Nonetheless, common wisdom in the publishing industry until the 1960s insisted that magazines amass the broadest possible circulation.[86] Thus, *Life*'s vision both responded to a perceived middle-class audience, and yet sought to make a widely accessible product.

In constructing images to appeal to a mass audience, *Life* presented an ideal with which it encouraged its readers to identify. This does not mean that *Life* created nuclear families, for many Americans in these years lived in family forms resembling *Life*'s families. Yet, even these people lived complex and multiply constructed lives, and their identification with a specific ideological position, religion, political party, or ethnic group varied according to the context. Recognizing oneself as belonging to a nuclear family, therefore, comes about in the active process of reading and viewing. *Life* urged its readers to identify with domesticity by focusing on the nuclear family as the representational ideal of American culture. As a form of representation, the nuclear family works so well because it blurs commercialism and consumer identity with seemingly voluntary ties of intimacy and affection.

Life's photographs of businessmen, politicians, and immigrants as self-made family men with their supportive wives and children constructed an ideologically meaningful portrait of the United States. Central to this vision was a narrative association between capitalism and democracy. Nationality often coalesces around ethnic or racial identities. In the United States, however, national identity is based on more abstract concepts of liberty, democracy, and citizenship. Family ideals and obligations function to mediate these abstract concepts and offer a source of identification because family is a site of emotional attachment and personal commitments. In the January 1953 special issue, which featured the cover photograph of Dale and Gladys Welling and their children, the editorial describes the American economy as "capitalism modified by democracy."[87] Complementing news stories about middle-class families, the editorial praises capitalism by labeling consumption as a democratic process. In this special issue, then, *Life* combines the family, democracy, and consumption in its portrait of the economic state of the nation. As Habermas suggests, *Life* turned to the patriarchal family and the American political tradition of democracy to legitimize the political economy at a time when it was undergoing significant transformations. Displacing political and social critiques, *Life* constructed an imagined community of middle-class families as the American nation.

When reporting on the intense social changes, political tensions, and economic upheavals of the postwar period, *Life* turned to an ideal of the middle-class family in order to direct a preferred reading about these events. Domestic ideology conceptualized the family as a private sphere distinct from the political arena. At the same time, *Life* continually relied on the family to represent domestic and political spheres. News photo-essays often negotiated ideological contestations between social conditions and consensus ideals through the intersection of these spheres. These intersections are explored in the next chapter, which examines the role of the public and private in *Life*'s news stories. Although public spaces and activities have more political weight in this society than activities centered around the home and family, the visual presence of the family in *Life*'s depictions of postwar America indicate that the public and private are interrelated rather than separate spheres.

Notes

1 Steven Mintz and Susan Kellogg, *Domestic Revolutions: A Social History of American Family Life* (New York: Free Press, 1988), 184.
2 John H. Mollenkopf, *The Contested City* (Princeton, NJ: Princeton University Press, 1983), 28.
3 Juan Ramon Garcia, *Operation Wetback: The Mass Deportation of Mexican Undocumented Workers in 1954* (Westport, Conn.: Greenwood Press, 1980), 23–36; Teresa L. Amott and Julie A. Matthaei, *Race, Gender, and Work: A Multicultural Economic History of Women in the United States* (Boston: South End Press, 1991), 79–80, 274–9.

4 David Halberstam, *The Powers That Be* (New York: Alfred A. Knopf, 1979), 60.

5 John Hartley and Martin Montgomery, "Representations and Relations: Ideology and Power in Press and TV News," in *Discourse and Communication: New Approaches to the Analysis of Mass Media Discourse and Communication*, ed. Teun A. van Dijk (Berlin: Walter de Gruyter, 1985), 260.

6 Among the growing theoretical literature on nationalism, see Anthony D. Smith, *The Ethnic Origins of Nations* (Oxford: Basil Blackwell, 1986); E. J. Hobsbawm, *Nations and Nationalism since 1780: Programme, Myth, Reality* (Cambridge: Cambridge University Press, 1990); and Benedict Anderson, *Imagined Communities: Reflections on the Origin and Spread of Nationalism*, rev. ed. (London: Verso, 1991).

7 Mary Layoun, "Telling Spaces: Palestinian Women and the Engendering of National Narratives," in *Nationalisms and Sexualities*, ed. Andrew Parker et al. (New York: Routledge, 1992), 411.

8 Anderson, *Imagined Communities*, 6–7; he argues that nationalism is not an ideology, but rather, that concepts of nation, like those of gender or kinship, are neither inherently reactionary or progressive. Eve Kosofsky Sedgwick similarly defines nationalism as an "underlying dimension of modern social functioning that could then be organized in a near-infinite number of different and even contradictory ways"; see "Nationalisms and Sexualities in the Age of Wilde," in *Nationalisms and Sexualities*, 238.

9 Anderson, *Imagined Communities*, 25.

10 Hobsbawm, *Nations and Nationalism*, 142.

11 Anderson, *Imagined Communities*, 144.

12 Stuart Hall, "Toad in the Garden: Thatcherism among the Theorists," in *Marxism and the Interpretation of Culture*, ed. Cary Nelson and Lawrence Grossberg (Urbana: University of Illinois Press, 1988), 35–73, esp. 58.

13 See John Taylor, *War Photography: Realism in the British Press* (London: Routledge, 1991), for an analysis of family imagery used by the British press during wartime. The American media also promoted family ideals during World War I but did not continue to use this iconography to the extent or with the cultural resonance that occurred after World War II.

14 Loudoun Wainwright, *Great American Magazine: An Inside History of LIFE* (New York: Alfred A. Knopf, 1986), 122.

15 "U.S. Joins War in Africa," and "Men Who Fought in Solomons Come Home Wounded," *Life*, Nov. 16, 1942, 42–3.

16 This policy changed as it became clear that the United States and its allies would win the war. The first photograph in *Life* of dead American soldiers was George Strock's Sept. 20, 1943, Picture of the Week of dead soldiers lying face down on a beach at Buna.

17 Anderson, *Imagined Communities*, 144.

18 Robert Westbrook, " 'I Want a Girl, Just Like the Girl That Married Harry James': American Women and the Problem of Political Obligation in World War II," *American Quarterly*, 42:4 (Dec. 1990), 587–614.

19 "Missing in Action," *Life*, July 6, 1942, 15–21.

20 See Michael Renov, "Advertising/Photojournalism/Cinema: The Shifting Rhetoric of Forties Female Representation," *Quarterly Review of Film and Video*, 11:1 (1989), 1–23, for an analysis of the image of woman in wartime advertising and its impact on film and other visual media during the 1940s.

21 Ad for Oneida Community Silverware, *Life*, June 14, 1943, 14.

22 "Letters to the Editor," *Life*, Oct. 16, 1944, 2–4.

23 Westbrook, " 'I Want a Girl, Just Like the Girl That Married Harry James,' " 599. For a discussion of *Life*'s depictions of the Japanese during the war, see Karen Huck, "Seeing Japanese: The Constitution of the Enemy Other in *Life* Magazine, 1937–1942," paper presented at the annual meeting of the American Studies Association, New York, 1987.

24 *Life*, Sept. 25, 1944, 75–6.

25 "Home: It's the Same as Ever," *Life*, Sept. 25, 1944, 86–9.

26 "Coast Japs Are Interned in Mountain Camp," *Life*, Apr. 6, 1942, 15–19. For a discussion of the photographs and conditions at one of these camps, see John Armor and Peter Wright, *Manzanar* (New York: Time Books, 1988).

27 "Tule Lake: At This Segregation Center Are 18,000 Japanese Considered Disloyal to U.S.," *Life*, Mar. 20, 1944, 25–35.

28 Among the extensive literature on this topic, see, e.g., Eleanor Straub, "United States Government Policy toward Civilian Women during World War II," *Prologue*, 5:4 (Winter 1973), 240–54; Susan M. Hartmann, *The Home Front and Beyond: American Women in the 1940s* (Boston: Twayne, 1982); and Karen Anderson, *Wartime Women: Sex Roles, Family Relations, and the Status of Women during World War II* (Westport, Conn.: Greenwood Press, 1981).

29 D'Ann Campbell, *Women at War with America: Private Lives in a Patriotic Era* (Cambridge, Mass.: Harvard University Press, 1984), 113–16; see also Hartmann, *Home Front and Beyond*, ch. 5.

30 The OWI joined forces with the War Manpower Commission to launch national campaigns to acquaint the public with the problems caused by the labor shortage. The national promotion, titled "America at War Needs Women at Work," employed all the major mass communications media including advertising, film, radio, magazines, newspapers, leaflets, posters, and brochures. For more on this campaign, see Maureen Honey, *Creating Rosie the Riveter: Class, Gender, and Propaganda during World War II* (Amherst: University of Massachusetts Press, 1984); and Leila J. Rupp, *Mobilizing Women for War: German and American Propaganda, 1939–1945* (Princeton, NJ: Princeton University Press, 1978).

31 Honey, *Creating Rosie the Riveter*, 179.

32 People section, *Life*, June 15, 1942, 44.

33 Honey, *Creating Rosie the Riveter*, esp. 97–108.

34 "Soldier's Wife at Work: Peoria Girl Takes Over Her Husband's Business," *Life*, Sept. 7, 1942, 39–42.

35 Honey, *Creating Rosie the Riveter*, 23.

36 For instance, the government only allocated $1.5 million for child-care services during the war. For a detailed discussion of the issues of child-care and support services, see J. F. Trey, "Women in the War Economy – World War II," *Review of*

Radical Political Economics, 4:3 (July 1972), 40–57; and Anderson, *Wartime Women*, ch. 4.

37   Hartmann, *Home Front and Beyond*, 24; William H. Chafe, *The American Woman: Her Changing Social, Economic, and Political Roles, 1920–1970* (New York: Oxford University Press, 1972), 180.

38   Hartmann, *Home Front and Beyond*, 189.

39   Henry R. Luce, "The American Century," *Life*, Feb. 17, 1941, 61–5.

40   For a discussion of the debates between isolationists and interventionists, see Robert A. Divine, *Second Chance: The Triumph of Internationalism in America during World War II* (New York: Atheneum, 1967). Even before Pearl Harbor, interventionists justified immediate military commitments by equating current objectives with future global objectives. Personnel at Time Inc. were among the intellectuals, politicians, and economic leaders who explored planning for a postwar society. In May 1947, for instance, *Fortune* published several pamphlets on postwar planning; see Robert T. Elson, *World of Time Inc.: An Intimate History of a Publishing Enterprise*, vol. 2: *1941–1960* (New York: Atheneum, 1973), 17–20.

41   David W. Noble, *The End of American History* (Minneapolis: University of Minnesota Press, 1985).

42   By June 1942, the conversion to war production had resulted in a 29 percent drop in the production of consumer goods. The projected loss of business to the advertising industry was 80 percent. In response, the advertising industry formed the War Advertising Council to work with the government. Consumer businesses, constrained from selling goods, were interested in cooperating with the government, as advertising enabled them to keep their name in the public eye – indeed the war effort offered companies a perfect opportunity to associate their name with national goals. Publicity also continued to stimulate consumer desires. The Treasury Department assisted businesses by allowing war contractors to deduct publicity expenses from taxable income. This meant that businesses engaged in government contracts could run propaganda ads partially underwritten by the government. For an in-depth analysis, see Honey, *Creating Rosie the Riveter*, 31–6.

43   Published in *Life*, Jan. 22, 1945, inside cover.

44   Published in *Life*, Oct. 9, 1944, 9. See Roland Marchand, *Advertising the American Dream: Making Way for Modernity, 1920–1940* (Berkeley: University of California Press, 1985), for a discussion of advertising typologies; and Bruce W. Brown, *Images of Family Life in Magazine Advertising: 1920–1978* (New York: Praeger Special Studies, 1981).

45   Kenneth T. Jackson, *Crabgrass Frontier: The Suburbanization of the United States* (New York: Oxford University Press, 1985), 273.

46   *Life*, Sept. 3, 1945, 30–3.

47   Hartmann, *Home Front and Beyond*, 24, 92.

48   John Patrick Diggins, *The Proud Decades: America in War and Peace, 1941–1960* (New York: W. W. Norton, 1988), 181.

49   Elaine Tyler May, *Homeward Bound: American Families in the Cold War Era* (New York: Basic Books, 1988); see also Andrew J. Cherlin, *Marriage, Divorce, Remarriage* (Cambridge, Mass.: Harvard University Press, 1981), who argues

similarly that scholars must combine cohort studies with analysis of the historical conditions of the period.

50 Jürgen Habermas, *Legitimation Crisis*, trans. Thomas McCarthy (Boston: Beacon Press, 1975).

51 Quoted in Wainwright, *Great American Magazine*, 165; see Clifford E. Clark, "Ranch-House Suburbia: Ideals and Realities," in *Recasting America: Culture and Politics in the Age of Cold War*, ed. L. May (Chicago: University of Chicago Press, 1989), 171–91, for a discussion of how suburban architecture represented cultural ideals.

52 "$15,000 'Trade Secrets' House," *Life*, Jan. 5, 1953, 8–15.

53 Jackson, *Crabgrass Frontier*, 209–18.

54 Marty Jezer, *The Dark Ages: Life in the United States 1945–1960* (Boston: South End Press, 1982), 179.

55 Mollenkopf, *Contested City*, 41.

56 Jackson, *Crabgrass Frontier*, 190–245.

57 *Life*, Dec. 17, 1945, 27–35.

58 "Letters to the Editor," *Life*, Jan. 7, 1946, 6.

59 George Lipsitz, *Class and Culture in Cold War America: "A Rainbow at Midnight"* (South Hadley, Mass.: Bergin & Garvey, 1982).

60 "The Great Train Strike: Railroad Shutdown Brings Wrath of People Down on All U.S. Labor," *Life*, June 3, 1946, 27–33.

61 Ibid., 32.

62 *Life* also uses this strategy on the first page of the essay when the writer quotes a dentist from Des Moines who said, "Labor is like a kid who gets too much money from his parents."

63 Hunt's attention to proper behavior is reminiscent of the relationship between respectability and nationalism that developed in conjunction with the rise of the bourgeoisie in modern Europe. See George L. Mosse, *Nationalism and Sexuality: Respectability and Abnormal Sexuality in Modern Europe* (New York: Howard Fettig, 1985), 8–9, who argues that respectability played a crucial role for the middle class by distinguishing it from both the aristocracy and lower classes, as well as providing stability amid the upheavals of industrialization and modernization.

64 "Letters to the Editor," *Life*, June 24, 1946, 6.

65 Jezer, *Dark Ages*, 119–22; Douglas F. Dowd, *The Twisted Dream: Capitalist Development in the United States since 1776* (Cambridge, Mass.: Winthrop, 1974), 65–75, 105–7.

66 Hartmann, *Home Front and Beyond*, 8.

67 Jezer, *Dark Ages*, 120.

68 Hartmann, *Home Front and Beyond*, 7–8.

69 Jezer, *Dark Ages*, 203.

70 Charles S. Maier, "The Politics of Productivity: Foundations of American International Economic Policy after World War II," *International Organization*, 31:4 (1977), 607–33.

71 *Life*, May 5, 1947, 27–33.

72 "They Pour in . . . and Family Shows Refugees Can Fit In," *Life*, Jan. 7, 1957, 20–7.

73 In an excellent discussion of Tom Wesselman's Pop Art images of "the economy of domesticity," Cecile Whiting analyzes an image that bears a resemblance to these pictures in their display of consumer goods on the kitchen table; see "Pop Art Domesticated: Class and Taste in Tom Wesselman's Collages," *Genders*, 13 (Spring 1992), 43–72.

74 See Judith Williamson, *Consuming Passions: The Dynamics of Popular Culture* (London: Marion Boyars, 1986), 115–16, who discusses the family in relation to Gramsci's concept of political and civil society, arguing that the family participates in both sectors.

75 Jezer, *Dark Ages*, 192–3.

76 "Letters to the Editor," *Life*, Apr. 10, 1944, 4.

77 "Letters to the Editor," *Life*, Feb. 11, 1946, 4.

78 George Lipsitz, "The Meaning of Memory: Family, Class, and Ethnicity in Early Network Television," *Time Passages: Collective Memory and American Popular Culture* (Minneapolis: University of Minnesota Press, 1990), 39–75.

79 This reading of how photographs secure identification derives from Judith Williamson's *Decoding Advertisements: Ideology and Meaning in Advertisements* (London: Marion Boyars, 1978), 44–5. She argues that advertisements work by combining unrelated signifiers, like a product and an actress, leaving the reader to make meaningful connections between the two. Thus, the advertisement draws the reader into the space of the signified so that the reader identifies with the message.

80 John Fiske, *Television Culture* (New York: Routledge, 1987), 169.

81 "GM Paces the U.S. Pension Parade," *Life*, June 5, 1950, 21–5.

82 The article appeared in *Life*, July 13, 1959, 16–25, as part of a series of articles titled "Old Age: Personal Crisis, U.S. Problem." The title indicates the perspective the magazine took on this topic.

83 See Lee Edelman, "Tearooms and Sympathy, or, The Epistemology of the Water Closet," in *Nationalisms and Sexualities*, 263–84, for an excellent discussion of Cold War attacks on homosexuality and the role of the media in promoting virulent homophobia. He examines *Life*'s first photo-essay on gays and lesbians, "Homosexuality in America," which appeared on June 26, 1964, 66–80.

84 John Hartley, "Invisible Fictions: Television Audiences, Paedocracy, Pleasure," in *Television Studies: Textual Analysis*, ed. Gary Burns and Robert J. Thompson (New York: Praeger, 1989), 223–43; see also Horace M. Newcomb, "On the Dialogic Aspects of Mass Communication," *Critical Studies in Mass Communications*, 1 (1984), 34–50.

85 See, e.g., *Life Study of Consumer Expenditures*, vols. 1–6, conducted for *Life* by Alfred Politz Research, Inc. (New York: Time Inc., 1957).

86 Curtis Prendergast, *The World of Time Inc.: The Intimate History of a Changing Enterprise*, vol. 3: *1960–1980* (New York: Atheneum, 1986), 53–4.

87 "What Makes the Economy Tick? Capitalism Modified by Democracy Has Room for Lots of Incentives – Including Money," *Life*, Jan. 5, 1953, 16.

8

Visual Culture and Working-Class Community: Photography and the Organizing of the Steelworkers' Union in Chicago

LARRY PETERSON

In the history of photography, 1936 was the year of *Life* magazine. According to the Time-Life corporation, photojournalism burst fully mature from its corporate womb to dominate the way Americans viewed the news for the next thirty years.[1] In the same year, documentary photographs of the New Deal's Farm Security Administration (FSA), such as Dorothea Lange's "Migrant Mother," Arthur Rothstein's "Fleeing a Dust Storm," and Walker Evans's portraits of Alabama sharecroppers, burned the image of rural destitution into America's consciousness. Virtually forgotten among historians, 1936 also marked the birth of *Steel Labor,* among a host of other richly illustrated newspapers in the newly formed Committee for Industrial Organization (CIO). Without corporate or government resources, these new labor newspapers nevertheless quickly succeeded in reaching millions of American workers. Readers found in them neither the news as propagated by Henry Luce nor the threatened values of a traditional rural and small-town America as pictured by the New Deal, but rather ordinary urban industrial workers. Workers saw themselves reflected, not through the slick gimmickry of a Margaret Bourke-White or the manipulated realism of the FSA,[2] but in

An earlier version of this article was presented at the Seventeenth Annual North American Labor History Conference on Community and Culture in Working Class History, Wayne State University, Detroit, October 19–21, 1995.

photographs familiar to them from their homes, communities, workplaces, and associations.

The founding of *Steel Labor* should have been noteworthy. For over a decade, since the decline of the Industrial Workers of the World (IWW) in the mid-1920s, no major American labor organization had tried to contest corporate domination of the burgeoning photographically illustrated press.[3] The periodicals of the American Federation of Labor (AFL) appeared as living fossils of an extinct visual culture, perpetuated by a dwindling constituency of older skilled craftsmen.[4] The CIO created a medium new to the labor movement that communicated directly to industrial workers in a visual language relevant to their lives.

Steel Labor chose the modern format of photographically illustrated newspapers, resolved the financial and technical problems that had long hobbled labor publications by ingeniously exploiting available resources, and selectively adapted pre-existing visual models to the organizing of industrial workers. The modern picture newspaper appealed to younger, American-born workers but was also accessible to immigrants and rural migrants who could not read English fluently. Whereas earlier industrial unions like the IWW addressed workers through their ethnic associations in a dozen or more languages, the CIO officially spoke English but used photography as its universal language. The picture format met other crucial organizing needs as well. *Steel Labor* challenged the monopoly of company magazines and plant newspapers over workplace news. It provided an alternative source of information about unions and strikes in a style independent of the commercial capitalist press. Most important, it showed how workers could reverse earlier defeats to organize a union successfully and improve their lives. Photo-essays laid out in practical steps how real workers unionized the most impregnable corporate fortresses. The keys to success lay, first, in responsible national leadership accountable to rank-and-file members through locally elected officials; second, in the unity of workers across ethnic, racial, gender, geographical, and occupational divisions; and, finally, through negotiation with employers and political action when possible, backed by members' militancy when necessary. Taken separately, the photographic types and styles and the graphic design used to communicate these messages were unremarkable. But, through selection and combination, *Steel Labor* and other CIO newspapers developed a distinctive, new kind of photography, quantitatively and qualitatively unlike anything American labor – or its European counterparts – had ever seen. How the CIO revitalized labor's visual culture can be illustrated through the example of the Steelworkers Organizing Committee (SWOC) and United Steelworkers of America (USWA) on the south side of Chicago from the mid-1930s to the mid-1950s.[5]

Overcoming Obstacles to a Labor Press

The creation of *Steel Labor* shortly after the founding of SWOC was by no means a foregone decision. SWOC was an organizing committee, not an established union, and in its early years lacked a large duespaying membership and stable organization.[6] Not even the CIO had its own newspaper in 1936. When organizers spread out through Chicago's steel communities, they at first passed out leaflets, sometimes targeted at individual factories. George Patterson, an organizer at US Steel's South Works, also sent news releases to neighborhood newspapers like the *Daily Calumet*, with some success.[7] He and others realized, however, that SWOC needed more substantial organizing materials. Contacted by the editor of the *People's Press*, Patterson suggested to SWOC leaders that organizers pass out this paper at factory gates. Published in a popular picture tabloid style similar to the Hearst papers, the *People's Press* had been successfully used by the United Electrical and Radio Workers of America (UE) on the east coast, and in 1936 its midwest edition, published in Chicago, reported extensively on SWOC's drive against US steel. SWOC ordered up to 20,000 copies in the summer of 1936, and the *People's Press* briefly published a special South Works edition.[8] Its photographs, however, were supplied by commercial news photo agencies and dwelled on movie stars, sports figures, and light human-interest stories. Workers were enticed to read about SWOC in eyecatching headlines about the organizing campaign, juxtaposed with pictures of Myrna Loy, Henry Fonda, and King Edward VIII. Its attempts to exploit mass culture to advance left-progressive causes did not challenge the bias of commercial photojournalism and could not meet SWOC's specific needs.[9]

SWOC thus opted to publish its own organ, *Steel Labor*, in August 1936. Vin Sweeney was appointed editor. A 1921 graduate of the University of Notre Dame, Sweeney was a professional journalist who had previously worked for the International News Service and several Pennsylvania newspapers, most recently the *Pittsburgh Press*. John L. Lewis recruited him as public relations director of the CIO in May 1936 before assigning him to *Steel Labor*. Unions later created their own press organizations, like the Midwest Labor Press Association, and the USWA eventually founded its own United Steel Workers Press Association, thus establishing a source of labor journalism independent of the commercial news media. Printed in Indianapolis in letterpress, *Steel Labor* was initially sent in bundles to steel centers for distribution at union meetings and factory gates. From December 1937 it was also mailed directly to members, shielding them from public exposure to company spies. As membership grew, circulation quickly increased, from 90,000–100,000 copies in 1936 to over 1 million after World War II.[10]

The choice of a picture format was also problematic. Steelworkers' positive reception of the *People's Press* underscored the popularity of picture papers. The picture format, moreover, projected SWOC as a dynamic new kind of union by breaking with the stiff formality of AFL journals. The financial backing of the United Mineworkers of America (UMWA) covered the higher cost of production. However, *Steel Labor* faced a much bigger problem that had long plagued labor publications: where to find a reliable source of pro-union photographs sufficiently large to fill its pages. When German Communists in the mid-1920s founded the *Arbeiter Illustrierte Zeitung*, the most famous and successful labor pictorial of the era, they quickly discovered that bias and subject matter made commercial news photographs useless. They had to found an association of amateur worker photographers to create their own supply of photographs; commercial photographs were effective only when critical photomontage exposed their bias.[11] The American left had similarly resorted to montage in the decade before World War I, while American Communists also copied the Germans, with less success, by encouraging left-wing camera clubs in the 1920s and supporting the Film and Photo League after 1930 and the Photo League after 1936.[12] *Steel Labor* did not have the resources either to hire its own staff photographers or to support a nationwide network of union camera clubs; montage could not make up for the lack of positive depictions of the union; and sympathetic amateur photographers in the Photo League were concentrated in New York, far from the centers of SWOC organizing.

Thus, like the IWW, *Steel Labor* at first relied on cartoons and drawings as much as on photographs. It rejected the expedient of commercial photojournalism and procured its own illustrations in the way pioneered by the IWW between 1912 and 1924. The union commissioned photographs locally from independent photographers who were known by and sympathetic to the workers.[13] However, this source was not big enough; the IWW's *One Big Union Monthly* and *Industrial Pioneer* had never been able to find photographs for more than 50 percent of their illustrations.[14] SWOC exploited two new sources, widely available only from the 1930s, that allowed it by 1940 to publish a fully photographic paper with its own pictures.

First, the rapid expansion of commercial photography in the 1920s and 1930s spawned a large number of small photographic studios in urban centers. In Chicago, they were centrally located in and around the Loop and thus readily accessible to the union's district organization. They were also highly competitive and welcomed commissions to cover union events. The steelworkers' District 31 frequently employed a dozen of these studios at the height of the studio system in the 1940s and 1950s. Occasionally, a photographer advertised himself as a "union photographer." Typically, these studios were run as partnerships and hired locally trained photographers to cover assignments and laboratory work. Moreover, some of their employees were workers who had even been employed earlier in the steel industry, had acquired their training and experience in New Deal programs or in the military during World War II, and lived or worked as part-time freelance photographers in the same neighborhoods organized by the steelworkers' union. They were thus especially suited to produce the kinds of photographs the union needed.[15]

Second, *Steel Labor* filled in gaps through the participation of union members. For example, in 1938–9 photojournalists striking the Hearst papers volunteered their services to SWOC, covering such events as the commemoration of the 1937 Memorial Day massacre.[16] Moreover, members took pictures of themselves. Snapshots of strikes date back to the Pullman strike of 1894 (though they were probably not taken by workers), and ownership of snapshot cameras was fairly common among skilled craftsmen by World War I (though they were used primarily to depict family rather than labor subjects).[17] William Johnson, a Pullman worker and member of a craft union who was elected several times as the Socialist candidate to represent Pullman's ward in Chicago's city council between 1903 and World War I, was also an amateur photographer. In the late 1890s and early 1900s he used photographs he had taken on trips and vacations in stereopticon lectures at Socialist and other political and union meetings to illustrate industrial conditions and inequality.[18] The IWW developed this approach more systematically. For example, during the Lawrence strike of 1912 it distributed handheld cameras to strikers, many of them women, so that they could take firsthand pictures of the strike events, and then published the photographs of industrial conditions, strike demonstrations, and military repression in the IWW and Socialist press.[19] Industrial workers took up snapshot photography extensively in the 1920s and especially the 1930s, while the development of inexpensive 35 mm cameras simultaneously made serious amateur photography more affordable to them.[20] So ubiquitous was photography by the late 1930s that even young, penniless workers in the Civilian Conservation Corps (CCC) memorialized their experience in snapshots.[21] From organizing drives in the late 1930s to union conventions and picnics in the 1940s to strikes in the 1950s, steelworkers substituted the Brownie camera when a professional photographer was unavailable. Local studios, often the same ones hired on other occasions, then processed the film and made 8 × 10 prints suitable for publication.[22]

Thus, *Steel Labor* relied on a loose web of social interconnections among small studios, independent neighborhood and freelance photographers, amateurs around local camera clubs, and simple snapshooters. These interconnections made it possible for the steelworkers' union to break free of commercial news monopolies and to create and control its own image. The union's locals, subdistricts, and districts as clients commissioned photographs of themselves as subjects, from photographers who as producers were at least independent and accommodating and usually sympathetic (if not workers themselves), for union publications that then sent the pictures back to workers as union messages.[23] Armed with its own photographs, *Steel Labor* rejected the dominant imagery of workers of the 1930s and 1940s – whether *Life* magazine-style photojournalism, or FSA social documentary, or corporate industrial photography. What picture did it create for steelworkers, and how does this picture relate to the visual culture of the American labor movement and industrial workers?

───────────────── **Renewing Labor Traditions** ─────────────────

From the labor movement, SWOC selectively revived photographic types, styles, and subjects developed a generation earlier by the IWW, but revised their content, while ignoring AFL imagery. The single most common photograph depicted local union officials and members, casually posed as a group participating in the union's activities at the local headquarters. Represented directly, informally, and unpretentiously as ordinary workers, they symbolized the rank-and-file base from which the union drew its strength. However, unlike the IWW's often anarchically folksy and humorous compositions, SWOC's group portraits sent a new organizational message. They included clearly identifiable members from all the ethnic, racial, gender, and other groups organized by SWOC so that each could see itself represented in the union. And local officials served as a visual link between members and district and national leaders. For example, coverage of district union conventions paired wide-angle shots of the local meeting hall, reflecting the diversity of members in the delegates' faces, with officials and organizers on stage, leading but accountable to the rank and file. SWOC offered steelworkers a picture of unity across diversity, then showed the kind of industrial organization that could achieve it.[24]

In some organizing campaigns, the union referred explicitly to its target audience, and just as explicitly wrapped its organizational message in American labor history. When the USWA won the NLRB election at the Pullman Car Works in January 1944, *Steel Labor* ran snapshots of the rank-and-file organizers behind the victory, including two women with Swedish surnames and a Polish man. They symbolized the two largest ethnic groups in the factory, as well as women's crucial activism during World War II alongside male old-timers. The accompanying full-page article presented the USWA as the successful culmination of the labor tradition begun by the American Railway Union (ARU), the first industrial union in the rail car industry: USWA Local 1834 reversed the ARU's defeat during the Pullman strike of

1894, still remembered by many Swedish workers whose fathers and grand-fathers had participated in the strike, and wrote a "new chapter in American labor history."[25]

SWOC also appropriated the IWW's iconology of industrial solidarity. Like the IWW after the Everett massacre of 1916, SWOC commemorated Chicago's 1937 Memorial Day massacre by combining the symbolism of two working-class rituals – the Sunday visit to the family cemetery plot and the holiday picnic – in a celebration of labor's martyrs.[26] Like the IWW, its photographs depicted the assembled workers as a fluid, inseparable sea of heads and signs. But, unlike the IWW, SWOC played down the event at the time it occurred. Whereas the IWW quickly protested and used photographs of the victims' corpses in the Everett morgue to arouse mass support, SWOC waited a full year until the first commemoration before publishing pictures related to the Memorial Day massacre, and ten years before reproducing news photographs of the actual event. In 1937 SWOC avoided the visual association of strikes with violence and defeat that had so damaged the IWW's attempts at indus-trial organization a generation earlier.[27]

SWOC similarly revived images of mass rank-and-file militancy and action. Photographs of picket lines at factory gates dated back to the Homestead strike of 1892 and Pullman strike of 1894, and drawings of labor demonstra-tions went back much further.[28] Between 1909 and 1913 the IWW and American Socialists appropriated and combined both types in a new symbol-ism of the mass strike and militant proletariat.[29] At first SWOC did not seize on this imagery. It began to use it extensively only in 1941 during the second drive to organize Little Steel, when it sought new approaches to make up for the setback of the 1937 Little Steel strike.[30] Photographs of mass demonstra-tions were used only occasionally once steelworkers were successfully organ-ized.[31] The picket line at the factory gate, in contrast, emerged as *the* image of rank-and-file militancy in every subsequent steel strike, large or small. The steelworkers' union expressed its challenge to corporate capital through the symbolic elements of rank-and-file workers holding signs with their demands and barring access to the main gate, thus silencing the factory in the back-ground. But again it added an organizational message. For example, during the 1956 strike one occasion for photographs was the visit of District 31 director Joseph Germano to the picket line at Youngstown Steel. To be successful, the rank and file had to be effectively organized and led. But union leaders also had to know and represent the members. In this case, Germano was no big shot with a photographer in his entourage looking for photo opportunities, but rather the first among equals, photographed by one of the workers with a simple Brownie camera. The snapshots were as much mementos that reflected the significance of the union in workers' lives as pictures that could be blown up for reproduction in *Steel Labor*.[32]

Finally, the steelworkers' union seized on a variety of other visual associations with progressive labor traditions. Super wide-angle portraits, reminiscent of the Socialist Party in the early twentieth century, commemorated the assembly of delegates at national conventions. Published in two-page spreads in *Steel Labor*, bought by delegates, and displayed to local members, such portraits reinforced the position of local officials as the linchpin of union organization.[33] Photo murals in union halls borrowed folk elements from New Deal public art and avant-garde montage but refocused both to show how the founding of the local union and the victory of the New Deal with union support enfranchised workers.[34] Most important, Philip Murray came to personify the union. Just as the American Railway Union had used the figure of Eugene Debs around which to rally its diverse membership, so *Steel Labor* cut across the many divisions among steelworkers by singling out Murray. Like Debs, Murray was genuinely revered by those who came in contact with him; *Steel Labor* responded to real sentiment among members. Local organizers, without prodding, wrote to Murray requesting large, exhibition-size portraits to hang in union halls, along with smaller autographed prints for themselves.[35] While formal studio portraits were sent out for

Figure 8.1. Renewing labor traditions: Delegates at Steelworkers Organizing Committee Roseland–Harvey Subdistrict Convention, Harvey, Illinois, October 20, 1940. Chicago Historical Society ICHi 35893

display, *Steel Labor* more typically showed Murray speaking in front of a microphone to workers at mass meetings or conventions or over the radio, updating the way Debs, the organizers of the 1919 steel strike, and even Big Bill Haywood had been depicted, but in sharp contrast to the AFL's preference for studio portraits that likened union officials to corporate managers.[36]

Challenging Welfare Capitalism

The selective development of labor traditions by itself was insufficient to promote the union. SWOC also needed to neutralize the influence of the steel companies and commercial news media over workers. To organize the steel companies, the problem was clear: it had to challenge welfare capitalism, seductively pictured each week and month in scores of plant newspapers and company magazines, and show that only by joining the union could workers realize the promised benefits. From the late 1930s to the mid-1950s, *Steel Labor* step by step appropriated every subject and type of photograph companies had traditionally used to promote welfare capitalism, then subtly altered details and stylistic elements to replace the companies' message with that of the union.

For example, corporations had long tried to convince workers that capitalist mass production was a rational, scientific form of industrial organization in which each class of employee fulfilled its function as part of a cooperative team and was fairly compensated for its contribution. This ideology was presented pictorially in photo-essays of the stages of production. Workers' position – defined by the layout of architecture and machinery, designed by managers, and directed by foremen – appeared as the necessary consequence of technical and economic logic, not as a social relation of subordination and control. *Steel Labor* never directly challenged this type of imagery and rarely published industrial photographs.[37] Rather, it more subtly transformed the stages of production into the stages of union organization, from the founding of a local and election of local officials, to the challenge against corporate resistance in NLRB elections and final victory in the signing of the first union contract. Instead of being boxed into the perspectival hierarchy of plant architecture, workers were shown actively organizing and enfranchising themselves. By filling the company's visual sequence with a new content, photographed in a different style, *Steel Labor* subverted the pretense of scientific objectivity and made the authority of managers and foremen appear as mutable social relations.[38]

Outside the workplace, companies used organized sports, along with other activities, to instill values of teamwork and discipline into workers and to subsume their leisure activities within a corporate community. As early as 1937 organizers in SWOC's Roseland–Harvey subdistrict in Chicago chose sports as the first welfare capitalist program to challenge and began to organize the union's own leagues in an alternative union community. Like companies, the USWA promoted its teams in photographs, but with subtle differences. First, all members were treated equally; the company, in contrast, promoted stars who were kept on the payroll in no-work jobs to win games. Union teams were open to all workers; company leagues were segregated. And union members played for fun and for their friends and families and often dressed and posed casually for pictures; company teams displayed a quasi-military discipline.[39] Some historians, arguing that unions reacted to company initiatives rather than making their own, have emphasized the unions' limited resources, inability to compete with well-funded corporate programs, and racial divisions.[40] However, the union leagues had one big, unquantifiable advantage over corporations. They played in local parks and high-school gymnasiums, where team members had first met and become friends. Moreover, many high schools in Chicago's steel communities – and

Figure 8.2. Challenging welfare capitalism: United Steelworkers of America District 31 Softball Team, Harvey, Illinois, 1950s, Chicago Historical Society ICHi 35894

221

their sports teams – were already racially integrated. Through its leagues, the USWA perpetuated and reinforced ties among members that grew directly out of the local working-class community. When District 31 held its annual basketball tournament at Thornton Fractional High School in Calumet City, Illinois, midway between the steel mills of South Chicago, northwestern Indiana, and Chicago's south industrial suburbs, and illustrated the program with photographs of teams from the competing locals, it underscored its differences with the company leagues: its roots in the community, the free and equal participation of its diverse membership, and steelworkers' ability through their union to make their own lives.[41]

Welfare capitalism promoted a general image of the corporate "family" whose benefit programs took care of workers from birth to death. As contracts progressively subjected benefits to collective bargaining, photographs illustrating them disappeared from company publications and reappeared, as union accomplishments, in *Steel Labor*. Between 1945 and 1960 the USWA appropriated virtually the entire package of company benefits, made them contractual obligations, and greatly expanded their value and coverage. Unable to tout welfare capitalism as in the past, but unwilling to relinquish the field to the union, many companies tenaciously pursued imagery that associated workers' real families with the company's imagined "family." The USWA countered with its own picture of the union family. For example, when the Pullman Car Works in the late 1940s seized on the idea of depicting multigenerational families of Pullman workers in its plant newspaper, *Steel Labor* countered with a snapshot of a union member attending a meeting of the local at Pullman's Bessemer, Alabama plant with his son. *Steel Labor* not only showed how members could pass on their organization and beliefs, but illustrated its message with an African-American worker, in contrast to Pullman, which had until recently excluded black workers from manufacturing jobs in Chicago and thus was unable to find multigenerational examples of black workers to include in its picture of "Pullman's big family."[42]

The USWA local at the Pullman Car Works also published its own monthly newspaper, in which it subverted some of Pullman's most cherished images, like the commemorative portraits of retired workers with their factory departments. Company departmental portraits were always rigidly composed according to a hierarchy of managers, foremen, and workers; the pensioners always sat front row center in suit and tie, usually holding a gift; the workers always wore their work clothes; and the location within the factory was always identifiable by the plant architecture. In the union's version, the hierarchy disappeared: there were no managers or foremen. The retiree, already known to union members, was not visually distinguished from his fellow workers. The workers changed into their street clothes, and many wore union buttons. And the location was not identifiable to outsiders; although the portraits may have been taken at Pullman's Market Hall, where the local rented office space, only workers from the local and the community would have recognized it. Though company and union department portraits used the same technique to commemorate the same milestone, the union altered the posing and details to appropriate and redefine a traditional type of corporate industrial photograph. In particular, whereas Pullman used visual elements to instruct workers about their position and benefits in the company, the union assumed its members' knowledge of context and emphasized the local's celebration of a major event in their working lives.[43]

The second major corporate influence over workers came from the commercial news media. With little exaggeration, one can reduce news photographs of union-related stories to a handful of stereotypes: the outside labor agitator; workers happily leaving the factory at the beginning of a strike like schoolchildren playing hookie; the violence and destruction of life and property that inevitably resulted from strikes; the destitution that awaited workers who let themselves be misled by unions; and vulgar, brutal, corrupt union bosses, visibly inferior to the civility of corporate managers.[44] SWOC was acutely aware that the capitalist press constantly reminded workers of past unsuccessful attempts to organize the steel industry. It went out of its way to overcome the wariness, born of past defeats, with which many workers initially greeted SWOC.[45] *Steel Labor* therefore contrasted different subjects and photographic types to commercial photojournalism: local officials chosen by workers from within their own community; peaceful yet vigilant picket lines at factory gates demanding participation in, not escape from, responsibility; improved living and working conditions won through collective bargaining; and the revered Philip Murray, who made the steel barons look like the brutal thugs. Photographs of violent strikes, even when the union was the innocent victim of corporate or police repression, were not printed. The 1937 Memorial Day massacre provides a telling contrast of commercial photojournalistic and labor strategies. In 1937, Chicago's newspapers filled their pages with photographs of the police attack on strikers, unsubtle reminders of what happened to workers who defied their employers by joining SWOC. In 1939, the Hearst photojournalists, now on strike themselves, covered the commemoration of the massacre in pictures of workers' unity, highlighting their solidarity with those who "died that the union may live."[46] Nevertheless, when resistance to company violence led to victory, as at Bethlehem Steel's Lackawanna plant in 1941, *Steel Labor* incorporated pictures of mass marches, demonstrations, and picketing into the stages of successful union organizing.[47] *Steel Labor* took the structure of its graphic design – the photographic format, full-page layouts, photo-essays – from the commercial press, but filled it with labor pictures to convey a union message.[48]

223

——— **Complementing the Working-Class Community** ———

Within the broader working-class community the steelworkers' union presented itself as a new institution that complemented rather than competed with older, trusted ones like churches, ethnic associations, and the family. Visually, it sought to establish the union's separate identity, but in styles that lent it the legitimacy of familiar institutions.

First, SWOC projected itself as a multi-ethnic organization. Although it sought the aid of ethnic associations in its organizing campaigns, it rarely took or used photographs that explicitly referred to them and thus broke with an earlier labor tradition. Unlike the IWW, it avoided establishing its locals' headquarters in or photographing members against the architectural backdrop of ethnic halls, even though many organizing drives, as at Pullman, revolved partly around them.[49] Unlike the steel organizers of 1919, it did not allow photographs of ethnic leaders addressing their compatriots for the union. SWOC was acutely aware both that it needed the general sympathy of local ethnic associations and that ethnic divisions had undermined earlier attempts at unionization. It therefore organized steelworkers across, not by, ethnicity, and its group portraits in particular emphasized ethnic mixing rather than separation by highlighting in captions the varied last names of the union's members and representatives.[50]

The two exceptions to this approach involved African-American and immigrant Mexican workers. Steel companies had historically employed both groups to divide workers and undermine unions, and many returned to this strategy in the late 1930s and during World War II.[51] Moreover, both groups, because of their specific histories, especially previous exclusion from organized labor, required reassurance to be won for the union. In Chicago, organizers made sure that photographs depicted the integration of members and local officials across racial and immigrant as well as ethnic divisions, and *Steel Labor* published photographs that highlighted their membership in the union. But under pressure from black members to redress the legacy of racial discrimination, the USWA also appointed an African-American international representative to deal specifically with the problems of black members, and *Steel Labor* ran frequent articles expressing the union's support for civil rights legislation, with photographs of its leaders, black and white, participating in conferences and other activities.[52] During World War II, *Steel Labor* temporarily reduced the number of photographs of African-Americans, probably in an effort to dampen the wartime increase in racial conflicts among members. It focused its attention instead on women, the union's strategic target in wartime organizing drives. But on a higher level the CIO published a well-illustrated pamphlet about the contributions of African-Americans to the war effort with the CIO's support, and on a lower level USWA locals continued to depict the integration of the union and its support for nondiscrimination in hiring and promotion.[53] Mexican workers, as the most recent immigrant group, were sometimes photographed with explicit references to their immigrant and foreign-language associations.[54] In both cases, the steelworkers' union emphasized the integration of equal members but recognized the need for separate African-American and Mexican organization in a way it avoided for older immigrant groups.

Once established, the USWA proceeded to make itself a vital presence in steel communities. The union hall, in particular, joined churches, ethnic halls, and civic associations as a center of community life. In some cases the location of a local's headquarters was so well known and provocative that visual reinforcement proved unnecessary. Local 1834 of the Pullman Car Works located its headquarters in Pullman's Market Hall, the center of George Pullman's model town one block from the main factory gate, where in 1894 the ARU could not rent space and shopkeepers had been coerced by the company into denying credit to striking workers. By the 1940s, long after being sold by the company, it had become the neighborhood's community center. In a further challenge to the company, the local defiantly named itself after Eugene V. Debs. His name on the masthead of each issue of the local's newspaper tacitly reminded members that the USWA finished the work begun by Debs by reclaiming the company town for its workers.[55] Elsewhere, USWA locals erected new buildings in similarly symbolic locations.[56] Their plain, functional, industrial architecture fit well in steel communities, and *Steel Labor* proudly published architectural photographs of each new one as it was dedicated.[57] *Steel Labor* further reported on the community services emanating from the union hall – volunteer work for hospitals, sponsorship of Little League teams, banquets for pensioners, college scholarships – primarily in photographs. Both photographic style and subject were familiar to workers from their church, ethnic, and civic associations.[58]

Finally, frequent use of snapshots associated the union with the visual culture of the family. Sometimes this association was explicit and obvious, as in pictures of Labor Day picnics published each fall in *Steel Labor*.[59] But often, as in the pictures of picket lines at factory gates, the association was purely subliminal: the snapshot form itself sent the message that the union was part of members' families and worked to improve their lives.[60] Perhaps the most interesting use of snapshots came from USWA conventions in Atlantic City. Seaside photographers snapped groups of delegates as they strolled along the boardwalk between sessions, reproduced by *Steel Labor* in full-page spreads along with more formal photographs of the proceedings. Here were ordinary workers, as capable as any working-class family of unpretentiously enjoying a popular ocean resort, but gathered to

Figure 8.3. Complementing the working-class community: United Steelworkers of America District 31 Scholarship Test, Thornton Township High School, Harvey, Illinois, May 1955. Chicago Historical Society ICHi 35892

carry on the serious business of representing the members and their families back home.[61]

Conclusions

Several conclusions can be drawn from the steelworkers' experience. Most basically, labor photography comprised a substantial proportion of photography's explosive growth in the mid 1930s. In a still unwritten chapter in the history of photography, the CIO made photography a tool to organize workers and develop their consciousness.[62] The steelworkers' union selectively renewed labor traditions, appropriated welfare capitalism, and complemented trusted institutions of the working-class community, while contrasting itself to professional photojournalism and rejecting social documentary.

Methodologically, historians should treat photographs critically, as documents in their own right, rather than naively as unproblematic sources of information or illustration.[63] Photography is a means of representation that conveys messages optically, rather than verbally or rationally, through specific visual techniques and forms. The steelworkers' union understood the power of visual representation. When monopolized by corporations, it hurt labor's cause, but in *Steel Labor* it helped unionize a previously unorganizable industry. While the photographs' ostensible subjects and descriptive detail reported on the progress of the union, photographic process, form, and context unconsciously passed on messages of labor's history and traditions and forged social and personal associations with workers' lives.

Viewed critically as documents, photographs alter interpretations of SWOC and the USWA. In a study of Chicago's industrial workers between the world wars, Lizabeth Cohen placed particular emphasis on changes in ethnic communities and on the influence of welfare capitalism in molding steelworkers' consciousness. This study of labor photography confirms many of her conclusions, as well as her analysis of the CIO's "culture of unity."[64] However, there is no room in her study for SWOC's repeated allusions to labor traditions. Contrary to Cohen's analysis, these traditions were emphasized most strongly precisely in the period when the steel industry was organized, from 1936 to 1944; the appropriation of welfare capitalism and the promotion of local union halls alongside existing ethnic institutions, in contrast, dated primarily from 1945 to 1960 and presupposed a consolidated union that could respectively incorporate and complement these rival influences. When SWOC harkened back to the visual culture of the IWW and other, mostly radical or militant, labor organizations, it thought workers would respond positively. This belief was reasonable because the photographs that perpetuated this culture were largely taken and supplied by the union's own locals. They suggested neither belief in a kind of "moral capitalism" fostered by corporate welfare programs nor support for SWOC born negatively out of broken corporate promises during the Depression, but rather an indigenous workers' consciousness with its own history, traditions, and meaning. Chicago's steelworkers wanted a more equal and democratic economy, society, and political system. The ideologies of capitalism or socialism were less important than workers' right to determine and benefit from their own labor, protected by legally enforceable safeguards. Steelworkers' persistent, untutored visualizations of free association and participation – what no welfare capitalist had ever allowed, least of all in industrial photographs – spoke equally to the supporters of Debsian socialism, radical industrial unionism, social Catholicism, social democratic industrial councils, and pure and simple collective bargaining. The CIO's culture of unity, in short, was rooted first and foremost in the rich traditions of American labor.

Finally, this study of the steelworkers' union offers a practical reminder. A crucial part of labor organizing involves breaking through the ideological influence of capitalist media over workers. In the twentieth century, commercial visual culture, especially the various photographic media, has played an ever-increasing role in propagating this ideological influence. Since the 1930s it has been all-pervasive. *Steel Labor* taught workers that they could draw on their own strengths and traditions but should adapt them to new conditions and opportunities. Mimicking the capitalist media, turning to professional middle-class social reformers, and relying on the goodwill of even sympathetic governments all leave visual culture in other people's control to serve their, not labor's, ends. The labor movement and workers already possessed the resources to make and represent themselves. In the depths of the Depression *Steel Labor* successfully challenged the Time-Life corporation and its imitators by listening and speaking to industrial workers in their own language. The news media could be similarly challenged today.

Notes

1 *Photojournalism* (New York: Time-Life Books, 1971). *Life* was in fact a latecomer to photojournalism. See Bodo von Dewitz and Robert Lebeck, *Kiosk: A History of Photojournalism 1839–1973* (Göttingen: Steidl Verlag, 2001).

2 Cf. Erskine Caldwell and Margaret Bourke-White, *You Have Seen Their Faces* (New York: Modern Age Books, 1937); James Curtis, *Mind's Eye, Mind's Truth: FSA Photography Reconsidered* (Philadelphia: Temple University Press, 1989).

3 For the IWW's pictorial magazines, see *The One Big Union Monthly* (1919) and *Industrial Pioneer* (1921–6).

4 See, for example, the *Railway Carmen's Journal* of the Brotherhood of Railway Carmen of America and *Machinists Monthly Journal* of the International Association of Machinists. These two AFL unions competed against the CIO at Pullman's rail car building plants and other steel factories on the far south side of Chicago.

5 This article is part of a broader study of photography at the Pullman Car Works and in the neighboring working-class communities of Pullman, Roseland, Kensington, West Pullman, and Fernwood.

6 Organizers had difficulty collecting dues in Chicago throughout SWOC's early years and had to organize additional fundraising events, such as union-sponsored dances. See Chicago Historical Society (CHS), United Steelworkers of America (USWA) District 31 Collection, Box 124, Folders 4–10, SWOC Field Workers Staff Meeting Minutes. See also David Brody, "The Origins of Modern Steel Unionism: The SWOC Era," and Mark McColloch, "Consolidating Industrial Citizenship: The USWA at War and Peace, 1939–46," both in Peter F. Clark, Peter Gottlieb, and Donald Kennedy (eds.), *Forging a Union of Steel: Philip Murray, SWOC, and the United Steelworkers* (Ithaca: ILR Press, 1987); Jonathan Rees, "'Giving with One Hand and Taking Away with the Other': The Failure of Welfare Capitalism at United States Steel, 1901–1937," *Labor's Heritage*, 9 (Fall 1997), 20–31, 48–57.

7 CHS, George Alexander Patterson Papers, Box 6, Folders 3, 4; Box 7, Folders 1, 3; Box 12, Folder 1.

8   CHS, Patterson Papers, Box 6, Folder 3, Frank L. Palmer (editor/publisher of the *People's Press*) to George A. Patterson, June 23, 26, 1936; George A. Patterson to John Matuszyk, Sept. 15, 1936. SWOC continued to pass out the *People's Press*, along with *Steel Labor*, as late as September 1937 during its first attempt to organize Pullman. (Communist organizers for SWOC passed out the *Daily Worker* as well.) Newberry Library, Pullman Company Archives, Record Group 06/Subgroup 01/Series 04, Box 25, Folder 25, reports of Pullman Company informants on union organizing.

9   See the *People's Press* for 1936–7. Editorially, the *People's Press* was left-progressive and labor-populist in orientation. Politically, it was associated with Communist union organizers and the CIO's left-led unions and projected a broad, non-partisan, popular front ideology. Stylistically, it descended from the reorganization and modernization of the international Communist press in the mid-1920s, influenced especially by Willi Münzenberg. Introduced first in Germany in 1925, this style combined sensationalistic headlines and photographs in the manner of tabloid pictorials with an explicit left political message. The *People's Press* was problematic for SWOC less for its political orientation and associations than because it followed too closely the model of commercial tabloids and because SWOC needed its own organ.

10 *Steel Labor*, Dec. 13, 1937, May 1961, May 1966, June 1967, Apr. 1973, July 1973.

11 Leah Ollman, *Camera as Weapon: Worker Photography between the Wars* (San Diego: Museum of Photographic Arts, 1991); *Creative Camera*, 197–8 (May–June 1981), 70–89; Heinz Willmann, *Geschichte der Arbeiter-Illustrierten-Zeitung 1921–1938* (Berlin: Dietz, 1974); Joachim Büthe et al., *Der Arbeiter-Fotograf: Dokumente und Beiträge zur Arbeiterfotografie, 1926–1932* (Cologne: Prometh, 1978); David Mellor (ed.), *Germany: The New Photography 1927–33* (London: Arts Council of Great Britain, 1978), 45–53, 92, 109–10.

12 Chicago *Socialist* and *Daily Socialist* (1908–12); Ollman, *Camera as Weapon*, 42–3; Anne Wilkes Tucker, Claire Cass, and Stephen Daiter, *This Was the Photo League: Compassion and the Camera from the Depression to the Cold War* (Chicago: Stephen Daiter Gallery, 2001); Lili Corbus Bezner, *Photography and Politics in America: From the New Deal into the Cold War* (Baltimore: Johns Hopkins University Press, 1999); *History of Photography*, 18 (Summer 1994); *Creative Camera*, 223–4 (July–Aug. 1983); Steve Hutkins, "Unemployed Worker with a Camera: Leo Seltzer and the Film and Photo League," *Center Quarterly*, 9 (Winter 1987–8), 8–11; *The Photo League 1936–1951* (New Paltz: State University of New York College at New Paltz/Photofind Gallery, n.d.); Naomi and Walter Rosenblum, "Camera Images of Labor – Past and Present," in Philip Foner and Reinhard Schulz (eds.), *The Other America: Art and the Labour Movement in the United States* (West Nyack: Journeyman Press, 1985), 130–5. The Photo League sponsored the first exhibition of John Heartfield's photomontages from the *Arbeiter Illustrierte Zeitung* in the US.

13 For the best documented example, see Walker C. Smith, *The Everett Massacre: A History of the Class Struggle in the Lumber Industry* (Chicago: IWW Publishing Bureau, [1917?]), with photographs by Seattle photographer J. J. Kneisle. For

other examples, see *Solidarity*, esp. 1912ff.; *Industrial Worker* (Seattle); *The One Big Union Monthly*; *Industrial Pioneer*; Ralph Chaplin, *The Centralia Conspiracy* (n.p., n.d.); Justus Ebert, *The Trial of a New Society* (Cleveland: IWW Publishing Bureau, [1913]); Joyce L. Kornbluh (ed.), *Rebel Voices: An IWW Anthology*, 2nd edn. (Chicago: Charles H. Kerr, 1988).

14 IWW publications evolved from no illustrations in the *Industrial Union Bulletin* (Chicago, 1907–9), to cartoons and drawings in *Solidarity* (1909–12), to a gradually increasing use of photographs (1912–18), culminating in the more heavily photographic monthlies, *The One Big Union Monthly* and *Industrial Pioneer* (1919–26). However, even in the 1920s drawings and cartoons usually outnumbered photographs by two to one. For a similar evolution, see *The Comrade: An Illustrated Socialist Monthly* (1901–5) and the *International Socialist Review* (1900–18). The latter adopted a more popular illustrated format in 1908, published its first photographs of IWW-led strikes in 1909, and was fully illustrated with a mix of drawings, cartoons, and photographs by 1911. The *International Socialist Review* obtained photographs from an eclectic mix of sources – photo agencies, social reform organizations, local photographers and newspapers, other magazines, and snapshots from subscribers. Cf. Allen Ruff, *"We Called Each Other Comrade": Charles H. Kerr & Company, Radical Publishers* (Urbana: University of Illinois Press, 1997).

15 Personal communication, Leslie E. Peterson. Peterson was the son and grandson of workers at the Pullman Car Works, was employed by Pullman from 1939 to 1942, lived and worked as a freelance photographer in and around Roseland, and was a photographer for the Lawrence-Phillip studio in Chicago's Loop from 1946 to 1950. In addition to the Lawrence-Phillip studio, USWA District 31 is known to have hired Mishkin Photo Service (union photographers UOPWA Local 24), Chicago Photographers, News-Ad Photography, Flash Foto Co. Photographers, Berger Studios, Kaufmann & Abry, Murray News Photos, and Burke & Dean Photographers in Chicago, Mercury Pictures in Hammond, Indiana, Van Buren Photo Finishers and Paul Vincent in Gary, Indiana, and (for USWA convention photographs) Central Studios in Atlantic City. CHS, Prints and Photographs, G1986.360, USWA District 31, Box 6; G1985.0394, George A. Patterson Collection, Box 8, Folder 10, USWA delegates at the CIO's Seventh Constitutional Convention, Stevens Hotel, Chicago, Nov. 20–25, 1944, taken by Alexander Archer, Union Photographer, 75 Fifth Avenue, NYC. George Patterson had various photographic work done at the Calumet Studio in South Chicago. CHS, Patterson Papers, Box 6, Folder 4, receipt dated Apr. 8, 1937, and photostats of Chicago *Daily News* photographs of the 1937 Memorial Day massacre; Box 6, Folder 8, receipt dated Jan. 1, 1938.

16 CHS, Prints and Photographs, G1986.360, USWA District 31, Box 6, Folders 2, 3, 8; Patterson Papers, Box 6, Folder 8, Dec. 29, 1938, Harvey D. Wohl (CIO Committee for the Guild's Hearst Strike) to George Patterson, Dec. 22, 1938, Minutes, CIO Committee for Guild's Hearst Strike. The Guild, in return, received publicity for its strike in CIO newspapers.

17 Ferdinand Schapper, *Southern Cook County before the Civil War: Views of Blue Island, Index of Early Settlers, Their Families, Etc.*, vol. 3 (1917), 1018, 1020 (in

CHS). Amateur photography among workers has not been studied extensively for the United States. My conclusions are based on family photographs of various workers from the Pullman–Roseland area and in public collections, especially University of Illinois at Chicago, Special Collections, Italian American Collection. For a German example, see Wulf Erdmann and Klaus-Peter Lorenz, *Die grüne Lust der roten Touristen: Das fotografierte Leben des Arbeiters and Naturfreundes Paul Schminke (1888–1966)* (Hamburg: Junius Verlag, 1985).

18 Newberry Library, Pullman Company Archives, Scrapbooks, Record Group 12/Series01/Volume 26, *Chicago Chronicle*, Apr. 9, 1903; *Inter-Ocean*, Apr. 17, 1903.

19 Ardis Cameron, *Radicals of the Worst Sort: Laboring Women in Lawrence, Massachusetts, 1860–1912* (Urbana: University of Illinois Press, 1993), 140, 159. The photographs appeared, for example, in *Solidarity*, the Chicago *Daily Socialist*, and the *International Socialist Review* during the strike, and in Ebert, *The Trial of a New Society* afterwards. Some of the Lawrence photographs, in addition to many others from other IWW-led strikes and activities, are in the Walter P. Reuther Library of Labor and Urban Affairs, Wayne State University, Detroit, IWW Collection. The AFL's United Textile Workers of America, the IWW's main competitor in the textile industry, took up the IWW's idea during the Fulton Bag and Cotton Mills strike in Atlanta, Georgia, in 1914–15, when one of the organizers, Ola Delight Smith, photographed similar scenes from this strike. Gary M. Fink, *The Fulton Bag and Cotton Mills Strike of 1914–15: Espionage, Labor Conflict, and New South Industrial Relations* (Ithaca: ILR Press, 1993); Robert C. McGrath, Jr., "History by a Graveyard: The Fulton Bag and Cotton Mills Records," and Gary M. Fink, "Labor Espionage: The Fulton Bag and Cotton Mills Strike of 1914–15," both in *Labor's Heritage*, 1 (Apr. 1989).

20 This subject has not been studied for the United States. On related themes concentrating more on the middle classes, see John Taylor, *A Dream of England: Landscape, Photography and the Tourist's Imagination* (Manchester: Manchester University Press, 1994), and Jo Spence and Patricia Holland (eds.), *Family Snaps: The Meaning of Domestic Photography* (London: Virago, 1991). Pullman in the 1920s encouraged amateur photography among its employees by having its company magazine sponsor a "Pullman Family Vacation Photo Contest," judged by the chief company photographer, John P. Van Vorst. See *Pullman News*, 4 (Oct. 1925), 194–5; 5 (Nov. 1925), cover and 219. However, very few factory workers enjoyed the benefit of paid vacations, and the contest attracted primarily white-collar employees and managers, with a smattering of senior skilled craftsmen. Of the sixteen winners, five were women, well above their proportion in Pullman's work force.

21 University of Illinois at Chicago, Special Collections, Italian American Collection, 55.48.2a–c, 55.50.1a–b, 55.50.2a–b. Cf. Maren Stange, "Publicity, Husbandry, and Technocracy: Fact and Symbol in Civilian Conservation Corps Photography," and Sally Stein, "Figures of the Future: Photography of the National Youth Administration," both in Pete Daniel et al., *Official Images: New Deal Photography* (Washington, DC: Smithsonian Institution Press, 1987).

22 CHS, Prints and Photographs, G1986.360, USWA District 31, Box 6, Folders 2, 12, 13: Walter P. Reuther Library, photographs by Mary Kovner of SWOC-led strikes in Ambridge, Pennsylvania (1938), Canton, Ohio (1937), Youngstown, Ohio (1937), and Jones & Laughlin (1937) and of SWOC organizing in Aliquippa, Pennsylvania (late 1930s).

23 For the theoretical significance of how photographs are commissioned, taken, and used, see David E. Nye, *Image Worlds: Corporate Identities at General Electric, 1890–1930* (Cambridge, MA: MIT Press, 1985), ch. 3.

24 For example, CHS, Prints and Photographs, G1986.360, USWA District 31, Box 6, Folders 1, 2, SWOC organizers and Calumet district convention, Harvey, Illinois, Oct. 20, 1940. Some of these photographs were published in *Steel Labor*, Nov. 29, 1940.

25 *Steel Labor*, Feb. 25, 1944.

26 In Chicago, celebrations of labor's martyrs dated back to the dedication of the Haymarket Memorial in 1893 and to Joe Hill's funeral in 1915, both at Waldheim Cemetery. Melissa Dabakis, *Visualizing Labor in American Sculpture: Monuments, Manliness, and the Work Ethic, 1880–1935* (New York: Cambridge University Press, 1999), ch. 2; Gibbs M. Smith, *Labor Martyr Joe Hill* (New York: Grosset & Dunlap, 1969), ch. 9; *International Socialist Review*, 16 (Jan. 1916), 400–5.

27 For Everett, see Smith, *The Everett Massacre*, 8, 55, 119, 235, 243, 252, 260, 264, 282, 290, 294; *Industrial Worker*, May 19, 1917. For the Memorial Day massacre, see CHS, Prints and Photographs, G1986.360, USWA District 31, Box 6, Folders 2, 3, 8; *Steel Labor*, June 1937, June 17, 1938, June 1947. After 1947 photographs of the massacre were regularly published around Memorial Day and Labor Day and in articles on the union's history. On the USWA's strategy in general, see Lizabeth Cohen, *Making a New Deal: Industrial Workers in Chicago, 1919–1939* (Cambridge: Cambridge University Press, 1990).

28 Library of Congress, Prints and Photographs, Lot 7105, LC-USZ62-12996, Strikers Watching for Scabs, Homestead, 1892; Chicago Public Library, Special Collections, Historic Pullman Collection, HPC 1.13, Workmen outside Gate, Pullman, 1894 (this photograph in fact dates from 1891, possibly from an earlier strike at the Pullman Car Works, but was reprinted as a drawing in the Chicago *Times*, June 20, 1894, and has been inaccurately attributed ever since to the 1894 strike); Theodore F. Watts, *The First Labor Day Parade: Media Mirrors to Labor's Icons* (Silver Spring: Phoenix Rising, 1983); Howard B. Rock, " 'All Her Sons Join in One Social Band': Visual Images of New York's Artisan Societies in the Early Republic," *Labor's Heritage*, 3 (July 1991), 4–21.

29 Ebert, *The Trial of a New Society*, opposite p. 114; *Solidarity*, Mar. 2, 1912; *Daily Socialist*, Jan. 24, 25, 1912, with coverage continuing into February and March; *International Socialist Review*, 10 (Sept. 1909), 193–202; 10 (Oct. 1909), 289–302; 12 (Mar. 1912), 533–43; 12 (Apr. 1912), 613–30; 13 (June 1913), 847–51.

30 On Bethlehem Steel, see *Steel Labor*, Jan. 31, Feb. 28, Mar. 20, Apr. 18, May 23, June 25, July 25, 1941.

31 In contrast, *FE News* placed much heavier emphasis on mass demonstrations and militancy. The Farm Equipment Workers Union (FE), an offshoot of SWOC with

a local at the International Harvester plant in West Pullman, was a left-led CIO union. Many of its leaders belonged to or sympathized with the Communist Party, and photographs in *FE News* reflected their greater reliance on mass rank-and-file action. *FE News* also differed from *Steel Labor* in photographs that promoted support of the Soviet Union during World War II, solidarity with other, especially left-led, CIO unions, and activities of the international workers' movement. Cf. Toni Gilpin, "Labor's Last Stand," *Chicago History*, 18 (Spring 1989), 42–59. Newspapers of weaker CIO unions, like the United Chemical Workers (which had a local at a Sherwin-Williams paint factory adjacent to the Pullman Car Works) published few photographs of any kind before the 1950s.

32 *Steel Labor* published full-page and double centerfold spreads of pickets during the 1946, 1949, 1952, 1956, and 1959 strikes, as well as single pictures of many smaller strikes. For the 1956 strike, see CHS, Prints and Photographs, G1986.360, USWA District 31, Box 6, Folder 12, 13; *Steel Labor*, August 1956.

33 Compare *Daily Socialist*, Feb. 7, 1908, pp. 2–3, with *Steel Labor*, Oct. 1956, pp. 8–9, Oct. 1958, pp. 12–13.

34 For example, the USWA local in Aliquippa, Pennsylvania. See McColloch, "Consolidating Industrial Citizenship," 85; James Green, "Democracy Comes to 'Little Siberia': Steel Workers Organize in Aliquippa, Pennsylvania, 1933–1937," *Labor's Heritage*, 5 (Summer 1993), 4–27. On the New Deal's mural art and photomontage, see Bonnie Yodelson, *The Committed Eye: Alexander Alland's Photography* (New York: Museum of the City of New York, 1991); Merry A. Foresta, "Art and Document: Photography of the Works Progress Administration's Federal Art Project," in Daniel et al., *Official Images*, pp. 148–93; Stein, "Figures of the Future," esp. plate 130, p. 147; Christopher Phillips, "Introduction," and Sally Stein, " 'Good Fences Make Good Neighbors': American Resistance to Photomontage between the Wars," both in Matthew Teitelbaum (ed.), *Montage and Modern Life 1919–1942* (Cambridge, MA: MIT Press, 1992); Karal Ann Marling, *Wall-to-Wall America: A Cultural History of Post Office Murals in the Great Depression* (Minneapolis: University of Minnesota Press, 1982); Marlene Park and Gerald E. Markowitz, *Democratic Vistas: Post Offices and Public Art in the New Deal* (Philadelphia: Temple University Press, 1984); Bruce I. Bustard, *A New Deal for the Arts* (Seattle: University of Washington Press, 1997). *Steel Labor* did not use photomontage until the mid-1950s.

35 CHS, Patterson Papers, Box 7, Folder 5, Apr. 3, 6, 1942, correspondence between George A. Patterson and Philip Murray. Cf. Clark, Gottlieb, and Kennedy (eds.), *Forging a Union of Steel*. For Debs, see Library of Congress, Prints and Photographs, Lot 4403, Broadside Collection, LC-USZ62-43971, American Railway Union Memento, ca. 1995; Larry Peterson, "Photography and the Pullman Strike: Remolding Perceptions of Labor Conflict by New Visual Communication," in Richard Schneirov, Sheldon Stromquist, and Nick Salvatore (eds.), *The Pullman Strike and the Crisis of the 1890s: Essays on Labor and Politics* (Urbana: University of Illinois Press, 1999), 87–129.

36 For example, *Steel Labor*, Dec. 31, 1937, Aug. 25, Oct. 27, 1939, May 24, 1940. After Murray died in 1952 and was replaced by David McDonald, this focus on the union's leader degenerated into a staged and retouched cult of personality.

37 It differed here from older left pictorials. For example, the *International Socialist Review* had run frequent articles on industrial and technological change after 1910, illustrated with industrial photographs. See *International Socialist Review*, 11 (Aug. 1910), 75–9, for the steel industry; 11 (May 1911), 690–4, for coke; 13 (Aug. 1912), 105–10, for timber; 15 (Jan. 1915), 406–12, for automobiles; 18 (Nov.–Dec. 1917), 288–91, for coalmining. Like the IWW, it paid close attention to changes in the means of production, rooted in a Marxist analysis of the economy, but had to resort to corporate imagery as the only readily available source of industrial photographs.

38 For example, compare the many production sequences in the *Pullman Car Works Standard* (1916–19), *Pullman News* (1922–40), *The Carbuilder* (1940–80), *Pullman Standard Carworker* (1943–1950s), and Joseph Husband, *The Story of the Pullman Car* (Chicago: A. C. McClurg, 1917), with *Steel Labor*, Jan. 5, 1937, May 26, 1939, Jan. 31–July 25, 1941, Oct. 31, 1941.

39 CHS, USWA District 31 Collection, Box 124, Folder 4, Oct. 4, 1937, and Folder 7, SWOC Field Workers Staff Meeting, Minutes; *Steel Labor*, June 23, 1939, June 28, July 26, 1940, Oct. 31, 1941; CHS, Prints and Photographs, G1986.360, USWA District 31, Box 6, Folder 7, District 31 Softball Team. *Steel Labor* began to report more regularly on USWA teams in 1945 and on its leagues in 1947, when it created a sports page. For an example of segregated company teams and leagues, see *Pullman-Standard Log* (1943–5).

40 Elizabeth Fones-Wolf, *Selling Free Enterprise: The Business Assault on Labor and Liberalism, 1945–1960* (Urbana: University of Illinois Press, 1994); Elizabeth Fones-Wolf, "Contested Play: Company, Union, and Industrial Recreation, 1945–1960," *Labor's Heritage*, 6 (Summer 1994), 4–21.

41 CHS, USWA District 31 Collection, Box 120, Folder 7, Program, US[W]A-CIO District 31 Steelworkers Basketball Tourney, Thornton Fractional H. S., Mar. 4, 11, 1951.

42 Compare *Pullman Standard Carworker*, June 3, 1949, Jan. 13, 1950, with *Steel Labor*, June 1949.

43 Compare group portraits of the passenger car paint department at the Pullman Car Works, 1939, 1942, 1945, and 1949, in the author's personal collection, with *1834 Streamliner*, 4 (Feb. 1954), 4, in CHS, USWA District 31 Collection, Box 184, Folder 3. The union's photograph also sent a message about how workers retired. Prior to unionization, workers commonly worked into old age, until they collapsed on the shopfloor and were taken home by stretcher or in the factory ambulance. Many died before they could collect their company pension. Those lucky enough to recover returned later to be photographed with their former department. With the union, many more workers formally retired while in reasonably good health and actually collected their pension. For an example of retirement before the union, see Mario Manzardo, "Liberi Cuori" [Liberated Hearts], in Alice and Staughton Lynd (eds.), *Rank and File: Personal Histories by*

234

Working-Class Organizers (Boston: Beacon Press, 1973), 136. The USWA made pensions its major contract demand in the 1949 strike, and thereafter *Steel Labor* reported frequently, with photographs, on the union's success in ensuring members a secure retirement at a reasonable age.

44 Cf. William J. Puette, *Through Jaundiced Eyes: How the Media View Organized Labor* (Ithaca: ILR Press, 1992); Harry R. Rubenstein, "Symbols and Images of American Labor: Dinner Pails and Hard Hats," *Labor's Heritage*, 1 (July 1989), 34–49; Peterson, "Photography and the Pullman Strike." One of the very few major dailies that reported sympathetically on SWOC's organizing drives was *PM* in New York. At least two of its staff photographers, Morris Engel and Arthur Leipzig, were also members of the Photo League. Engel was one of the photographers who covered CIO organizing. Paul Milkman, *PM: A New Deal in Journalism, 1940–1948* (New Brunswick: Rutgers University Press, 1997).

45 Cf. Cohen, *Making a New Deal*; Clark, Gottlieb, and Kennedy (eds.), *Forging a Union of Steel*.

46 CHS, Patterson Papers, Box 6, Folders 4, 8; CHS, Prints and Photographs, G1986.360, USWA District 31, Box 6, Folders 2, 3, 8.

47 *Steel Labor*, Jan. 31–July 25, 1941. For an exception in the commercial media, see Milkman, *PM*, 128–31. *PM*'s coverage of SWOC's drive against Bethlehem steel in 1941, photographed by staff photographers Mary Morris and Alan Fisher, was similar to the photographs published in *Steel Labor*.

48 SWOC/USWA ignored the related field of social documentary altogether. On the rare occasions when it published documentary photographs, they did not depict steelworkers but rather subjects, like agriculture, associated with the FSA-style documentary of the 1930s. See *Steel Labor*, July 1959, p. 20, "In Pennsylvania, Migrant Farm Workers Face 'Slave Labor' Condition." Although social documentary had a rich tradition in the steel industry, dating back to Lewis Hine's work for the Pittsburgh Survey, its middle-class bias and target audience and its negative imagery made it unsuitable for the union. On social reform imagery, *Steel Labor* again broke with older left pictorials like the *International Socialist Review*, which printed photographs by Lewis Hine and from *The Survey*. *International Socialist Review*, 10 (Apr. 1910), 899ff., on Pittsburgh industry; 12 (Dec. 1911), 327–33, on Gary, Indiana. See also Margaret Byington, *Homestead: The Households of a Mill Town* (New York: Russell Sage Foundation, 1910); Maren Stange, *Symbols of Ideal Life: Social Documentary Photography in America 1890–1950* (Cambridge: Cambridge University Press, 1989); Grant H. Kester, "When Figures Are Facts: Visuality and Class in the Pittsburgh Survey," *Afterimage*, 21 (Apr. 1994), 5–9; Curtis, *Mind's Eye, Mind's Truth*.

49 *Industrial Pioneer*, 1 (Mar. 1924), 27, photograph of Philadelphia Marine Transport Workers and their headquarters in the Lithuanian National Hall; CHS, USWA District 31 Collection, Box 102, Folder 3, List of Polish associations and their leaders in Roseland; Box 124, Folder 4, SWOC Field Workers Staff Meeting Minutes; Newberry Library, Pullman Company Archives, Record Group 06/Subgroup 01/Series 04, Box 25, Folder 25, reports of Pullman Company informants on union organizing; William Adelman, *Touring Pullman* (Chicago: Illinois Labor

History Society, 1977), 34–5; Cohen, *Making a New Deal*. For a rare exception, see *Steel Labor*, Jan. 21, 1938, "Polish Committee Aids SWOC" (at Carnegie–Illinois Steel South Works).

50 See such regular features in *Steel Labor* as "News of SWOC Local Unions in Pictures," begun in 1940 and continued thereafter under a variety of headings.

51 For example, after 1937 the Pullman Car Works opened manufacturing jobs to African-Americans for the first time and also hired a significant number of Mexican immigrants (employed in small numbers since the 1920s). This change in employment policy followed the first, unsuccessful attempt by SWOC to organize a local at the Pullman Car Works in 1936–7. When racial divisions failed to keep SWOC from unionizing Pullman's Chicago area plants between 1942 and 1944, Pullman added southern whites to its employment mix in an apparent attempt to spark racial conflict. Cf. National Archives, Great Lakes Region, RG 228, Records of the Committee of Fair Employment Practices (Entry 70), Pullman Standard Car Manufacturing Company. I would like to thank Beverly Watkins for calling my attention to this file. See also CHS, USWA District 31 Collection, Box 124, Folders 4–10, SWOC Field Workers Staff Meeting Minutes; Box 184, Folder 3, LU 1834 Pullman-Standard Car Mfg. Co.; Claude A. Barnett Papers, Box 41, Folder 1, Press Releases, Associated Negro Press, Dec. 13, 1944. The earliest extant photographic evidence of black manufacturing workers at the Pullman Car Works dates from 1939. Group portrait, passenger car paint department, dated 10-6-39, in the author's personal collection.

52 McColloch, "Consolidating Industrial Citizenship," esp. pp. 58–61.

53 *The Negro in 1944*, published by the National Political Action Committee of the CIO; *Pullman-Standard Log*, Oct. 6, 1944, p. 1, "Union and Management Join in V-Day Committee."

54 For example, CHS, Prints and Photographs, G1986.360, USWA District 31, Box 6, Folder 2, ICHi 20951.

55 *1834 Streamliner*, 4 (Feb., Mar. 1954), in CHS, USWA District 31 Collection, Box 184, Folder 3.

56 For example, USWA Local 1033 in South Chicago established its headquarters across the street from the site of the 1937 Memorial Day massacre and later added a commemorative plaque and memorial hall. *Steel Labor*, May 1967, cover; Oct. 1969, p. 7. The USWA local of the John A. Roebling's Sons plant in Roebling, New Jersey, a planned company town built in 1905 that was similar in many respects to Pullman, located its new headquarters on the main street one block from the factory gate. Cf. *Steel Labor*, Nov. 1955, p. 7; Clifford W. Zink and Dorothy White Hartman, *Spanning the Industrial Age: The John A. Roebling's Sons Company, Trenton, New Jersey, 1848–1974* (Trenton: Trenton Roebling Community Development Corporation, 1992), 105–27, 157–63.

57 For example, *Steel Labor*, Sept. 1952, p. 10; Apr. 1957, p. 1; Dec. 1958, p. 13; May 1959, p. 7.

58 For example, *Steel Labor*, May 1957, cover and pp. 4–5; Mar. 1958, p. 16; Apr. 1958, pp. 12, 16. For the photography of Chicago's ethnic groups, see University of Illinois at Chicago, Special Collections, Italian American Collection; Giovanni

Schiavo, *The Italians in Chicago: A Study in Americanization* (Chicago: Italian American Publishing Company, 1928); *Poles of Chicago: A History of One Century of Polish Contribution to the City of Chicago* (Chicago: Polish Pageant, 1937); Dominic A. Pacyga, *Polish Immigrants and Industrial Chicago: Workers on the South Side, 1880–1922* (Columbus: Ohio State University Press, 1991); Rod Sellers and Dominic A. Pacyga, *Chicago's Southeast Side* (Charleston: Arcadia Publishing, 1998); Dominic Candeloro, *Italians in Chicago* (Chicago: Arcadia Publishing, 2001); Maureen O'Brien Will, "Bessemer Park," *Chicago History*, 19 (Spring–Summer 1990), 52–69; Catherine Sardo Weidner, "Building a Better Life," *Chicago History*, 18 (Winter 1989–90), 4–25. The photographs were similar because unions and ethnic associations hired the same kinds of photographers for a similar range of assignments.

59 For example, *Steel Labor*, Sept. 1954, p. 10, "*Steel Labor* Visits a Local Picnic." Even more explicit was the cover story of *Steel Labor*, Sept. 1957, on a day in the life of a woman member of the USWA local at the Trenton plant of John A. Roebling's Sons. The cover photograph depicted the subject stretched out on her living-room floor arranging snapshots in her family album, and the photograph was framed with black photocorners typical of albums in the 1950s. The story continued on the "Women's Corner" page with more photographs, following her as she left for work, discussed union affairs with the local's president, worked in the factory office, bought flowers on her way home, helped her mother prepare dinner, and ate dinner with her parents.

60 During the 1952 and 1956 strikes, *Steel Labor*, July 1952, p. 12, and Aug. 1956, pp. 8–9, carried the snapshot allusions even further. The strikes occurred during summer heatwaves, and members were photographed as they tried to stay cool – playing cards, sitting in the shade of factory gates, drinking refreshments, and sunbathing in front of the factories – as on a family holiday.

61 CHS, Prints and Photographs, G1986.360, USWA District 31, Box 6, Folders 1, 2, 13; *Steel Labor*, June 1946, p. 12; June 1950, p. 16; Oct. 1956, pp. 8–9. On seaside photography, see Taylor, *A Dream of England*, ch. 3; Audrey Linkman, *The Victorians: Photographic Portraits* (London: Tauris Parke Books, 1993), 167–73.

62 Among the few studies that touch on labor photography are McGrath, "History by a Graveyard"; Fink, *The Fulton Bag and Cotton Mills Strike*; and Harry R. Rubenstein, "Symbols and Images of Labor: Badges of Pride," *Labor's Heritage*, 1 (Apr. 1989), 36–51.

63 Cf. Curtis, *Mind's Eye, Mind's Truth*.

64 Cf. Cohen, *Making a New Deal*.

Sit-coms and Suburbs:
Positioning the 1950s Homemaker

MARY BETH HARALOVICH

T he suburban middle-class family sit-com of the 1950s and 1960s
centered on the family ensemble and its home life: breadwinner
father, homemaker mother, and growing children placed within the
domestic space of the suburban home. Structured within definitions of
gender and the value of home life for family cohesion, these sit-coms drew
upon particular historical conditions for their realist representation of family
relations and domestic space. In the 1950s, a historically specific social
subjectivity of the middle-class homemaker was engaged by suburban
housing, the consumer product industry, market research, and the lifestyle
represented in popular "growing family" sit-coms such as *Father Knows Best*
(1954–1963) and *Leave It to Beaver* (1957–1963). With the reluctant and
forced exit of women from positions in skilled labor after World War II and
during a period of rapid growth and concentration of business, the middle-
class homemaker provided these institutions with a rationale for establishing
the value of domestic architecture and consumer products for quality of life
and the stability of the family.

The middle-class homemaker was an important basis of this social economy – so much so that it was necessary to define her in contradictions which
held her in a limited social place. In her value to the economy, the homemaker
was at once central and marginal.[1] She was marginal in that she was positioned within the home, constituting the value of her labor outside of the
means of production. Yet she was also central to the economy in that her
function as homemaker was the subject of consumer product design and

Mary Beth Haralovich, "Sit-coms and Suburbs: Positioning the 1950s Homemaker," *Quarterly Review of Film and Video*, 11 (1989): 61–83. Reprinted with permission of Taylor &
Francis, Inc., http://www.routledge-ny.com

marketing, the basis of an industry. She was promised psychic and social satisfaction for being contained within the private space of the home; and in exchange for being targeted, measured, and analyzed for the marketing and design of consumer products, she was promised leisure and freedom from housework.

These social and economic appeals to the American homemaker were addressed to the white middle class whom Stuart and Elizabeth Ewen have described as "landed consumers," for whom "suburban homes were stand-ardized parodies of independence, of leisure, and most important of all, of the property that made the first two possible."[2] The working class is marginalized in and minorities are absent from these discourses and from the social economy of consumption. An ideal white and middle-class home life was a primary means of reconstituting and resocializing the American family after World War II. By defining access to property and home ownership within the values of the conventionalized suburban family, women and minorities were guaranteed economic and social inequality. Just as suburban housing provided gender-specific domestic space and restrictive neighborhoods, con-sumer product design and market research directly addressed the class and gender of the targeted family member, the homemaker.

The relationship of television programming to the social formation is crucial to an understanding of television as a social practice. Graham Murdock and Peter Golding argue that media reproduce social relations under capital through "this persistent imagery of consumerism conceal[ing] and compensat[ing] for the persistence of radical inequalities in the distribu-tion of wealth, work conditions and life chances." Stuart Hall has argued that the ideological effects of media fragment classes into individuals, masking economic determinacy and replacing class and economic social relations with imaginary social relations.[3] The suburban family sit-com is dependent upon this displacement of economic determinations onto imaginary social relations that naturalize middle-class life.

Despite its adoption of historical conditions from the 1950s, the suburban family sit-com did not greatly proliferate until the late 1950s and early 1960s. While *Father Knows Best*, in 1954, marks the beginning of popular discussion of the realism of this program format, it was not until 1957 that *Leave It to Beaver* joined it on the schedule. In the late 1950s and early 1960s, the format multiplied, while the women's movement was seeking to release homemakers from this social and economic gender definition.[4] This "nostalgic" lag between the historical specificity of the social formation and the popularity of the suburban family sit-com on the prime-time schedule underscores its ability to mask social contradictions and to naturalize woman's place in the home.

The following is an analysis of a historical conjuncture in which institutions important to social and economic policies defined women as homemakers:

suburban housing, the consumer product industry, and market research. *Father Knows Best* and *Leave It to Beaver* mediated this address to the homemaker through their representations of middle-class family life. They appropriated historically specific gender traits and a realist *mise en scène* of the home to create a comfortable, warm, and stable family environment. *Father Knows Best*, in fact, was applauded for realigning family gender roles, for making "polite, carefully middle-class, family-type entertainment, possibly the most non-controversial show on the air waves."[5]

"Looking through a Rose-Tinted Picture Window into Your Own Living Room"

After four years on radio, *Father Knows Best* began the first of its six seasons on network television in 1954. This program about the family life of Jim and Margaret Anderson and their children, Betty (age 15), Bud (age 13), and Kathy (age 8), won the 1954 Sylvania Award for outstanding family entertainment. After one season the program was dropped by its sponsor for low ratings in audience polls. But more than twenty thousand letters from viewers protesting the program's cancellation attracted a new sponsor (the Scott Paper Company), and *Father Knows Best* was promptly reinstated in the prime-time schedule. It remained popular even after first-run production ended in 1960 when its star, Robert Young, decided to move on to other roles. Reruns of *Father Knows Best* were on prime time for three more years.[6]

Contemporary writing on *Father Knows Best* cited as its appeal the way it rearranged the dynamics of family interaction in situation comedies. Instead of the slapstick and gag-oriented family sit-com with a "henpecked simpleton" as family patriarch (this presumably refers to programs such as *The Life of Riley*), *Father Knows Best* concentrated on drawing humor from parents raising children to adulthood in suburban America. This prompted the *Saturday Evening Post* to praise the Andersons for being "a family that has surprising similarities to real people":

> The parents...manage to ride through almost any family situation without violent injury to their dignity, and the three Anderson children are presented as decently behaved children who will probably turn into useful citizens.[7]

These "real people" are the white American suburban middle-class family, a social and economic arrangement valued as the cornerstone of the American social economy in the 1950s. The verisimilitude associated with *Father Knows Best* is derived not only from the traits and interactions of the middle-class family, but also from the placement of that family within the promises that suburban living and material goods held out for it. Even while the role of Jim Anderson was touted as probably "the first intelligent father permitted on radio or TV since they invented the thing,"[8] the role of Margaret Anderson in relation to the father and the family – as homemaker – was equally important to post-World War II attainment of quality family life, social stability, and economic growth.

Leave It to Beaver was not discussed as much or in the same terms as *Father Knows Best*. Its first run in prime-time television was from 1957 to 1963, overlapping the last years of *Father Knows Best*. Ward and June Cleaver raise two sons (Wally, 12; Theodore, the Beaver, 8) in a single-family suburban home which, in later seasons, adopted a nearly identical floor plan to that of the Andersons. Striving for verisimilitude, the stories were based on the "real life" experiences of the scriptwriters in raising their own children. "In recalling the mystifications that every adult experienced when he [sic] was a child, 'Leave It to Beaver' evokes a humorous and pleasurably nostalgic glow."[9]

Like *Father Knows Best*, *Leave It to Beaver* was constructed around an appeal to the entire family. The Andersons and the Cleavers are already assimilated into the comfortable environment and middle-class lifestyle that housing and consumer products sought to guarantee for certain American families. While the Andersons and the Cleavers are rarely (if ever) seen in the process of purchasing consumer products, family interactions are closely tied to the suburban home. The Andersons' Springfield and the Cleavers' Mayfield are ambiguous in their metropolitan identity as suburbs in that the presence of a major city nearby is unclear, yet the communities exhibit the characteristic homogeneity, domestic architecture, and separation of gender associated with suburban design.

Margaret Anderson and June Cleaver, in markedly different ways, are two representations of the contradictory definition of the homemaker in that they are simultaneously contained and liberated by domestic space. In their placement as homemakers, they represent the promises of the economic and social processes that established a limited social subjectivity for homemakers in the 1950s. Yet there are substantial differences in the character traits of the two women, and these revolve around the degree to which each woman is contained within the domestic space of the home. As we shall see, June is more suppressed in the role of homemaker than Margaret is, with the result that June remains largely peripheral to the decision-making activities of family life.

These middle-class homemakers lead a comfortable existence in comparison with television's working-class homemakers. In *Father Knows Best* and *Leave It to Beaver*, middle-class assimilation is displayed through deep-focus photography exhibiting tasteful furnishings, tidy rooms, appliances, and gender-specific functional spaces: dens and workrooms for men, the "family space" of the kitchen for women. Margaret Anderson and June

Cleaver have a lifestyle and domestic environment radically different from that of their working-class sister, Alice Kramden, in *The Honeymooners*. The suburban home and accompanying consumer products have presumably liberated Margaret and June from the domestic drudgery that marks Alice's daily existence.

The middle-class suburban environment is comfortable, unlike the cramped and unpleasant space of the Kramdens' New York City apartment. A major portion of the comedy of *The Honeymooners'* (1955–1956) working-class urban family is derived from Ralph and Alice Kramden's continual struggle with outmoded appliances, their lower-class taste, and the economic blocks to achieving an easy assimilation into the middle class through home ownership and the acquisition of consumer goods. Ralph screams out of the apartment window to a neighbor to be quiet; the water pipe in the wall breaks, spraying plaster and water everywhere. The Kramdens' refrigerator and stove predate the postwar era.

One reason for this comedy of *mise en scène* is that urban sit-coms such as *I Love Lucy* (1951–1957) and *The Honeymooners* tended to focus on physical comedy and gags generated by their central comic figures (Lucille Ball and Jackie Gleason) filmed or shot live on limited sets before studio audiences.[10] *Father Knows Best* and *Leave It to Beaver*, on the other hand, shifted the source of comedy to the ensemble of the nuclear family as it realigned the roles within the family. *Father Knows Best* was praised by the *Saturday Evening Post* for its "outright defiance" of "one of the more persistent clichés of television script-writing about the typical American family... the mother as the iron-fisted ruler of the nest, the father as a blustering chowderhead and the children as being one sassy crack removed from juvenile delinquency." Similarly, *Cosmopolitan* cited the program for overturning television programming's "message... that the American father is a weak-willed, predicament-inclined clown [who is] saved from his doltishness by a beautiful and intelligent wife and his beautiful and intelligent children."[11]

Instead of building family comedy around slapstick, gags and clowning, the Andersons are the modern and model American suburban family, one in which – judging from contemporary articles about *Father Knows Best* – viewers saw themselves. The *Saturday Evening Post* quoted letters from viewers who praised the program for being one the entire family could enjoy; they could "even learn something from it." In *Cosmopolitan*, Eugene Rodney, the producer of *Father Knows Best*, identified the program's audience as the middle-class and middle-income family. "It's people in that bracket who watch us. They don't have juvenile delinquent problems. They are interested in family relations, allowances, boy and girl problems."[12] In 1959 *Good Housekeeping* reported that a viewer had written to the program to thank *Father Knows Best* for solving a family problem:

Last Monday my daughter and I had been squabbling all day. By evening we were both so mad that I went upstairs to our portable TV set, leaving her to watch alone in the living room. When you got through with us, we both felt like fools. We didn't even need to kiss and make up. You had done it for us. Thank you all very much.

Good Housekeeping commented fondly on the program's "lifelike mixture of humor, harassment, and sentiment that literally hits home with some 15 million mothers, fathers, sons, and daughters. Watching it is like looking through a rose-tinted picture window into your own living room." In this last season, *Father Knows Best* ranked as the sixth most popular show on television.[13]

The verisimilitude of *Father Knows Best* and *Leave It to Beaver* was substantially reinforced by being based at major movie studios (Columbia and Universal, respectively), with sets that were standing replications of suburban homes. The *Saturday Evening Post* described the living environment of *Father Knows Best*:

> The set for the Anderson home is a $40,000 combination of illusion and reality. Its two floors, patio, driveway and garage sprawl over Columbia Pictures Stage 10. One room with interchangeable, wallpapered walls, can be made to look like any of the four different bedrooms. The kitchen is real, however.... If the script calls for a meal or a snack, Rodney insists that actual food be used.... "Don't give me too much food," [Young said] "Jim leaves quickly in this scene and we can't have fathers dashing off without cleaning their plates."

The home is a space not for comedy riffs and physical gags but for family cohesion, a guarantee that children can be raised in the image of their parents. In *Redesigning the American Dream*, Dolores Hayden describes suburban housing

> as an architecture of gender, since houses provide settings for women and girls to be effective social status achievers, desirable sex objects, and skillful domestic servants, and for men and boys to be executive breadwinners, successful home handy men, and adept car mechanics.[14]

——— "The Home Is an Image . . . of the Household and ——— of the Household's Relation to Society"

As social historians Gwendolyn Wright and Dolores Hayden have shown, housing development and design are fundamental cornerstones of social order. Hayden argues that "the home is an image . . . of the household, and of the household's relation to society."[15] The single-family detached suburban home was architecture for the family whose healthy life would be guaranteed by a nonurban environment, neighborhood stability, and separation of family functions by gender. The suburban middle-income family was the primary locus of this homogeneous social formation.

When President Harry Truman said at the 1948 White House Conference on Family Life that "children and dogs are as necessary to the welfare of this country as is Wall Street and the railroads," he spoke to the role of home ownership in transforming the postwar American economy. Government policies supported suburban development in a variety of ways. The 41,000 miles of limited-access highways authorized by the Federal Aid Highway Act of 1956 contributed to the development of gender-specific space for the suburban family: commuter husbands and homemaker mothers. Housing starts became, and still continue to be, an important indicator of the well-being of the nation's economy. And equity in homeownership is considered to be a significant guarantee of economic security in the later years of life.[16]

But while the Housing Act of 1949 stated as its goal "a decent home and a suitable living environment for every American family," the Federal Housing Administration (FHA) was empowered with defining "neighborhood character." Hayden argues that the two national priorities of the postwar period – removing women from the paid labor force and building more housing – were conflated and tied to

> an architecture of home and neighborhood that celebrates a mid-nineteenth century ideal of separate spheres for women and men ... characterized by segregation by age, race, and class that could not be so easily advertised.[17]

In order to establish neighborhood stability, homogeneity, harmony, and attractiveness, the FHA adopted several strategies. Zoning practices prevented multi-family dwellings and commercial uses of property. The FHA also chose not to support housing for minorities by adopting a policy called "red-lining," in which red lines were drawn on maps to identify the boundaries of changing or mixed neighborhoods. Since the value of housing in these neighborhoods was designated as low, loans to build or buy houses were considered bad risks. In addition, the FHA published a technical bulletin titled "Planning Profitable Neighborhoods," which gave advice to developers on how to concentrate on homogeneous markets for housing. The effect was to "green-line" suburban areas, promoting them by endorsing loans and development at the cost of creating urban ghettos for minorities.[18]

Wright discusses how the FHA went so far as to enter into restrictive or protective covenants to prevent racial mixing and "declining property values." She quotes the 1947 manual:

If a mixture of user groups is found to exist, it must be determined whether the mixture will render the neighborhood less desirable to present and prospective occupants. Protective covenants are essential to sound development of proposed residential areas, since they regulate the use of the land and provide a basis for the development of harmonious, attractive neighborhoods.

Despite the fact that the Supreme Court ruled in favor of the NAACP's case against restrictive covenants, the FHA accepted written and unwritten agreements in housing developments until 1968.[19]

The effect of these government policies was to create homogeneous and socially stable communities with racial, ethnic, and class barriers to entry. Wright describes "a definite sociological pattern to the household that moved out to the suburbs in the late 1940s and 1950s": the average age of adult suburbanites was 31 in 1950; there were few single, widowed, divorced, and elderly; there was a higher fertility rate than in the cities; and 9% of suburban women worked, as compared to 27% in the population as a whole. According to Hayden, five groups were excluded from single-family housing through the social policies of the late 1940s: single white women; the white elderly working and lower class; minority men of all classes; minority women of all classes; and minority elderly.[20]

The suburban dream house underscored this homogeneous definition of the suburban family. Domestic architecture was designed to display class attributes and reinforce gender-specific functions of domestic space. Hayden describes Robert Woods Kennedy, an influential housing designer of the period, arguing that the task of the housing architect was "to provide houses that helped his clients to indulge in status-conscious consumption... to display the housewife 'as a sexual being'... and to display the family's possessions 'as proper symbols of socio-economic class,' claiming that [this] form of expression [was] essential to modern family life." In addition to the value of the home for class and sexual identity, suburban housing was also therapeutic for the family. As Hayden observes, "whoever speaks of housing must also speak of home; the word means both the physical space and the nurturing that takes place there."[21]

A popular design for the first floor of the home was the "open floor plan," which provided a whole living environment for the entire family. With few walls separating living, dining, and kitchen areas, space was open for family togetherness. This "activity area" would also allow children to be within sight and hearing of the mother. Father could have his own space in a den or workroom and a detached garage for his car, while mother might be attracted to a modern model kitchen with separate laundry room. Bedrooms were located in the "quiet zone," perhaps on the second floor at the head of a stairway, away from the main activities of the household. While children might have the private space of individual bedrooms, parents shared the "master bedroom," which was larger and sometimes equipped with walk-in closets and dressing areas.[22]

This housing design, built on a part of an acre of private property with a yard for children, allowed the postwar middle-class family to give their children a lifestyle that was not so commonly available during the Depression and World War II. This domestic haven provided the setting for the socialization of girls into women and boys into men, and was paid for by the labor of the breadwinner father and maintained by the labor of the homemaker mother. The homemaker, placed in the home by suburban development and housing design, was promised release from household drudgery and an aesthetically pleasing interior environment as the basis of the consumer product industry economy.

"Leisure *Can* Transform her Life even if Good Design Can't"

Like housing design and suburban development, the consumer product industry built its economy on defining the social class and self-identity of women as homemakers. But this industrial definition of the homemaker underwent significant changes during the 1950s as suburban housing proliferated to include the working class. Two significant shifts marked discussions among designers about the role of product design in social life. The first occurred in 1955, when, instead of focusing on practical problems, the Fifth Annual Design Conference at Aspen drew a record attendance to discuss theoretical and cultural aspects of design. Among the topics discussed were the role of design in making leisure enjoyable and the possibility that mass communications could permit consumer testing of products before the investment of major capital. Design was no longer simply a matter of aesthetically pleasing shapes, but "part and parcel of the intricate pattern of twentieth-century life." The second shift in discussion occurred in early 1958, when *Industrial Design* (a major trade journal in the field) published several lengthy articles on market research, which it called "a new discipline – sometimes helpful, sometimes threatening – that is slated to affect the entire design process."[23]

Prior to the prominence of market research in the United States, designers discussed the contribution of product design to an aesthetically pleasing lifestyle, to the quality of life, and to making daily life easier. The homemaker was central to the growth and organization of the consumer product industry, but the editors of *Industrial Design* introduced the journal's fourth annual design review (December 1957) with an article positioning the homemaker as a problematic recipient of the benefits of design. Entitled "Materialism, Leisure and Design," this essay is worth quoting at some length. It first summarized the contribution of design to the leisure obtained from consumer products:

> We care very much about this world of things, partly because we are design-conscious and partly because we are American: this country is probably unique in that a review of the year's products is actually a measure of the material improvement in the everyday life of most citizens.... We think there is a good side [to American materialism], and that it does show up here – in quality, in availability and in the implication of increased leisure. Traditionally American design aims unapologetically at making things easier for people, at freeing them.

The article went on to respond to cynics who questioned whether homemakers *should* be freed from housework. *Industrial Design* argued for the potentially beneficial emancipation of the homemaker gained by product design:

> Automatic ranges and one-step washer-dryers leave the housewife with a precious ingredient: time. This has come to be regarded as both her bonus and her right, but not everyone regards it with unqualified enthusiasm. Critics belonging to the woman's-place-is-in-the-sink school ask cynically what she is free *for*. The bridge table? Afternoon TV? The lonely togetherness of telephone gossip? The analyst's couch? Maybe. But is this the designer's problem? Certainly it is absurd to suggest that he has a moral responsibility *not* to help create leisure time because if he does it is likely to be badly used. More choice in how she spends her time gives the emancipated woman an opportunity to face problems of a larger order than ever before, and this *can* transform her life, even if good design can't. In any case, the designer does have a responsibility to fill leisure hours, and *any* hours, with objects that are esthetically pleasing.[24]

These attempts to equate design aesthetics with leisure for the homemaker were occasionally challenged because they marginalized lifestyles other than the middle class. When Dr. Wilson G. Scanlon, a psychiatrist, addressed the 1957 meeting of the Southern New England Chapter of the Industrial Designers Institute, he argued that the act of "excessive purchasing of commodities [was] a form of irrational and immature behavior," that new purchases and increased leisure have not put anxieties to rest, and that "acceptance of some eccentricity rather than emphasis on class conformity should make for less insecurity [and for] a nation that is emotionally mature."[25]

Esther Foley, home services editor of MacFadden Publications, "shocked and intrigued" her audience at the "What Can the Consumer Tell Us?" panel at the 1955 conference of the American Society of Industrial Designers by discussing working-class homemakers. The flagship magazine of MacFadden

Publications was *True Story*, with a circulation of two million nearly every year from 1926 through 1963. In addition to the confessional stories in the company's *True Romance*, *True Experience*, and other *True* titles, in the 1950s and 1960s some MacFadden publications were "family behavior magazines," appealing to working-class homemakers who were "not reached by the middle-class service magazine such as *McCalls* and *Ladies Home Journal*."[26]

Foley introduced a "slice of life" into the theoretical discussions of design by showing color slides of the homes of her working-class readers. She showed

> their purchased symbols – the latest shiny "miracle" appliances in badly arranged kitchens, the inevitable chrome dinette set, the sentimental and unrelated living room furnishings tied together by expensive carpets and cheap cotton throw rugs.[27]

While Scanlon complained of the psychological damage to the nation from class conformity through consumerism (an issue the women's movement would soon raise), Foley illustrated the disparity between the working class and an aesthetics of product design articulated for the middle class. These criticisms recognized the social and economic contradictions in the growing consumer economy.

In the mid-1950s, *Industrial Design* began to publish lengthy analyses of product planning divisions in consumer product corporations. The journal argued that changes in industrial organization would be crucial to the practice of design. There were three important issues: (1) how large corporations could summon the resources necessary for analyzing consumer needs and habits in order to succeed in the increasingly competitive market for consumer products; (2) how product designers must become aware of the role of design in business organizations; and (3) how industrial survival in the area of consumer goods would increasingly depend on defining new consumer needs.[28]

The close relationship between research and design is illustrated by GE's 1952 "advance industrial design group" test of a wall-mounted refrigerator. The first stages of design testing measured the "maximum reach-in for average housewife's height." The article was illustrated with a picture of a woman standing with arm outstretched into a cardboard mockup of the refrigerator. While at first glance this is an amusing notion, the homogeneity of suburban development and housing design suggests that this physical identification of "the average housewife" is consistent with her placement within limited social definitions.[29]

This need for the consumer product industry to define the homemaker and, through her, its value to home life is well illustrated by a 1957 discussion among television set designers on whether to design television sets as furniture or as functional instruments like appliances. The designers talked about three aspects of this problem: (1) how to define the role and function of television in many aspects of daily life, not solely as part of living room viewing; (2) how to discover the needs of the consumer in television set design; and (3) the necessity of recognizing the role of television set design as part of an industry with a mass market. Whether modeled upon furniture or appliances, television set design should help the homemaker integrate the receiver into the aesthetics of interior decoration.[30]

The case for television as furniture was based on "better taste" on the part of consumers and the rapidly expanding furniture industry. Television set purchases exhibited a trend toward "good taste" and away from the "18th-century mahogany and borax-modern cabinets." In the previous year (1956), the furniture industry had had its best sales year in history. Given television's rapid installation rate in the 1950s (by 1960 it was in 87% of American households), designers agreed that people were spending more time at home and were more interested in the home's appearance. Designers needed to consider how the television set would play an important role in home redecoration and how they could assist homemakers in making aesthetic decisions concerning this new piece of furniture:

> There is not a homemaker who has not faced the problem of a proper room arrangement, lighting, color and decoration for television viewing – and even hi-fi listening. Yet let's be honest: the industry has not made an effort to solve this problem.[31]

The case for television as an instrument rested on its portability. Recent developments in the technology of television allowed for smaller, lighter sets that could be easily integrated into outdoor activities (on the deck behind the house) as well as into the kitchen decor (on the kitchen counter, color-coordinated with the appliances). For cues on how to proceed to fill this consumer need, television set designers suggested looking to the appliance industry, which had already proved effective in integrating products into complete and efficient packages for the kitchen.[32]

The consumer product design industry was aware of the significance of the homemaker in the economics of marketing and design. Before the introduction of systematic market research, her "needs" as a homemaker were partially determined by simply asking her what she wanted and then analyzing her responses. The 1957 Design Symposium at Silvermine invited five home-makers as conference participants, rather than merely as topics of discussion. They were not "typical housewives but five women with the ability to give serious thought and attention to shopping." These women helped the design-ers to analyze the way irons, washing machines, foreign cars, vacuum cleaners, and ranges functioned in their lives. But the feminine voice of the housewife was not the only voice heard at Silvermine. Four male "experts" discussed the need for consumers to communicate their "needs and wants" and described how the federal highway program, which fostered suburban expansion, would contribute to the development of a new mode of consumption: the shopping center. They also observed that deciding what product to buy produces tension that must be relieved.[33]

Hayden points out that housework is status-producing labor for the family, but at the same time it lowers the status of the homemaker by separating her from public life. The "psychological conflict" engendered by "guarantee[ing] the family's social status at the expense of her own...increases when women...come up against levels of consumption" that lie outside their potential for upward mobility.[34] Market research based its strength on turning these tensions around, placing them in the service of the consumer economy.

———— "Women Respond with Favorable Emotions ———— to the Fresh, Creamy Surface of a Newly Opened Shortening Can"

By 1958, the "feminine voice" of the homemaker was even further enmeshed in expert opinion from the field of consumer science and psychology. With high competition in the consumer product industry, it was no longer adequate to determine the conscious needs of the homemaker through interviewing. Instead, market researchers sought to uncover the unconscious processes of consumption. *Industrial Design* described the market researcher as "a man with a slide rule in one hand and a copy of Sigmund Freud in the other," who quantified the unconscious motivations in purchasing.[35]

The class- and gender-related tensions inherent in consumer decisions could be identified through market research and alleviated through design. The status of the home and the identity of the homemaker, two important subjects of this research, were based on the development of suburban housing and the concomitant change in shopping patterns. With impersonal supermarkets replacing small retailers, market researchers argued that "sales talk had to be built into product and packaging."[36] Survey research, depth or motivational research, and experimental research sought to link design with class and gender characteristics, and ultimately to determine how product design could appeal to upward mobility and confirm the self-identity of homemakers. Survey research also helped to correlate the "social image" of products with their users in order to design products that would attract new groups as well as retain current buyers. The Index of Social Position, developed by August Hollingshead of Yale University, organized data on consumers into an estimation of their social status in the community. A multi-factor system rated residential position (neighborhood), power position (occupation), and taste level (education). The total score, he argued, would reveal a family's *actual* place in the community, replacing subjective judgments by interviewers.[37]

Other types of market research focused on the function of women as homemakers. Thus the economic responsibility for class status lay with the father while the mother was addressed through emotional connotations associated with homemaking. Depth research looked into the psychic motivations of consumers and revealed, for example, that "women reacted with favorable emotions to [the] fresh, creamy surface of a newly opened shortening can." Ernest Dichter redesigned the Snowdrift shortening label with this emotional response in mind. A swirl of shortening formed the letter S emerging from the can on a wooden spoon (to further associations with traditional cooking). The *s*-shape integrated the name of the product with the emotional appeal of the texture of the shortening. Proof of these researcher deductions and, presumably, the typicality of homemaker emotions was provided by IBM data-processing equipment, which could handle large samples and quantify the results.[38]

Experimental research included projective techniques that would elicit unconscious responses to market situations, on the theory that consumers would impute to others their own feelings and motivations. These techniques included word-association, cartoons in which word balloons were filled in, narrative projection in which a story was finished, role-playing, and group discussions. For example, women were shown the following two grocery lists and asked to describe the woman who used each list.

Shopping List 1	*Shopping List 2*
pound and a half of hamburger	pound and a half of hamburger
2 loaves of Wonder Bread	2 loaves of Wonder Bread
bunch of carrots	bunch of carrots
1 can Rumford's Baking Powder	1 can Rumford's Baking Powder
Nescafe instant coffee (drip)	1 lb. Maxwell House Coffee (ground)
2 cans Del Monte peaches	2 cans Del Monte peaches
5 lbs. potatoes	5 lbs. potatoes

Of the women polled, 48% described the first shopper as lazy, while only 4% attached that label to the second shopper. Women who considered using instant coffee a trait of the lazy housewife were less likely to buy it, "indicating that personality image was a motive in buying choice."[39]

In perception tests, machines measured the speed with which a package could be identified and how much of the design's "message" could be retained. Role-playing at shopping and group discussions at the Institute for Motivational Research's "Motivational Theater" were "akin to... 'psycho-drama'" in that consumers would reveal product-, class-, and gender-related emotions that researchers would elicit and study. These techniques, it was noted in a contemporary article, "stimulate expression" by putting the subject "in another's position – or in one's own position under certain circumstances, like shopping or homemaking."[40]

Some designers complained that this application of science to design inhibited the creative process by substituting testable and quantifiable elements for aesthetics. In an address to the 1958 Aspen Conference, sociologist C. Wright Mills criticized designers for "bringing art, science and learning into a subordinate relation with the dominant institutions of the capitalist economy and the nationalist state." Mills's paper was considered to be "so pertinent to design problems today" that *Industrial Design* ran it in its entirety rather than publishing a synopsis of its major points, as it typically did with conference reports.[41]

Mills complained that design helped to blur the distinction between "human consciousness and material existence" by providing stereotypes of meaning. He argued that consumer products had become "the Fetish of human life" in the "virtual dominance of consumer culture." Mills attacked designers for promulgating "The Big Lie" of advertising and design, the notion that "we only give them what they want." He accused designers and advertisers of determining consumer wants and tastes, a procedure characteristic "of the current phase of capitalism in America... creat[ing] a panic for status, and hence a panic of self-evaluation, and... connect[ing] its relief with the consumption of specified commodities." While Mills did not specifically address the role of television, he did cite the importance of distribution in the postwar economy and "the need for the creation and maintenance of the national market and its monopolistic closure."[42]

Televisual Life in Springfield and Mayfield

One way that television distributed knowledge about a social economy that positioned women as homemakers was through the suburban family sit-com. These sit-coms promoted an image of the housewife and a mode of feminine subjectivity similar to those put forth by suburban development and the consumer product industry. In their representation of middle-class family life, series such as *Father Knows Best* and *Leave It to Beaver* mobilized the discourses of other social institutions. Realistic *mise en scène* and the character traits of family members naturalized middle-class home life, masking the social and economic barriers to entry into that privileged domain.

The heterogeneity of class and gender that market research analyzed is not manifested in either *Father Knows Best* or *Leave It to Beaver*. The Andersons and the Cleavers would probably rank quite well in the Index of Social Position. Their neighborhoods have large and well-maintained homes; both families belong to country clubs. Jim Anderson is a well-respected insurance agent with his own agency (an occupation chosen because it would not tie him to an office). Ward Cleaver's work is ambiguous, but both men carry a briefcase and wear a suit and tie to work. They have the income that easily provides their families with roomy, comfortable, and pleasing surroundings and attractive clothing; their wives have no need to work outside the home. Both men are college-educated; the programs often discuss the children's future college education.

Father Knows Best and *Leave It to Beaver* rarely make direct reference to the social and economic means by which the families attained and maintain their middle-class status. Their difference from other classes is not a subject of these sit-coms. By effacing the separations of race, class, age, and gender that produced suburban neighborhoods, *Father Knows Best* and *Leave It to Beaver* naturalize the privilege of the middle class. Yet there is one episode of *Leave It to Beaver* from the early 1960s that lays bare its assumptions about what constitutes a good neighborhood. In doing so, the episode suggests how narrowly the heterogeneity of social life came to be defined.

Wally and Beaver visit Wally's smart-aleck friend, Eddie Haskell, who has moved out of his family's home into a rooming house in what Beaver describes as a "crummy neighborhood." Unlike the design of suburban developments, this neighborhood has older, rambling two-story (or more) houses set close together. The door to one house is left ajar, paper debris is blown about by the wind and left on yards and front porches. Two men are working on an obviously older model car in the street, hood and trunk open, tire resting against the car; two garbage cans are on the sidewalks; an older man in sweater and hat walks along carrying a bag of groceries. On a front lawn, a rake leans against a bushel basket with leaves piled up; a large canvas-covered lawn swing sits on a front lawn; one house has a sign in the yard: "For sale by owner – to be moved."

Wally and Beaver are uneasy in this neighborhood, one which is obviously in transition and in which work activities are available for public view. But everyone visible is white. This is a rare example of a suburban sit-com's demarcation of good and bad neighborhoods. What is more typical is the assumption that the homes of the Andersons and the Cleavers are representative of the middle class.

In different ways, the credit sequences that begin these programs suggest recurring aspects of suburban living. The opening of *Father Knows Best* begins with a long shot of the Anderson's two-story home, a fence separating the front lawn from the sidewalk, its landscape including trellises with vines and flowers. A cut to the interior entryway shows the family gathering together. In earlier seasons, Jim, wearing a suit and with hat in hand, prepares to leave for work. He looks at his watch; the grandfather clock to the left of the door shows the time as nearly 8:30 A.M. Margaret, wearing a blouse, sweater, and skirt, brings Jim his briefcase and kisses him goodbye. The three Anderson children giggle all in a row on the stairway leading up to the second-floor bedrooms. In later seasons, after the long shot of the house, the Anderson family gathers in the entryway to greet Jim as he returns from work. Margaret, wearing a dress too fancy for housework, kisses him at the doorway as the children cluster about them, uniting the family in the home.

The opening credits of *Leave It to Beaver* gradually evolved from an emphasis on the younger child to his placement within the neighborhood and then the family. The earliest episodes open with childlike etchings drawn in a wet concrete sidewalk. Middle seasons feature Beaver walking home along a street with single-family homes set back behind manicured, unfenced lawns. In later seasons, the Cleaver family is shown leaving their two-story home for a picnic trip: Ward carries the thermal cooler, June (in a dress, even for a picnic) carries the basket, and Wally and Beaver climb into the Cleavers' late model car. While *Father Knows Best* coheres around the family ensemble, *Leave It to Beaver* decenters the family around the younger child, whose rearing provides problems that the older child has either already surmounted or has never had.

The narrative space of these programs is dominated by the domestic space of the home. *Father Knows Best* leaves the home environment much less often than does *Leave It to Beaver*, which often focuses on Beaver at school. This placing of the family within the home contributes in large measure to the ability of these programs to "seem real." During the first season of *Leave It to Beaver*, the Cleavers' home was an older design rather than a suburban dream house. The kitchen was large and homey, with glass and wood cabinets. The rooms were separated by walls and closed doors. By the 1960s, the Cleavers, like the Andersons, were living in the "open floor plan," a popular housing design of the 1950s. As you enter the home, to your far left is the den, the private space of the father. To the right of the den is the stairway leading to the "quiet zone" of the bedrooms. To your right is the living room, visible through a wide and open entryway the size of two doors. Another wide doorway integrates the living room with the formal dining room. A swinging door separates the dining room from the kitchen. The deep-focus photography typical of these sit-coms displays the expanse of living space in this "activity area."

While the Cleaver children share a bedroom, it is equipped with a private bathroom and a portable television set. Ward and June's bedroom is small, with twin beds. Since it is not a site of narrative activity, which typically takes place in the boys' room or on the main floor of the home, the parents' bedroom is rarely seen. These two small bedrooms belie the scale of the house when it is seen in long shot.

The Andersons' home makes more use of the potential of the bedrooms for narrative space. With four bedrooms, the Anderson home allows each of the children the luxury of his or her own room. Jim and Margaret's "master" bedroom, larger than those of their children, has twin beds separated by a nightstand and lamp, a walk-in closet, a dressing table, armchairs, and a small alcove. In this design, the "master" bedroom is conceived as a private space for parents, but the Anderson children have easy access to their parents' bedroom. The Andersons, however, have only one bathroom. Betty has commented that when she gets married she will have three bathrooms because "there won't always be two of us."

The Andersons and the Cleavers also share aspects of the decor of their homes, displaying possessions in a comfortably unostentatious way. Immediately to the left of the Andersons' front door is a large free-standing grandfather clock; to the right and directly across the room are built-in bookcases filled with hardcover books. In earlier seasons of *Leave It to Beaver*, the books (also hardbound) were on shelves in the living room. Later, these books were relocated to Ward's study, to line the many built-in bookshelves behind his desk.

The two families have similar tastes in wall decorations and furnishings. Among the landscapes in heavy wood frames on the Cleavers' walls are pictures of sailing vessels and reproductions of "great art," such as "Pinkie" by Sir Thomas Lawrence. While the Andersons do not completely share the Cleavers' penchant for candelabra on the walls and tables, their walls are tastefully decorated with smaller landscapes. Curiously, neither house engages in the prominent display of family photographs.

The large living room in each home has a fireplace. There is plenty of room to walk around the furniture, which is overstuffed and comfortable or of hardwood. The formal dining room in both homes includes a large wooden table and chairs that can seat six comfortably. It is here that the families have their evening meals. A sideboard or hutch displays dishes, soup tureens, and the like. The kitchen contains a smaller, more utilitarian set of table and chairs, where breakfast is eaten. Small appliances such as a toaster, mixer, and electric coffeepot sit out on counters. A wall-mounted roll of paper towels is close to the sink. The Andersons' outdoor patio has a built-in brick oven, singed from use.

While both homes establish gender-specific areas for women and men, *Father Knows Best* is less repressive in its association of this space with familial roles. Both Jim Anderson and Ward Cleaver have dens; Ward is often shown doing ambiguous paperwork in his, the rows of hardcover books behind his desk suggesting his association with knowledge and mental work. June's forays into Ward's space tend to be brief, usually in search of his advice on how to handle the boys. As Ward works on papers, June sits in a corner chair sewing a button on Beaver's shirt. Ward's den is often the site of father-to-son talks. Its doorway is wide and open, revealing the cabinet-model television that Beaver occasionally watches. While Jim also has a den, it is much less often the site of narrative action, and its door is usually closed.

Workrooms and garages are also arenas for male activity, providing storage space for paint or lawn care equipment or a place to work on the car. The suburban homemaker does not have an equivalent private space. Instead, the woman shares her kitchen with other family members, while the living and dining rooms are designated as family spheres. In typical episodes of *Leave It to Beaver*, June's encounters with family members generally take place in the kitchen, while Ward's tend to occur throughout the house. As her sons pass through her space, June is putting up paper towels, tossing a salad, unpacking groceries, or making meals. Margaret, having an older daughter, is often able to turn this family/female space over to her. She is also more often placed within other domestic locations: the patio, the attic, the living room.

Both Margaret and June exemplify Robert Woods Kennedy's theory that housing design should display the housewife as a sexual being, but this is accomplished not so much through their positioning within domestic space as through costume. June's ubiquitous pearls, stockings and heels, and cinch-waisted dresses are amusing in their distinct contradiction of the realities of housework. While Margaret also wears dresses or skirts, she tends to be costumed more casually, and sometimes wears a smock when doing house-work. Margaret is also occasionally seen in relatively sloppy clothes suitable for dirty work but marked as inappropriate to her status as a sexual being.

In one episode of *Father Knows Best*, Margaret is dressed in dungarees, sweatshirt, and loafers, her hair covered by a scarf as she scrubs paint from her youngest daughter, Kathy. When Betty sees her, she laughs, "If you aren't a glamorous picture!" As Jim arrives home early, Betty counsels Margaret, "You can't let Father see you like this!" Betty takes over scrubbing and dressing Kathy while Margaret hurries off to change before Jim sees her. But Margaret is caught, embarrassed at not being dressed as a suburban object of desire. Jim good-naturedly echoes Betty's comment: "If you aren't a glamor-ous picture!" He calms Margaret's minor distress at being seen by her husband in this departure from her usual toilette: "You know you always look great to me."

As this example shows, the agreement among Jim, Margaret, and Betty on the proper attire for the suburban homemaker indicates the success with which Betty has been socialized within the family. Yet even though both programs were created around "realistic" storylines of family life, the nurturing function of the home and the gender-specific roles of father and mother are handled very differently in *Father Knows Best* and *Leave It to Beaver*.

By 1960, Betty, whom Jim calls "Princess," had been counseled through adolescent dating and was shown to have "good sense" and maturity in her relations with boys. Well-groomed and well-dressed like her mother, Betty could easily substitute for Margaret in household tasks. In one episode, Jim and Margaret decide that their lives revolve too much around their children ("trapped," "like servants") and they try to spend a weekend away, leaving Betty in charge. While Betty handles the situation smoothly, Jim and Margaret are finally happier continuing their weekend at Cedar Lodge with all of the children along.

Bud, the son, participates in the excitement of discovery and self-definition outside of personal appearance. A normal boy in the process of becoming a man, he gets dirty at sports and tinkering with engines, replaces blown fuses, and cuts the grass. Unlike Betty, Bud has to be convinced that he can handle dating; Jim counsels him that this awkward stage is normal and one that Jim himself has gone through.

Kathy (whose pet name is "Kitten"), in contrast to her older sister, is a tomboy and is interested in sports. By 1959, *Good Housekeeping* purred that

> Kathy seems to have got the idea it might be more fun to appeal to a boy than to be one. At the rate she's going, it won't be long before [Jim and Margaret] are playing grandparents.[43]

Film and television writer Danny Peary was also pleased with Kathy's development, but for a very different reason: in the 1977 *Father Knows Best* "Reunion" show, Kathy was an unmarried gym teacher. Peary also felt that *Father Knows Best* was different from other suburban family sit-coms in its representation of women. "The three Anderson females . . . were intelligent, proud, and resourceful. Margaret was Jim's equal, loved and respected for her wisdom."[44] The traits that characterize Margaret in her equality are her patience, good humor, and easy confidence. Unlike Ward Cleaver, Jim is not immune to wifely banter.

In one episode, Jim overhears Betty and her friend Armand rehearsing a play, and assumes they are going to elope. Margaret has more faith in their daughter and good-naturedly tries to dissuade Jim from his anxiety: "Jim, when are you going to stop acting like a comic-strip father?" In the same episode, Jim and Margaret play Scrabble, an activity that the episode suggests they do together often. "Dad's getting beat at Scrabble again," observes Bud. Kathy notices, "He's stuck with the Z again." Margaret looks up Jim's Z word in the dictionary, doubting its existence. Margaret is able to continually best Jim at this word game and Jim is willing to play despite certain defeat.

In contrast to this easy-going family with character traits allowing for many types of familial interaction, *Leave It to Beaver* tells another story about gender relations in the home. June does not share Margaret's status in intelligence. In a discussion of their sons' academic performances, June remarks, "We can't all be *A* students; maybe the boys are like me." Ward responds, "No, they are *not* like you" and then catches himself. Nor does June share Margaret's witty and confident relationship with her husband. She typically defers to Ward's greater sense for raising their two sons. Wondering how to approach instances of boyish behavior, June positions herself firmly at a loss. She frequently asks, mystified, "Ward, did boys do this when you were their age?" Ward always reassures June that whatever their sons are doing (brothers fighting, for example) is a normal stage of development for boys, imparting to her his superior social and familial knowledge. Like her sons, June acknowledges the need for Ward's guidance. Unlike Margaret, June is structured on the periphery of the socialization of her children, in the passive space of the home.

Ward, often a misogynist, encourages the boys to adopt his own cynical attitude toward their mother and women in general. In an early episode, Ward is replacing the plug on the toaster. He explains to Beaver that "your mother" always pulls it out by the cord instead of properly grabbing it by the plug. Beaver is impressed by Ward's knowledge of " 'lectricity," to which Ward responds by positioning his knowledge as a condition of June's ineptness. "I know enough to stay about one jump ahead of your mother." Unlike *Father Knows Best*, *Leave It to Beaver* works to contain June's potential threat to patriarchal authority. When June asks why Beaver would appear to be unusually shy about meeting a girl, Ward wonders as well: "He doesn't know enough about life to be afraid of women."

In the episode in which Eddie Haskell moves out of the home, Ward sides with the Haskells by forbidding both his sons to visit Eddie's bachelor digs. As Ward telephones another father to ask him to do the same, June timidly asks (covering a bowl to be put in the refrigerator), "Ward, aren't you getting terribly involved?" Ward answers that if this were their son he would appreciate the support of other parents. June murmurs assent as Ward and June continue the process of defining June's function within the family in terms of passivity and deference.

While *Father Knows Best* and *Leave It to Beaver* position the homemaker in family life quite differently, both women effortlessly maintain the domestic space of the family environment. In their representation of women's work in the home, these programs show the great ease and lack of drudgery with which Margaret and June keep their homes tidy and spotlessly clean. In any episode, these homemakers can be seen engaged in their daily housework. June prepares meals, waters plants, and dusts on a Saturday morning. She brings in groceries, wipes around the kitchen sink, and asks Wally to help her put away the vacuum cleaner (which she has not been shown using). Margaret prepares meals, does dishes, irons, and also waters plants. While June is often stationary in the kitchen or sewing in the living room, Margaret is usually moving from one room to another, in the process of ongoing domestic activity.

While one could argue that this lack of acknowledgment of the labor of homemaking troubles the verisimilitude of these sit-coms, the realist *mise en scène* that includes consumer products suggests the means by which the comfortable environment of quality family life can be maintained. Margaret and June easily mediate the benefits promised by the consumer product industry. They are definitely not women of leisure, but they are women for whom housework is neither especially confining nor completely time-consuming.

The visible result of their partially visible labor is the constantly immaculate appearance of their homes and variously well-groomed family members. (The older children are more orderly because they are further along in the process of socialization than are the younger ones.) The "real time" to do piles of laundry or the daily preparation of balanced meals is a structured absence of the programs. The free time that appliances provide for Margaret and June is attested to by their continual good humor and the quality of their interactions with the family. Unrushed and unpressured, Margaret and June are not so free from housework that they become idle and self-indulgent. They are well-positioned within the constraints of domestic activity and the promises of the consumer product industry.

We have seen how the homemaker was positioned in the postwar consumer economy by institutions that were dependent on defining her social subjectivity within the domestic sphere. In the interests of family stability, suburban development and domestic architecture were designed with a particular definition of family economy in mind: a working father who could, alone, provide for the social and economic security of his family; a homemaker wife and mother who maintains the family's environment; children who grow up in neighborhoods undisturbed by heterogeneity of class, race, ethnicity, and age.

The limited address to the homemaker by the consumer product industry and market research is easily understood when seen within this context of homogeneity in the social organization of the suburban family. Defined in terms of her homemaking function for the family and for the economy, her life could only be made easier by appliances. The display of her family's social status was ensured by experts who assuaged any uncertainties she may have had about interior decor by designing with these problems in mind. By linking her identity as a shopper and homemaker to class attributes, the base of the consumer economy was broadened, and her deepest emotions and insecurities were tapped and transferred to consumer product design.

The representation of suburban family life in *Father Knows Best* and *Leave It to Beaver* also circulated social knowledge that linked the class and gender identities of homemakers. Realist *mise en scène* drew upon housing architecture and consumer products in order to ground family narratives within the domestic space of the middle-class home. The contribution of the television homemaker to harmonious family life was underscored by the ease with which she negotiated her place in the domestic arena.

This brief social history has placed one television format – the suburban family sit-com – within the historical context from which it drew its conventions, its codes of realism, and its definitions of family life. Yet we must also ask about resistances to this social subjectivity by recognizing the heterogeneity of the social formation. For example, in the late 1950s and 1960s, when the suburban family sit-com proliferated on prime-time television, the women's movement was resisting these institutional imperatives, exposing the social and economic inequalities on which they were based.[45]

Oppositional positions point to the inability of institutions to conceal completely the social and economic determinations of subjectivity. But the durability of the suburban family sit-com indicates the degree of institutional as well as popular support for ideologies that naturalize class and gender identities. Continuing exploration of the relationship between the historical specificity of the social formation and the programming practices of television contributes to our understanding of the ways in which popular cultural forms participate in the discourses of social life and diverge from the patterns of everyday experience.

Notes

1 In *Women: The Longest Revolution* (London: Virago, 1984), 18, Juliet Mitchell argues that women are bound up in this contradiction: "[Women] are fundamental to the human condition, yet in their economic, social, and political roles, they are marginal. It is precisely this combination – fundamental and marginal at one and the same time – that has been fatal to them."

2 Stuart Ewen and Elizabeth Ewen, *Channels of Desire: Mass Images and the Shaping of American Consciousness* (New York: McGraw-Hill, 1982), 235.

3 Graham Murdock and Peter Golding, "Capitalism, Communication and Class Relations," and Stuart Hall, "Culture, Media and the 'Ideological Effect,'" in *Mass Communication and Society*, ed. James Curran, Michael Gurevitch, and Janet Woollacott (Beverly Hills: Sage, 1979), 12, 36, 336–9.

4   I began this study by considering prime-time network sit-coms with runs of three seasons or more from 1948 through 1960. Fourteen of these thirty-five sit-coms were structured around middle-class families living in suburban single-family dwellings. Eight of these fourteen defined the family unit as a breadwinner father, a homemaker mother, and children growing into adults: *The Ruggles* (1949–1952), *The Aldrich Family* (1949–1953), *The Stu Erwin Show* (1950–1955), *The Adventures of Ozzie and Harriet* (1952–1966), *Father Knows Best* (1954–1963), *Leave It to Beaver* (1957–1963), *The Donna Reed Show* (1958–1966), and *Dennis the Menace* (1959–1963).

The other six suburban family sit-coms shared some of these traits, but centered their narratives on situations or characters other than the family ensemble: *Beulah* (1950–1953) focused on a black maid to an apparently broadly caricatured white middle-class family; *December Bride* (1954–1961) concerned an attractive, dating widow living with her daughter's family; *The Bob Cummings Show* (1955–1959) concentrated on the adventures of a playboy photographer living with his widowed sister and nephew in a suburban home; *I Married Joan* (1952–1955) focused on the zany adventures of the wife of a domestic court judge; *My Favorite Husband* (1953–1957) had a couple working for social status in the suburbs; and *Bachelor Father* (1957–1962) featured an attorney who cared for his young niece in Beverly Hills.

This information was derived from the following sources: Tim Brooks and Earle Marsh, *The Complete Directory of Prime Time Network Television Shows, 1946–Present* (New York: Ballantine Books, 1981); Les Brown, *The New York Times Encyclopedia of Television* (New York: Times Books, 1977); Henry Castleman and Walter J. Podrazik, *The TV Schedule Book* (New York: McGraw-Hill, 1984).

5   Kenneth Rhodes, "Father of *Two* Families," *Cosmopolitan* (Apr. 1956), 125.

6   Ibid.; Bob Eddy, "Private Life of a Perfect Papa," *Saturday Evening Post* (Apr. 27, 1957), 29; Brooks and Marsh, *Complete Directory*, 245–6.

7   Rhodes, "Father," 125; Eddy, "Private Life," 29.

8   Newspaper critic John Crosby, quoted in Eddy, "Private Life," 29.

9   "TV's Eager Beaver," *Look* (May 27, 1958), 68.

10 Brooks and Marsh, *Complete Directory*, 340–1, 352–3.

11 Eddy, "Private Life," 29; Rhodes, "Father," 126.

12 Eddy, "Private Life," 29; Rhodes, "Father," 127.

13 "Jane Wyatt's Triple Threat," *Good Housekeeping* (Oct. 1959), 48.

14 Eddy, "Private Life," 176; Dolores Hayden, *Redesigning the American Dream: The Future of Housing, Work and Family Life* (New York: Norton, 1984), 17.

15 Hayden, *American Dream*, 40; see also Gwendolyn Wright, *Building the Dream: A Social History of Housing in America* (Cambridge: MIT Press, 1981).

16 Hayden, *American Dream*, 35, 38, 55; Wright, *Building the Dream*, 246, 248.

17 Hayden, *American Dream*, 41–2; Wright, *Building the Dream*, 247.

18 Wright, *Building the Dream*, 247–8.

19 Ibid., 248.

20 Hayden, *American Dream*, 55–6; Wright, *Building the Dream*, 256.

21 Hayden, *American Dream*, 63, 109.

22 Hayden, *American Dream*, 17–18; Wright, *Building the Dream*, 254–5.

23 "The fifth international design conference at Aspen found 500 conferees at the crossroads, pondering the direction of the arts, and, every now and then, of the American consumer," *Industrial Design*, 2:4 (Aug. 1955), 42; Avrom Fleishman, "M/R, a Survey of Problems, Techniques, Schools of Thought in Market Research: Part 1 of a Series," *Industrial Design*, 5:1 (Jan. 1958), 33–4.

24 "Materialism, Leisure and Design," *Industrial Design*, 4:12 (Dec. 1957), 33–4.

25 Dr. Wilson G. Scanlon, "Industrial Design and Emotional Immaturity," *Industrial Design*, 4:1 (Jan. 1957), 68–9.

26 "Eleventh Annual ASID Conference: Three Days of Concentrated Design Discussion in Washington, D.C.," *Industrial Design*, 2:6 (Dec. 1955), 128; Theodore Peterson, *Magazines in the Twentieth Century* (Urbana: University of Illinois Press, 1964), 255, 298, 301–2.

27 "Eleventh Annual ASID Conference," 123.

28 Richard Tyler George, "The Process of Product Planning," *Industrial Design*, 3:5 (Oct. 1956), 97–100. See also Deborah Allen, Avrom Fleishman, and Jane Fiske Mitarachi, "Report on Product Planning," *Industrial Design*, 4:6 (June 1957), 37–81; "Lawrence Wilson," *Industrial Design*, 2:5 (Oct. 1955), 82–3; "Sundberg-Ferar," *Industrial Design*, 2:5 (Oct. 1955), 86–7; "10 Work Elements of Product Planning," *Industrial Design*, 4:6 (June 1957), 47.

29 Avrom Fleishman, "M/R: Part 2," *Industrial Design*, 5:2 (Feb. 1958), 42.

30 "IDI Discusses TV, Styling and Creativity," *Industrial Design*, 4:5 (May 1957), 67–8.

31 A. C. Nielsen Company, "The Nielsen Ratings in Perspective" (1980), 20; "IDI Discusses TV," 67–8.

32 "IDI Discusses TV," 67–8. On television technology and set design, see "Design Review," *Industrial Design*, 6:9 (Aug. 1959), 89; "TV Sets Get Smaller and Smaller," *Industrial Design*, 4:1 (Jan. 1957), 39–43; "Redesign: Philco Crops the Neck of the Picturetube to Be First with Separate-Screen Television," *Industrial Design*, 5:6 (June 1958), 52; "Design Review," *Industrial Design*, 6:9 (Aug. 1959), 88; Tenite advertisement, *Industrial Design*, 6:7 (July 1959), 23; Tenite advertisement, *Industrial Design*, 8:11 (Nov. 1961), 25.

33 "The Consumer at IDI," *Industrial Design*, 4:11 (Nov. 1957), 68–72.

34 Hayden, *American Dream*, 50.

35 Fleishman, "M/R, a Survey of Problems," 27, 29. While Fleishman recognized Paul Lazarsfeld's contribution to market research, this article did not mention Lazarsfeld's work in the television industry or his development of The Analyzer, an early instrument for audience measurement, for CBS. See Laurence Bergreen, *Look Now, Pay Later* (New York: New American Library, 1981), 170–1.

36 Fleishman, "M/R, a Survey of Problems," 27.

37 Ibid., 35.

38 Ibid., 37.

39 Ibid., 40.

40 Ibid., 41–2.

41 Fleishman, "M/R: Part 2," 34–5; C. Wright Mills, "The Man in the Middle," *Industrial Designs*, 5:11 (Nov. 1958), 70; Don Wallace, "Report from Aspen," *Industrial Design*, 5:8 (Aug. 1958), 85.

42 Mills, "Man in the Middle," 72–4.

43 "Jane Wyatt's Triple Threat," 48.

44 Danny Peary, "Remembering 'Father Knows Best,'" in *TV Book*, ed. Judy Fireman (New York: Workman, 1977), 173–5.

45 Long-running suburban family sit-coms that ran on network prime time during the early years of the women's movement were *Father Knows Best* (1954–1963), *Leave It to Beaver* (1957–1963), *The Donna Reed Show* (1958–1966), *The Dick Van Dyke Show* (1961–1966), *Hazel* (1961–1966), *Dennis the Menace* (1959–1963), and *The Adventures of Ozzie and Harriet* (1952–1966). This information was obtained from Brooks and Marsh, *Complete Directory*, 15–16, 193, 199–200, 211, 245–6, 322, 423–4.

The Eye of Difference: The Politics of Appearance

10

The Zoot-Suit and Style Warfare

STUART COSGROVE

—— **Introduction: The Silent Noise of Sinister Clowns** ——

What about those fellows waiting still and silent there on the platform, so still and silent they clash with the crowd in their very immobility, standing noisy in their very silence; harsh as a cry of terror in their quietness? What about these three boys, coming now along the platform, tall and slender, walking with swinging shoulders in their well-pressed, too-hot-for-summer suits, their collars high and tight about their necks, their identical hats of black cheap felt set upon the crowns of their heads with a severe formality above their conked hair? It was as though I'd never seen their like before: walking slowly, their shoulders swaying, their legs swinging from their hips in trousers that ballooned upward from cuffs fitting snug about their ankles; their coats long and hip-tight with shoulders far too broad to be those of natural western men. These fellows whose bodies seemed – what had one of my teachers said of me? – 'You're like one of those African sculptures, distorted in the interest of design.' Well, what design and whose?[1]

The zoot-suit is more than an exaggerated costume, more than a sartorial statement, it is the bearer of a complex and contradictory history. When the nameless narrator of Ellison's *Invisible Man* confronted the subversive sight of three young and extravagantly dressed blacks, his reaction was one of fascination not of fear. These youths were not simply grotesque dandies parading the city's secret underworld, they were 'the stewards of something uncomfortable',[2] a spectacular reminder that the social

Stuart Cosgrove, "The Zoot-Suit and Style Warfare," *History Workshop Journal*, 18 (Autumn 1984): 77–91. Reprinted with permission of Oxford University Press.

Figure 10.1. Clyde Duncan, a bus-boy from Gainesville, Georgia, who appeared on the front page of the *New York Times* at the height of the zoot-suit riots. Reprinted courtesy of Stuart Cosgrove and Oxford University Press

order had failed to contain their energy and difference. The zoot-suit was more than the drape-shape of 1940s fashion, more than a colourful stage-prop hanging from the shoulders of Cab Calloway, it was, in the most direct and obvious ways, an emblem of ethnicity and a way of negotiating an identity. The zoot-suit was a refusal: a subcultural gesture that refused to concede to the manners of subservience. By the late 1930s, the term 'zoot' was in common circulation within urban jazz culture. Zoot meant something worn or performed in an extravagant style, and since many young blacks wore suits with outrageously padded shoulders and trousers that were fiercely tapered at the ankles, the term zoot-suit passed into everyday usage. In the sub-cultural world of Harlem's nightlife, the language of rhyming slang succinctly described the zoot-suit's unmistakable style: 'a killer-diller coat with a drapeshape, reat-pleats and shoulders padded like a lunatic's cell'. The study of the relationships between fashion and social action is notoriously underdeveloped, but there is every indication that the zoot-suit riots that erupted in the United States in the summer of 1943 had a profound effect on a whole generation of socially disadvantaged youths. It was during his period as a young zoot-suiter that the Chicano union activist Cesar Chavez first came into contact with community politics, and it was through the experiences of participating in zoot-suit riots in Harlem that the young pimp 'Detroit Red' began a political education that transformed him into the Black radical leader Malcolm X. Although the zoot-suit occupies an almost mythical place within the history of jazz music, its social and political importance has been virtually ignored. There can be no certainty about when, where or why the zoot-suit came into existence, but what is certain is that during the summer months of 1943 'the killer-diller coat' was the uniform of young rioters and the symbol of a moral panic about juvenile delinquency that was to intensify in the post-war period.

At the height of the Los Angeles riots of June 1943, the *New York Times* carried a front page article which claimed without reservation that the first zoot-suit had been purchased by a black bus worker, Clyde Duncan, from a tailor's shop in Gainesville, Georgia.[3] Allegedly, Duncan had been inspired by the film 'Gone with the Wind' and had set out to look like Rhett Butler. This explanation clearly found favour throughout the USA. The national press forwarded countless others. Some reports claimed that the zoot-suit was an invention of Harlem night life, others suggested it grew out of jazz culture and the exhibitionist stage-costumes of the band leaders, and some argued that the zoot-suit was derived from military uniforms and imported from Britain. The alternative and independent press, particularly *Crisis* and *Negro Quarterly*, more convincingly argued that the zoot-suit was the product of a particular social context.[4] They emphasised the importance of Mexican-American youths, or *pachucos*, in the emergence of zoot-suit style and, in tentative ways, tried to relate their appearance on the streets to the concept of *pachuquismo*.

In his pioneering book, *The Labyrinth of Solitude*, the Mexican poet and social commentator Octavio Paz throws imaginative light on *pachuco* style and indirectly establishes a framework within which the zoot-suit can be understood. Paz's study of the Mexican national consciousness examines the changes brought about by the movement of labour, particularly the generations of Mexicans who migrated northwards to the USA. This movement, and the new economic and social patterns it implies, has, according to Paz, forced young Mexican-Americans into an ambivalent experience between two cultures.

> What distinguishes them, I think, is their furtive, restless air: they act like persons who are wearing disguises, who are afraid of a stranger's look because it could strip them and leave them stark naked.... This spiritual condition, or lack of a spirit, has given birth to a type known as the pachuco. The pachucos are youths, for the most part of Mexican origin, who form gangs in southern cities; they can be identified by their language and behaviour as well as by the clothing they affect. They are instinctive rebels, and North American racism has vented its wrath on them more than once. But the pachucos do not attempt to vindicate their race or the nationality of their forebears. Their attitude reveals an obstinate, almost fanatical will-to-be, but this will affirms nothing specific except their determination...not to be like those around them.[5]

Pachuco youth embodied all the characteristics of second generation working-class immigrants. In the most obvious ways they had been stripped of their customs, beliefs and language. The *pachucos* were a disinherited generation within a disadvantaged sector of North American society; and predictably their experiences in education, welfare and employment alienated them from the aspirations of their parents and the dominant assumptions of the society in which they lived. The *pachuco* subculture was defined not only by ostentatious fashion, but by petty crime, delinquency and drug-taking. Rather than disguise their alienation or efface their hostility to the dominant society, the *pachucos* adopted an arrogant posture. They flaunted their difference, and the zoot-suit became the means by which that difference was announced. Those 'impassive and sinister clowns' whose purpose was 'to cause terror instead of laughter,'[6] invited the kind of attention that led to both prestige and persecution. For Octavio Paz the *pachuco*'s appropriation of the zoot-suit was an admission of the ambivalent place he occupied. 'It is the only way he can establish a more vital relationship with the society he is antagonising. As a victim he can occupy a place in the world that previously ignored him; as a delinquent, he can become one of its wicked heroes.'[7] The zoot-suit riots of 1943 encapsulated this paradox. They emerged out of the dialectics of delinquency and persecution, during a period in which American society was undergoing profound structural change.

The major social change brought about by the United States' involvement in the war was the recruitment to the armed forces of over four million civilians and the entrance of over five million women into the war-time labour force. The rapid increase in military recruitment and the radical shift in the composition of the labour force led in turn to changes in family life, particularly the erosion of parental control and authority. The large scale and prolonged separation of millions of families precipitated an unprecedented increase in the rate of juvenile crime and delinquency. By the summer of 1943 it was commonplace for teenagers to be left to their own initiatives whilst their parents were either on active military service or involved in war work. The increase in night work compounded the problem. With their parents or guardians working unsocial hours, it became possible for many more young people to gather late into the night at major urban centres or simply on the street corners.

The rate of social mobility intensified during the period of the zoot-suit riots. With over 15 million civilians and 12 million military personnel on the move throughout the country, there was a corresponding increase in vagrancy. Petty crimes became more difficult to detect and control; itinerants became increasingly common, and social transience put unforeseen pressure on housing and welfare. The new patterns of social mobility also led to congestion in military and industrial areas. Significantly, it was the overcrowded military towns along the Pacific coast and the industrial conurbations of Detroit, Pittsburgh and Los Angeles that witnessed the most violent outbreaks of zoot-suit rioting.[8]

'Delinquency' emerged from the dictionary of new sociology to become an everyday term, as wartime statistics revealed these new patterns of adolescent behaviour. The *pachucos* of the Los Angeles area were particularly vulnerable to the effects of war. Being neither Mexican nor American, the *pachucos*, like the black youths with whom they shared the zoot-suit style, simply did not fit. In their own terms they were '24-hour orphans', having rejected the ideologies of their migrant parents. As the war furthered the dislocation of family relationships, the *pachucos* gravitated away from the home to the only place where their status was visible, the streets and bars of the towns and cities. But if the *pachucos* laid themselves open to a life of delinquency and detention, they also asserted their distinct identity, with their own style of dress, their own way of life and a shared set of experiences.

—————— **The Zoot-Suit Riots: Liberty, Disorder** ——————
and the Forbidden

The zoot-suit riots sharply revealed a polarization between two youth groups within wartime society: the gangs of predominantly black and Mexican youths who were at the forefront of the zoot-suit subculture, and the predominantly white American servicemen stationed along the Pacific coast. The riots invariably had racial and social resonances but the primary issue seems to have been patriotism and attitudes to the war. With the entry of the United States into the war in December 1941, the nation had to come to terms with the restrictions of rationing and the prospects of conscription. In March 1942, the War Production Board's first rationing act had a direct effect on the manufacture of suits and all clothing containing wool. In an attempt to institute a 26% cut-back in the use of fabrics, the War Production Board drew up regulations for the wartime manufacture of what *Esquire* magazine called, 'streamlined suits by Uncle Sam.'[9] The regulations effectively forbade the manufacture of zoot-suits and most legitimate tailoring companies ceased to manufacture or advertise any suits that fell outside the War Production Board's guide lines. However, the demand for zoot-suits did not decline and a network of bootleg tailors based in Los Angeles and New York continued to manufacture the garments. Thus the polarization between servicemen and *pachucos* was immediately visible: the chino shirt and battledress were evidently uniforms of patriotism, whereas wearing a zoot-suit was a deliberate and public way of flouting the regulations of rationing. The zoot-suit was a moral and social scandal in the eyes of the authorities, not simply because it was associated with petty crime and violence, but because it openly snubbed the laws of rationing. In the fragile harmony of wartime society, the zoot-suiters were, according to Octavio Paz, 'a symbol of love and joy or of horror and loathing, an embodiment of liberty, of disorder, of the forbidden.'[10]

The zoot-suit riots, which were initially confined to Los Angeles, began in the first few days of June 1943. During the first weekend of the month, over 60 zoot-suiters were arrested and charged at Los Angeles County jail, after violent and well publicized fights between servicemen on shore leave and gangs of Mexican-American youths. In order to prevent further outbreaks of fighting, the police patrolled the eastern sections of the city, as rumours spread from the military bases that servicemen were intending to form vigilante groups. The *Washington Post*'s report of the incidents, on the morning of Wednesday 9 June 1943, clearly saw the events from the point of view of the servicemen.

> Disgusted with being robbed and beaten with tire irons, weighted ropes, belts and fists employed by overwhelming numbers of the youthful hoodlums, the

uniformed men passed the word quietly among themselves and opened their campaign in force on Friday night.

At central jail, where spectators jammed the sidewalks and police made no efforts to halt auto loads of servicemen openly cruising in search of zoot-suiters, the youths streamed gladly into the sanctity of the cells after being snatched from bar rooms, pool halls and theaters and stripped of their attire.[11]

During the ensuing weeks of rioting, the ritualistic stripping of zoot-suiters became the major means by which the servicemen re-established their status over the *pachucos*. It became commonplace for gangs of marines to ambush zoot-suiters, strip them down to their underwear and leave them helpless in the streets. In one particularly vicious incident, a gang of drunken sailors rampaged through a cinema after discovering two zoot-suiters. They dragged the *pachucos* on to the stage as the film was being screened, stripped them in front of the audience and as a final insult, urinated on the suits.

The press coverage of these incidents ranged from the careful and caution-ary liberalism of the *Los Angeles Times* to the more hysterical hate-mongering of William Randolph Hearst's west coast papers. Although the practice of stripping and publicly humiliating the zoot-suiters was not prompted by the press, several reports did little to discourage the attacks:

> ...zoot-suits smouldered in the ashes of street bonfires where they had been tossed by grimly methodical tank forces of service men.... The zooters, who earlier in the day had spread boasts that they were organized to 'kill every cop' they could find, showed no inclination to try to make good their boasts.... Searching parties of soldiers, sailors and Marines hunted them out and drove them out into the open like bird dogs flushing quail. Procedure was standard: grab a zooter. Take off his pants and frock coat and tear them up or burn them. Trim the 'Argentine Ducktail' haircut that goes with the screwy costume.[12]

The second week of June witnessed the worst incidents of rioting and public disorder. A sailor was slashed and disfigured by a pachuco gang; a policeman was run down when he tried to question a car load of zoot-suiters; a young Mexican was stabbed at a party by drunken Marines; a trainload of sailors were stoned by *pachucos* as their train approached Long Beach; streetfights broke out daily in San Bernardino; over 400 vigilantes toured the streets of San Diego looking for zoot-suiters, and many individuals from both factions were arrested.[13] On 9 June, the *Los Angeles Times* published the first in a series of editorials designed to reduce the level of violence, but which also tried to allay the growing concern about the racial character of the riots.

> To preserve the peace and good name of the Los Angeles area, the strongest measures must be taken jointly by the police, the Sheriff's office and Army and

Navy authorities, to prevent any further outbreaks of 'zoot suit' rioting. While members of the armed forces received considerable provocation at the hands of the unidentified miscreants, such a situation cannot be cured by indiscriminate assault on every youth wearing a particular type of costume.

It would not do, for a large number of reasons, to let the impression circulate in South America that persons of Spanish-American ancestry were being singled out for mistreatment in Southern California. And the incidents here were capable of being exaggerated to give that impression.[14]

The Chief, the Black Widows and the Tomahawk Kid

The pleas for tolerance from civic authorities and representatives of the church and state had no immediate effect, and the riots became more frequent and more violent. A zoot-suited youth was shot by a special police officer in Azusa, a gang of *pachucos* were arrested for rioting and carrying weapons in the Lincoln Heights area; 25 black zoot-suiters were arrested for wrecking an electric railway train in Watts, and 1000 additional police were drafted into East Los Angeles. The press coverage increasingly focused on the most 'spectacular' incidents and began to identify leaders of zoot-suit style. On the morning of Thursday 10 June 1943, most newspapers carried photographs and reports on three 'notorious' zoot-suit gang leaders. Of the thousands of *pachucos* that allegedly belonged to the hundreds of zoot-suit gangs in Los Angeles, the press singled out the arrests of Lewis D. English, a 23-year-old black, charged with felony and carrying a '16-inch razor sharp butcher knife;' Frank H. Tellez, a 22-year-old Mexican held on vagrancy charges, and another Mexican, Luis 'The Chief' Verdusco (27 years of age), allegedly the leader of the Los Angeles *pachucos*.[15]

The arrests of English, Tellez and Verdusco seemed to confirm popular perceptions of the zoot-suiters widely expressed for weeks prior to the riots. Firstly, that the zoot-suit gangs were predominantly, but not exclusively, comprised of black and Mexican youths. Secondly, that many of the zoot-suiters were old enough to be in the armed forces but were either avoiding conscription or had been exempted on medical grounds. Finally, in the case of Frank Tellez, who was photographed wearing a pancake hat with a rear feather, that zoot-suit style was an expensive fashion often funded by theft and petty extortion. Tellez allegedly wore a colourful long drape coat that was 'part of a $75 suit' and a pair of pegged trousers 'very full at the knees and narrow at the cuffs' which were allegedly part of another suit. The caption of the Associated Press photograph indignantly added that 'Tellez holds a medical discharge from the Army'.[16] What newspaper reports tended to suppress was information on the Marines who were arrested for inciting riots, the existence of gangs of white American zoot-suiters, and the opinions of Mexican-American servicemen stationed in California, who were part of the war-effort but who refused to take part in vigilante raids on *pachuco* hangouts.

As the zoot-suit riots spread throughout California, to cities in Texas and Arizona, a new dimension began to influence press coverage of the riots in Los Angeles. On a day when 125 zoot-suited youths clashed with Marines in Watts and armed police had to quell riots in Boyle Heights, the Los Angeles press concentrated on a razor attack on a local mother, Betty Morgan. What distinguished this incident from hundreds of comparable attacks was that the assailants were girls. The press related the incident to the arrest of Amelia Venegas, a woman zoot-suiter who was charged with carrying, and threatening to use, a brass knuckleduster. The revelation that girls were active within *pachuco* subculture led to consistent press coverage of the activities of two female gangs: the Slick Chicks and the Black Widows.[17] The latter gang took its name from the members' distinctive dress, black zoot-suit jackets, short black skirts and black fish-net stockings. In retrospect the Black Widows, and their active part in the subcultural violence of the zoot-suit riots, disturb conventional understandings of the concept of *pachuquismo*.

As Joan W. Moore implies in *Homeboys*, her definitive study of Los Angeles youth gangs, the concept of *pachuquismo* is too readily and unproblematically equated with the better known concept of *machismo*.[18] Undoubtedly, they share certain ideological traits, not least a swaggering and at times aggressive sense of power and bravado, but the two concepts derive from different sets of social definitions. Whereas *machismo* can be defined in terms of male power and sexuality, *pachuquismo* predominantly derives from ethnic, generational and class-based aspirations, and is less evidently a question of gender. What the zoot-suit riots brought to the surface was the complexity of *pachuco* style. The Black Widows and their aggressive image confounded the *pachuco* stereotype of the lazy male delinquent who avoided conscription for a life of dandyism and petty crime, and reinforced radical readings of *pachuco* subculture. The Black Widows were a reminder that ethnic and generational alienation was a pressing social problem and an indication of the tensions that existed in minority, low-income communities.

Although detailed information on the role of girls within zoot-suit sub-culture is limited to very brief press reports, the appearance of female *pachucos* coincided with a dramatic rise in the delinquency rates amongst girls aged between 12 and 20 years old. The disintegration of traditional family relationships and the entry of young women into the labour force undoubtedly had an effect on the social roles and responsibilities of female adolescents, but it is difficult to be precise about the relationships between changed patterns of social experience and the rise in delinquency. However, war-time society brought about an increase in unprepared and irregular sexual intercourse, which in turn led to significant increases in the rates of abortion, illegitimate births and venereal diseases. Although statistics are difficult to trace, there are many indications that the war years saw a remarkable increase in the numbers of young women who were taken into social care or referred to penal institutions, as a result of the specific social problems they had to encounter.

Later studies provide evidence that young women and girls were also heavily involved in the traffic and transaction of soft drugs. The *pachuco* sub-culture within the Los Angeles metropolitan area was directly associated with a widespread growth in the use of marijuana. It has been suggested that female zoot-suiters concealed quantities of drugs on their bodies, since they were less likely to be closely searched by male members of the law enforcement agencies. Unfortunately, the absence of consistent or reliable information on the female gangs makes it particularly difficult to be certain about their status within the riots, or their place within traditions of feminine resistance. The Black Widows and Slick Chicks were spectacular in a sub-cultural sense, but their black drape jackets, tight skirts, fish net stockings and heavily emphasised make-up, were ridiculed in the press. The Black Widows clearly existed outside the orthodoxies of war-time society: playing no part in the industrial war effort, and openly challenging conventional notions of feminine beauty and sexuality.

Towards the end of the second week of June, the riots in Los Angeles were dying out. Sporadic incidents broke out in other cities, particularly Detroit, New York and Philadelphia, where two members of Gene Krupa's dance band were beaten up in a station for wearing the band's zoot-suit costumes; but these, like the residual events in Los Angeles, were not taken seriously. The authorities failed to read the inarticulate warning signs proffered in two separate incidents in California: in one a zoot-suiter was arrested for throwing gasoline flares at a theatre; and in the second another was arrested for carrying a silver tomahawk. The zoot-suit riots had become a public and spectacular enactment of social disaffection. The authorities in Detroit chose to dismiss a zoot-suit riot at the city's Cooley High School as an adolescent imitation of the Los Angeles disturbances.[19] Within three weeks Detroit was in the midst of the worst race riot in its history.[20] The United States was still involved in the war abroad when violent events on the home front signalled the beginnings of a new era in racial politics.

Official Fears of Fifth Column Fashion

Official reactions to the zoot-suit riots varied enormously. The most urgent problem that concerned California's State Senators was the adverse effect that the events might have on the relationship between the United States and Mexico. This concern stemmed partly from the wish to preserve good international relations, but rather more from the significance of relations with Mexico for the economy of Southern California, as an item in the *Los Angeles Times* made clear. 'In San Francisco Senator Downey declared that the riots may have 'extremely grave consequences' in impairing relations between the United States and Mexico, and may endanger the program of importing Mexican labor to aid in harvesting California crops.'[21] These fears were compounded when the Mexican Embassy formally drew the zoot-suit riots to the attention of the State Department. It was the fear of an 'international incident'[22] that could only have an adverse effect on California's economy, rather than any real concern for the social conditions of the Mexican-American community, that motivated Governor Warren of California to order a public investigation into the causes of the riots. In an ambiguous press statement, the Governor hinted that the riots may have been instigated by outside or even foreign agitators:

> As we love our country and the boys we are sending overseas to defend it, we are all duty bound to suppress every discordant activity which is designed to stir up international strife or adversely affect our relationships with our allies in the United Nations.[23]

The zoot-suit riots provoked two related investigations; a fact finding investigative committee headed by Attorney General Robert Kenny and an un-American activities investigation presided over by State Senator Jack B. Tenney. The un-American activities investigation was ordered 'to determine whether the present zoot-suit riots were sponsored by Nazi agencies attempting to spread disunity between the United States and Latin American countries'.[24] Senator Tenney, a member of the un-American Activities committee for Los Angeles County, claimed he had evidence that the zoot-suit riots were 'axis-sponsored' but the evidence was never presented.[25] However, the notion that the riots might have been initiated by outside agitators persisted throughout the month of June, and was fuelled by Japanese propaganda broadcasts accusing the North American government of ignoring the brutality of US marines. The arguments of the un-American activities investigation were given a certain amount of credibility by a Mexican pastor based in Watts, who according to the press had been 'a pretty rough customer himself, serving as a captain in Pancho Villa's revolutionary army.'[26] Reverend Francisco Quintanilla, the pastor of the Mexican Methodist church, was convinced the riots were the result of fifth columnists. 'When boys start attacking servicemen it means the enemy is right at home. It means they are being fed vicious propaganda by enemy agents who wish to stir up all the racial and class hatreds they can put their evil fingers on.'[27]

The attention given to the dubious claims of nazi-instigation tended to obfuscate other more credible opinions. Examination of the social conditions of *pachuco* youths tended to be marginalized in favour of other more 'newsworthy' angles. At no stage in the press coverage were the opinions of community workers or youth leaders sought, and so, ironically, the most progressive opinion to appear in the major newspapers was offered by the Deputy Chief of Police, E. W. Lester. In press releases and on radio he provided a short history of gang subcultures in the Los Angeles area and then tried, albeit briefly, to place the riots in a social context.

> The Deputy Chief said most of the youths came from overcrowded colorless homes that offered no opportunities for leisure-time activities. He said it is wrong to blame law enforcement agencies for the present situation, but that society as a whole must be charged with mishandling the problems.[28]

On the morning of Friday, 11 June 1943, the *Los Angeles Times* broke with its regular practices and printed an editorial appeal, 'Time For Sanity,' on its front page. The main purpose of the editorial was to dispel suggestions that the riots were racially motivated, and to challenge the growing opinion that white servicemen from the Southern States had actively colluded with the police in their vigilante campaign against the zoot-suiters.

> There seems to be no simple or complete explanation for the growth of the grotesque gangs. Many reasons have been offered, some apparently valid, some farfetched. But it does appear to be definitely established that any attempts at curbing the movement have had nothing whatever to do with race persecution, although some elements have loudly raised the cry of this very thing.[29]

A month later, the editorial of July's issue of *Crisis* presented a diametrically opposed point of view:

> These riots would not occur – no matter what the instant provocation – if the vast majority of the population, including more often than not the law enforcement officers and machinery, did not share in varying degrees the belief that Negroes are and must be kept second-class citizens.[30]

But this view got short shrift, particularly from the authorities, whose initial response to the riots was largely retributive. Emphasis was placed on arrest and punishment. The Los Angeles City Council considered a proposal from Councillor Norris Nelson, that 'it be made a jail offense to wear zoot-suits with reat pleats within the city limits of LA',[31] and a discussion ensued for over

an hour before it was resolved that the laws pertaining to rioting and disorderly conduct were sufficient to contain the zoot-suit threat. However, the
council did encourage the War Production Board (WPB) to reiterate its
regulations on the manufacture of suits. The regional office of the WPB
based in San Francisco investigated tailors manufacturing in the area of
men's fashion and took steps 'to curb illegal production of men's clothing
in violation of WPB limitation orders.' Only when Governor Warren's fact-
finding commission made its public recommendations did the political
analysis of the riots go beyond the first principles of punishment and pro-
scription. The recommendations called for a more responsible co-operation
from the press; a programme of special training for police officers working in
multi-racial communities; additional detention centres; a juvenile forestry
camp for youth under the age of 16; an increase in military and shore police;
an increase in the youth facilities provided by the church; an increase in
neighbourhood recreation facilities and an end to discrimination in the use of
public facilities. In addition to these measures, the commission urged that
arrests should be made without undue emphasis on members of minority
groups and encouraged lawyers to protect the rights of youths arrested for
participation in gang activity. The findings were a delicate balance of punishment and palliative; it made no significant mention of the social conditions of
Mexican labourers and no recommendations about the kind of public spending that would be needed to alter the social experiences of *pachuco* youth. The
outcome of the zoot-suit riots was an inadequate, highly localized and
relatively ineffective body of short term public policies that provided no
guidelines for the more serious riots in Detroit and Harlem later in the
same summer.

The Mystery of the Signifying Monkey

> The pachuco is the prey of society, but instead of hiding he adorns himself to
> attract the hunter's attention. Persecution redeems him and breaks his solitude:
> his salvation depends on him becoming part of the very society he appears to
> deny.[32]

The zoot-suit was associated with a multiplicity of different traits and conditions. It was simultaneously the garb of the victim and the attacker, the
persecutor and the persecuted, the 'sinister clown' and the grotesque dandy.
But the central opposition was between the style of the delinquent and that of
the disinherited. To wear a zoot-suit was to risk the repressive intolerance
of wartime society and to invite the attention of the police, the parent
generation and the uniformed members of the armed forces. For many

pachucos the zoot-suit riots were simply hightimes in Los Angeles when momentarily they had control of the streets; for others it was a realization that they were outcasts in a society that was not of their making. For the black radical writer, Chester Himes, the riots in his neighbourhood were unambiguous: 'Zoot Riots are Race Riots.'[33] For other contemporary commentators the wearing of the zoot-suit could be anything from unconscious dandyism to a conscious 'political' engagement. The zoot-suit riots were *not* 'political' riots in the strictest sense, but for many participants they were an entry into the language of politics, an inarticulate rejection of the 'straight world' and its organization.

It is remarkable how many post-war activists were inspired by the zoot-suit disturbances. Luis Valdez of the radical theatre company, El Teatro Campesino, allegedly learned the 'chicano' from his cousin the zoot-suiter Billy Miranda.[34] The novelists Ralph Ellison and Richard Wright both conveyed a literary and political fascination with the power and potential of the zoot-suit. One of Ellison's editorials for the journal *Negro Quarterly* expressed his own sense of frustration at the enigmatic attraction of zoot-suit style.

> A third major problem, and one that is indispensable to the centralization and direction of power is that of learning the meaning of myths and symbols which abound among the Negro masses. For without this knowledge, leadership, no matter how correct its program, will fail. Much in Negro life remains a mystery; perhaps the zoot-suit conceals profound political meaning; perhaps the symmetrical frenzy of the Lindy-hop conceals clues to great potential powers, if only leaders could solve this riddle.[35]

Although Ellison's remarks are undoubtedly compromised by their own mysterious idealism, he touches on the zoot-suit's major source of interest. It is in everyday rituals that resistance can find natural and unconscious expression. In retrospect, the zoot-suit's history can be seen as a point of intersection, between the related potential of ethnicity and politics on the one hand, and the pleasures of identity and difference on the other. It is the zoot-suit's political and ethnic associations that have made it such a rich reference point for subsequent generations. From the music of Thelonious Monk and Kid Creole to the jazz-poetry of Larry Neal, the zoot-suit has inherited new meanings and new mysteries. In his book *Hoodoo Hollerin' Bebop Ghosts*, Neal uses the image of the zoot-suit as the symbol of Black America's cultural resistance. For Neal, the zoot-suit ceased to be a costume and became a tapestry of meaning, where music, politics and social action merged. The zoot-suit became a symbol for the enigmas of Black culture and the mystery of the signifying monkey:

Figure 10.2. A Los Angeles police officer pretends to clip the "Argentine" hairstyle of a young *pachuco* zoot-suiter. Reprinted courtesy of Stuart Cosgrove and Oxford University Press

But there is rhythm here
Its own special substance:
I hear Billie sing, no Good Man, and dig Prez, wearing the Zoot suit of life, the
Porkpie hat tilted at the correct angle; through the Harlem smoke of beer and
whisky, I understand the mystery of the Signifying Monkey.[36]

Notes

1 Ralph Ellison, *Invisible Man* (New York, 1947), 380.
2 Ibid., 381.
3 'Zoot Suit Originated in Georgia,' *New York Times*, 11 June 1943, 21.
4 For the most extensive sociological study of the zoot-suit riots of 1943 see Ralph H. Turner and Samuel J. Surace, 'Zoot Suiters and Mexicans: Symbols in Crowd Behaviour,' *American Journal of Sociology*, 62 (1956), 14–20.

5   Octavio Paz, *The Labyrinth of Solitude* (London, 1967), 5–6.

6   Ibid., 8.

7   Ibid.

8   See K. L. Nelson (ed.), *The Impact of War on American Life* (New York, 1971).

9   O. E. Schoeffler and W. Gale, *Esquire's Encyclopaedia of Twentieth-Century Men's Fashion* (New York, 1973), 24.

10 Paz, *Labyrinth of Solitude*, 8

11 'Zoot-Suiters Again on the Prowl as Navy Holds Back Sailors,' *Washington Post*, 9 June 1943, 1.

12 Quoted in S. Menefee, *Assignment USA* (New York, 1943), 189.

13 Details of the riots are taken from newspaper reports and press releases for the weeks in question, particularly from the *Los Angeles Times*, *New York Times*, *Washington Post*, *Washington Star* and *Time Magazine*.

14 'Strong Measures Must be Taken Against Rioting,' *Los Angeles Times*, 9 June 1943, 4.

15 'Zoot-Suit Fighting Spreads On the Coast,' *New York Times*, 10 June 1943, 23.

16 Ibid.

17 'Zoot-Girls Use Knife in Attack,' *Los Angeles Times*, 11 June 1943, 1.

18 Joan W. Moore, *Homeboys: Gangs, Drugs and Prison in the Barrios of Los Angeles* (Philadelphia, 1978).

19 'Zoot Suit Warfare Spreads to Pupils of Detroit Area,' *Washington Star*, 11 June 1943, 1.

20 Although the Detroit Race Riots of 1943 were not zoot-suit riots, nor evidently about 'youth' or 'delinquency', the social context in which they took place was obviously comparable. For a lengthy study of the Detroit riots see R. Shogun and T. Craig, *The Detroit Race Riot: A Study in Violence* (Philadelphia and New York, 1964).

21 'Zoot Suit War Inquiry Ordered by Governor,' *Los Angeles Times*, 9 June 1943, p. A.

22 'Warren Orders Zoot Suit Quiz; Quiet Reigns After Rioting,' *Los Angeles Times*, 10 June 1943, 1.

23 Ibid.

24 'Tenney Feels Riots Caused by Nazi Move for Disunity,' *Los Angeles Times*, 9 June 1943, p. A.

25 Ibid.

26 'Watts Pastor Blames Riots on Fifth Column,' *Los Angeles Times*, 11 June 1943, p. A.

27 Ibid.

28 'California Governor Appeals for Quelling of Zoot Suit Riots,' *Washington Star*, 10 June 1943, p. A3.

29 'Time for Sanity,' *Los Angeles Times*, 11 June 1943, p. 1.

30 'The Riots,' *The Crisis*, July 1943, p. 199.

31 'Ban on Freak Suits Studied by Councilmen', *Los Angeles Times*, 9 June 1943, p. A3.

32 *Labyrinth of Solitude*, 9.

33 Chester Himes, 'Zoot Riots are Race Riots,' *The Crisis* (July 1943); reprinted in Himes, *Black on Black: Baby Sister and Selected Writings* (London, 1975).

34 El Teatro Campesino presented the first Chicano play to achieve full commercial Broadway production. The play, written by Luis Valdez and entitled *Zoot Suit*, was a drama documentary on the Sleepy Lagoon murder and the events leading to the Los Angeles riots. (The Sleepy Lagoon murder of August 1942 resulted in 24 *pachucos* being indicted for conspiracy to murder.)

35 Quoted in Larry Neal, 'Ellison's Zoot Suit,' in J. Hersey (ed.), *Ralph Ellison: A Collection of Critical Essays* (New Jersey, 1974), 67.

36 From Larry Neal's poem 'Malcolm X: An Autobiography', in L. Neal, *Hoodoo Hollerin' Bebop Ghosts* (Washington, DC, 1974), 9.

11

Looking Jewish, Seeing Jews

MATTHEW FRYE JACOBSON

The Jew can be unknown in his Jewishness. He is not wholly what he is. One hopes, one waits. His actions, his behavior are the final determinant. He is a white man, and, apart from some rather debatable characteristics, he can sometimes go unnoticed...One has only not to be a nigger. Granted, the Jews are harassed – what am I thinking of? They are hunted down, exterminated, cremated. But these are little family quarrels.

Frantz Fanon, *Black Skin, White Masks* (1952)

I like the idea of having a Jewish officer – what's his name, Jacobs – in Burma. See that you get a good clean-cut American type for Jacobs.

Jack Warner's casting instructions for *Objective Burma* (1945)

Whaen Johann Blumenbach sat down to delineate *The Natural Varieties of Man* in 1775, he lighted upon the "racial face" of the Jews as the most powerful example of "the unadulterated countenance of nations." The principle of stable racial types was illustrated "above all [by] the nation of the Jews, who, under every climate, remain the same as far as the fundamental configuration of face goes, remarkable for a racial character almost universal, which can be distinguished at the first glance even by those little skilled in physiognomy."[1]

The racial character of Jewishness in the New World ebbed and flowed over time. The saga of Jewishness-as-difference in North America properly begins as early as 1654, when Peter Stuyvesant wrote to the Amsterdam Chamber of

Matthew Frye Jacobson, "Looking Jewish, Seeing Jews," in Jacobson, *Whiteness of A Different Color: European Immigrants and the Alchemy of Race.* Cambridge, MA: Harvard University Press, 1998: 171–99. © 1998 by the President and Fellows of Harvard College. Reprinted with permission.

the Dutch West India Company that Christian settlers in New Amsterdam had "deemed it useful to require [Jews] in a friendly way to depart." Stuyvesant went on to pray "that the deceitful race, – such hateful enemies and blasphemers of the name of Christ, – be not allowed further to infect and trouble this new colony."[2] In the early republic Jewishness was most often taken up as a matter not of racial difference marked by physicality, but of religious difference marked by a stubborn and benighted failure to see Truth. Jews were "un-Christian," as in the laws limiting the right of office-holding in Maryland; they were "infidels" in more heated rhetoric. Then, like other non-Anglo-Saxon immigrants who entered under the terms of the 1790 naturalization law, Jews were increasingly seen as a racial group (in their case as Orientals, Semites, or Hebrews) in the mid to late nineteenth century – particularly as the demographics of immigration tilted away from German and other West European Jews, and toward the Yiddish-speaking Jews of Eastern Europe. Finally, again like other non-Anglo-Saxon immigrants, Jews gradually became Caucasians over the course of the twentieth century.

Thus anti-Semitism and the racial odyssey of Jews in the United States are neither wholly divisible from nor wholly dependent upon the history of whiteness and its vicissitudes in American political culture. When Henry James writes, "There were thousands of little chairs and almost as many little Jews; and there was music in the open rotunda, over which Jews wagged their big noses," it is useful to know that he is drawing upon a long European tradition of anti-Jewish imagery buttressed by arrangements of institutional power and political custom. It is also useful to know, however, that James's sensibilities could be as easily unsettled by a gang of Italian "ditchers" or a variety of other immigrant arrivals. After a visit to "the terrible little Ellis Island" in 1906, James ventured that the sight would bring "a new chill in [the] heart" of any long-standing American, as if he had "seen a ghost in his supposedly safe old house." American natives, he wrote, had been reduced to a state of "*un*settled possession" of their own country; and it was not the Jew alone, but the "inconceivable alien" in general, who had him so worried.[3]

Yet as with Irish immigrants, who came ashore already carrying the cultural and political baggage of Saxon oppression, the Jews' version of becoming Caucasian cannot be understood apart from their particular history of special sorrows in the ghettos of Eastern Europe, apart from the deep history of anti-Semitism in Western culture, apart from anti-Semitic stereotypes that date back well before the European arrival on North American shores, or apart, finally and most obviously, from the historic cataclysm of the Holocaust.

The thick traces of this history and the Jewish discomfort with it are nicely captured in the exchange with which this study opened, a scene from *The Counterlife* in which two of Philip Roth's characters argue over whether or not Jews are Caucasian. In an era when religious orthodoxy has been eroded by the tides of secularization, and when race has been rendered unspeakable by the atrocities in Nazi Germany, what does Jewishness consist in? This is a point of no small disagreement, even as the twentieth century comes to a close. On the one hand, in a short story like "My Jewish Face" (1990), the Jewish writer Melanie Kaye/Kantrowitz can depict the recognition and public acknowledgment of one's own "Jewish face" as a powerful sign of cultural resistance or political maturation. In popular, street-level conversation among Jewish insiders, too, a common joke has it that so-and-so "doesn't look like a Jew – he looks like *two* Jews." And yet on the other hand, as Roth's Nathan Zuckerman uneasily remarks, "Some nasty superstitions always tend to crop up when people talk about a Jewish race." The touchiness of the very question of Jewish visibility in the late twentieth century denotes the searing and complicated history of "the Jewish race."[4]

My interest in physicality here has primarily to do with the relationship between race as a conceptual category and race as a perceptual category. From a historical standpoint, looking Jewish (or Irish or Levantine or Italian or Cape Verdean) is not terribly interesting in and of itself. But there is a dynamic relationship between visible "difference" on the one hand, and deep social and political meaning on the other. Recall Charles Dudley Warner's peculiar but telling description of his encounter with a group of Moslem mourners in *In the Levant*:

> You would not see in farthest Nubia a more barbarous assemblage, and not so fierce an one. In the presence of these wild mourners the term 'gentler sex' has a ludicrous sound...most of them were flamingly ugly, and – *to liken them to what they most resembled* – physically and mentally the type of the North American squaws.[5]

The emphasized phrase here signals a double task of first "recognizing" (that is, *assigning*) resemblance and then, second, reifying that resemblance by "likening" the two disparate objects of perception. The phrase "to liken them to what they most resembled" does not merely represent an awkward rendering on Warner's part, but conveys the crucial cognitive work of racial perception. Warner interpolates a group of actual Moslem mourners into his own, preexisting conception of "barbarism" and "wildness" – a conception that is evidently inflected by notions of "ugliness" and "womanliness," and that already comprises "Nubians" and "North American squaws." This cognitive act of "likening," of course, silently entails other, equally portentous acts of "differentiating."

Here, then, is a rudimentary model for thinking about the complex interplay between social distinctions and racial perceptions. Like Irishness, Italianness, Greekness, and other probationary whitenesses, visible Jewishness in American culture between the mid-nineteenth and mid-twentieth centuries represented a complex process of social value *become* perception: social and political meanings attached to Jewishness generate a kind of physiognomical surveillance that renders Jewishness itself discernible as a particular pattern of physical traits (skin color, nose shape, hair color and texture, and the like) – what Blumenbach called "the fundamental configuration of face." The visible markers may then be interpreted as outer signs of an essential, immutable, inner moral-intellectual character; and that character, in its turn – attested to by physical "difference" – is summoned up to explain the social value attached to Jewishness in the first place. The circuit is ineluctable. Race is social value become perception; Jewishness seen is social value naturalized and so enforced.

This is not to say that people all "really" look alike; rather, it is to argue that those physical differences which register in the consciousness as *"difference"* are keyed to particular social and historical circumstances. (We might all agree that Daniel Patrick Moynihan "looks Irish," for instance; but unlike our predecessors, we at the turn of the twenty-first century are not likely to note his Irishness first thing.) Thus a writer defending the "better" Jews (what a later generation would tellingly call "white Jews") in the *North American Review* in 1891 could collapse the distinction between behavior and physicality, arguing that "among cultured Jews the racial features are generally less strongly defined." (When Jews are of the "better" type, that is, the observing eye need not scout their Jewishness.)[6] That same year, meanwhile, in *The Witch of Prague*, the novelist Marion Crawford could thoroughly fuse physicality and inner character in his portrait of Jewish evil. In the Jewish quarter one encountered

> throngs of gowned men, crooked, bearded, filthy, vulture-eyed . . . hook-nosed and loose-lipped, grasping fat purses, in lean fingers, shaking greasy curls that straggled out under caps of greasy fur, glancing to the left and right with quick, gleaming looks that pierced the gloom like fitful flashes of lightening . . . a writhing mass of humanity, intoxicated by the smell of gold, mad for its possession, half hysteric with fear of losing it, timid, yet dangerous, poisoned to the core by the sweet sting of money, terrible in intelligence, vile in heart, contemptible in body, irresistible in the unity of their greed – the Jews of Prague.[7]

Nor, indeed, have conceptions of a racial Jewishness necessarily been confined to negative depictions. The point is a critical one. As I have argued elsewhere, Yiddish writers like Abraham Cahan and Morris Winchevsky were as quick as their non-Jewish contemporaries to assign a distinctly racial integrity to Jewishness and Jews. Racial perceptions of Jewishness are not simply a subject for the annals of anti-Semitism, in other words; nor does racial ascription necessarily denote a negative assessment of a given group in every case. Among the secularized Jews of the *haskala*, or Jewish enlightenment, responses to "the Jewish Question" (such as Zionism, or bundist Yiddish socialism) rested solidly upon *racial* notions of a unified Jewish "peoplehood." In the sciences, too, it was not only the virulent Madison Grants and the Lothrop Stoddards, but Jewish scientists like Maurice Fishberg and Joseph Jacobs, who advanced the scholarly idea of Jewish racial purity.[8] (Nor, for that matter, were Jewish versions of Jewish racial difference in every instance *positive*, either: as the *American Hebrew* remarked in response to the immigrant waves from further east in Europe [1894], the acculturated German Jew "is closer to the christian sentiment around him than to the Judaism of these miserable darkened Hebrews.")[9]

Thus the history of racial Jewishness is not merely the history of anti-Semitism; it encompasses the ways in which both Jews and non-Jews have construed Jewishness – and the ways in which they have *seen* it – over time. It encompasses not only arguments, like Madison Grant's, that "the mixture of a European and a Jew is a Jew," or the view of Jews as "mud people" – the progenitors of all nonwhites – which circulates in far right theology in the 1990s.[10] It also comprises the race pride of a Morris Winchevsky or a Leon Kobrin, and the social forces under whose influence such conceptions of peoplehood have largely given way. By 1950 Ludwig Lewisohn could assert that "no sane man regards Jewish characteristics as 'racial.'"[11] And yet as late as the 1970s Raphael Patai would still be trying to dispel "the myth of the Jewish race"; and later still Philip Roth would be wincing at the "nasty superstitions" attached to racial Jewishness.

A few remarks on the strategy of the present inquiry are in order. The definition of "Jewishness" under investigation here is quite narrow. Surely religion and culture can figure prominently in the ascription of Jewishness by Jews or non-Jews, anti-Semites or philo-Semites. This discussion does not seek to exhaust Jewishness in all of its dimensions or in its full range of possibilities; rather, it investigates strictly ethnoracial conceptions and perceptions of Jewishness (answers to the question, is Jewishness a parcel of biological, heritable traits?). Such conceptions, and the inevitable debates over them, have been central to some Jews themselves as they pondered their common destiny irrespective of religious devotion, and to non-Jews wrestling with questions of immigration, intergroup relations, and the smooth functioning of the polity. I begin by sketching the emergence of a visible, physical – biological – Jewishness in common American understanding during the period preceding the mid-twentieth century. This history loosely parallels the chronology laid out for whiteness in general in part one, although in the case of Jews World War II will present a sharper turning point than 1924 in the final transformation toward Caucasian whiteness.

The investigation ends, then, with a close reading of Arthur Miller's *Focus* (1945), a sustained inquiry into the properties of Jewishness rendered at precisely that post-Nazi moment – like *Gentleman's Agreement* – when "racial" Jewishness was still a live, yet a newly intolerable, conception.

"Are Jews white?" asks Sander Gilman. The question gets at the fundamental instability of Jewishness as racial difference, but so does its wording fundamentally misstate the contours of whiteness in American political culture.[12] From 1790 onward Jews were indeed "white" by the most significant measures of that appellation: they could enter the country and become naturalized citizens. Given the shades of meaning attaching to various racial classifications, given the nuances involved as whiteness slips off toward Semitic or Hebrew and back again toward Caucasian, the question is not *are* they white, nor even how white are they, but how have they been both white and Other? What have been the historical terms of their probationary whiteness?

Jews in American Culture

The idea of a unique Jewish physicality or Jewish "blood" was not new to nineteenth-century America. As James Shapiro has recently argued, theology heavily influenced early modern conceptions of both racial and national difference in Europe, and so the alien Jew figured prominently in European discussion as early as the sixteenth century. In 1590 Andrew Willet argued that "Jews have never been grafted onto the stock of other people." In 1604 the Spaniard Prudencio de Sandoval combined a protoracialist argument of hereditary Jewish evil with a kind of racialism-by-association with the other Other, the Negro: "Who can deny that in the descendants of the Jews there persists and endures the evil inclination of their ancient ingratitude and lack of understanding, just as in Negroes [there persists] the inseparability of their blackness?" Such ideas evidently crossed the Atlantic early on in the settlement of the New World, assuming even more directly racialist overtones in Increase Mather's comments on the "blood" of nations and the purity of the Jews in 1669:

> The providence of God hath suffered other nations to have their blood mixed very much, as you know it is with our own nation: there is a mixture of British, Roman, Saxon, Danish, [and] Norman blood. But as for the body of the Jewish nation, it is far otherwise. Let an English family live in Spain for five or six hundred years successively, and they will become Spaniards. But though a Jewish family live in Spain a thousand years, they do not degenerate into Spaniards (for the most part).[13]

Until the second half of the nineteenth century, however, it was generally not their "blood" but their religion that marked the Jews as a people apart. The Jew was the perpetual "Historical Outsider," in Frederic Jaher's phrase, whose perceived difference derived above all from "Christian hostility." The Jew's difference was primarily cast in terms of the "infidel" or the "blasphemer" (one Jacob Lambrozo was indicted in Maryland for denouncing Jesus as a "necromancer," for example), and discussion was occasionally infused with a dose of long-standing European rumor (such as the twelfth-century "blood libel" that Jews needed Christian blood for certain holiday fêtes) or stereotypes of Jews as well-poisoners and usurers. Although the popular view of Jews was "amply negative" in the colonies, by Jaher's account, it was far better there than in Europe; and their status was characterized by a general state of toleration disrupted only by occasional anti-Semitic outbursts, as when the New York Assembly disfranchised them in 1737, or when Savannah freeholders resisted the expansion of a Jewish cemetery in 1770.[14]

These religiously grounded ideas about the Jewish alien could occasionally take on a racialist cast in the new nation, just as they had in early modern Europe. In a rabid denunciation of the Jacobin propensities of the Democratic Society in 1795, for instance, one Federalist publisher asserted that the democrats would be "easily known by their physiognomy"; they seem to be "of the tribe of Shylock: they have that leering underlook and malicious grin."[15] But generally Jews remained "free [though unchristian] white persons" in the early republic, and the overt depictions of the Jew as a racial Other rose sharply only in the second half of the nineteenth century, particularly in the decades after what John Higham has called "a mild flurry of ideological anti-Semitism" during the Civil War. Now it was not only that Jews could be known in their greed (or their Jacobinism or their infidelism or their treachery) by their physiognomy, but that their physiognomy itself was significant – denoting, as it did, their essential unassimilability to the republic. Only now did the "Israelitish nose" stand for something in and of itself – not greed, or usury, or infidelism, or well-poisoning, but simply "difference." Only now was the dark Jew equated with "mongrelization," that catch-all term for "unfitness" in American political culture.[16] Thus a century after Johann Blumenbach introduced as scientific fact the remarkable stability of the Jews when it came to "the fundamental configuration of face," the New York *Sun* offered this vernacular explanation of "why the Jews are kept apart" (1893):

Other races of men lose their identity by migration and by intermarrying with different peoples, with the result that their peculiar characteristics and physiognomies are lost in the mess. The Jewish face and character remain the same as they were in the days of PHARAOH. Everybody can distinguish the Jewish features in the most ancient carvings and representations, for they are the same as those seen at this day. Usually a Jew is recognizable as such by sight. In whatever country he is, his race is always conspicuous...After a few generations other immigrants to this country lose their race identity and become Americans only. Generally the Jews retain theirs undiminished, so that it is observable by all men.[17]

Others, as we have seen, strongly contested the blithe assertion that "other immigrants to this country lose their race identity," but the *Sun* was nonetheless expressing a point of impressive consensus on the unassimilability of the Jews.

This intensifying perception of a distinctly racial Jewishness coincided with two entangling developments between the 1850s and the early twentieth century: the rise of the racial sciences, and the rise of what John Higham has called "discriminatory" (as opposed to "ideological") anti-Semitism.[18] Popular accounts of the racial Otherness of Jews, that is, at once framed, and were framed by, a scientific discourse of race on the one hand, and a set of social practices (including hiring and admissions patterns, and the barring of Jews from certain Saratoga resorts) on the other. This coincidence of scientific racialism, discriminatory practice, and the popular expression of racial Jewishness attests to the centrality of race as an organizer of American social life. It also attests to the similarity between the Jewish odyssey from white to Hebrew and, say, the Irish odyssey from white to Celt. Despite its capacity to absorb and adapt unique, long-standing anti-Semitic notions of Jewish greed and the like, the racial ideology encompassing Jewishness in the United States in the latter half of the nineteenth century did set Jews on a social trajectory similar to that traveled by many other probationary "white persons." The full texture of anti-Semitism in this country thus combined strains of an international phenomenon of Jew-hatred with the mutability of American whiteness.[19]

The rise of races and phenotypes in scientific discourse, as described earlier, was a creature of the age of European expansionism and exploration. Non-European races were "discovered" and became "known" through the technologies of conquest; then scientific accounts of these races, in their turn, justified and explained colonial domination and slavery. But Jews received a fair amount of attention even in this context, in part because of the mutual accommodations of scientific and religious understandings of genesis (or Genesis) and "difference," and in part because, as somewhat anomalous Europeans, Jews put stress upon the ideas of consanguinity and race which undergirded emergent European nationalisms. Just as the alien Jew raised questions as to who could or could not be truly "English" in Shakespeare's England, so romantic nationalisms of the nineteenth century had to come to terms with the anomalous Jew in any effort to theorize and police the "imagined community" of the nation. As one scholar puts it, science itself was "often either motivated by or soon annexed to political causes."[20] Just as the plunder of exploration and slavery formed the context within which Africans became "known" to Western science, so Jewish emancipation, debates over citizenship, and the emergence of modern nationalism formed the context within which science comprehended "the Jewish race." Were "Jewish traits" properly attributed to social isolation, environment, or immutable character? Could Jews be compatriots of non-Jews? Could they be redeemed as Europeans?

Thus from the outset scientific writings on Jews in Europe tended to focus upon questions of assimilation, most often emphasizing the race's stubborn immutability – which is to say, its unassimilability. As Gobineau wrote in his essay *Sur l'Inegalité des Races Humaines*, the "Jewish type" has remained much the same over the centuries; "the modifications it has undergone ... have never been enough, in any country or latitude, to change the general character of the race. The warlike Rechabites of the Arabian desert, the peaceful Portuguese, French, German, and Polish Jews – they all look alike ... The Semitic face looks exactly the same as it appears on the Egyptian paintings of three or four thousand years ago."[21] The Jews may be incorporated, but they will forever be Jews. In *Races of Man* (1850), Robert Knox similarly noted Jews' essential physicality, leaving little doubt as to the further question of racial merit:

> Brow marked with furrows or prominent points of bone, or with both; high cheek-bones; a sloping and disproportioned chin; and elongated, projecting mouth, which at the angles threatens every moment to reach the temples; a large, massive, club-shaped, hooked nose, three or four times larger than suits the face – these are features which stamp the African character of the Jew, his muzzle-shaped mouth and face removing him from certain other races ... Thus it is that the Jewish face never can [be], and never is, perfectly beautiful.[22]

The presumed immutability of the Jews became a staple of American science by mid-century as well, even though slavery and the question of Negro citizenship still dominated racial discussion. In *Types of Mankind* (1855) Josiah Nott remarked that the "well-marked Israelitish features are never beheld out of that race"; "The complexion may be bleached or tanned ... but the Jewish features stand unalterably through all climates." In *Natural History of the Human Races* (1869) John Jeffries, too, argued that "the Jews have preserved their family type unimpaired; and though they number over five million souls, each individual retains the full impress of his primitive typical ancestors."[23] And of course we have already seen where these "observations" on Jewish racial integrity tended in the age of eugenics.

In this connection the British scholar Joseph Jacobs deserves special attention. A Jew himself, Jacobs was, as he announced in the preface to *Studies in Jewish Statistics* (1891), "inclined to support the long-standing belief in the substantial purity of the Jewish race."[24] For Jacobs, according to the historian John Efron, Jewish race science represented "a new form of Jewish self-defense" and his own work a new genre of political resistance, "the scientific apologia." But if aimed toward the redemption, rather than the renunciation, of racial Jewishness, Jacobs's work rests upon the same logic of "difference" as the most virulent of his anti-Semitic contemporaries. Indeed, it is in Jacobs's work perhaps above all that we glimpse the depth of "difference" associated with Jewish racial identity in this period. "Even more in Jewesses than in Jews," he wrote, "we can see that cast of face in which the racial so dominates the individual that whereas of other countenances we say, 'That is a kind, a sad, a cruel, or a tender face,' of this our first thought is, 'That is a Jewish face.'... Even the negroes of Surinam, when they see a European and a Jew approaching, do not say, 'Here are two whites,' but, 'Here is a white and a Jew.'"[25]

Just as earlier scientific approaches to the righteousness of slavery (the work of Josiah Nott and John Van Evrie, for instance) had seized upon the degeneracy of the "mulatto" as proof of the unbridgeable divide separating black from white, so Jacobs went into great detail on the "infertility of mixed marriages" between Jews and non-Jews, on the basis of statistics kept in Prussia and Bavaria between 1875 and 1881. The variance in fecundity, according to Jacobs, was an average of 4.41 children for Jewish–Jewish marriages to 1.65 for Jewish–Gentile marriages in Prussia; and 4.7 to 1.1 in Bavaria. He also charted various physical characteristics of Jews and non-Jews in different regions, including the color of eyes, hair, and skin. (Only 65.4 percent of Austrian Jews had "white" skin, he found, as compared with more than 80 percent of the Gentiles.)[26]

Like conceptions of Anglo-Saxon, Celtic, or Teutonic racial character, scientific observations on the Hebrew passed from the rarified discourse of ethnological journals into the American vernacular and the American visual lexicon of race as well. Racial depiction did not necessarily entail a negative judgment; racially accented declarations of *philo*-Semitism were common enough. William Cullen Bryant lamented that Edwin Booth's rendering of Shylock, for instance, failed to do justice to "the grandeurs of the Jewish race." He later sang of "the wonderful working of the soul of the Hebrew."[27] James Russell Lowell, in an ambivalent twist, couched highly sympathetic remarks on Jewishness in a language of physicality and character, but also drew upon the common, anti-Semitic imagery of his day. "All share in government of the world was denied for centuries to perhaps the ablest, certainly the most tenacious, race that ever lived in it," he wrote compassionately in

"Democracy" (1884), "...a race in which ability seems as natural and hereditary as the curve of their noses...We drove them into a corner, but they had
their revenge...They made their corner the counter and banking house of the
world, and thence they rule it and us with the ignoble scepter of finance."[28]
Lowell's respect for "perhaps the ablest" race is the basis for an indictment
of Christian political conduct, and particularly its lamentable exclusions.
Even if blame lies at the doorstep of Christians, however, the Jewish
"revenge" Lowell envisions taps the popular currents of nineteenth-century
anti-Semitism.

More positive a view still, yet no less racial, is Oliver Wendell Holmes's
philo-Semitic paean "At the Pantomime" (1874):

> Amidst the throng the pageant drew
> Were gathered Hebrews, not a few,
> Black bearded, swarthy, – at their side
> Dark, jewelled women, orient-eyed.
>   . . .
> Next on my left a breathing form
> Wedged up against me, close and warm;
> The beak that crowned the bistred face
> Betrayed the mould of Abraham's race, –
> That coal-black hair, that smoke-brown hue, –
> Ah, cursed, unbelieving Jew!
> I started, shuddering, to the right,
> And squeezed – a second Israelite!

Over the course of ten stanzas the narrator has a change of heart, and as he
recognizes his Hebrew neighbors as distant kinsmen of Jesus Christ, his racial
hatred gives way to racial glorification:

> Thou couldst scorn the peerless blood
> That flows unmingled from the flood, –
> Thy scutcheon spotted with the stains
> Of Norman thieves and pirate Danes!
> The New World's foundling, in thy pride
> Scowl on the Hebrew at thy side,
> And lo! the very semblance there
> The Lord of Glory deigned to wear!

Holmes concludes, perhaps with as much self-congratulation as contrition,
"Peace be upon thee, Israel!"[29]

In *The Ambivalent Image*, her study of Jews in American cultural imagery,
Louise Mayo has amassed an invaluable compendium of racial figures of
Jewishness across time. Although Mayo's project did not entail theorizing

the relationship between racial Jewishness and the American social order, her work supports the trajectory of Anglo-Saxondom and its Others sketched out above. Racial depictions of Jews would become most urgent, of course, as immigration figures climbed in the decades following Russia's May Laws of 1881. Nonetheless, as Mayo has so nicely laid bare in her cultural excavations, Hebrews appeared as a counterpoint to Anglo-Saxons in American cultural representation long before actual Hebrews began to disembark in huge numbers at Castle Garden and Ellis Island toward the end of the century. This seems part of the reflex toward an Anglo-supremacist exclusivity beginning in the 1840s. Thus in the cosmos of American popular literature, for instance, George Lippard could remark in *Quaker City* (1844), "Jew was written on his face as though he had fallen asleep for three thousand years at the building of the Temple"; in Peter Hamilton Meyers's *The Miser's Heir* (1854), a certain character's "features ... proclaim him a Jew"; and in J. Richter Jones's *Quaker Soldier* (1866), a Jew is characterized by the "hereditary habits of his race."[30] By the early twentieth century a Jewish group could organize a grassroots boycott of certain New York theaters, protesting their "scurrilous and debasing impersonations of the Hebrew type." Judge Hugo Pam, the leader of the boycott, argued that the theater was fostering "race prejudice" because so many theater goers "get their impressions of the race from the stage Jew." (Significantly, this group took its cue from Irish activists, who, Pam said, had succeeded in eliminating "stage lampoons of the Celtic race" from popular theater.)[31]

Racial depictions of Jewishness circulated not only in cultural productions themselves, but also in cultural commentary, as when *Harper's Weekly* reported that the audience of the Yiddish theater was "remarkably strange in appearance to an Anglo-Saxon," or when *Bookman* reviewed Abraham Cahan's *Yekl* as a penetrating look at the Yiddish immigrant's "racial weakness." William Dean Howells, too, discussed Cahan's novella in racial terms, identifying Cahan as a "Hebrew" and his ghetto sketches as "so foreign to our race and civilization."[32]

Wherever "difference" was cast as race, certainly, the weight of the culture in general tended most often toward negative depiction. Nativist discussion of immigration restriction in the 1890s and the eugenics movement of the earlier twentieth century, of course, stated Jewish difference most boldly. Sounding the familiar chord of race and republicanism, Henry Cabot Lodge warned that Jews "lack the nobler abilities which enable a people to rule and administer and to display that social efficiency in war, peace, and government without which all else is vain." The *Illustrated American* was blunter still, crying in 1894 that "the inroad of the hungry Semitic barbarian is a positive calamity." In a piece on immigration and anarchism, the New York *Times*, too, lamented the arrival of "unwashed, ignorant, unkempt, childish semi-savages," and remarked upon the "hatchet-faced, sallow, rat-eyed young men of the Russian Jewish colony." In response to Franz Boas's innovative argument that in fact no biological chasm did separate new immigrants from America's "old stock," Lothrop Stoddard dismissed his views as "the desperate attempt of a Jew to pass himself off as 'white.'"[33]

Franz Boas's argument notwithstanding, increasingly in the years after the Russian May Laws and the pogroms of 1881, Jews, too, embraced race as a basis for unity. This was particularly true among some Zionists and freethinkers for whom religion had ceased meaningfully to explain their ties to the "folk." The "Jewish Question" as it was posed during the period of pogroms in the East and the Dreyfus Affair in the West generated new secular and political notions of Jewish peoplehood in response. It was in this period, for instance, that Joseph Jacobs began his forays into Jewish race science in Europe. And, as John Efron has amply documented, the *racial* individuality of the Jews as a people was of particular interest within the budding Zionist movement. Aron Sandler's *Anthropologie und Zionismus* (1904), for instance, mobilized the scientific language of a distinct racial genius in order to press the necessity of a Jewish territory where that genius could properly take root and develop.[34]

Indeed, a much longer tradition entwined Jewish nationalism with Jewish racialism. The proto-Zionist Moses Hess, in *Rome and Jerusalem* (1862), had flatly announced that "Jewish noses cannot be reformed, nor black, curly, Jewish hair be turned through baptism or combing into smooth hair. The Jewish race is a primal one, which had reproduced itself in its integrity despite climatic influences... The Jewish type is indestructible."[35] The American proto-Zionist Emma Lazarus, too, wrote in *Epistle to the Hebrews* (1887) that Judaism was emphatically *both* a race and a religion. She rhapsodized over the Jews' "fusion of Oriental genius with Occidental enterprise and energy," "the fire of our Oriental blood," and "the deeper lights and shadows of [Jews'] Oriental temperament." She lamented that Jews in America tended to be condemned "as a race" for failings of a single individual. At once demonstrating her own commitment to racialism, yet marking the extent to which race was a contested concept, she lamented the Jews' lack of unanimity on their own racial status: "A race whose members are recognized at a glance, whatever be their color, complexion, costume or language, yet who dispute the cardinal fact as to whether they are a race, cannot easily be brought into unanimity upon more doubtful propositions," she sighed.[36]

In the 1890s and early 1900s immigrant writers in the United States like Abraham Cahan, Leon Kobrin, Abraham Liessen [Abraham Wald], and Bernard Gorin also lighted upon race both as a way of understanding their own secular Jewishness and as a way of couching their (socialist) appeals to the Yiddish masses. And even as late as the 1920s and 1930s a literature of

Jewish assimilation toyed with race in its exploration of Jewish destiny in the New World.[37] "What of today and of America?" asked Ludwig Lewisohn. "Were the Jews Germans? Are they Americans?...I am not talking about citizenship and passports or external loyalties. What are the inner facts?"[38]

The Island Within (1928), an immigrant saga tracing several generations of a German-Jewish family from Germany in the mid-nineteenth century to the United States in the early twentieth, is Lewisohn's exploration of precisely these "inner facts." "How was it," the novel's young hero, Arthur, wants to know, "that, before they went to school, always and always, as far back as the awakening of consciousness, the children knew that they were Jews?...There was in the house no visible symbol of religion and of race." What does Jewishness consist in? What is its basis, especially in the crucible of a transnational history in which questions of national belonging are so vexed?

Arthur vows to understand. Along the way in this ethnoracial *Bildungsroman*, he takes up anthropology and studies the "variableness of racial types" (but later discovers, to his distaste, that his professor rather undemocratically believes in "fixed qualitative racial differences," and so he searches elsewhere). A neighbor, Mrs. Goldman, provides a simple formula: "Jews always have been Jews and they always will be." The tautology actually foreshadows Arthur's own resolution at the end of the novel.[39]

Throughout the quest, race is central both to Arthur's crisis and to its resolution; for him it becomes a measure of his own alienation. He first registers the degree of his assimilation when he discovers that his own father "looks Jewish" to him: "His father's profile under the hat, pale and unwontedly sorrowful, looked immemorially Jewish...Arthur realized instantly that this perception of his was itself an un-Jewish one and showed how he had grown up to view his very parents slightly from without and how, indeed, in all thoughts and discussions, he treated the Jews as objects of his discourse." Some two hundred pages later, after a good deal of soul-searching and after many tortured conversations on the subject of Jewishness, Arthur discovers and reclaims his own "island within" – his own immutable, unshakable Jewishness. "You didn't know you were going to resurrect the Jew in you?" asks his Gentile wife, Elizabeth. He responds, "You're quite right...But really I didn't even have to resurrect the Jew. I just put away a pretense." Thus eternal Jewishness (what a generation of Yiddish speakers had called *dos pintele yid*, "the quintessence of the Jew"), if racially ambiguous, does have distinctly racial connotations. "It's kind of an argument, isn't it, against mixed marriages?" asks Elizabeth. "I'm afraid it is."[40]

In *I Am a Woman – and a Jew* (1926), Leah Morton [Elizabeth Stern], too, recounted her marriage to a non-Jew, her foray into the world of social work, her secularization, and her eventual re-embrace of Jewishness (if not exactly of Judaism), all in the terms of her relationship to the "race." The authenticity of this narrative has recently been questioned; but it is nonetheless significant that this public embrace of her Jewish identity – however real or imagined – is cast in the thoroughly racial terms of the period's public discourse of Jewishness as difference.[41] Of New York's Bohemia, she wrote, "They were frankly Jewish. They had Jewish names, Jewish faces and the psychology of the Jew." Upon her first taste of public life in the settlement house movement, Leah came to realize that "here, in this office, I was not a girl representing a race. I was not a Jewish maiden responsible to a race, as at home." This fairly conveys Morton's own version of that Jewish immutability so stressed by writers from Knox and Gobineau to Jacobs and Cahan. "Was there a Jewish 'race'?" she asks. "Scientists were taking sides, saying, yes, or no, as they decided. What did it matter to us who were Jews? There was a Jewish people, something that belonged to us, so unchanging that we could not destroy it." The biological basis of that "something that belonged to us," in Morton's estimation, finally comes through when she discovers and embraces "all that we, who are Jews, 'part Jews' or 'all Jews' share." This is Morton's version of the "island within": "We Jews are alike. We have the same intensities, the sensitiveness, poetry, bitterness, sorrow, the same humor, the same memories. The memories are not those we can bring forth from our minds: they are centuries old and are written in our features, in the cells of our brain."[42]

This, then, was the vision of difference that the blackface of an Al Jolson or an Eddie Cantor sought to efface. *The Jazz Singer* marks the beginning of the drift by which American Jews became racial Caucasians and illustrates Frantz Fanon's contention that, when it comes to race-hatred or race-acceptance, "one has only not to be a nigger."[43] As with all racial transformations, the next leg of the Jews' odyssey – the cultural trek from Hebrew to Caucasian – would be a gradual affair, glacial rather than catastrophic. A new paradigm was in ascendance in the 1920s and after; perhaps nothing demonstrates so well the power of that paradigm in redefining Jews as the odd, archaic ring that so much of the material in the foregoing pages now has. Whether it is Leah Morton writing proudly of the features and the brain cells of the eternal Jew, or Lothrop Stoddard commenting upon the slim prospects of Franz Boas's passing himself off as "white," these commentators from the mid-nineteenth century to the early twentieth were clearly speaking from a racial consciousness not our own.

Arthur Miller's *Focus*

Jews did not disappear from racial view overnight in the mid-1920s, nor had racial Jewishness vanished completely even by the 1940s. An *Atlantic Monthly* piece entitled "The Jewish Problem in America" (1941) could still assert that the Jew had become European "only in residence; by nature he did not become an Occidental; he could not possibly have done so." Comparing Jews to another problematic "Oriental" group, Armenians, this writer went on to wonder "whether [differences] can be faded out by association, *miscegenation*, or other means of composition."[44] When Nazi policy began to make news in the 1930s and early 1940s, too, headlines in journals like the *Baltimore Sun* and the *Detroit Free Press* revealed the extent to which Americans and Germans shared a common lexicon of racial Jewishness: American papers unself-consciously reported upon the Nazis' "steps to solve [the] race problem," "laws restricting [the] rights of Hebrews," and the "persecution of members of the Jewish race." Hearst papers remarked upon the "extermination of an ancient and cultured race," while the Allentown (Pennsylvania) *Chronicle and News* commented upon Jews' inability to assimilate with "any other race."[45]

World War II and the revelations of the horrors of Nazi Germany were in fact part of what catapulted American Hebrews into the community of Caucasians in the mid-twentieth century. [...] The feverish and self-conscious revision of "the Jewish race" was at the very heart of the scientific project to rethink the "race concept" in general – the racial devastation in Germany, that is, was largely responsible for the mid-century ascendance of "ethnicity."

Changes wrought in the U.S. social order by the war itself and by the early Cold War, too, helped to speed the alchemy by which Hebrews became Caucasian. From A. Phillip Randolph's threatened march on Washington, to African-Americans' campaign for Double Victory, to the major parties' civil rights planks in 1944 and the rise of the Dixiecrats in 1948, the steady but certain ascendance of Jim Crow as *the* pressing political issue of the day brought the ineluctable logic of the South's white-black binary into play with new force in national life. Postwar prosperity and postindustrial shifts in the economy, too, tended to disperse Jews geographically, either to outlying suburbs or toward sunbelt cities like Los Angeles and Miami – in either case, to places where whiteness itself eclipsed Jewishness in racial salience. As scholars like Deborah Dash Moore and Karen Brodkin Sacks have written, Jews became simply "white or Anglo" in the regional racial schemes of the sunbelt; and racially tilted policies like the GI Bill of Rights and the Federal Housing Authority's "whites only" approach to suburban housing loans re-created Jews in their new regime of racial homogenization. Nikhil Singh has rightly called the postwar suburban boom a case of "state sponsored apartheid"; its hardening of race along exclusive and unforgiving lines of color held tremendous portent for Jews and other white races.[46] And finally, ironically, if racialism had historically been an important component of Zionism, the establishment of a Jewish state ultimately had the opposite effect of whitening the Jews in cultural representations of all sorts: America's client state in the Middle East became, of ideological necessity and by the imperatives of American nationalism, a *white* client state. This revision was popularized not only in mainstream journalism, but in Technicolor extravaganzas on Middle Eastern history like *The Ten Commandments* and *Exodus*.[47]

Given these many historical changes, and given the dawning horror of Nazi Germany and the overtly racial state policy that was its basis, it is not surprising that the 1940s produced a profound revision in the taxonomy of the world's races. Among nonscientific intellectuals, the revision included, most notably, Laura Z. Hobson's *Gentleman's Agreement* (1947) and Arthur Miller's *Focus* (1945). Both of these novels took up Jewishness-as-difference in the racial terms of physiognomy or visibility. Both novels self-consciously undermined that notion of stable Jewish physicality by plot devices of mistaken or assumed identity and racial interchangeability: both involved central characters who, although Gentile in fact, "looked Jewish" and so discovered the social cost attached to that physiognomical circumstance.

Focus, Miller's second novel, shares a good deal with the spirit of *Gentleman's Agreement*, but this work more thoroughly disentangles the skein of race and perception. *Focus* is perhaps the most thoroughgoing meditation ever produced on the questions of American justice and Jewish racial difference – on "looking Jewish." The novel is a brilliant piece of social commentary, at once a psychological study of the dynamics of hatred and desire, and a nuanced exploration of Jewish "difference." In this novel Jewish physicality is a dual phenomenon of "appearing" and "seeing." The plot turns on the fate of an anti-Semitic Milquetoast named Newman who, because he happens to "look Jewish," himself becomes the victim of anti-Semitism. He loses his job; he runs afoul of the local Christian Front; his house is vandalized; he is assaulted. Ultimately Newman embraces his fate as an honorary Jew, thus literally becoming a "new man" – a newly minted social Jew and a newly converted racial liberal.

The plot device at the center of this ironic turn of events is a creation of wry genius: Newman, a corporate personnel officer whose job it is to screen prospective employees (that is, to discriminate) slips up and hires someone who appears to be a Jew. Reprimanded by his boss and rattled by this rare mistake on his part, he gets a new pair of glasses so that he might be more discriminating in the future. But if the new glasses help Newman to see Jews, they also happen to make him look Jewish. "Since you got the glasses," remarks an affable neighbor, "you got to admit you do look a little Hebey." Even his mother confirms his worst suspicions: "you almost look like a Jew."[48]

Despite the whimsicality of its plot construction, *Focus* offers a profound analysis of anti-Semitism as an instrument of economic and political power. (In this respect *Focus* has more in common with Carey McWilliams's *Mask for*

Privilege than with *Gentleman's Agreement*.) Miller addresses the *work* of anti-Semitism from the standpoint of political economy through the character of Finkelstein, a Jew in Newman's neighborhood who witnesses Newman's victimization at the hands of the (mistaken) Christian Front. According to Finkelstein, "the Jew" is not so much the *object* of anti-Semitism as its mode of operation. The object of Jew-hatred, that is, is an allocation of economic and social resources based upon a spontaneous popular allegiance to anti-Semitic leadership and a web of discriminatory practices. "What the hell can [the Christian Front] get out of the Jews?" he asks Newman.

> "There's a hundred and thirty million people in this country and a couple million is Jews. It's you they want, not me. I'm...I'm," he started to stutter in his fury, "I'm chicken feed, I'm nothin'. All I'm good for is they can point to me and everybody else will give them their brains and their money, and then they will have the country. It's a trick, it's a racket."[49]

Miller demonstrates the principle in action by the string of misfortunes Newman suffers (and thus, the string of *fortunes* some unnamed "non-Jew" enjoys) as a result of his looking Jewish.

Finkelstein has evidently come to his own understanding of anti-Semitism by way of an East European parable he recalled while visiting his father's grave. The parable, an eight-page story-within-the-story, involves a Jewish peddler in Poland named Itzik. After a fearsome uprising in which the serfs have murdered their overseer and plundered a certain baron's estate, the baron ingeniously lures Itzik into a position not only to recover the riches for him, but to dampen the dangerous fervor of the rebellious serfs: "I am changing my policy," he tells a naïve and uninformed Itzik, "and will allow you to sell your wares among the peasants." Itzik enters the gates of the manor, and indeed for his meager wares he finds ready buyers, who pay with the money they have earlier stolen from the estate. Soon enough Itzik is predictably stripped of the million Kroner after the baron's army has wracked the peddler's village and destroyed his family in a horrific pogrom. Thus does Itzik function as a "middle-man" not only in the East European economy, but in its *political* economy; the Jewish merchant is a living buffer between the grasping Gentile nobility and the exploited Gentile peasantry. "From that day onward Itzik the peddler was insane."[50]

The story had puzzled Finkelstein as a child, and his father had offered no interpretation. As he ponders the tale at his father's graveside, however, he is struck not so much by the diabolism with which the baron has diverted the wrath of the serfs by offering up Itzik and his wares, as by the tragic willingness with which Itzik has allowed himself to be scripted in on the baron's terms, first as an errand-boy and finally as a scapegoat. The meaning of the story, Finkelstein now concludes, "was that this Itzik should never have allowed himself to accept a role that was not his, a role that the baron had created for him." "They are not going to make an Itzik out of me," he resolves.[51]

The parable of Itzik gathers its force when, on his way out of the cemetery where his father is buried, Finkelstein discovers a headstone that has been toppled by hoodlums and defaced with a yellow swastika. "In America *noch*" [In America yet], Finkelstein thinks, thus bringing European and American history to unbearable proximity, both by the literal sense of the sentence and by its poignant bilingualism. The toppled gravestone and the swastika, indeed, symbolize the occasion for *Focus* itself, just as Finkelstein's resolve never to be made "an Itzik" condenses the sense of the novel to its purest form. The tale of Itzik in Poland provides the deep genealogy of that "racket" which Finkelstein deems anti-Semitism; the stone and the swastika are the immediate, concrete emblems of that racket and its contemporary sway.[52]

This sociopolitical dimension of "being made an Itzik" has its psychological analogues as well; and the two dimensions of anti-Semitism will come together over the course of the novel in Miller's treatment of the ways in which the social category "Jew" becomes aligned with the visual category "Jew." Layered atop this foundation of political exploitation, in Miller's scheme, is a superstructure of Jew-hatred deriving in large part from a psychology of *self*-hatred. If the motive for anti-Semitic practice is largely economic, in other words, the venom of anti-Semitic belief is largely psychological.

Miller develops this most clearly in a scene involving Newman's interview with an applicant named Gertrude Hart when he is still working in the personnel office. Newman's mistaken hire, Miss Kapp (whom he now refers to matter-of-factly as "Kapinsky"), has been fired; Newman now has his new glasses, and he is eager to prove himself and his sharpness of vision by hiring the "perfect girl" – someone whose visual credentials as a Gentile are above reproach. In this frame of mind he scrutinizes Gertrude Hart, whom he takes to be a Jew. But as a result of this scrutiny on his part he also thinks he discerns her scrutinizing *him*. Miss Hart seems to be taking him for a Jew, and his uneasy posture under her suspicious gaze leads Newman into the house of mirrors of his own hatreds and fears. He cannot bring himself to rebut her unspoken racial accusation, and in his own embarrassment and discomfiture – his acquiescent *imposture* – he feels her eyes actually transforming him into a Jew, for "to him Jew had always meant impostor": "poor Jews pretended they were poorer than they were, the rich richer... Their houses smelled, and when they did not it was only because they wanted to seem like gentiles. For him, whatever they did that was pleasing was never done naturally, but out of a desire to ingratiate themselves... And when he encountered an open-handed

Jew... in the Jew's open-handedness he saw only trickery or self-display. Pretenders, impostors. Always." Under Gertrude Hart's gaze Newman comes to feel the impostor, which is to say, he comes to feel the Jew.[53]

This passage is a compelling study of the hatred that can attach to race – virtually no piece of evidence is enough to reverse its course. What follows is a stunning treatment of the complex processes of projection, ascription, and reification, as the anti-Semite contemplates one whom he supposes to be "the Jew" and slowly recognizes the desire he feels for her.

> He was sitting there in the guilt of the fact that the evil nature of the Jews and their numberless deceits, especially their sensuous lust for women – of which fact he had daily proof in the dark folds of their eyes and their swarthy skin – all were the reflections of his own desires with which he had invested them... her eyes had made a Jew of him; and his monstrous desire was holding back his denial.

As he continues to scan her face he pegs her racially, first as looking "almost Irish," but he then notices a "Hebrew dip to the nose," and he can finally conclude comfortably, "She had the vitriol of the Hebrews... and their lack of taste."[54]

For Arthur Miller the manner in which a particular class of people comes to "look Jewish" is crucial to the internal dynamic of anti-Semitism. Like Hobson, Miller could not take up the question of Jewishness and justice without taking up the elusive problem of Jewishness-as-difference itself. But whereas Hobson would interrogate the static category "Jews" under an epistemological regime of race and "difference," Miller investigates racial Jewishness itself as a dynamic *process* that is set in motion, in part, by the conventions of an anti-Semitism whose purpose is not hatred but profit. The novel thus aims primarily to illumine the complex relationship between appearance and vision, between the physiognomy of the Jew and the eye of the beholder. Gertrude's "eyes made a Jew of [Newman]" in their first interview. "You ought to have more sense than to make a Jew out of me," Newman objects to his neighbor, Fred. "No one makes a Jew out of me and gets away with it," Gertrude later tells Newman.[55] This drumming on the theme of "making a Jew out of me" by acts of perception and social intercourse lends a second dimension to Finkelstein's notion of "making an Itzik of me" by acts of political coercion. In order to be exploited as an Itzik on the American scene the Jew must first be seen and known; but it is the seeing and knowing themselves that render the Jew racially Jewish.

Miller introduces the relationship between essential "difference" and social modes of perception when Newman first examines himself in the mirror with his new glasses on: "In the mirror in his bathroom, the bathroom he had used for nearly seven years, he was looking at what might very properly be called the face of a Jew. A Jew, in effect, had gotten into his bathroom." Newman's own preconceived notion of Jewish physicality is reflected back to him as Jewishness. It is not that now his face merely looks Jewish; in looking like the face of a Jew, it "might very properly be called the face of a Jew." The anti-Semitic gaze and the Semitic physiognomy meet at the mirror's surface to produce a "Jew" where before there had been none. That Jew is now loose in Newman's house.[56]

Although there seems an optical trickery at work in his newly discovered visual Jewishness – "He took the glasses off and slowly put them on again to observe the distortion" – Newman's torrent of associations confounds the notions of objectivity and subjectivity, revealing his presumptive "Jewishness" as a complicated interplay of physicality and character:

> He tried his smile. It was the smile of one who is forced to pose before a camera, but he held it and it was no longer his smile. Under such bulbous eyes it was a grin, and his teeth which had always been irregular now seemed to insult the smile and warped it into a cunning, insincere mockery of a smile, an expression whose attempt at simulating joy was belied, in his opinion, by the Semitic prominence of his nose, the bulging set of his eyes, the listening posture of his ears. His face was drawn forward, he fancied, like the face of a fish.[57]

By a density of description and a confusion of logic this passage renders two distinct recitations at once: the account of Newman's own unhappiness to find himself a Jew, and an account of Newman's presuppositions about Jewishness, now reflected back to him as physiognomical facts in his own Jewish face. The extent to which Newman is "making a Jew of himself" is indicated in the first two lines quoted here, where "his smile" becomes "no longer his smile" as Newman "forces" himself to "pose." In Newman's world-view, as we come to find, "being forced" and "posing" are the chief conditions marking the Jew's movement in the social world. As he stands smiling before the mirror under the harsh command of his own inspection, he literally *becomes* someone who "is forced" and who "poses" – a Jew. This recognition of his own Jewish posture, then, comes back to Newman as observable fact. Although the presence of the anti-Semitic gaze is marked throughout the passage by phrases like "seemed," "in his opinion," and "he fancied," Newman registers only the observable facts of a "cunning, insincere mockery of a smile," a "Semitic" nose, "bulbous" eyes, "listening" ears – the "face of a fish." This physiognomical condition, and the state it represents, "belie" the pretense of "joy." There *can* be no joy for the Jew; and indeed, for Newman there *is* no joy *as* a Jew – a fact he sees as plainly as the nose on his face.

Similarly, when Newman loses a job opportunity because of his Semitic appearance, he muses over the way in which he has been artificially but nonetheless irretrievably interpolated as a racial Jew. "Is it possible...that Mr. Stevens looked at me and thought me untrustworthy, or grasping, or loud because of my face?" he wonders. His reflection on this injustice stirs an inchoate protest against a regime of social perception that renders individuals so utterly knowable by their outward appearance. For the moment, however, Newman's capacity for protest is limited by his own stubborn adherence to that very regime.

> *He* was not his face. Nobody had a right to dismiss him like that because of his face. Nobody! He was *him*, a human being with a certain definite history and he was not this face which looked like it had grown out of another alien and dirty history.

On the one hand, back when he was working in the personnel office, "no proof, no documents, no words could have changed the shape of a face that he himself suspected," and hence he now understands as well as anyone the power of racial suspicions to generate their own racial objects. And yet, on the other hand, even as he is beginning to recognize the process by which racial Jews are created, he still does not recognize the Jewish race as a creation of that process. Rather, Jews are products of an "alien and dirty history."[58]

The latter half of this equation will ultimately shift for Newman; the Jews' history comes to seem neither alien nor dirty, as his own victimization as a Jew forces the realization that racial "Jewishness" is not the stable essence he had always supposed, but a highly unstable categorical convention based upon certain social practices and ways of seeing. By the novel's end Newman the sometime anti-Semite could perhaps say of the Jews, after Theodore Herzl, "We are one people – our enemies have made us one without our consent."[59] Unlike Herzl, however, Newman could note that not all those who had been rendered members in this unified Jewish people had originally been Jews in fact. The Jews, according to the bottom-line definition in Newman's evolving cosmos, are people who are treated in a particular way, socially and politically; and anyone so treated is "in effect" a Jew. "Jewish" identity is thus unhinged from any stable notions of race – *anybody* can turn out to be Jewish – but neither can Jewishness be entirely uncoupled from the question of looking and being seen a certain racially charged way.

The twin themes of political and psychological Jewishness ("making an Itzik" and "making a Jew") converge in the ironic early history of Newman and Gertrude Hart. In his capacity as personnel officer, Newman has refused to hire Gertrude because she looked Jewish, because she seemed to take him for a Jew, because he experienced a monstrous desire for her, because his desire for her (a Jewess) was indeed monstrous, and because in his very monstrousness he in fact became the Jew she took him to be. After Newman himself has lost his job, their paths cross again in another interview at a second firm – this time he is the Jewish-looking applicant and she is working in the personnel office. Gertrude understands that Newman had taken her for a Jew, and she comments simply that he must have been looking at her "cockeyed" before. Her remark causes Newman to focus upon Gertrude's changeability and upon his own vision:

> It was like seeing a face in a movie change and dissolve, taking on a new character and yet remaining the same face ... Her eyes in which he had detected that mocking secretiveness were now simply the darkened eyes of a woman who had done a lot of crying. And yet they were the same eyes. Her nose ... it occurred to him that the Irish often had a dip in their noses, and he thought now that it became her well ... As a Jewess she had seemed vitriolic and pushy and he had hated himself even as he was drawn fearfully to her, but now he no longer feared her.

Once again later on, after the two are married, Newman changes Gertrude back and forth from Jewish to Gentile, like a Nekar cube or a figure-ground puzzle, by sheer effort of mind: "There she was ..., Jewish. Now he changed her back again ... Here she was, Gertrude, his wife, gentile, as easily under-standable as his own mother."[60]

Like other works that interrogate conventional notions of "difference" only by mobilizing the very categories they seek to undermine (*Pudd'nhead Wilson* and *Black No More*, for instance), *Focus* refuses to sit completely still for analysis. Is there such a thing as a Jewish race, by this account? Miller does define anti-Semitism as a peculiar brand of madness – "People were in asylums for being afraid that the sky would fall, and here were millions walking around as insane as anyone could be who feared the shape of a human face." And yet that "shape of a human face" is so fundamental to the phenomenon of anti-Semitism as Miller sees it that one cannot dispense with the notion of race and races in unraveling the complexities involved either in "making Jews" or "making Itziks" in the American social order. Race is a self-sustaining feature of the social landscape, and no less so in its moments of self-collapse. Newman – like Phil Green in *Gentleman's Agree-ment* – can make a muddle of the notion of a Jewish race by "looking Jewish" without in fact *being* Jewish. But "looking Jewish" is the baseline reality that Newman must approximate in order to call into question the idea of Jewish physicality; and so just as Phil Green proves the racial basis of Jewishness by failing to pass, so Newman reifies the Jewish "look" by assuming it. (Nor are Jews alone among white races in *Focus*: when Newman makes his report against the Christian Front, the beat cop whom he deals with has a "broad Irish face.")[61]

At bottom *Focus* and *Gentleman's Agreement* are predicated on the same assumption of interchangeability, and subject to the same limitations of that assumption. Just as the Gentile Green can volunteer to be victimized by anti-Semitism (or so, at least, would Hobson like to think), so the Gentile Newman can be *in*voluntarily victimized by it. But the way in which both works are structured by the Jewish "look" is symptomatic of their production amid the historic flux of stable Semitic racial character and newly consolidated Caucasian whiteness: that there *is* in fact such a thing as "looking Jewish" is, paradoxically, precisely why Green cannot pass and why Newman can.

Finally, it is less the theme of mistaken identity than Newman's dramatic decision simply to go ahead and be a Jew that aligns Miller's novel with *Gentleman's Agreement*. Newman turns out not to be Philip Green's inverted double, but Professor Lieberman's. Whereas Lieberman is a Jew marked by classically Jewish physiognomy who goes forth to proclaim, "I am *not* a Jew," Newman is a *non*-Jew marked by classically Jewish physiognomy who goes forth to proclaim, "I *am* a Jew" – a reverse variation on Lieberman's "new principle." By setting the more radical shape-shifter at the center of his work, Miller thus makes *Focus* a novel less about Jewishness than about social conscience and justice generally – a theme embodied as well in the character of Finkelstein.

It is worth pausing, in closing, to consider the nexus established here between justice and race, especially in the mid-1940s, the era of the March on Washington Movement and the Fair Employment Practices Committee (FEPC), the campaign for Double Victory, Chicago's housing covenant wars, and early federal promises "to secure these rights" for American Negroes. Miller could not write about race and justice in 1945 and avoid the question of the color line. If, as Carey McWilliams had it, anti-Semitism had been a "mask for privilege" in the decades before the 1940s, then the racial revision of Jewishness into Caucasian whiteness would become the invisible mask of *Jewish* privilege in the decades *after* the 1940s. (Jews, for instance, would move in next door to Gentiles in the suburban neighborhoods that Federal Housing Authority policy so vigilantly preserved for members of "the same social and racial classes." If Jewishness never faded altogether as a social distinction, it did fade considerably in these years as a *racial* one.)[62] No less than Laura Z. Hobson's disquieting assertion of equality based upon literal interchangeability, *Focus*, by its revision of racial Jewishness, raises the question of the relationship between real justice and real "difference."

The novel offers but fleeting commentary on the meaning of the sharpening American color line for the prospect of Jewish racial identity. After the

Christian Front had vandalized his property by strewing garbage across his lawn, Newman stood "white and clean in his pajamas on the porch, [staring] down the stoop at the glistening of some wet food leavings that were scattered in the grass." The reference to Newman's whiteness here could be, like the logic of justice based upon sameness that governs *Gentleman's Agreement*, a protest against the unjust treatment, not of a citizen or neighbor, but of a specifically *white* citizen and neighbor. But if so, this seems Newman's sentiment, not Arthur Miller's. Later, as Newman reflects upon his alienation from his own (lily-white) neighborhood, he recalls an earlier evening when a Puerto Rican maid had been accosted on his street, and no one had come to her aid.

> She could have been murdered, clubbed to death out here that night. No one would have dared outdoors to help, to even say she was a human being. Because all of them watching from their windows knew she was not white.
> But he was white. A white man, a neighbor. He *belonged* here. Or did he? Undoubtedly they all knew the rumor by now. Newman is a Jew.[63]

The compelling indeterminacy here – "He belonged here. Or did he?" – may mark the ambiguous racial status of the Jewish pariah in 1945, but it also signals Miller's refusal to take refuge in whiteness. The novel's notable silence on the African-American presence and on antiblack racism as a phenomenon related in some way to anti-Semitism does leave lingering questions about the overall politics of race envisioned here. Yet this treatment still does not seek to efface the physicality of the white races; nor does Miller lay claim to a simpler, self-assured whiteness. In this respect *Focus* represents a more progressive political impulse than either of the dominant approaches to the Jewish race in more recent decades – that is, scientific rebuttals to racially inflected anti-Semitism, like Raphael Patai and Jennifer Wing's *Myth of the Jewish Race* (1975), or politically spirited disavowals of whiteness and white privilege, like Michael Lerner's "Jews Are Not White" (1993).[64] In other words, Miller neither reifies race by arguing the biogenetic specifics of Jewishness nor dodges the issue of white privilege that surely undergirds the history of Jews in the United States. Rather, he locates the phenomenon of race in the eye of the beholder – in disparate acts of perception engendered by the contingencies of political economy and power relations.

Newman's racial conversion or awakening at the end of *Focus*, indeed, represents one of the few models extant for a truly progressive politics based upon the deconstruction of race: it is a progressive politics on the coalition model, and yet it is coalition rooted not in a reification of categories, but in a recognition of their logical nonsense. When questioning Newman in the wake of the Christian Front's assault, a policeman asks him to name all the Jews in the neighborhood.

"There are the Finkelsteins on the corner..."
"Just them and yourself?" interrupted the policeman.
"Yes. Just them and myself."[65]

Newman recognizes his own Jewishness as a product of the perception of others, and he decides to band together with others so perceived. *This* is a solidarity uniquely attuned to race, not as a biological bond, but as a historical process; it is a solidarity founded upon a keen understanding of race, perception, and the vicissitudes of whiteness – the cultural and historical contingencies of looking Jewish and seeing Jews.

* * *

In Saratoga in 1877 Joseph Seligman discovered just how racially distant were the Hebrew and the Anglo-Saxon, even if contemporary circumstances in the frontier West and the Reconstruction South pulled for a homogenized political whiteness. Across the latter half of the nineteenth century Jews, by common consensus, did represent a distinct race; but by the mid-twentieth such certainties had evaporated. Miller and Hobson could now toy with and undermine notions of distinct Jewish racial character, though the older view still left traces on their work. If the core concern for "fitness for self-government" determined the broad patterns of racial perception over time in the United States from 1790 to the 1840s to the post-1924 period, these instances of racial instability and indeterminacy reveal the social, political, and psychological circuitry by which history has divided the polity along racial lines that, paradoxically, can be as unforgiving as they are unreliable. The racial contradictions of 1877 and the racial odyssey of American Jews from "white persons" to "Hebrews" to "Caucasians" illustrate how historical circumstance, politically driven categorization, and the eye of the beholder all conspire to create distinctions of race that are nonetheless experienced as *natural* phenomena, above history and beyond question.

Notes

1 Johann Friedrich Blumenbach, *On the Natural Varieties of Mankind* [1775, 1795] (New York: Bergman, 1969), 234.
2 In Morris U. Schapps (ed.), *A Documentary History of Jews in the United States, 1654–1875* (New York: Schocken, 1950, 1971), 1–2.
3 Henry James, "Glasses," *Atlantic Monthly* (Feb. 1896), 145; William Boelhower, *Through a Glass Darkly: Ethnic Semiosis in American Literature* (New York: Oxford, 1987), 17–40, 21; Henry James, *The American Scene* [1906] (n.l.: Library of

America, 1993), 425–7. See also Karen Brodkin Sacks, "How Did Jews Become White Folks?" in Steven Gregory and Roger Sanjek (eds.), *Race* (New Brunswick: Rutgers University Press, 1994), 79–85.

4 Melanie Kaye/Kantrowicz, *My Jewish Face and Other Stories* (San Francisco: Spinster-Aunt Lute, 1990); Philip Roth, *The Counterlife* (New York: Penguin, 1988), 79.

5 Charles Dudley Warner, *In the Levant* [1877] (New York: Houghton Mifflin, 1901), 177–8. Emphasis added.

6 *North American Review*, 152 (1891), 128. On "white Jews" see Louis Binstock, "Fire-Words," *Common Ground* (Winter 1947), 83–4, and Laura Z. Hobson, *Gentleman's Agreement* (New York: Simon & Schuster, 1947), 154–5.

7 F. Marion Crawford, *The Witch of Prague* [1891] (London: Sphere Books, 1974), 186.

8 Matthew Frye Jacobson, *Special Sorrows: The Diasporic Imagination of Irish, Polish, and Jewish Immigrants in the United States* (Cambridge: Harvard University Press, 1995), 102–5, and "'The Quintessence of the Jew': Polemics of Nationalism and Peoplehood in Turn-of-the-Century Yiddish Fiction," in Werner Sollors and Marc Schell (eds.), *Multilingual America* (New York: New York University Press, 1998); John Efron, *Defenders of the Race: Jewish Doctors and Race Science in Fin-de-Siècle Europe* (New Haven: Yale University Press, 1994).

9 Hasia Diner, *In the Almost Promised Land: American Jews and Blacks, 1915–1935* [1977] (Baltimore: Johns Hopkins University Press, 1995), 8–9.

10 Madison Grant, *The Passing of the Great Race: or, The Racial Basis of European History* (New York: Scribner's, 1916), 15–16; James William Gibson, *Warrior Dreams: Violence and Manhood in Post-Vietnam America* (New York: Hill & Wang, 1994), 72.

11 Ludwig Lewisohn, *The American Jew: Character and Destiny* (New York: Farrar, Straus & Co., 1950), 23.

12 Sander Gilman, *The Jew's Body* (New York: Routledge, 1991), ch. 7; Sacks, "How Did Jews Become White Folks?"

13 James Shapiro, *Shakespeare and the Jews* (New York: Columbia University Press, 1996), 36, 168, 169, 170; see pp. 167–93 on early modern English conceptions of nationality and the Jewish alien.

14 Frederic Cople Jaher, *A Scapegoat in the New Wilderness: The Origins and Rise of Anti-Semitism in America* (Cambridge: Harvard University Press, 1994), 17, 82, 87–8, 106, 112. For Jaher's view of the Christian roots of the Jew as "Historical Outsider," see pp. 17–81 passim.

15 Jaher, *Scapegoat*, 133.

16 Ibid., 222, 232; on the worsening image, see pp. 170–241; on the proto-racialism of older stereotypes, see pp. 192–4. John Higham, *Send These to Me: Immigrants in Urban America* [1975] (Baltimore: Johns Hopkins University Press, 1984), 123. Jeffrey Melnick notes an interesting swing in American discourse between the Jew as "mongrel" and the Jew as racially "pure" – both are bad. *A Right to Sing the Blues* (Cambridge: Harvard University Press, 1999).

17 New York *Sun*, Apr. 24, 1893, 6.

18 Higham, *Send These to Me*, 117–52. On Jews and the racial sciences see Robert Singerman, "The Jew as Racial Alien: The Genetic Component of American Anti-Semitism," in David Gerber (ed.), *Anti-Semitism in American History* (Urbana: University of Illinois Press, 1987), 103–28, and below.

19 John Higham, "Ideological Anti-Semitism in the Gilded Age," and "The Rise of Social Discrimination," in *Send These to Me*, 95–116, 117–52. On "status panic" and American anti-Semitism, see p. 141.

20 Efron, *Defenders*, 63.

21 Michael Bediss (ed.), Arthur Comte de Gobineau, *Selected Political Writings* (New York: Harper & Row, 1970), 102; William Stanton, *The Leopard's Spots: Scientific Attitudes toward Race in America, 1815–59* (Chicago: University of Chicago Press, 1960), 147–8; George Stocking (ed.), *Bones, Bodies, Behavior: Essays on Biological Anthropology* (Madison: University of Wisconsin Press, 1988); Thomas Gossett, *Race: The History of an Idea in America* (New York: Schocken, 1963).

22 Quoted in Efron, *Defenders*, 51.

23 Josiah Nott, *Types of Mankind* (Philadelphia: Lippincott, 1855), 117, 118; John P. Jeffries, *Natural History of the Human Races* (New York: Edward O. Jenkins, 1869), 123.

24 Joseph Jacobs, *Studies in Jewish Statistics, Social, Vital, and Anthropometric* (London: D. Nutt, 1891), p. xxx.

25 Ibid., p. xxviii; Efron, *Defenders*, 58–90, 59.

26 Jacobs, *Jewish Statistics*, pp. v, xiv; Efron, *Defenders*, 79–80; Maurice Fishberg, *The Jews: A Study of Race and Environment* (n.l.: Walter Scott, 1911); Sander Gilman, *The Case of Sigmund Freud: Medicine and Identity at the Fin de Siècle* (Baltimore: Johns Hopkins University Press, 1993), 11–68; Sander Gilman, *Freud, Race, and Gender* (Princeton: Princeton University Press, 1993), 12–48.

27 Quoted in Louise Mayo, *The Ambivalent Image: Nineteenth-Century America's Perception of the Jew* (Rutherford: Fairleigh Dickinson University Press, 1988), 77.

28 James Russell Lowell, "Democracy" [1884], in *Essays, Poems, and Letters* (New York: Odyssey Press, 1948), 153.

29 Oliver Wendell Holmes, "At the Pantomime" [1874], in *The Poetical Works of Oliver Wendell Holmes* (Boston: Houghton, Mifflin & Co., 1949), vol. 2, pp. 210–13.

30 Mayo, *Ambivalent Image*, 44, 53, 54.

31 New York *Times*, Apr. 25, 1913, 3.

32 Mayo, *Ambivalent Image*, 75–6, 154; Howells quoted in Bernard Richards, "Abraham Cahan Cast in a New Role," in Cahan, *Yekl, the Imported Bridegroom, and Other Stories* (New York: Dover, 1970), p. vii.

33 Mayo, *Ambivalent Image*, 58, 156, 172; Stoddard quoted in Michael Rogin, *Blackface, White Noise: Jewish Immigrants in the Hollywood Melting Pot* (Berkeley: University of California Press, 1996), 89. The Dillingham Commission was uncharacteristically sanguine regarding Jews' prospects for assimilation in 1911, asserting that "the Jews of to-day are more truly European than Asiatic or Semitic." Nonetheless, the report did note that "Israelites" were "preserving their own individuality to a marked degree." *Reports of the Immigration Commis-*

sion: Dictionary of Races and Peoples (Washington, DC: Government Printing Office, 1911), 73, 74.

34 Efron, *Defenders*, 123–74.

35 Quoted in Gilman, *The Jew's Body*, 179.

36 Emma Lazarus, *An Epistle to the Hebrews* [1887] (New York: Jewish Historical Society, 1987), 9, 20, 21, 78, 80.

37 Jacobson, *Special Sorrows*, 97–111; Melnick, *A Right to Sing the Blues*.

38 Ludwig Lewisohn, *The Island Within* (New York: Modern Library, 1928), 43.

39 Ibid., 103–4, 146, 154–5, 168.

40 Ibid., 148, 346.

41 Laura Browder, "*I Am a Woman – And a Jew*: Ethnic Imposter Autobiography and the Creation of Immigrant Identity," paper delivered at the ASA annual conference, Kansas City, Nov. 1, 1996.

42 Leah Morton [Elizabeth Stern], *I Am a Woman – and a Jew* [1926] (New York: Markus Wiener, 1986), 347, 62, 193, 360. The text also contains racialized references to Irish and Polish immigrants and to Nordic natives, pp. 175, 245, 299.

43 Frantz Fanon, *Black Skin, White Masks* [1952] (New York: Grove Wiedenfeld, 1967), 115.

44 Albert Nock, "The Jewish Problem in America," *Atlantic Monthly* (July 1941), 69 (emphasis added). In rebuttal, see Marie Syrkin, "How Not to Solve the 'Jewish Problem,'" *Common Ground* (Autumn 1941), 77.

45 Deborah Lipstadt, *Beyond Belief: The American Press and the Coming of the Holocaust, 1933–1945* (New York: Free Press, 1986), 59–60, 88, 93, 157. See also Elazar Barkan, *The Retreat of Scientific Racism: Changing Concepts of Race in Britain and the United States between the World Wars* (Cambridge: Cambridge University Press, 1992), ch. 6; Stefan Kuhl, *The Nazi Connection: Eugenics, American Racism, and German National Socialism* (New York: Oxford, 1994).

46 Deborah Dash Moore, *To the Golden Cities: Pursuing the American Jewish Dream in Miami and L.A.* (New York: Free Press, 1994), 55; Sacks, "How Did Jews Become White Folks?" 86–98; Rogin, *Blackface, White Noise*, 265; Nikhil Pal Singh, "'Race' and Nation in the American Century: A Genealogy of Color and Democracy" (Ph.D. diss., Yale University, 1995); Douglass Massey and Nancy Denton, *American Apartheid: Segregation and the Making of the Underclass* (Cambridge: Harvard University Press, 1993), 51–4.

47 Moore, *Golden Cities*, 227–61; Alan Nadel, *Containment Culture: American Narratives, Postmodernism, and the Atomic Age* (Durham: Duke University Press, 1995), 90–116. On the racial dynamics of American involvement in the Middle East, see also Soheir A. Morsy, "Beyond the Honorary 'White' Classification of Egyptians: Societal Identity in Historical Context," in Gregory and Senjak, *Race*, 175–98.

48 Arthur Miller, *Focus* (New York: Reynal & Hitchcock, 1945), 175, 26.

49 Ibid., 182.

50 Ibid., 142–50, 147.

51 Ibid., 149, 150.

52 Miller, *Focus*, 142–50, 149, 150. The issue was pressing in Finkelstein's America just as it was in Itzik's Poland: according to the historian Hasia Diner, more than a hundred anti-Semitic organizations formed in the United States in the 1930s. Diner, *Almost Promised Land*, 241.

53 Miller, *Focus*, 33, 28–35.

54 Ibid., 34–5.

55 Ibid., 34, 174, 117.

56 Ibid., 24.

57 Ibid., 25.

58 Ibid., 67, 66.

59 Theodore Herzl, *The Jewish State* [1896] (New York: Dover, 1988), 92.

60 Miller, *Focus*, 82–3, 134.

61 Ibid., 215, 216.

62 Rogin, *Blackface, White Noise*, 265–6; Sacks, "How Did Jews Become White Folks?" 92–8.

63 Miller, *Focus*, 138, 177.

64 Raphael Patai and Jennifer Wing, *The Myth of the Jewish Race* (New York: Scribner's, 1975); Michael Lerner, "Jews Are Not White," *Village Voice*, May 18, 1993, 33–4.

65 Miller, *Focus*, 217.

Troubling Sights (Sites): Visual Maps and America's "Others"

12

The Photograph as an Intersection of Gazes

CATHERINE A. LUTZ AND JANE L. COLLINS

If photographs are messages, the message is both transparent and mysterious.

(Sontag 1977: 111)

All photographs tell stories about looking. In considering the *National Geographic's* photographs, we have been struck by the variety of looks and looking relations that swirl in and around them. These looks – whether from the photographer, the reader, or the person photographed – are ambiguous, charged with feeling and power, central to the stories (sometimes several and conflicting) that the photo can be said to tell. By examining the "lines of sight" evident in the *Geographic* photograph of the non-Westerner, we become aware that it is not simply a captured view of the *other*, but rather a dynamic site at which many gazes or viewpoints intersect. This intersection creates a complex, multidimensional object; it allows viewers of the photo to negotiate a number of different identities both for themselves and for those pictured; and it is one route by which the photograph threatens to break frame and reveal its social context. We aim here to explore the significance of "gaze" for intercultural relations in the

Catherine A. Lutz and Jane L. Collins, "The Photograph as an Intersection of Gazes," in Lutz and Collins, *Reading National Geographic*. Chicago: University of Chicago Press, 1993: 187–216. © 1993 by the University of Chicago. Reprinted with permission.

photograph and to present a typology of seven kinds of gaze that can be found in the photograph and its social context: the photographer's gaze (the actual look through the viewfinder); the institutional magazine gaze, evident in cropping, picture choice, and captioning; the reader's gaze; the non-Western subject's gaze; the explicit looking done by Westerners who may be framed with locals in the picture; the gaze returned or refracted by the mirrors or cameras that are shown in local hands; and our own academic gaze.

The Gaze and its Significance

The photograph and the non-Western person share two fundamental attributes in the culturally tutored experience of most Americans; they are objects at which we *look*. The photograph has this quality because it is usually intended as a thing of either beauty or documentary interest and surveillance. Non-Westerners draw a look, rather than inattention or interaction, to the extent that their difference or foreignness defines them as noteworthy yet distant. A look is necessary to cross the span created by the perception of difference, a perception which initially, of course, also involves looking. When people from outside the Western world are photographed, the importance of the look is accentuated.[1]

A number of intellectual traditions have dealt with "the gaze," looking or spectating as they occur in photography and art. Often these types of analysis have focused on the formal features of the photograph alone, excluding history and culture. While we are critical of several of the perspectives on gaze that we review below, to view photographs as having a certain structure can be consistent with an emphasis on an active and historical reader. In other words, we will argue that the lines of gaze perceptible in the photograph suggest the multiple forces at work in creating photographic meaning, one of the most important of which is readers' culturally informed interpretive work. One objective of our research has been to test the universal claims of certain of these theories about gaze by looking at actual cases of photographs being taken, edited, and read by individuals in real historical time and cultural space. Nonetheless, the interethnic looking that gets done in *National Geographic* photos can be conceptualized by drawing on a number of the insights of these analyses.

Feminist film theory, beginning with Mulvey (1985), has focused on the ways in which looking in patriarchal society is, in her words, "split between active/male and passive/female. The controlling male gaze projects its phantasy on to the female figure which is styled accordingly (1985: 808). The position of spectator, in this view, belongs to the male and allows for the construction of femininity. John Berger (1972) has treated the gaze as masculine. He points out that contemporary gender ideologies envisage men as active doers and define women as passive presence, men by what they do to others, women by their attitudes toward themselves. This has led to women's focusing on how they appear before others and so to fragmenting themselves into "the surveyor and the surveyed. . . . One might simplify this by saying *men act* and *women appear*. Men look at women. Women watch themselves being looked at . . . [and] the surveyor of woman in herself is male" (1972: 46–7; see also Burgin 1986).

Mulvey and Berger alert us to the ways in which the position of spectator has the potential to enhance or articulate the power of the observer over the observed. Representations produced by the artist, the photographer, and the scientist in their role as spectators have permanent, tangible qualities and are culturally defined as quasi-sacred. Both Mulvey and Berger point out that it is the social context of patriarchy, rather than a universal essential quality of the image, that gives the gaze a masculine character.

Recent critiques of these views take issue with the simple equation of the gaze with the masculine, with the psychoanalytic emphasis of this work and its concomitant tendency to universalize its claims and to ignore social and historical context, as well as its neglect of race and class as key factors determining looking relations (de Lauretis 1987; Gaines 1988; Green 1984; Jameson 1983; Tagg 1988; Williams 1987). These critiques make a number of proposals useful in examining *National Geographic* photographs. They suggest, first, that the magazine viewer operates within a racial system in which there are taboos on certain kinds of looking, for example, black men looking at white women. Gaines (1988) forcefully suggests that we need to rethink ideas about looking "along more materialist lines, considering, for instance, how some groups have historically had the license to 'look' openly while other groups have 'looked' illicitly" (1988: 24–5). She also argues that those who have used psychoanalytic theory claim to treat looking positions (viewer/viewed) as distinct from actual social groups (male/female) even while they are identified with gender, and in so doing, "keep the levels of the social ensemble [social experience, representational systems, and so on] hopelessly separate."

Work on women as spectators suggests that viewers may have several possible responses to images, moving toward and away from identification with the imaged person and sometimes "disrupt[ing] the authority and closure of dominant representations" (Williams 1987: 11; compare Burgin 1982). This research suggests that looking need not be equated with control-ling; Jameson argues that there may be legitimate pleasures in looking at others that are not predicated on the desire to control, denigrate, or distance oneself from the other. More broadly, we can say that the social whole in which photographers, editors, and a diversity of readers look at the non-Western

313

world allows no simple rendering of the spectator of the magazine, including the spectator's gender.

Much feminist analysis of the power of gaze has drawn on the psychoanalytic theorizing of Lacan (1981). While it carries the dangers of a universalizing focus, Lacan's view of the gaze can be helpful as a model for the *potential* effects of looking. Lacan speaks of gaze as something distinct from the eye of the beholder and from simple vision: it is that "something [which] slips... and is always to some degree eluded in it [vision]" (1981: 73); it is "the lack." The gaze comes from the other who constitutes the self in that looking, but the gaze the self encounters is "not a seen gaze, but a gaze imagined by me in the field of the Other" (1981: 84). Ultimately, however, the look that the self receives is "profoundly unsatisfying" because the other does not look at the self in the way that the self imagines it ought to be looked at. The photograph of the non-Westerner can be seen as at least partially the outcome of a set of psychoculturally informed choices made by photographers, editors, and caption writers who pay attention at some level to their own and the other's gaze. Their choices may be made in such a way as to reduce the likelihood of the kind of disappointment Lacan mentions. What can be done in the photograph is to manipulate, perhaps unconsciously, the gaze of the other (by way of such processes as photo selection) so that it allows us to see ourselves reflected in their eyes in ways that are comfortable, familiar, and pleasurable. Photographs might be seen as functioning in the way Lacan says a painting can, which is by pacifying the viewer. What is pacified is the gaze, or rather the anxiety that accompanies the gap between our ideal identity and the real. This taming of the gaze occurs when we realize that the picture does not change as our gaze changes. In Lacan's view, we are desperate for and because of the gaze, and the power of the pictorial representation is that it can ease that anxiety. Photos of the ethnic other can help relieve the anxiety provoked by the ideal of the other's gaze and estimation of us.[2]

Homi Bhabha (1983), on the other hand, argues that the gaze is not only crucial to colonial regimes, but that a tremendous ambivalence and unsettling effect must accompany colonial looking relations because the mirror which these images of the other hold up to the colonial self is "problematic, for the subject finds or recognizes itself through an image which is simultaneously alienating and hence potentially confrontational" (29). "There is always the threatened return of the look" (1983: 33). In Bhabha's terms, the look at the racial other places the viewer in the uncomfortable position of both recognizing himself or herself in the other and denying that recognition. Denial leaves "always the trace of loss, absence. To put it succinctly, the recognition and disavowal of 'difference' is always disturbed by the question of its re-presentation or construction" (1983: 33). From this perspective, which borrows from Lacan and Freud, colonial social relations are enacted largely through a "regime of visibility," in which the look is crucial both for identifying the other and for raising questions of how racist discourse can enclose the mirrored self as well as the other within itself. The photograph and all its intersections of gaze, then, is a site at which this identification and the conflict of maintaining a stereotyped view of difference occurs.[3]

Foucault's analysis of the rise of surveillance in modern society is also relevant to understanding the photographic gaze, and recent analyses (Green 1984; Tagg 1988) have sharply delineated ways in which photography of the other operates at the nexus of knowledge and power that Foucault identified. Foucault pointed to psychiatry, medicine, and legal institutions as primary sites in which control over populations was achieved. His novel contribution was to see these institutions as exercising power not only by coercive control of the body but by creating knowledge of the body and thereby forcing it "to emit signs" or to conform physically and representationally to the knowledge produced by these powerful institutions. The crucial role of photography in the exercise of power lies in its ability to allow for close study of the other and to promote, in Foucault's words, the "normalizing gaze, a surveillance that makes it possible to qualify, to classify and to punish. It establishes over individuals a visibility through which one differentiates them and judges them" (1977: 25).

In the second half of the nineteenth century, photography began to be used to identify prisoners, mental patients, and racial or ethnic types. According to Tagg, its efficacy lies not so much in facilitating social control of those photographed but in representing these others to an audience of "non-deviants" who thereby acquire a language for understanding themselves and the limits they must observe to avoid being classed with those on the outside. Foucault's analysis might suggest that the gaze of the *Geographic* is part of the "capillary system" of international power relations allowing for the surveillance, if not the control, of non-Western people. The magazine's gaze at the third world operates to represent it to an American audience in ways that can but do not always shore up a Western cultural identity or sense of self as modern and civilized. The gaze is not, however, as singular or monolithic as Foucault might suggest. In itself, we might say, a look can mean anything, but lines and types of gaze, in social context, tend to open up certain possibilities for interpreting a photograph and to foreclose others. They often center on issues of intimacy, pleasure, scrutiny, confrontation, and power.[4]

A Multitude of Gazes

Many gazes can be found in every photograph in the *National Geographic*. This is true whether the picture shows an empty landscape; a single person looking straight at the camera; a large group of people, each looking in a different direction but none at the camera; or a person in the distance whose eyes are tiny or out of focus. In other words, the gaze is not simply the look given by or to a photographed subject. It includes seven kinds of gaze.[5]

The photographer's gaze

This gaze, represented by the camera's eye, leaves its clear mark on the structure and content of the photograph. Independently or constrained by others, the photographer takes a position on a rooftop overlooking Khartoum or inside a Ulithian menstrual hut or in front of a funeral parade in Vietnam. Photo subject matter, composition, vantage point (angle or point of view), sharpness and depth of focus, color balance, framing, and other elements of style are the results of the viewing choices made by the photographer or by the invitations or exclusions of those being photographed (Geary 1988).

Susan Sontag argues that photographers are usually profoundly alienated from the people they photograph, and may "feel compelled to put the camera between themselves and whatever is remarkable that they encounter" (1977: 10). *Geographic* photographers, despite an expressed fundamental sympathy with the third world people they meet, confront them across distances of class, race, and sometimes gender. Whether from a fear of these differences or the more primordial (per Lacan) insecurity of the gaze itself, the photographer can often make the choice to insert technique between self and his or her subjects, as can the social scientist (Devereux 1967).

Under most circumstances, the photographer's gaze and the viewer's gaze overlap. The photographer may treat the camera eye as simply a conduit for the reader's look, the "searchlight" (Metz 1985) of his or her vision. Though these two looks can be disentangled, the technology and conventions of photography force the reader to follow that eye and see the world from its position.[6] The implications of this fact can be illustrated with a photo that shows a Venezuelan miner selling the diamonds he has just prospected to a middleman (August 1976 [Figure 12.1]). To take his picture, the photographer has stood inside the broker's place of business, shooting out over his back and shoulder to capture the face and hands of the miner as he exchanges his diamonds for cash. The viewer is strongly encouraged to share the photographer's interest in the miner, rather than the broker (whose absent gaze may be more available for substitution with the viewer's than is the miner's), and in fact to identify with the broker from whose relative position the shot has been taken and received. The broker, like the North American reader, stands outside the frontier mining world. Alternative readings of this photograph are, of course, possible; the visibility of the miner's gaze may make identification with him and his precarious position more likely. Ultimately

Figure 12.1. The gaze of the camera is not always exactly the same as the gaze of the viewer, but in most *Geographic* photographs the former structures the latter in powerful ways. In this August 1976 photograph of a Venezuelan diamond transaction, the viewer is strongly encouraged to share the photographer's interest in the miner rather than in the broker. Photograph by Robert Madden. © by National Geographic Society. Reprinted courtesy of National Geographic Society

what is important is the question of how a diverse set of readers respond to such points of view in a photograph.

The magazine's gaze

This is the whole institutional process by which some portion of the photographer's gaze is chosen for use and emphasis. It includes (1) the editor's decision to commission articles on particular locations or issues; (2) the editor's choice of pictures; and (3) the editor's and layout designer's decisions about cropping the picture, arranging it with other photos on the page to bring out the desired meaning, reproducing it in a certain size format to emphasize or downplay its importance, or even altering the picture. The reader, of course, cannot determine whether decisions relating to the last two choices are made by editor or photographer. The magazine's gaze is more evident and accessible in (4) the caption writer's verbal fixing of a vantage on the picture's meaning. This gaze is also multiple and sometimes controversial, given the diverse perspectives and politics of those who work for the *Geographic.*

The magazine readers' gazes

As Barthes has pointed out, the "photograph is not only perceived, received, it is *read*, connected more or less consciously by the public that consumes it to a traditional stock of signs" (1977: 19). Independently of what the photographer or the caption writer may intend as the message of the photo, the reader can imagine something else. This fact, which distinguishes the reader's gaze from that of the magazine, led us to investigate the former directly by asking a number of people to look at and interpret our set of photos. Certain elements of composition or content may make it more likely that the reader will resist the photographic gaze and its ideological messages or potentials. These include whatever indicates that a camera (rather than the reader's eye alone) has been at work – jarring, unnatural colors, off-center angles, and obvious photo retouching.

What *National Geographic* subscribers see is not simply what they get (the physical object, the photograph) but what they imagine the world is about before the magazine arrives, what imagining the picture provokes, and what they remember afterwards of the story they make the picture tell or allow it to tell. The reader's gaze, then, has a history and a future, and it is structured by the mental work of inference and imagination, provoked by the picture's inherent ambiguity (Is that woman smiling or smirking? What are those people in the background doing?) and its tunnel vision (What is going on outside the picture frame? What is it, outside the picture, that she is looking at?). Beyond that, the photo permits fantasy ("Those two are in love, in love like I am with Stuart, but they're bored there on the bench, bored like I have been even in love" or "That child. How beautiful. She should be mine to hold and feed.").

The reader's gaze is structured by a large number of cultural elements or models, many more than those used to reason about racial or cultural difference. Cultural models that we have learned help us interpret gestures such as the thrown-back shoulders of an Argentinean cowboy as indicative of confidence, strength, and bravery. Models of gender lead to a reading of a picture of a mother with a child as a natural scenario, and of the pictured relationship as one of loving, relaxed nurturance; alternatively, the scene might have been read as underlaid with tensions and emotional distance, an interpretation that might be more common in societies with high infant mortality. There is, however, not one reader's gaze; each individual looks with his or her own personal, cultural, and political background or set of interests. It has been possible for people to speak of "the [singular] reader" only so long as "the text" is treated as an entity with a single determinate meaning that is simply consumed (Radway 1984) and only so long as the agency, enculturated nature, and diversity of experience of readers are denied.

The gaze of the *National Geographic* reader is also structured by photography's technological form, including a central paradox. On the one hand, photographs allow participation in the non-Western scene through vicarious viewing. On the other, they may also alienate the reader by way of the fact that they create or require a passive viewer and that they frame out much of what an actual viewer of the scene would see, smell, and hear, thereby atomizing and impoverishing experience (Sontag 1977). From another perspective, the photograph has been said (Metz 1985) to necessarily distance the viewer by changing the person photographed into an object – we know our gaze falls on a two-dimensional object – and promoting fantasy. Still, the presumed consent of the other to be photographed can give the viewer the illusion of having some relationship with him or her.

Finally, this gaze is also structured by the context of reading. How and where does the reader go through the magazine – quickly or carefully, alone or with a child? [...] In a less literal sense, the context of reading includes cultural notions about the magazine itself, as high middlebrow, scientific, and pleasurable. Readers' views of what the photograph says about the other must have something to do with the elevated class position they can assume their reading of *National Geographic* indicates. If I the reader am educated and highbrow in contrast to the reader of *People* magazine or the daily newspaper, my gaze may take on the seriousness and appreciative stance a high-class cultural product requires.

The non-Western subject's gaze

There is perhaps no more significant gaze in the photograph than that of its subject. It is how and where the other looks that most determines the differences in the message a photograph can give about intercultural relations. The gaze of the other found in *National Geographic* can be classified into at least four types; she or he can confront the camera, look at something or someone within the picture frame, look off into the distance, or not look at anything at all.

The gaze confronting camera and reader comprises nearly a quarter of the photos that have at least some non-Western locals in them.[7] What does the look into the camera's eye suggest to readers about the photographic subject? A number of possibilities suggest themselves.

The look into the camera must at least suggest acknowledgment of photographer and reader. Film theorists have disagreed about what this look does, some arguing that it short circuits the voyeurism identified as an important component of most photography: there can be no peeping if the other meets our gaze. The gaze can be confrontational: "I see you looking at me, so you cannot steal that look." Others, however, have argued that this look, while acknowledging the viewer, simply implies more open voyeurism: the return gaze does not contest the right of the viewer to look and may in fact be read as the subject's assent to being watched (Metz 1985: 800–1).

This disagreement hinges on ignoring how the look is returned and on discounting the effects of context inside the frame and in the reader's historically and culturally variable interpretive work. Facial expression is obviously crucial. The local person looks back with a number of different faces, including friendly smiling, hostile glaring, a vacant or indifferent glance, curiosity, or an ambiguous look. Some of these looks, from some kinds of ethnic others, are unsettling, disorienting, and perhaps often avoided. In *National Geographic*'s photos, the return look is, however, usually not a confrontational or challenging one. The smile plays an important role in muting the potentially disruptive, confrontational role of this return gaze. If the other looks back at the camera and smiles, the combination can be read by viewers as the subject's assent to being surveyed. In 38 percent of the pictures of locals where facial expressions are visible (N = 436), someone is smiling (although not all who smile are looking into the camera), while a higher 55 percent of all pictures in which someone looks back at the camera include one or more smiling figures.

The camera gaze can also establish at least the illusion of intimacy and communication. To the extent that *National Geographic* presents itself as bringing together the corners of the world, the portrait and camera gaze are important routes to those ends. The other is not distanced, but characterized

320

as approachable; the reader can imagine the other is about to speak to him or her. The photographers commonly view the frontal shot as a device for cutting across language barriers and allowing for intercultural communication. The portrait is, in the words of one early *Geographic* photographer, "a collaboration between subject and photographer" (National Geographic Society 1981: 22). In published form, of course, the photographed person is still "subjected to an unreturnable gaze" (Tagg 1988: 64), in no position to speak.

The magazine's goal of creating intimacy between subject and reader contradicts to some extent its official goal of presenting an unmanipulated, truthful slice of life from another country. Virtually all the photographers and picture editors we spoke with saw the return gaze as problematic and believed that such pictures ought to be used sparingly because they are clearly not candid, and potentially influenced by the photographer. They might also be "almost faking intimacy," one editor said. Another mentioned that the use of direct gaze is also a question of style, suggesting more commercial and less gritty values. The photographer can achieve both the goals of intimacy and invisibility by taking portraits which are not directly frontal, but in which the gaze angles off to the side of the camera.

To face the camera is to permit close examination of the photographed subject, including scrutiny of the face and eyes, which are in commonsense parlance the seat of the soul – feelings, personality, or character. Frontality is a central technique of a documentary rhetoric in photography (Tagg 1988: 189); it sets the stage for either critique or celebration, but in either case evaluation, of the other as a person or type. Editors at the magazine talked about their search for the "compelling face" in selecting photos for the magazine.

Racial, age, and gender differences appear in how often and how exactly the gaze is returned and lend substance to each of these perspectives on the camera gaze. To a statistically significant degree, women look into the camera more than men, children and older people look into the camera more often than other adults, those who appear poor more than those who appear wealthy, those whose skin is very dark more than those who are bronze, those who are bronze more than those whose skin is white, those in native dress more than those in Western garb, those without any tools more than those who are using machinery.[8] Those who are culturally defined as weak – women, children, people of color, the poor, the tribal rather than the modern, those without technology – are more likely to face the camera, the more powerful to be represented looking elsewhere. There is also an intriguing (but not statistically significant) trend toward higher rates of looking at the camera in pictures taken in countries that were perceived as friendly towards the United States.[9]

To look out at the viewer, then, would appear to represent not a confrontation between the West and the rest, but the accessibility of the other. This interpretation is supported by the fact that historically the frontal portrait has been associated with the rougher classes, as the Daumier print points out. Tagg (1988), in a social history of photography, argues that this earlier class-based styling was passed on from portraiture to the emerging use of photography for the documentation and surveillance of the criminal and the insane. Camera gaze is often associated with full frontal posture in the *Geographic*; as such, it is also part of frontality's work as a "code of social inferiority" (Tagg 1988: 37). The civilized classes, at least since the nineteenth century, have traditionally been depicted in Western art turning away from the camera and so making themselves less available.[10] The higher-status person may thus be characterized as too absorbed in weighty matters to attend to the photographer's agenda. Facing the camera, in Tagg's terms, "signified the bluntness and 'naturalness' of a culturally unsophisticated class [and had a history which predated photography]" (1988: 36).

These class-coded styles of approach and gaze before the camera have continued to have force and utility in renderings of the ethnic other. The twist here is that the more civilized quality imparted to the lighter-skinned male in Western dress and to adult exotics who turn away from the camera is only a relative quality. Full civilization still belongs, ideologically, to the Euroamerican.

Whether these categories of people have actually looked at the camera more readily and openly is another matter. If the gaze toward the camera reflected only a lack of familiarity with it, and curiosity, then one would expect rural people to look at the camera more than urban people. This is not the case. One might also expect some change over time, as cameras became more common everywhere, but there is no difference in rate of gaze when the period from 1950 to 1970 is compared with the later period. The heavy editorial hand at the *Geographic* argues that what is at work is a set of unarticulated perceptions about the kinds of non-Westerners who make comfortable and interesting subjects for the magazine. *National Geographic* editors select from a vast array of possible pictures on the basis of some notion about what the social/power relations are between the reader and the particular ethnic subject being photographed. These aesthetic choices are outside explicit politics but encode politics nonetheless. A "good picture" is a picture that makes sense in terms of prevailing ideas about the other, including ideas about accessibility and difference.

In a second form of gaze by the photographed subject, the non-Westerner looks at someone or something evident within the frame. The ideas readers get about who the other is are often read off from this gaze, which is taken as an index of interest, attention, or goals. The Venezuelan prospector who looks at the diamonds as they are being weighed by the buyer is interested in selling, in making money, rather than in the Western viewer or other compatriots. The caption supplies details: "The hard-won money usually flies fast in gambling and merry-making at primitive diamond camps, where riches-to-rags tales abound." [A] picture of the Marcos family...shows both Ferdinand and Imelda happily staring at their children, assuring the audience of their family-oriented character.

A potential point of interest in our set of photographs is the presence of a Western traveler. In 10 percent of such pictures, at least one local looks into the camera. Yet in 22 percent of the pictures in which only locals appear, someone looks into the camera. To a statistically significant degree, then, the Westerner in the frame draws a look away from those Westerners beyond the camera, suggesting both that these two kinds of Westerners might stand in for each other, as well as indexing the interest they are believed to have for locals.

Third, the other's gaze can run off into the distance beyond the frame. This behavior can suggest radically different things about the character of the subject. It might portray either a dreamy, vacant, absent-minded person or a forward-looking, future-oriented, and determined one. Compare the photo of three Argentinean gauchos as they dress for a rodeo (October 1980) with the shot of a group of six Australian aborigines as they stand and sit in a road to block a government survey team (November 1980). Two of the gauchos, looking out the window at a point in the far distance, come across as thoughtful, pensive, and sharply focused on the heroic tasks in front of them. The aboriginal group includes seven gazes, each heading off in a different direction and only one clearly focused on something within the frame, thus giving the group a disconnected and unfocused look. It becomes harder to imagine this group of seven engaged in coordinated or successful action; that coordination would require mutual planning and, as a corollary, at least some mutual gazing during planning discussions. Other elements of the photograph which add to this impression include their more casual posture, three of them leaning on the truck behind them, in contrast with the gaucho picture in which each stands erect. In addition, the gaze of the aborigines is by no means clear, with gaze having to be read off from the direction of the head. The fuzzy gaze is a significant textual device for reading off character, alienation, or availability. Character connotations aside, the out-of-frame look may also have implications for the viewer's identification with the subject, in some sense connecting with the reader outside the frame (Metz 1985: 795).

Finally, in many pictures no gaze at all is visible, either because the people in them are tiny figures lost in a landscape or in a sea of others, or because the scene is dark or the person's face covered by a mask or veil. We might read this kind of picture (14 percent of the whole sample) as being about the landscape or activity rather than the people or as communicating a sense of nameless others or group members rather than individuals. While these pictures do not increase in number over the period, there has been a sudden spate of recent covers in which the face or eyes of a non-Western person photographed are partly hidden (November 1979, February 1983, October 1985, August 1987, October 1987, November 1987, July 1988, February 1991, December 1991). Stylistically, *National Geographic* photographers may now have license to experiment with elements of the classical portrait with its full-face view, but the absence of any such shots before 1979 can also be read as a sign of a changing attitude about the possibilities of cross-cultural communication. The covered face can tell a story of a boundary erected, contact broken.

A direct Western gaze

In its articles on the non-Western world, the *National Geographic* has frequently included photographs that show a Western traveler in the local setting covered in the piece. During the postwar period, these Western travelers have included adventurers, mountain climbers, and explorers; anthropologists, geographers, botanists, and archaeologists; United States military personnel; tourists; and government officials or functionaries from the United States and Europe, from Prince Philip and Dwight Eisenhower to members of the Peace Corps. These photographs show the Westerners viewing the local landscape from atop a hill, studying an artifact, showing a local tribal person some wonder of Western technology (a photograph, a mirror, or the camera itself), or interacting with a native in conversation, work, or play. The Westerner may stand alone or with associates, but more often is framed in company with one or more locals.

These pictures can have complex effects on viewers, for they represent more explicitly than most the intercultural relations it is thought or hoped obtain between the West and its global neighbors. They may allow identification with the Westerner in the photo and, through that, more interaction with, or imaginary participation in, the photo. Before exploring these possibilities, however, we will speculate on some of the functions these photographs serve in the magazine.

Most obviously, the pictures of Westerners can serve a validating function by proving that the author was *there*, that the account is a first-hand one, brought from the field rather than from library or photographic archives. In this respect the photography sequences in *National Geographic* resemble traditional ethnographic accounts, which are written predominantly in the third person but often include at least one story in the first person that portrays the anthropologist in the field (Marcus and Cushman 1982). For this purpose, it does not matter whether the Westerner stands alone with locals.

To serve the function of dramatizing intercultural relations, however, it is helpful to have a local person in the frame. When the Westerner and the other are positioned face-to-face, we can read their relationship and their natures from such features as Goffman (1979) has identified in his study of advertising photography's representation of women and men – their relative height, the leading and guying behaviors found more often in pictured males, the greater emotional expressiveness of the women, and the like.[11] What the Westerners and non-Westerners are doing, the relative vantage points from which they are photographed, and their facial expressions give other cues to their moral and social characters.

Whether or not the gaze of the two parties is mutual provides a comment on who has the right and/or the need to look at whom. When the reader looks out at the world through this proxy Westerner, does the other look back? Rich implications can emerge from a photo showing two female travelers looking at an Ituri forest man in central Africa (February 1960 [Figure 12.2]). Standing in the upper left-hand corner, the two women smile down at the native figure in the lower right foreground. He looks toward the ground in front of them, an ambiguous expression on his face. The lines of their gaze have crossed but do not meet; because of this lack of reciprocity, the women's smiles appear bemused and patronizing. In its lack of reciprocity, this gaze is distinctly colonial. The Westerners do not seek a relationship but are content, even pleased, to view the other as an ethnic object. The composition of the picture, structured by an oblique line running from the women down to the man, shows the Westerners standing over the African; the slope itself can suggest, as Maquet (1986) has pointed out for other visual forms, the idea of *descent* or decline from the one (the Western women) to the other.

A related function of this type of photo lies in the way it prompts the viewer to become self-aware, not just in relation to others but as a viewer, as one who looks or surveys. Mulvey (1985) argues that the gaze in cinema takes three forms – in the camera, in the audience, and in the characters as they look at each other or out at the audience. She says that the first two forms have to be invisible or obscured if the film is to follow realist conventions and bestow on itself the qualities of "reality, obviousness and truth" (1985: 816). The viewer who becomes aware of his or her own eye or that of the camera will develop a "distancing awareness" rather than an immediate unconscious involvement. Applying this insight to the *Geographic* photograph, Mulvey might say that bringing the Western eye into the frame promotes distancing rather than immersion. Alvarado (1979/80) has also argued that such intrusion can reveal contradictions in the social relations of the West and the rest that are otherwise less visible, undermining the authority of the photographer by showing the photo being produced, showing it to be an artifact rather than an unmediated fact.[12]

Photographs in which Westerners appear differ from others because we can be more aware of ourselves as actors in the world. Whether or not Westerners

Figure 12.2. Photographs in which Western travelers are present encode complete messages about intercultural relations. The nonreciprocal gazes in this February 1960 picture encode distinctly colonial social relations. Photograph by Lowell Thomas, Jr. Reprinted courtesy of National Geographic Society

appear in the picture, we *are* there, but in pictures that include a Westerner, we may see ourselves being viewed by the other, and we become conscious of ourselves and relationships. The act of seeing the self being seen is antithetical to the voyeurism which many art critics have identified as intrinsic to most photography and film (Alloula 1986; Burgin 1982; Metz 1985).

This factor might best account for Westerners retreating from the photographs after 1969. Staffers in the photography department said that pictures including authors of articles came to be regarded as outdated and were discontinued. Photographer and writer were no longer to be the stars of the story, we were told, although text continued to be written in the first person. As more and more readers had traveled to exotic locales, the *Geographic* staff realized that the picture of the intrepid traveler no longer looked so intrepid. While the rise in international tourism may have had this effect, other social changes of the late 1960s contributed as well. In 1968 popular American protest against participation in the Vietnam War reached a critical point. Huge antiwar demonstrations, the police riot at the Democratic convention, and especially the Viet Cong's success in the Tet offensive convinced many that the American role in Vietnam and, by extension, the third world, would have to be radically reconceptualized. The withdrawal or retreat of American forces came to be seen as inevitable, even though there were many more years of conflict over how, when, and why. American power had come into question for the first time since the end of World War II. Moreover, the assassinations of Malcolm X and Martin Luther King, and the fire of revolt in urban ghettoes, gave many white people a sense of changing and more threatening relations with people of color within the boundaries of the United States.

Most of the non-*Geographic* photos now considered iconic representations of the Vietnam War do not include American soldiers or civilians. The girl who, napalmed, runs down a road towards the camera; the Saigon police chief executing a Viet Cong soldier; the Buddhist monk in process of self-immolation – each of these photographs, frequently reproduced, erases American involvement.

The withdrawal of Americans and other Westerners from the photographs of *National Geographic* may involve a historically similar process. The decolonization process accelerated in 1968 and led Americans (including, one must assume, the editors of *National Geographic*) to see the third world as a more dangerous place, a place where they were no longer welcome to walk and survey as they pleased. The decreasing visibility of Westerners signaled a retreat from a third world seen as a less valuable site for Western achievement, more difficult of access and control. The decolonization process was and is received as a threat to an American view of itself. In Lacan's terms, the other's look could threaten an American sense of self-coherence, and so in this historic moment the Westerner, whose presence in the picture makes it possible for us to see ourselves being seen by that other, withdraws to look from a safer distance, behind the camera.

The refracted gaze of the other: to see themselves as others see them

In a small but nonetheless striking number of *National Geographic* photographs, a native is shown with a camera, a mirror, or mirror equivalent in his or her hands. Take the photograph of two Aivilik men in northern Canada sitting on a rock in animal skin parkas, one smiling and the other pointing a camera out at the landscape (November 1956). Or the picture that shows two Indian women dancing as they watch their image in a large wall mirror. Or the picture of Governor Brown of California on Tonga showing a group of children the Polaroid snapshots he has just taken of them (March 1968).

Mirror and camera are tools of self-reflection and surveillance. Each creates a double of the self, a second figure who can be examined more closely than the original – a double that can also be alienated from the self, taken away, as a photograph can be, to another place. Psychoanalytic theory notes that the infant's look into the mirror is a significant step in ego formation because it permits the child to see itself for the first time as an other. The central role of these two tools in American society – after all, its millions of bathrooms have mirrors as fixtures nearly as important as their toilets – stems at least in part from their self-reflective capacities. For many Americans, self-knowledge is a central life goal; the injunction to "know thyself" is taken seriously.

The mirror most directly suggests the possibility of self-awareness, and Western folktales and literature provide many examples of characters (often animals like Bambi or wild children like Kipling's Mowgli) who come upon the mirrored surface of a lake or stream and for the first time see themselves in a kind of epiphany of newly acquired self-knowledge. Placing the mirror in non-Western hands makes an interesting picture for Western viewers because this theme can interact with the common perception that the non-Western native remains somewhat childlike and cognitively immature. Lack of self-awareness implies a lack of history (Wolf 1982); he or she is not without consciousness but is relatively without self-consciousness. The myth is that history and change are primarily characteristic of the West and that self-awareness was brought to the rest of the world by "discovery" and colonization.[13]

In the article "Into the Heart of Africa" (August 1956) a magazine staff member on expedition is shown sitting in his Land-Rover, holding open a *National Geographic* magazine to show a native woman a photograph of a woman of her tribe [Figure 12.3]. Here the magazine serves the role of reflecting glass, as the caption tells us: "Platter-lipped woman peers at her look-alike in the mirror of *National Geographic*." The *Geographic* artist smiles as he watches the woman's face closely for signs of self-recognition; the fascination evident in his gaze is in the response of the woman, perhaps the question of how she "likes" her image, her own self. An early version of this type of photo a quarter of a century earlier shows an explorer in pith helmet who, with a triumphant smile, holds up a mirror to a taller native man [Figure 12.4]. He dips his head down to peer into it, and we, the viewers, see not his expression but a redundant caption: "His first mirror: Porter's boy seeing himself as others see him." By contrast with the later photo, the explorer's gaze is not at the African but out toward the camera, indicating more interest in the camera's reception of this amusing scene than in searching the man's face for clues to his thinking. It also demonstrates the importance of manipulating relative height between races to communicate dominance. In the same genre, a Westerner in safari clothes holds a mirror up to a baboon (May 1955). Here as well, the *Geographic* plays with boundaries between nature and culture. The baboon, like third-world peoples, occupies that boundary in the popular culture of white Westerners (see Haraway 1989); its response to the mirror can only seem humorously inadequate when engaged in the ultimately human and most adult of activities, self-reflection.

The mirror sometimes serves as a device to tell a story about the process of forming national identity. National self-reflection is presumed to accompany

Figure 12.3. A surprising number of *Geographic* photographs feature mirrors and cameras, with Westerners offering third-world peoples glimpses of themselves. In this August 1956 picture, a staff artist in what was then French Equatorial Africa shows a woman "her look-alike." Photograph by Volkmar Kurt Wentzel. © by National Geographic Society. Reprinted courtesy of National Geographic Society

development, with the latter term suggesting a process that is both technological and psychosocial. The caption to a 1980 picture of a Tunisian woman looking into a mirror plays with this confusion between individual and nation, between the developing self-awareness of mature adults and historically emergent national identity: "A moment for reflection: Mahbouba Sassi glances in the mirror to tie her head-band. A wife and mother in the village of Takrouna, she wears garb still typical of rural women in the region. Step by step, Tunisia has, by any standards, quietly but steadily brought herself into the front rank of developing nations."

Cameras break into the frame of many *National Geographic* photographs. In some, a Westerner is holding the camera, showing a local group the

Figure 12.4. This February 1925 photograph is captioned "His first mirror: Porter's boy seeing himself as others see him," suggesting that self-awareness comes with Western contact and technology. Photography by Felix Shay. © by National Geographic Society. Reprinted courtesy of National Geographic Society

photograph he has just taken of them. Here the camera, like the mirror, shows the native himself. Frequently the picture is handed to children crowding happily around the Western cameraman. Historically it was first the mirror and then the camera that were thought to prove the superiority of the Westerner who invented and controls them (Adas 1989). In many pictures of natives holding a mirror or camera, the magazine plays with what McGrane (1989) identifies with the nineteenth century European mind, the notion "of a low threshold of the miraculous [in the non-Western native], of a seemingly childish lack of restraint" (1989: 50).

In other pictures, the native holds the camera. In one sense, this violates the prerogative of the Western surveyor to control the camera, long seen as a form of power. In an analysis of photographs of Middle Eastern women,

Graham-Brown (1988) provides evidence that colonial photographers were motivated to keep local subjects "at the lens-end of the camera" and quotes one who, in 1890, complained, "It was a mistake for the first photographer in the Pathan [Afghanistan] country to allow the natives to look at the ground glass screen of the camera. He forgot that a little learning is a dangerous thing" (1988: 61). The camera could be given to native subjects only at the risk of giving away that power.

Pictures in *National Geographic* that place the camera in other hands, however, merely suggest that the native's use of the camera is amusing or quaint. A broad smile graces the face of the Aivilik man above who uses the camera lens to view the landscape with a companion. At least one caption suggests that, although the subject goes behind the camera – in 1952 a young African boy looking through the viewfinder – what he looks out at is the imagined self at whom the Western photographer has been looking moments before: "Young Lemba sees others as the photographer sees him."

Such pictures were more common in the 1950s. We can detect a change, as decolonization proceeded, in the simple terms with which the problem is depicted in an amazing photograph from August 1982 [Figure 12.5]. It sits on the right-hand side of the page in an article entitled "Paraguay, Paradox of South America." The frame is nearly filled with three foreground figures – a white female tourist standing between an Amerindian woman and man, both in native dress, both bare-chested. The three stand close together in a line, the tourist smiling with her arm on the shoulder of the sober-faced native woman. The tourist and the man, also unsmiling, face off slightly toward the left where a second camera (besides the one snapping the photo for the magazine) takes their picture. The caption asks us to look at the natives as photographic subjects: "Portraits for pay: A tourist poses with members of the Macá Indian tribe on Colonia Juan Belaieff Island in the Paraguay River near Asunción. The Indians charge 80 cents a person each time they pose in a photograph."

This rare photograph invites us into a contradictory, ambiguous, but, in any case, highly charged scene. It is not a pleasant picture, in contrast with more typical *Geographic* style, because it depicts the act of looking at unwilling subjects, suggesting the voyeurism of the photograph of the exotic, a voyeurism *doubled* by the presence of a second photographer. Further, the picture's ambiguity lies in its suggestion that we are seeing a candid shot of a posed shot, and that we are looking at the other look at us though in fact the Indian gaze is diverted twenty degrees from ours. This unusual structure of gaze draws attention to the commodified nature of the relationship between looker and looked-at. The Indians appear unhappy, even coerced; the tourist satisfied, presumably with her catch. Here too an apparent contradiction – the diverted gaze and its candid appearance suggest that the *National Geographic*

Figure 12.5. A rare picture from August 1982 draws attention to the presence of the camera by photographing people being photographed for pay. Photography by O. Louis Mazzatenta. © by National Geographic Society. Reprinted courtesy of National Geographic Society

photographer took this picture without paying, unlike the tourists; the caption suggests otherwise.

The photograph's potentially disturbing message for *National Geographic* readers is muted when one considers that the camera has not succeeded so much in representing the returned gaze of indigenous peoples as it has in taking the distance between Western viewer and non-Western subject one step farther and in drawing attention to the photographer (and the artifice) between them. A symptom of alienation from the act of looking even while attention is drawn to it, this photo may exemplify a principle that Sontag says operates in all photography: "The photographer is supertourist, an extension of the anthropologist, visiting natives and bringing back news of their exotic doings and strange gear. The photographer is always trying to colonize new experiences or find new ways to look at familiar subjects – to fight against boredom. For boredom is just the reverse side of fascination: both depend on being outside rather than inside a situation, and one leads to the other" (1977: 42). Avoiding boredom is crucial to retaining readers' interest and therefore membership.

One could also look at the photograph from a 1990 issue on Botswana showing a French television crew – in full camera-and-sound gear and from a distance of a few feet – filming two Dzu Bushmen in hunting gear and authentic dress. The Frenchmen enthusiastically instruct the hunters in stalking posture, and the caption critiques them, noting that they have dressed up the natives (who otherwise wear Western clothing) for the benefit of European consumers. While this photograph is valuable in letting the reader see how images are constructed rather than found, its postmodern peek behind the scenes may also do what Gitlin notes contemporary journalism has done: engaged in a demystifying look at how image makers control the face political candidates put forward, they encourage viewers to be "cognoscenti of their own bamboozlement" (1990).

Ultimately the magazine itself is a mirror for the historical, cultural, and political-economic contexts of its production and use. That context is reflected in the magazine's images, but not in a simple, reflective way, as either the objectivist myth of the nature of cameras and mirrors or as the Althusserian notion of a "specular," or mirrorlike ideology (in which the subject simply recognizes him- or herself) would have it. It is perhaps more in the form of a rippled lake whose many intersecting lines present a constantly changing and emergent image.

The academic spectator

In one sense, this gaze is simply a subtype of the reader's gaze. It emerges out of the same American middle-class experiential matrix with its family of other cultural representations, its formal and informal schooling in techniques for interpreting both photograph and cultural difference, and its social relations. We read the *National Geographic* with a sense of astonishment, absorption, and wonder, both as children and, in a way that is different only some of the time, as adults. All of the looks embedded in the pictures are ultimately being filtered for you the reader through this, our own gaze. At times during this project, we have looked at the reader of an American magazine who is looking at a photographer's looking at a Western explorer who is looking at a Polynesian child who is looking at the explorer's photographed snapshot of herself moments earlier. While this framing of the seventh look might suggest that it is simply a more convoluted and distanced voyeurism, it can be distinguished from other kinds of readers' gazes, including the voyeuristic and the hierarchic, by both its distinctive intent and the sociological position (white, middle class, female, academic) from which it comes. Its intent is not aesthetic appreciation or formal description, but critique of the images in spite of, because of, and in terms of their pleasures. We aim to make the pictures tell a different story than they were originally meant to tell, one about their makers and readers rather than their subjects.[14] The critique arises out of a desire "to anthropologize the West," as Rabinow (1986) suggests we might, and to denaturalize the images of difference in the magazine in part because those images and the institution which has produced them have historically articulated too easily with the shifting interests and positions of the state. The strong impact of the magazine on popular attitudes suggests that anthropological teaching or writing purveys images that, even if intended as oppositional (certainly not always the case), may simply be subsumed or bypassed by the *National Geographic* view of the world.

A suspicion of the power of images is inevitable, as they exist in a field more populated with advertising photography than anything else. The image is experienced daily as a sales technique or as a trace of the commodity. That experience is, at least for us and perhaps for other readers, transferred to some degree to the experience of seeing *National Geographic* images.

Our reading of theory has tutored our gaze in distinctive ways, told us how to understand the techniques by which the photographs work, how to find our way to something other than an aesthetic or literal reading, suggesting that we view them as cultural artifacts. It also suggested that we avoid immersion in the many pleasures of the richly colored and exotically peopled photographs, as in Alloula's reading of Algerian colonial period postcards. He notes his analytic need to resist the "aestheticizing temptation" (1986: 116) to see beauty in those cards, a position predicated in part on a highly deterministic view of their hegemonic effect. Alternative, more positive views of the political implications of visual pleasure exist, a view which Jameson (1983) and others argue is achieved in part by unlinking a disdain for popular culture products from the issue of pleasure. Validating both seemingly contradictory views, however, would seem to be the fact that the seductiveness of the pictures both captures and instructs us. We are captured by the temptation to view the photographs as more real than the world or at least as a comfortable substitute for it, to imagine at some level a world of basically happy, classless, even noble others in conflict neither with themselves nor with "us." These and other illusions of the images we have found in part through our own vulnerability to them. The pleasures are also instructive, however. They come from being given views, without having to make our own efforts to get them, of a world different, however slightly, from the American middle-class norm. The considerable beauty with which those lives are portrayed can potentially challenge that norm.

Conclusion

The many looking relations represented in all photographs are at the foundation of the kinds of meaning that can be found or made in them. The multiplicity of looks is at the root of a photo's ambiguity, each gaze potentially suggesting a different way of viewing the scene. Moreover, a visual illiteracy leaves most of us with few resources for understanding or integrating the diverse messages these looks can produce. Multiple gaze is the source of many of the photograph's contradictions, highlighting the gaps (as when some gazes are literally interrupted) and multiple perspectives of each person involved in the complex scene. It is the root of much of the photograph's dynamism as a cultural object, and the place where the analyst can perhaps most productively begin to trace its connections to the wider social world of which it is a part. Through attention to the dynamic nature of these intersecting gazes, the photograph becomes less vulnerable to the charge that it masks or stuffs and mounts the world, freezes the life out of a scene, or violently slices into time. While the gaze of the subject of the photograph may be difficult to find in the heavy crisscrossing traffic of the more privileged gazes of producers and consumers, contemporary stories of contestable power are told there nonetheless.

--- **Notes** ---

1 The same of course can be said for other categories of people who share a marked quality with the non-Westerner, including physical deviants (Diane Arbus's pictures, for example), the criminal (Tagg 1988), and, most commonly, women (Goffman 1979).

2 The differences between painting and photography are also important. The gaze cannot be altered at will or completely to taste, and so the looks that are exchanged in *National Geographic* photographs can be seen as more disappointing and less pacifying than are, for example, Gauguin's pictures of Polynesian women.

3 This analysis resembles the less psychoanalytically freighted work of Sider on the stereotype in Indian–white relations. Sider frames the problem as one of "the basic contradiction of this form of domination – *that it cannot both create and incorporate the other as an other* – thus opening a space for continuing resistance and distancing" (1987: 22).

4 Ellsworth's research (e.g., 1975) on gaze in natural and experimental contacts between people (conducted in the United States) has been central in making the argument for a thoroughly contextual view of looking relations in the discipline of psychology.

5 An early typology of the gaze from a colonial and racist perspective is found in Sir Richard Burton's accounts of his African expeditions, during which he felt himself to be the victim of "an ecstasy of curiosity." Wrote Burton: "At last my experience in staring enabled me to categorize the infliction as follows. Firstly is the stare furtive, when the starer would peep and peer under the tent, and its reverse, the open stare. Thirdly is the stare curious or intelligent, which generally was accompanied with irreverent laughter regarding our appearance. Fourthly is the stare stupid, which denoted the hebete incurious savage. The stare discreet is that of

Sultans and greatmen; the stare indiscreet at unusual seasons is affected by women and children. Sixthly is the stare flattering – it was exceedingly rare, and equally so was the stare contemptuous. Eighthly is the stare greedy; it was denoted by the eyes restlessly bounding from one object to another, never tired, never satisfied. Ninthly is the stare peremptory and pertinacious, peculiar to crabbed age. The dozen concludes with the stare drunken, the stare fierce or pugnacious, and finally the stare cannibal, which apparently considered us as articles of diet" (Burton in Moorehead 1960: 33). One can imagine a similarly hostile categorization of white Westerners staring at exotics over the past centuries.

6   Some contemporary photographers are experimenting with these conventions (in point of view or framing) in an effort to undermine this equation. Victor Burgin, for example, intentionally attempts to break this down by making photographs that are "'occasions for interpretation' rather than ... 'objects of consumption'" and that thereby require a gaze which more actively produces itself rather than simply accepting the photographer's gaze as its own. While one can question whether any *National Geographic* photograph is ever purely an object of consumption, the distinction alerts us to the possibility that the photographer can encourage or discourage, through technique, the relative independence of the viewer's gaze.

7   This figure is based on 438 photographs coded in this way, 24% of which had a subject looking at the camera.

8   These analyses were based on those photos where gaze was visible, and excluded pictures with a Westerner in the photo. The results were, for gender (N = 360) $x^2 = 3.835$, df = 1, p < .05; for age (N = 501) $x^2 = 13.745$, df = 4, p < .01; for wealth (N = 507) $x^2 = 12.950$, df = 2, p < .01; for skin color (N = 417) $x^2 = 8.704$, df = 3, p < .05; for dress style (N = 452) $x^2 = 12.702$, df = 1, p < .001; and for technology (N = 287) $x^2 = 4.172$, df = 1, p < .05. Discussing these findings in the photography department, we were given the pragmatic explanation that children generally are more fearless in approaching photographers, while men often seem more wary of the camera than women, especially when it is wielded by a male photographer.

9   In the sample of pictures from Asia in which gaze is ascertainable (N = 179), "friendly" countries (including the PRC after 1975, Taiwan, Hong Kong, South Korea, Japan, and the Philippines) had higher rates of smiling than "unfriendly" or neutral countries ($x^2 = 2.101$, df = 1, p = .147). Excluding Japan, which may have had a more ambiguous status in American eyes, the relationship between gaze and "friendliness" reaches significance ($x^2 = 4.14$, df = 1, p < .05).

10 Tagg (1988) notes that the pose was initially the pragmatic outcome of the technique of the Physionotrace, a popular mechanism used to trace a person's profile from shadow onto a copper plate. When photography took the place of the Physionotrace, no longer requiring profiles, the conventions of associating class with non-frontality continued to have force.

11 Goffman (1979) draws on ethological insights into height and dominance relations when he explains why women are almost always represented as shorter than men in print advertisements. He notes that "so thoroughly is it assumed that

differences in size will correlate with differences in social weight that relative size can be routinely used as a means of ensuring that the picture's story will be understandable at a glance" (1979: 28).

12 The documentary filmmaker Dennis O'Rourke, whose films *Cannibal Tours* and *Half Life: A Parable for the Nuclear Age* explore third-world settings, develops a related argument for the role of reflexivity for the image maker (Lutkehaus 1989). He consistently includes himself in the scene but distinguishes between simple filmmaker self-revelation and rendering the social relations between him and his subjects, including capturing the subject's gaze in such a way as to show his or her complicity with the filmmaker. O'Rourke appears to view the reader's gaze more deterministically (for instance, as "naturally" seeing the complicity in a subject's gaze) than do the theorists considered above.

13 Compare the pictures of natives looking into a mirror with that of an American woman looking into the shiny surface of the airplane she is riveting in the August 1944 issue. It is captioned, "No time to prink [primp] in the mirror-like tail assembly of a Liberator." The issue raised by this caption is not self-knowledge (Western women have this) but female vanity, or rather its transcendence by a woman who, manlike, works in heavy industry during the male labor shortage of World War II. Many of these mirror pictures evoke a tradition in Western art in which Venus or some other female figure gazes into a mirror in a moment of self-absorption. Like those paintings, this photo may operate "within the convention that justifies male voyeuristic desire by aligning it with female narcissistic self-involvement" (Snow 1989: 38).

14 Our interviews with readers show that they do not always ignore the frame but also sometimes see the photograph as an object produced by someone in a concrete social context.

References

Adas, Michael. 1989. *Machines as the Measure of Men*. Ithaca: Cornell University Press.

Alloula, Malek. 1986. *The Colonial Harem*. Minneapolis: University of Minnesota Press.

Alvarado, Manuel. 1979/80. Photographs and narrativity. *Screen Education* (Autumn/Winter), 5–17.

Barthes, Roland. 1977. The Photographic Message. In *Image–Music–Text*, trans. S. Heath. Glasgow: Fontana.

Berger, John. 1972. *Ways of Seeing*. London: British Broadcasting Corporation and Penguin Books.

Bhabha, Homi K. 1983. The Other Question – Homi K. Bhabha Reconsiders the Stereotype and Colonial Discourse. *Screen*, 24:6, 18–36.

Burgin, Victor (ed.). 1982. *Thinking Photography*. London: Macmillan.

Burgin, Victor. 1986. *The End of Art Theory: Criticism and Post-modernity*. London: Macmillan.

De Lauretis, Teresa. 1987. *Technologies of Gender: Essays on Theory, Film, and Fiction.* Bloomington: Indiana University Press.

Devereux, George. 1967. *From Anxiety to Method in the Behavioral Sciences.* The Hague: Mouton.

Ellsworth, Phoebe. 1975. Direct Gaze as Social Stimulus: The Example of Aggression. In P. Pliner, L. Krames, and T. Alloway (eds.), *Nonverbal Communication of Aggression*, 53–75. New York: Plenum.

Gaines, Jane. 1988. White Privilege and Looking Relations: Race and Gender in Feminist Film Theory. *Screen*, 29:4, 12–27.

Geary, Christaud M. 1988. *Images from Barnum: German Colonial Photography at the Court of King Njoya, Cameroon, West Africa, 1902–1915.* Washington, DC: Smithsonian Institution Press.

Gitlin, Todd. 1990. Blips, Bites and Savvy Talk. *Dissent*, 37, 18–26.

Goffman, Erving. 1979. *Gender Advertisements.* New York: Harper & Row.

Graham-Brown, Sarah. 1988. *Images of Women: The Portrayal of Women in Photography of the Middle East, 1860–1950.* London: Quartet Books.

Green, David. 1984. Classified Subjects. *Ten/8*, 8:14, 30–7.

Haraway, Donna. 1989. *Primate Visions: Gender, Race, and Nature in the World of Modern Science.* New York: Routledge.

Jameson, Fredric. 1983. Pleasure: A Political Issue. In Fredric Jameson (ed.), *Formations of Pleasure*, 1–14. London: Routledge.

Lacan, Jacques. 1981. *The Four Fundamental Concepts of Psycho-Analysis.* New York: Norton.

Lutkehaus, Nancy. 1989. "Excuse me, everything is not airight": On Ethnography, Film, and Representation. An Interview with Filmmaker Dennis O'Rourke. *Cultural Anthropology* 4, 422–37.

Maquet, Jacques. 1986. *The Aesthetic Experience.* New Haven: Yale University Press.

Marcus, George, and Dick Cushman. 1982. Ethnographies as Texts. *Annual Review of Anthropology*, 11, 25–69.

McGrane, Bernard. 1989. *Beyond Anthropology: Society and the Other.* New York: Columbia University Press.

Metz, Christian. 1985. From *The Imaginary Signifier.* In G. Mast and M. Cohen (eds.), *Film Theory and Criticism: Introductory Readings*, 782–802. New York: Oxford University Press.

Moorehead, Alan. 1960. *The White Nile.* New York: Harper & Brothers.

Mulvey, Laura. 1985. Visual Pleasure and Narrative Cinema. In G. Mast and M. Cohen (eds.), *Film Theory and Criticism: Introductory Readings*, 803–16. New York: Oxford University Press.

National Geographic Society. 1981. *Images of the World: Photography at the National Geographic.* Washington, DC: National Geographic Society.

Rabinow, Paul. 1986. Representations Are Social Facts: Modernity in Anthropology. In J. Clifford and G. Marcus (eds.), *Writing Culture*, 234–61. Berkeley and Los Angeles: University of California Press.

Radway, Janice. 1984. *Reading the Romance.* Chapel Hill: University of North Carolina Press.

Sider, Gerald. 1987. When Parrots Learn to Talk, and Why They Can't: Domination, Deception, and Self-Deception in Indian–White Relations. *Comparative Studies in Society and History*, 29, 3–23.

Snow, Edward. 1989. Theorizing the Male Gaze: Some Problems. *Representations*, 25 (Winter), 30–41.

Sontag, Susan. 1977. *On Photography*. New York: Dell.

Tagg, John. 1988. *The Burden of Representation: Essays on Photographies and Histories*. Amherst: University of Massachusetts Press.

Williams, Anne. 1987. Untitled. *Ten/8*, 11, 6–11.

Wolf, Eric. 1982. *Europe and the People without History*. Berkeley and Los Angeles: University of California Press.

13

When Strangers Bring Cameras:
The Poetics and Politics of Othered Places

ARDIS CAMERON

It is not down in any map;
True places never are.
Herman Melville

Like all narratives of identity, stories of place take shape and derive meaning in and through a system of differences. This is who we are, and more importantly perhaps, this is who and what we are not. "True places," where authenticity and realness are said to dwell, find expression in the discursive imaginary topographies of Otherness and so come down, not in maps, but in stories of alterity that mark *home* from *away*. A place without a story is really nowhere at all.

It comes as no surprise then that highly storied regions like northern New England and Appalachia enter into the national imaginary as worlds apart. Bounded by images of rugged coastlines, pristine lighthouses, and lobster boats, the conceptual borders of Maine take shape in opposition to the desolate "hollers," rusty cars, and soot-encrusted miners of eastern Kentucky. But if places like these are conceived and translated through a prism of differences, modern practices of image-making and the kinds of looking relations they help shape underscore the degree to which northern New

Ardis Cameron, "When Strangers Bring Cameras: The Poetics and Politics of Othered Places," *American Quarterly*, 54:3 (September 2002): 411–35. © 2002 by the American Studies Association. Reprinted with permission of the Johns Hopkins University Press.

England and Appalachia share a common past as deeply othered places. Rural, poor, and historically dominated by outside interests, they have been shaped less by their geographical location in America's hinterlands than by the weight of visual excess that has historically bounded them as separate and apart from stories of "America." Topographies of strangeness overstuffed with desire and dread, othered places like these have long defined a particular kind of rupture in American narratives of modernity and progress: a breech that anthropologist Kathleen Stewart describes as "a space on the side of the road."[1] If stories of place accentuate regional differences, the poetics of othered places underscore the shared legacy of America's unassimilated regions whose unquiet images hang like phantasmagoric dream spaces over American narratives of self and other, center and margin, "in here" and "out there."[2]

Two recent documentary films provide a useful way to explore such spaces and investigate the kinds of poetics they perform. *Belfast, Maine*, a four-hour film by Fred Wiseman that inchworms its way through a blue-collar New England town, and *Stranger with a Camera*, a self-reflective look by Kentucky filmmaker Elizabeth Barret at documentary film practices in her home state, are at once stories of place and problematic performances of otherness. Given the history of northern New England and Appalachia, they could hardly be otherwise. Both regions emerged in the voyeuristic practices of cosmopolitan storytellers who found in the "hidden pockets" of turn-of-the-century America places of authenticity and cultural intensity seemingly absent from the home they called "America." Increasingly fetishized as a zone of difference – a particular place and a peculiar people – each entered the cultural imaginary in terms long familiar to students of regional fiction: as ethnographically colorful, pre-modern, and temporally frozen so as to fix in place old world dialects, gestures, and customs. Marketable as stories to a new class of readers, both regions afforded as well and array of consumerist possibilities as tourists sought relief from "over-civilization" and as new professions emerged to document and distribute images of "out there" to those tied down by "here." In the process both places became important staging grounds where would-be image-makers could find more accessible routes into creative careers than were ordinarily available to them. Not unlike the genre of regional fiction (studied so perceptively by Richard Brodhead) which extended authorship to those "traditionally distanced from literary lives," the commodification of othered places produced in the twentieth century "the opportunity it offered."[3] As early as the 1930s the two regions fostered a thriving culture industry that catered to consumerist desires for non-modern cultural experiences and vernacular authenticity.[4] New subjects of representation emerged and new categories of artistic self-fashioning, including most recently "the documentary arts," found ready access to public places and a privileged location in the art-culture system.[5] As both films suggest, albeit in radically different ways, the stranger with a camera had become in Maine and Kentucky a common, and by the 1960s, an increasingly troubling figure in the landscape.

Barret begins her story here in the complicated history of looking relations that shaped the Kentucky of her childhood and called forth the documentary practices she embraced as an adult. "I grew up in a place inundated with picture takers of the creeks, hollows, houses, and people of Appalachia," the filmmaker tells viewers as they watch with her eyes the TV poverty pictures made famous by the 1960s "war on poverty." "I didn't think about them. After all, what did those images have to do with me?"

It is the story of one particular picture taker, Canadian filmmaker Hugh O'Connor, that calls Barret to question anew the pull of these images and to reexamine her own relationship to them. O'Connor had come to Kentucky in the fall of 1967 when Barret was a young schoolgirl growing up in Whitesburg, the daughter of middle-class parents. Like many journalists and writers, he and his small crew had turned their focus on Letcher County where images of barefooted children, toothless women, and soot-faced miners were both in abundance and in demand as supporting evidence in the fight to fund much-needed but controversial welfare programs. Stopping down the road in Jeremiah, O'Connor asked and was granted permission to film a tenant miner and his family. But before they could finish shooting the scene, word had spread around the country of the film crew's presence. Soon, Hobart Ison, whose family had owned land in eastern Kentucky for generations and who then owned the property O'Connor was filming, drove up, looked at the camera crew, and fired a round of gunshot. Two bullets lodged in the camera. A third made a gaping hole in O'Connor's chest, killing him almost instantly.

As a teenager, the killing of Hugh O'Connor seemed remote to Barret: school had started; it was homecoming week; she was Homecoming Queen. Like others in Letcher County, Barret was embarrassed and insulted by the poverty tours that brought into her hometown busloads of journalists, filmmakers, and politicians eager to show an affluent nation the "other America." Most townspeople sympathized with Ison, and it was difficult to find a jury impartial to the landlord's feeling of rage, humiliation, and exploitation. Daniel Boone Smith, the prosecuting attorney, eventually found his dozen, but it was the camera and the invasive practices of the strangers who aimed them that stood trial. In one of the film's most moving scenes, Barret focuses on Richard Black, a member of O'Connor's film crew who, as a witness to the murder, recalls the hostility directed towards him during the trial – hostile glares, epithets, death threats – and yet even he was moved by the closing arguments of Ison's attorney. "The defense was a poem, a beautiful poem," Black muses, not about murder or about Ison, but "about eastern Kentucky." It was Kentucky's tarnished image, the defense implied, that Ison shot in self-defense; an image created in the eyes of the jury, not by poverty or corporate greed, but rather by the very processes that brought these things into public view. Sentenced to ten years in prison, Ison was paroled after serving twelve months.

Stranger with a Camera is an attempt to understand this murder from the point of view of someone who has stood on both sides of the camera, a perspective that allows Barret to resist the kinds of representational essentializing that are inextricably wound up with ethnographic traditions of film-making. Eschewing the search for the "real" Appalachia, it is less a story of place than of travel. Barret shows us eastern Kentucky as a space of occupation and encounter – of *roots* and of *routes* – to borrow a metaphor from the anthropologist James Clifford. In Clifford's formulation, *roots* conjures up a grounded, organic community marked by its lack of external relations and displacements. *Routes*, on the other hand, conveys an imagined geographic site at once a cultural and physical encounter – less a locale than an exchange – a site Clifford describes as one of dwelling *and* travel.[6] Clifford thus uses the metaphor of travel to "shake up" the persistent localization of the ethnographer's "field." He calls attention away from placeness and towards "sites of displacement, interference, and interaction." Barret follows his lead.

The film begins with an image of a man with a camera. Bent over an ancient viewfinder, he is taking pictures of a family event – a baptism perhaps. The image is small, reduced on the screen to a postage stamp size of color amidst a large blackened screen. The man with the camera shoots his film. Slowly new images are added, each the product of a separate camera. Some are still photographs of migrant workers made famous during the 1930s. Others are familiar documentary styled moving images of Appalachian "folklife." A few seem right out of *National Geographic*. Collectively they invite the audience to stand on both sides of the camera alternately showing camera crews filming others and then turning the lens towards the audience as the camera "shoots" it. In one lingering final image that acts as a transition into the story of "the killing," a dark skinned man peers intensely into the lens of the camera. His puzzlement invites the audience to ponder as well the strangeness of picture taking as he fervently looks to see what might be inside and behind the scope pointed at him.

Juxtaposing images with image-makers allows Barret to keep the audience focused on the contested nature of camera work and the kinds of visual skirmishes it has historically produced. From there, she turns to a more conventional style of interviewing informants who collectively introduce the story of O'Connor's murder. A retired miner, his face deeply lined with wrinkles, appears on screen. With a slight stutter, he recalls that fall day when he stood on the front porch of his rented cabin and posed for the camera. Others tell the story from where they stood. A colleague of

O'Connor's, whose visit to the Kentucky film school, Appalshop, "cast a shadow" over Barret's profession, tells of how the crew tried to get away from the enraged Ison. Calvin Trillin reads from his 1969 *New Yorker* story of the same title, and the audience learns of O'Connor's death. Then Barret makes the story her own as the soft southern lilt of her voice-over introduces the audience to "the hills I grew up in" and to her own position as "someone who lives in the community I document." We learn that the small five-frame images Barret employed at the beginning of the film are a technique made famous by IMAX and developed by O'Connor for the 1967 Montreal Exposition. The miner, who begins the story, was the same one O'Connor was shooting when Ison shot him. The insider voice of the Kentucky-born Barret then gives way to the stranger she too has become as she struggles to understand why it happened. "What brought these two men, Hobart Ison with his gun, and Hugh O'Connor with his camera, face to face in September, 1967?" Dislodged from the "gist" of this place, viewers watch as Kentucky fragments into a set of competing images powerful enough to bring these two men together.

Like many filmmakers who went to Kentucky, O'Connor's route into Appalachia was through the poverty pictures that migrated north during the 1960s. Barret takes us there. Stark black and white photos fill up the screen as *The Crusader*, a muckraking television show produced by the BBC, documents the Kentucky poor. Then there is a rush of images and voice-overs from the National Council of Churches and *The New York Times*. We go "On the Road" with Charles Kurault to uncover "Christmas in Appalachia." We watch President Johnson resting on the porch of a destitute family, then we see Bobby Kennedy as he travels through the muddy streets of Hazard to witness firsthand the hunger, the poverty, and the misery of eastern Kentucky. Embarrassed by the poverty pictures of her youth, Barret was nonetheless aware that life could be harsh in Letcher County. In 1965, one half of the county lived below the poverty line, where malnutrition, illiteracy, and tarpaper shacks were as common as the mustard brown slag heaps that poured down the hills. Using clips from the broadcasts she watched as a child, Barret shows their power as visual evidence against the exploitative practices of the coal mining industry and the corrupt policies of local government. "What did you eat for breakfast?" Charles Kurault asked the wife of a miner living along the oozing banks of Pert Creek. Pointing to her husband she responds, "he gits gravy, eggs and bacon." She and her children had coffee and cigarettes.

Barret tells the story of Kentucky's working poor through the eyes of Mason Eldridge, the tenant miner O'Connor had stopped to film. Living in the midst of enormous natural wealth, Eldridge worked six twelve-hour shifts to earn $6.00 per day. We see his hunched profile as he calmly and precisely recalls the 1967 price of $2.98 per ton of coal, the twenty-five tons required to reach six dollars a day, and the sixteen bucks he received for it each week. His face is deeply lined, teeth are not where they should be; his skin has the texture of leather and is pasty white. Then we see Eldridge as he appeared that autumn day to Hugh O'Connor whose camera recorded a tall, lanky, young man, his face still black from his work day, his baby swinging in strong arms. "It was murder, no doubt about that," he opines, and one is left to wonder if he means O'Connor's death or his life in the coalmines of Letcher County.

As Benedict Anderson has argued, the hold of a place begins in the imagination and, as *Stranger* makes clear, images are the mental maps that turn geographical location into a culture longing – dirt into dread and desire. For Hobart Ison, looks could kill, and looking became in turn an excuse for murder. For others in Whiteburg, however, image making and image reading opened up new possibilities for re-imagining and re/presenting the ecological devastation brought about by the timber and mining interests. "Look what man hath wrought on *that* purple mountain's majesty," Whitesburg native Harry Caudill declared as he showed reporters what the mine owners and the local politicians who protected them had done to "America the Beautiful."[7] Caudill was no stranger to Letcher County. His great-great-great-grandfather was the first white man to settle there, and the Caudill name runs through Pine Mountain and along the Kentucky River like the white oaks and towering poplars that once dominated the landscape.[8] We are introduced to Caudill through moving images taken by the BBC in 1964 shortly after the publication of his first book, *Night Comes to the Cumberlands*. A detailed and wrenching account of the destruction brought about by the giant coal augers and bulldozers that ripped out one hundred million tons of coal every year from the Kentucky mountains, the book stood in sharp contrast to popular impressions of moonshining "hillbillies," cartoon mountain daughters, and tourist inspired images of Daniel Boone log cabins and coonskin hats. *The New York Times* sent down a reporter to see if Caudill was a crank. The camera shows them Pert Creek. It takes the BBC to a hollow down the road. It leads the Council of Churches on a pilgrimage to the riverbeds where dirty yellow coal silt moved like lava down the bank. "Harry's horror tours," they were called. His widow picks up her husband's book and reads a passage from it. "The eyes of the 'furrin' timber hunters must have popped with amazement," Caudill writes in *Night Comes*, and the Kentucky of "Goliath-sized pencil-straight poplars, some of them towering one hundred and seventy-five feet and achieving a diameter of seven or eight feet," comes into view. With his horror tours, Caudill turned the nation's eyes to the repugnant spectacle that replaced this rare old growth.

Images of excess, whether of bulging bounty or grotesque deprivation, were not new to American encounters with Appalachia, for it was always the function of othered places to provide in the national imaginary a space of both desire and dread – of "authenticity and the degraded state of nature" as Stewart puts it.[9] But the images Barret presents call attention as well to the new symbolic power Appalachia attained as the war against poverty gained momentum. Like the inner city that was re-imagined "a culture of poverty," Appalachia became in the mind's eye of the nation a bounded culture defined less by the failures of post-World War II capitalism than by its own separation from the material promises it offered "our" nation. Poverty, these pictures seemed to suggest, was not made by bad economics but was instead spawned by a culture both insular and deficient – a culture comprised, as Charles Kurault put it, by "the permanent poor." Certainly Barret was not alone in thinking these pictures had nothing to do with her or her life in Whitesburg. As her impoverished neighbors electronically traveled to New York City and beyond, she found herself part of a national TV audience who watched in mutual fascination the comings and goings to the "Other" America. Like the "outsiders-who-make-the-insiders-insiders," described by Foucault, Kentucky's poor constituted in their wretched surroundings and physical imperfections, a visual cartography through which a white middle-class America could map the borders of home and nation. Even to Barret, Kentucky seemed far away.

While Barret never fully develops the totalizing practices of the 1960s poverty pictures, she resists the documentary urge to particularize the Kentucky hills as a zone of difference. It is, as the title suggests, a place of exchanges – of traveling picture takers and of migrating pictures. She recognizes that she is part of that exchange and uses a set of questions to negotiate her position as the legitimizing voice of the film and the subject it treats. "These kids lived only a few miles away from me," Barret explains. "How did they feel having their pictures on TV?" In the trafficking of images, "Who gets to tell the communities' story? What are the storyteller's responsibilities?" And, "What is the difference between how people see their own place and how others represent it?" Questions like these help undercut the traditional position of the socially oriented filmmaker, whose role in the construction of meaning is, as film critic Trinh T. Minh-ha points out, easily obscured by its "righteous mission."[10] Hoping to learn something from this story "now that I have stood on both sides of the camera," Barret brings to center stage the camera's complicity in constituting the very subjects it purports to represent.

For social historians, *Stranger* is an especially welcome alternative to documentary practices that tend to serve up "ordinary people" as a way to signify the authenticity of "this place" and generate topographies of strangeness.[11] Class position becomes for Barret a way to complicate notions of regional identity and subvert the ethnographic tendency to conflate othered places with cultural but not social difference. She shows a set of photographs of herself as a stylish homecoming queen, bubbling cheerleader, and honor student. She interviews neighbors, miners, government officials, Vista volunteers, newspaper reporters, and others who remember Hobart Ison and the pictures that turned him into a murderer. Not all of Whitesburg middle classes welcomed the picture takers and not just a few of the miners sided with Hobart Ison. But mostly, Barret agues, "social status affected how people see the place they live in and how they want others to see it." Strip mining, Barret makes clear, was and still is a difficult issue since most of the mining in Kentucky is carried out by small independent operators who, having lost the land they now work, hold on more tightly to an imagined past easily threatened by those who do not share it. "The same system that brought prosperity to some impoverished others," Barret explains. "Some filmmakers wanted to show that contrast to help bring about social change. Others mined the images the way the companies had mined the coal." Cameras could rob people too.

It is Barret's ability to show us the ongoing complicity of camera work – its power to rob, to plunder, to produce, to shape, to reveal, and to distort, to inspire – that makes *Stranger* such an important and useful film. However one looks at it, filmmaking is never benign or neutral. "The camera is like a gun," a colleague remarks. "It's threatening. It's invasive, exploitive...and not always true." The Kentucky "we see" is always and also a partial truth, and while Barret never condones the murder of Hugh O'Connor, she "could understand where [Ison's] rage was coming from." Ultimately, it is this richly layered confrontation between Ison and O'Connor that allows Barret to sidestep binaries like "home" and "away," "us" and "them," "insider" and "outsider," and focus instead on the visual skirmishes that historically gave them shape and meaning. Like Stewart's "space on the side of the road," *Stranger* works to displace the urge to *know* Kentucky by understanding instead narrative formations of othered places and the kinds of graphic knowledges that get "caught up" in them.[12] As Barret's title suggests, looking is always a form of encounter, "place" an incessant story of travel.

Thirty years after Hugh O'Connor journeyed south to film the hills of eastern Kentucky, Cambridge filmmaker Frederick Wiseman headed north to the blue-collar town of Belfast, Maine. A self-described voyeur, Wiseman explained to the press that he sought to document the "unstaged reality of 'ordinary life,'" and a coastal town of sixty-five hundred seemed an ideal location. Like O'Connor, Wiseman traveled light, using portable hand-held equipment and a crew of two. And, also like the Canadian, he and his crew generated intense debate in the county over the kinds of pictures they took. Belfast is Waldo County's largest town, and like most of Maine, it was undergoing a new and brutal phase of de-industrialization as manufacturing jobs closed or moved across the border. What kinds of jobs would replace them was hotly contested. So was the "culture industry" that had begun to find Downeast to be "the other Maine," what the *New York Times* recently defined as "the large unseen social reality of the majority of the inhabitants of vacationland." Vacationland is a reference to the tourist directed motto that adorns the state's automobile license plates, which has come to define for many artists the polar opposite of "real Maine."[13] Equipped with cameras, tape recorders, field books, and sketchpads, a coterie of "new realists" came to the state to document what one documentary field school defined as "the really important people of Maine." Wiseman joined them in the fall of 1997.

The film is slow moving and takes viewers on a four-hour and eight-minute trip through the town. We see a sardine factory, a potato-processing plant, a group of hunters jawing, a trapper, a lobster fisherman, welfare clients, welfare case workers, a soup kitchen, a garden club, a drama group, a choir, trailers, old cars. What we never see, however, is the stranger or his camera. If Barret opens up othered places to viewer scrutiny and locates Kentucky in the historicized gaps between looking and knowing, Wiseman returns them to the totalizing gaze of the filmmaker's "innocent eye." *Belfast, Maine* snaps into view unencumbered by even the slightest sense of how it, or "we," got there. Rooted in the traditions of visual anthropology, the film is thus more about "being there" than about "getting there," less about looking than being "looked at." The *routes* of things – the complex migratory life of images and image-makers – disappear from view as the filmmaker puts his camera between himself and the *root* of blue-collar places. Never in sight, the camera urges viewers to follow and identify with its distancing gaze. In the process, *Belfast* reinscribes a familiar landscape of regional differences and cultural strangeness. Displaced by a poetics of otherness, social conflict, class difference, and the meaning-making processes of social documentary, morph into ruminative visions of *gritty* small town America and the kinds of hardscrabble lives that linger like a cultural ache, if not a social problem, on the national consciousness. Released last year to international acclaim, the film underscores the persistent appeal of othered places as they travel through the modern art/culture system still "producing the opportunities they offer" to strangers and their cameras.

Belfast is Frederick Wiseman's thirty-first film in thirty-three years, and he is considered by many to be the dean of the American documentary film. "No other documentarian since Robert Flaherty," noted one reviewer, "has enjoyed such widespread, superlative-laced praise."[14] Best known perhaps for his 1967 film, *Titicut Follies*, a chilling portrayal of patients at Massachusetts' Bridgewater State Hospital for the criminally insane, the Cambridge filmmaker began his career as something of a reformer, although issues of inmate privacy led to the film being banned in the state until 1991. With *Titicut*, however, Wiseman established himself as a devotee of *cinéma-vérité*, a documentary film style that he continues to defend, although he sounds increasingly uncomfortable with its claims to unmediated truth. "One of the things we're trying to do," Wiseman told reporters, "is create the illusion that we're telling the truth – and, well, that may coincide with the truth."[15] Nevertheless, *Belfast* works hard to maintain the illusion of objective observation, and most reviewers saw in it the grand synthesis of Wiseman's formidable career. Comparing it to the art of Walt Whitman, filmmaker Errol Morris proclaimed *Belfast* "a vision, a simulacrum of the world."[16] The Film Society of Lincoln Center declared the film a "triumph of unsurpassed ethnography" and a "microcosm of American life."[17] It has been shown to enthusiastic crowds at film festivals in England, Scotland, Canada, and the Netherlands, and last year it became the centerpiece of a Wiseman retrospective where the film-maker was honored with the Irene Diamond Lifetime Achievement Award for his commitment to human rights. "Frederick Wiseman," wrote the doyenne of American film criticism Pauline Kael, "is probably the most sophisticated intelligence to enter the documentary field."[18] Like "outsider art," which in the eyes of sophisticated collectors has come to epitomize a culture unsullied by contact with the metropolis, *Belfast* puts on display the visual artifacts of an American marginalia. A metonym for small town USA, *Belfast* works best in the big city.

Frequently described as a "professional observer," Wiseman uses a fly-on-the-wall documentary style to bring "this place" upfront by keeping the camera off stage. Like a "searchlight," the camera presents itself as no more than an aid for the eye of the viewer.[19] To enhance this impression, Wiseman uses few interpretive devices. There is no music in his film, no explanatory voiceovers. There are no interviews, reenactments, or flashbacks. No identifying information of any kind seems to intrude into Wiseman's story and viewers are presented with a film "pieced" together and devoid of a narrative script. As Wiseman puts it, "his films – and his subjects – speak for themselves."[20] What you see, the filmmaker insists, is Belfast, Maine the town, not *Belfast, Maine* the movie.

The film begins where othered places often do – in the imaginary dream spaces that press against the center's order of things and sit like a kind of hope against hope that "this place" is still within "our" grasp. "A Place," as Stewart explains, "to which 'we' might return."[21] It is dawn in a snug harbor: a lobster boat heads out to sea; a fisherman gracefully hauls his traps; the cries of herring gulls pierce the silence. It is silent, peaceful – the sea turns a serene blue. It is a long lingering take, constituting almost nine minutes of screen time, and Wiseman uses it to set the stage and establish temporality. Unlike Barret, who is constantly trying to query the illusions of ethnographic *vérité*, Wiseman uses techniques like this to shore them up. Long-form sequences of men fishing lobster, women packing sardines, a baker making doughnuts, a hunter finding his perch, an old woman in bed – are meant to suggest that cinematic time can be as authentic as "real time." They provide the "you are there" effect that brings to disparate viewers the cohesion of the tour. Viewers become audience.

Because Wiseman positions himself as the "ethnographic eye" that takes *us* to the semi-exotic and picturesque, he has at times been compared to Robert Flaherty, whose work ushered in the *âge d'or* of the romantic ethnographic documentary. With Wiseman, however, the picturesque, so important to films like Flaherty's influential *Nanook of the North* (1922), is employed in *Belfast* less to preserve a vanishing "folk" culture than to signal what anthropologist Johannes Fabian called the "ethnographic present," a mode of representation in the third person that works to "mark an Other outside the dialogue."[22] While Fabian was most concerned with practices of ethnographic writing, recent scholars have demonstrated the ways in which ethnographic cinema works in similar ways. In *Belfast*, long protracted shots, tight angled close-ups, and a preference for both "local" rituals and the shabby *mise-en-scène* help distance viewer from subject: "them" from "us," "our" time from "theirs" (Figure 13.1). In one particularly gruesome scene, a coyote is shown in a frenzy of pain, his leg snared in a steel trap. The writhing pain of the animal

Figure 13.1. Deer kill, the fundamental referent of rural authenticity. From *Belfast, Maine*

reinforces the illusion of unmediated observation – who could watch such a thing and not intervene – and establishes an ethnographic peephole into a present *we* no longer inhabit. A man drives his pickup down a long dusty road that leads to the trap in the open field. He pauses to watch the animal, then, very slowly he lifts his rifle and shoots the quivering coyote in the head. The viewer watches transfixed by what urbanization has moved away from: the ritualistic enactment of "the hunt" that so often gives to othered places the sanguine whiff of rural authenticity and cold-blooded truth.

Wiseman links scenes like this with decaying piers, tumble-down trailers, autumn woods, aging factories, and a workforce both elderly and infirm. Cars whiz by this place abandoned by both time and youth. Here *we* enter a place not of return, but of fascination: a territory of the unassimilated who stayed behind. In this sense Wiseman creates a picturesque more in keeping with the original meaning of the word that, among nineteenth-century regionalists, conjured up the wild, irregular, yet charming places off the beaten track.[23] From the sublime world of ocean fishing, Wiseman thus turns his camera on the unfolding "everyday" where storekeepers open their shops, dry cleaners press clothes, bakers turn dough into "donuts," factory workers can sardines and process potatoes, a teacher lectures to his silent students, and a cadre of welfare workers, visiting nurses, and volunteers minister to the obese, the alcoholic, the malnourished, the mentally challenged, the elderly poor. Viewed through the pale northern light of autumn, scenes like these mark Belfast not simply as a geographic place, but as a particular kind of *landscape* – a poetic terrain of gritty, hardscrabble others who live stoically, humbly, nobly, in the rustic places just beyond the border. The overall effect is suggestive of Foucault's "normalizing gaze" in that "it establishes over individuals a visibility through which one differentiates them and judges them."[24] In the rhetoric of viewers, *Belfast* was never discussed as an "our town" but rather as a town of *those* people, *that sort*, and *their kind*. Wiseman referred to the town as, "a place like that." One local viewer wrote, "It was as interesting as a trip to a foreign country. I felt like I could be a thousand miles away without ever leaving home."[25] Another Belfast native told the press, "It was really good that Fred Wiseman came and illustrated that I really live in a place where I have never been." A portrait of the ordinary, Belfast viewers looked into the screen and saw a landscape of otherness. "They left out the more normal aspects of life," a local viewer complained, "the population that was just normal."

It is this ability of documentary filmmaking to shape categories of difference and erase the traces of representation, which has made the ethnographic documentary so problematic and so interesting to scholars. "Progressive" filmmaking contains an additional set of challenges as stories of the "down and out" obscure the meaning-making apparatus they produce. As one theorist points out, when "the silent common people" become the "fundamental referent of the social," the position of the socially oriented filmmaker in the production of meaning goes unchallenged, "skillfully masked as it is by its righteous mission."[26] As Wiseman creates a place that seems "Other" even to those who live there, he represents it to audiences as an unmediated cultural real expunged of ideology, if not moral certainty. The Harry Potter of documentary filmmaking, Wiseman is a cinematic wizard who, in the service of the unexpressed, uses the camera like a wand. And because Wiseman is so good at what he does and occupies such an influential position in the filmmaking world, it makes sense to use some of the tools of cultural criticism to explore in some detail how an othered place like *Belfast* works to obscure the "bottom up" world it sets out to reveal and protest against.

Once again, temporality proves critical in *Belfast* not only as a way to establish an ethnographic present but as a way to decontextualize and dehistoricize the two activities. Wiseman puts wage labor and social services at the center of his film. Consider, for example a scene taken at the local fish-processing plant where women workers are shown skillfully and speedily sniping off the heads and tails of sardines. Fingers, sliced and bandaged, seem to fly over the fish as they pack the truncated bodies into tins. It is, as critics point out, a remarkable sequence. Altogether it takes up more than nine minutes of screen time and is made up of two hundred and seventy shots. "I tried to edit the shots," Wiseman explains, "so they tell you something about the technological nature of the sardine factory and something about the nature of work...and connections to other factories and other work."[27] Yet the scene, despite its industrialized setting, strongly invokes the past. The workers are uniformly old; they are all white and female. Their gendered skills seem oddly redundant in an automated world, their whiteness an anomaly in the "new" economy. The conveyor belt winds and twists its way along the shop in a kind of Rube Goldberg sequence that makes it seem a folksy throwback to the 1920s. There are no supervisors in sight, no punch clocks, no workplace rules, no bells, no union halls. No one shouts or looks idle; not one worker looks up to eyeball the camera. The tedium and monotony of the job give way to a sense of placidity, even contentment, among the workforce. Technology seems beside the point as the antiquated machinery forces attention instead to the faded position of the industry that hovers like a ghost over the decayed ports of Downeast Maine. Sardines, potatoes, and chickens *are* history – as in sadly but inevitably gone – rather than *in* history as part of the larger decision-making processes involved in the reorganization of the local economy.

Like many of the "new realists," Wiseman uses rough physical labor to code the town blue-collar. Waitresses, seamstresses, crab pickers, cashiers, day care workers, and retail clerks, are all out of sight in *Belfast*. Women seem to enter the economy as either elderly factory hands or middle-class health care providers. With few exceptions, wage labor itself seems almost a nostalgic afterthought taking up only a small fraction of the film's "work" scenes, while ignoring the family economy that stitches together much of the rural livelihood. With the exception of the factory operatives, most of those coded as working-class are instead engaged in quirky male defined jobs like taxidermy and donut making, or running independent businesses, or fishing. In one early morning scene reminiscent of the Dunkin' Donut advertisement whose baker knows "it's time to make the doughnuts," an independent grocer downtown puts dough to fat. The sequence underscores the film's aversion to malls, fast food chains, and corporate employers like the controversial MBNA that take up less than two minutes of film time. The service industry is almost totally absent despite Maine's growing dependence upon it. Dunkin' Donuts, the mall, and McDonald's never make it to the big screen despite their proximity to downtown. When read along with other work places – a fish pier, a taxidermy shop, a country store, a trawler, a local dry cleaner's – laboring *Belfast* conjures up a pre-industrial world unsullied by their presence.

The anti-modern impulse, of course, has always moved in tandem with stories of othered places. Rural work and workplaces, even in the rusty towns like Belfast, are constantly summoned to signal a collective sense of loss – of seasonality, of hand skills, of endurance, of geographical closeness, of community. It is not the future we see in *Belfast* but a remembrance of things forgotten and missed. In the endless images of rotting piers, decaying factories, threadbare workers, back wood roads, and tumble down mobile homes, viewers are invited to witness the nostalgia of ruins rather the economics of regional labor markets or the decisions of policy makers. For *The New York Times*, the poetics of hardscrabble places translated into an "elegiac vision of a small town that works." "What *Belfast* really wants to do," a reviewer explained to readers, "is capture a deeper, more timeless sense of the town as a hardy organism more closely tied to nature than many other more affluent American communities."[28] Not surprisingly, sequences of natural settings play important roles in the film – fields, woods, the sea, dawn, pumpkins, sunset, and autumn in New England. The social structures of community enter as well with clips of choir practice, a gardening club, a drama group, a town meeting. It is a place where people still care, a "place where place still matters."[29]

Visual clues like these take on added importance since Wiseman never uses identifying titles or captions of any kind. Viewers must depend upon certain familiar markers to understand the action or story Wiseman wants to tell or not tell. Workers carrying the code "blue collar" can be found most commonly in places of employment, while middle-class members of the community appear more often in social situations, alone, or in small intimate groups: a garden club learning to arrange flowers, an amateur theater group, a gay-lesbian pot luck, a city council meeting, a church choir, or simply an artist in his studio. In their study of photographs from *National Geographic*, Catherine Lutz and Jane Collins noted that people of color were "less often the subject of individualized photographic accounts." Like *Belfast*'s wage earners, they appeared more often as part of a mass grouping less subject to "biographic" attentiveness. Lutz and Collins argue that such groupings suggest to readers "that they had relatively undifferentiated feelings, hopes, or needs."[30] In the visual lexicon of *Belfast*, laboring people come into focus without social complexity or agency, their images constituting an incessant narrative of human toil: a fundamental referent of hardscrabble lives emptied of collective or personal history (Figure 13.2). "There is something deeply reassuring," writes one reviewer, "in watching how a product is made from scratch by silent, dedicated workers patiently executing their mechanical tasks in hygienic settings."[31] Frozen in time and severed from history, workers in *Belfast* collapse into a generic, undifferentiated, visual topography that Carolyn Chute proudly calls, "a people of the tribal class."[32]

When modernity does enter *Belfast* the film, it comes in the form of the social welfare system. Images of social workers and their clients take up almost as much cinematic space as do scenes of work. They appear in a seemingly

Figure 13.2. *"Belfast, ME, The Movie,"* cartoon by Darryl Smith. Reprinted with permission

random order; there is no attempt to link them to outmoded factories or vanishing sources of employment that might explain their protracted presence on the screen. But if poor people seem as plentiful in Belfast as in Whitesburg, Kentucky during the 1960s, they "look" very different when viewed through Wiseman's camera. Unlike the poverty pictures Barret presents, these images avoid frontal shots that allow for much scrutiny of the face or eyes where, visual scholars tell us, "the seat of soul – feelings, personality, or character" are located.[33] Wiseman prefers to shoot people at an angle so that his subjects never "eyeball" the camera. In part, this accentuates the illusion of "being there," for how could the subjects not see "us" if the camera stood in front of their eyes? It confirms as well the purposefulness of the subjects' activity in that they are engaged in the "unstaged" reality of "life" rather than in the stranger who observes them. Moving images are far more suggestive, of course, and lend themselves to many different and often unanticipated readings. But when viewed in comparison to the poverty pictures of Appalachia, they reinforce Wiseman's claim to invisibility and truthfulness. This is no reporter telling stories or asking questions. So too can the relentless avoidance of "the seat of soul" be read as a move away from portraiture and towards typology. In place of feelings, personality, and character, viewers confront a representational type that lacks both individuation and personal history. *They* sit; *they* stand; *they* complain; *they* hurt; *they* never look *us* in the face. Each image tells the same story. Just as *Belfast* workers flatten out into an undifferentiated "tribe," welfare recipients melt into a categorical image of "the rural poor," a northern "white trash" that easily becomes a displaced sign of cultural rather than economic conditions. A young woman on anti-psychotic drugs tells her caseworker how she tries to stay sober, but "Dad wants us to get high with him." She complains that there is too much "crap with the state." In one of the most noted scenes, a social worker picks nits from a client's hair. The comb pulls and tugs at tangled wild tuffs of hair from a woman whose front teeth are missing. The social worker explains to her that she needs to keep her daughters out of her bed, or she'll re-infect them. What about the youngest daughter's cramps? The client stumbles over the word "menstrual." A visual code for the gritty realism of the "Other," images like this confirm our entry into the culture of "this place." Privy to the *gist* of things, viewers again become all-knowing audience.

Because "culture" is for Wiseman a precipitant of lived experiences, poverty emerges less as a problem to war against than as a cultural expression to contemplate. "You look misery in the eye," writes Pauline Kael, "and you realize there's nothing to be afraid of."[34] A man sits half naked in his trailer as a nurse wraps his swollen feet; he laughs and kids the nurse. A woman is wheeled into the emergency ward, her huge belly exposed. She says nothing. A painfully thin woman in her eighties graciously waits as the health care worker finds a pulse. Her bed is worn, the windows dirty. She calmly talks of death. A wizened old man silently lines up for food at the soup kitchen. "I make movies," Wiseman explains, "not offer solutions to society's complex problems."[35] Images like these, however, are not without motive force. They float in an ethnographic present that helps affirm the timeless quality of poverty. "I think you find that everywhere," a viewer noted when asked about the numerous scenes of poor people, "it's part of life."[36] The poor will always be with *us*. Wiseman pounds the viewer with images of poor people and because they circulate and are read in relation to each other, they preclude questions of causality or the contemplation of alternatives. Poverty seems strangely unencumbered by any active sense of how it came to be. We enter trailers and backwood shacks, never the homes of the middle classes. "There are no glaring class differences," a reviewer noted approvingly. Unlike the poverty pictures of Appalachia, *Belfast* situates poor people in an environment where caregivers address the needs of uncomplaining clients. "Their patience," a critic found, "is mirrored by the forbearance of the social and welfare workers calmly quieting clients about their health, medication, living habits, and states of mind."[37] Here is a world less open to change than to rumination. There is "a contemplative manner in *Belfast, Maine*," writes Kael, who, like many viewers, left the theater with a new appreciation for the "meditative almost pastoral side to Mr. Wiseman."

As a filmmaker, Wiseman eschews any claims to truth making. Half-jokingly he describes his work as "reality fiction." For the most part, *Belfast* avoids explanation, preferring instead reality pictures open to interpretation. But as a "professional observer," Wiseman also wants "to get it right." It took six weeks to film *Belfast* and ten months to edit it. Wiseman wants us to know certain things about the town. The most didactic scene is at the Waldo County Health Commission where a lecturer gives the audience a few facts: Waldo County ranks third in the nation for the number of smokers between the ages of eighteen and thirty-four. Another third of adults are overweight, an increase of 8 percent in ten years. More troubling, however, she reports, are lifestyle issues that lead to the poor health of County residents. She reads them in the order of priority: "Teen pregnancy, poor parenting, dysfunctional family behavior, alcoholism, tobacco." It is a curious sequence in a film stridently opposed to narration and explanation. Yet the explanatory power of the scene is hard to miss. Even progressive magazines and newspapers referred to Belfast's laboring population as "these damaged, self-injuring workers."[38] Part of a cultural experience that marks *Belfast* as a gritty, working-class Other, poverty becomes a personal rather than a social issue. There are no scenes of contaminated lakes, no talk of wage scales, lay offs, shut downs. No one mentions summer people or those "from away" who have made housing almost unaffordable among "locals." Homelessness, which increased throughout Maine by 69 percent between 1993 and 2000, is either never mentioned or remains on the cutting room floor. In such a context, *Belfast* travels into the imaginary of viewers not as "news," or as Barret insisted as a problematic form of looking, but rather as a new aesthetic, one that tends to equate the poor with a certain documentary fascination for different places and other people. The "unflinching eye" becomes, for viewers like Kael, less a call to arms than a self-referential call to order. As the photographer Martha Rosler has suggested, "Documentary is a little like horror movies, putting a face on fear and transforming threat into fantasy, into imagery. One can handle imagery by leaving it behind. (It is them [*sic*], not us.) One may even, as a private person, support causes."

Not everyone cooperates. One man, it might be argued, looked back. It is Halloween in a Belfast soup kitchen. The camera scans the cheery, decorated room then alights on a client. He is a tall, stooped, middle-aged patron who patiently waits in line for a Halloween meal. At first he appears like the others we have seen: quiet, reticent, passively accepting help. A chirpy, middle-aged woman, obviously enjoying her role as volunteer, stands with a knife before a pumpkin-shaped cake and jokingly asks, "Would you like an eyeball, a nose, or what?" The man's rheumy eyes sharpen into focus, his face hardens, and his voice takes on an edge that is new in this town. "I'll take whatever I can get," he says. The volunteer laughs nervously then suddenly stops when she looks him in the eye, and he turns his towards the screen. For a fleeting moment the safety of observation loosens and we wonder, "what does this man see when he looks at us?" How does hunger look offstage? The scene reminds us that the appeal of ethnographically othered places also resides in the very cracks and fissures of official discourse and fictions of rescue. Images are hard things to "get right" or to leave behind. As a rare, unstaged and unanticipated moment in the film, the image disrupts and refuses in ways still being thought out by picture takers and scholars, the ideological closure that so often accompanies the righteous mission of the ethnographic documentary. That Wiseman cannot see this is *Belfast*'s failure and Belfast's loss.

For historians of the "bottom up," who have long shared with anthropologists, sociologists, regionalists, and professional observers of all sorts an affinity for documenting and knowing "the *gist* of a place," *Stranger* and *Belfast* force into view an epistemology of the Other that makes visible our own tracks as *les chasseurs d'images*. In different ways Barret and Wiseman compel us to suspend our longing "to get it right" so that we might instead "see it" as the re-presentation it also and always is. And, like all texts that provoke, *Belfast* and *Stranger* raise as well a set of questions that help historians of all sorts put "the visual" on the ground where it rubs up against the material conditions of cultural production and is put to work in the service of those offstage. How, for example, do class differences and rural wage laborers enter into public discourse when stories of place take shape in the popular imagination as zones of difference and strangeness? If, as Wiseman's promoters argue, it is the supposed absence of mediation that accounts for his status as documentary "artist," what happens to the status of the poor as they become "art"? How do images like those produced in Maine and Kentucky find value and meaning as they migrate from the material conditions of a place and into the fetishized "local" of othered places? And, as a few literary scholars have asked, what happens to the "natives" as their images leave home and travel into a second home sited in a decontextualized milieu of aesthetics or ethnographic knowledge? Do these images travel as the displaced signs of cultural or economic differences? As an exploited class or an exotic ethnicity? Do they signify regional trouble or cosmopolitan longing? And finally, there is Barret's question which leads viewers to all the others: "What are the responsibilities of any of us who take the images of other people and put them to our own uses?"

Like all "true places," northern New England and Appalachia elude the best of maps, but their images can direct us to the performative spaces that linger "on the side of the road" where ideology and looking collide and the politics of othered places begin. For historians of "the bottom up," it is a space worth imagining, and as Stewart perceptively points out, "the very motive for telling the story and its point in the end."[39]

Notes

1 Kathleen Stewart, *A Space on the Side of the Road: Cultural Poetics in an "Other" America* (Princeton, NJ: Princeton University Press, 1996).
2 I use the language of Stewart to describe the kinds of poetics othered places enact. See ibid., esp. ch. 2.
3 Richard Brodhead, *Cultures of Letters: Scenes of Reading and Writing in Nineteenth-Century America* (Chicago: University of Chicago Press, 1994), 116, 119.
4 See especially Dona Brown, *Inventing New England: Regional Tourism in the Nineteenth Century* (Washington, DC: Smithsonian Institution Press, 1995); David Whisnant, *All That is Native and Fine: The Politics of Culture in an American Region* (Chapel Hill, NC: University of North Carolina Press, 1983); Henry Shapiro, *Appalachia On Our Mind: The Southern Mountains and Mountaineers in the American Consciousness, 1870–1920* (Chapel Hill, NC: University of North Carolina Press, 1978); Steven Nissenbaum, "New England as a Region and Nation," in Edward Ayers and Pete Onuf, *All Over the Map: Rethinking American Regions* (Baltimore: Johns Hopkins University Press, 1996); George H. Lewis, "The Maine That Never Was: The Construction of Popular Myth in Regional Culture," *Journal of American Culture*, 16 (Summer 1993), 91–9.

5 The term "art-culture system" is used by anthropologist historian James Clifford to describe how in the last century material objects, especially non-Western and tribal artifacts, accrued value and authenticity in "western systems of exchange, disciplinary archives, and discursive traditions." See James Clifford, *The Predicament of Culture: Twentieth-Century Ethnography, Literature, and Art* (Cambridge, MA: Harvard University Press, 1988), esp. ch. 10.

6 Clifford, *Routes: Travel and Translation in the Late Twentieth Century* (Cambridge, MA: Harvard University Press, 1997), esp. ch. 1. For a provocative critique of the kinds of representational essentializing performed by Western localizing strategies and disciplinary practices, see also Caren Kaplan, *Questions of Travel: Postmodern Discourses of Displacement* (Durham, NC: Duke University Press, 1998); Arjun Appadurai, "Introduction: Place and Voice in Anthropological Theory," *Cultural Anthropology*, 3 (1988), 16–20.

7 Harry Caudill, quoted in Calvin Trillin, "A Stranger with a Camera," *The New Yorker*, Apr. 12, 1969, p. 179.

8 For a detailed history of Caudill and his fight against the coal interests, see, David G. McCullough, "The Lonely War of a Good Angry Man," *American Heritage*, 21 (Dec. 1969), 97–113.

9 Stewart, *A Space on the Side*, 119. See also Peter Stallybrass and Allon White, *The Politics and Poetics of Transgression* (Ithaca, NY: Cornell University Press, 1986), esp. ch. 3.

10 Trinh T. Minh-ha, "The Totalizing Quest of Meaning," in Michael Renov, *Theorizing Documentary* (New York: Routledge, 1993), 96.

11 For a provocative discussion of the documentary use of "the silent common people" see Trinh T. Minh-ha, "The Totalizing Quest," esp. pp. 96–7.

12 Stewart, *Space*, 11.

13 Anthony Walton, "A Life in the Other Maine," *New York Times Book Review*, Aug. 20, 2000, p. 26.

14 Stuart Klawans, "As Maine Goes, So Goes..." *The Nation*, Feb. 14, 2000, p. 34.

15 Wiseman Interview in Stephen Holden, "Seaside Town Under a Microscope," quoted in *The New York Times*, Jan. 28, 2000, Sec. E, p. 17.

16 Errol Morris, quoted in Philip Lepate, "Composing an American Epic," in *The New York Times*, Jan. 3, 2000, p. 11.

17 *New York Times*, Jan. 31, 2000; *The Nation*, Jan. 31, 2000. See also David Sterritt, "Penetrating *Belfast, Maine*, Gets Inside Small Town," in *The Christian Science Monitor*, Jan. 28, 2000, p. 15; Eddie Cockrell, "Belfast, Maine," in *Daily Variety*, Sept. 7, 1999, p. 8.

18 Chris Wright, "Belfast, Maine," *Boston Phoenix*, Jan. 31, 2000; see also *The New York Times*, Feb. 3, 2000, p. 22.

19 The term is from Christian Metz, quoted in Catherine Lutz and Jane Collins, *Reading National Geographic* (Chicago: University of Chicago Press, 1993), 193.

20 Wiseman, quoted in *The Boston Phoenix*, Jan. 31, 2000.

21 Stewart, *Space*, 5.

22 Johannes Fabian, *Time and the Other: How Anthropology Makes Its Object* (New York: Columbia University Press, 1983), 84–7. The comparison to Flaherty

is skillfully made by Fatimah Tobing Rony, "Robert Flaherty's *Nanook of the North*: The Politics of Taxidermy and Romantic Ethnography," in Daniel Berardi (ed.), *The Birth of Whiteness: Race and the Emergence of U.S. Cinema* (New Brunswick, NJ: Rutgers University Press, 1996), 301–28, esp. 305.

23 I use this term in its original meaning as a word used to designate "wild, irregular, but charming landscapes." For a helpful discussion see Brown, *Inventing New England*, 52–3. Brown also explains the emergence of the term "landscape" and provides a perceptive analysis of how the term infused into the materiality of location the poetics of cultural and economic value, what Raymond Williams famously called the "conspicuous aesthetic consumption" of scenery.

24 Michel Foucault, *Discipline and Punish: The Birth of the Prison*, trans. A. Sheridan (New York: Pantheon Books, 1977), 25.

25 Steve Olson, quoted in *Belfast Republican*, Feb. 10, 2000.

26 Trinh T. Minh-ha, "The Totalizing Quest," 96.

27 Georgeanne Davis, "Belfast, Maine," *The Free Press*, Jan. 20, 2000.

28 Holden, *New York Times*, Jan. 28, 2000, Sec. E, p. 17.

29 Stewart, *Space*, 41.

30 Lutz and Collins, *Reading National Geographic*, 163.

31 Holden, *New York Times*.

32 Carolyn Chute, quoted in Jules Crittenden, "Author Leads Crusade vs. 'Bad Government,'" *Boston Herald*, June 1, 1977, p. 6.

33 Lutz and Collins, *Reading National Geographic*, 199.

34 Pauline Kael, quoted in Phillip Lopate, "Composing an American Epic," *New York Times*, Jan. 23, 2000, p. 11.

35 Wiseman, quoted in Catherine Russel, "Persistence of Vision," *Maine Times*, Jan. 20, 2000, p. 16.

36 Kathy Messier, *Belfast Republican Journal*, Feb. 10, 2000.

37 Holden, *New York Times*.

38 See especially Klawans, "As Maine Goes, So Goes."

39 Stewart, *Space*, 211.

Part III, 1940–2000:
Suggested Readings

What is the relationship between Home and Away? And how do images of each help shape how we see ourselves and establish who "we" are? The following readings explore the performative nature of looking relations as the contentious gaze of the "All-American" takes ethnic, gender, and sexual shape amidst the rhetoric of hot and Cold Wars and the global politics of difference, cultural hybridity, and post-colonial Otherness.

Judith Smith, *Visions of Belonging: Family Stories, Popular Culture and Postwar Democracy, 1940–1960* (2004).

Hong Zhang, *America Perceived: The Making of Chinese Images of the United States, 1945–1953* (2002).

Mark Neumann, *On the Rim: Looking for the Grand Canyon* (1999).

Lauren Berlant, *The Queen of America Goes to Washington City: Essays on Sex and Citizenship* (1997).

Ann E. Kaplan, *Looking for the Other: Feminism, Film, and the Imperial Gaze* (1997).

Victor Burgin, *In/Different Spaces: Place and Memory in Visual Culture* (1996).

James Faris, *Navajo and Photography: A Critical History of the Representation of an American People* (1996).

Fatimah Tobing Rony, *The Third Eye: Race, Cinema, and Ethnographic Spectacle* (1996).

Kathleen Stewart, *A Space on the Side of the Road: Cultural Poetics in an "Other" America* (1996).

Deborh Willis, *Picturing Us: African American Identity in Photographs* (1994).

Melissa Banta and Curtis M. Hinsley (eds.), *From Site To Site: Anthropology, Photography, and the Power of Imagery* (1986).

Johannes Fabian, *Time and the Other: How Anthropology Makes its Object* (1983).

Appendix A:
"Reading the Visual Record"

ELSPETH H. BROWN

As historians move toward including the visual record as a site for evidence about the past, we face new challenges in historical methodology. How can historians, and their students, develop useful questions when faced with the mute visual record? While many students have learned strategies for analyzing textual documents, such as identifying the author's use of metaphor or imagery, few history students have been trained in parallel methodologies for reading visual records. This essay is designed to suggest one method, among many, that history and American studies students might use in analyzing visual texts, with a special attention to photography.[1]

Stage 1: Description

The first step to analyzing an image and its historically contingent meanings is to *see* the image. Viewers have a tendency to quickly process visual information into cultural meanings which may, or may not, be warranted by the visual evidence: a quick glance at a found snapshot of a smiling woman cradling an infant seems to confirm the cultural assumption of a young mother and her newborn child. In fact, however, the image itself provides no direct reference for this cultural relationship. The image might actually be showing, for example, a childcare worker and a child; or the child's aunt cradling her niece for the first time. A key step in mining the image for what it can tell us, on its own terms, without inferences and assumptions, is to slow down and describe what you see, using *only* the visual evidence present in the image. This crucial step can be frustrating, in that you might feel it is "obvious" what's in the image, but I guarantee that your understanding of what you see will often vary from another viewer's, since seeing is a subjective experience. We don't all, in fact, see the same things, nor draw the same meanings from what we see; history, politics, and culture inform every aspect of seeing and interpretation. So step one: describe what you see, without recourse to any analyses or assumptions that cannot be verified by evidence drawn from the image itself. Resist the impulse to skip ahead to an analysis of the image's meaning: describe what you see, first, no matter how boring or obvious this might seem. Here are three specific steps in the description stage of an image analysis, with reference to Figure A1.

First, note and describe the physical and material aspects of the image. Is the image printed on paper, on a coffee mug, or composed of pixels encountered in a digital environment? Describe the material articulation of the image, including its size and, for digital images, its resolution. At this stage, you might not in fact know what the materiality of the image might be: the coffee mug might look like porcelain to you, for example, but it might in fact be white stoneware. Nonetheless, make your best effort; you can always research later.

Second, describe the content of the image. Here, you are mostly concerned with subject matter. What does the image depict, in the most obvious sense? Include a mention of any text embedded in the image as well. In Figure A1, for example, a simple description of the image's content might be that the image depicts a smiling young woman in a semi-kneeling position holding a bouquet of what appears to be flowers. Don't describe her as "Hawaiian," since though the rest of the image urges you to read her as "Hawaiian," you in fact have no independent knowledge that she is. For all you know, she might be an underemployed actress, not of Hawaiian descent, who's picked up a modeling job on Madison Avenue. Include here a brief discussion of any text in the images, such as the Matson Line "card" in the bottom right of the image, or the text at the upper right part of the image.

Finally, describe the visual character of the image in what's known as a formal analysis. A formal analysis is a very close reading of a text or object, which uses an understanding of form as basis for interpretation. A formal analysis of an image doesn't mean that one cannot also perform other types of readings, such as those informed by feminism, history, queer theory, or post-structuralism; these theoretical and historical frameworks can be extremely important, but come in at a slightly later stage of the image analysis, after you have had a chance to explore, see, and understand the image's formal elements. Start with describing the image's composition, beginning with two-dimensional organization. Isolate vertical lines, then horizontal lines, then diagonal lines. Count them up, describe all of them, where they begin and end. How is your eye encouraged to move through the image? Do the lines lead, and then entrap or release, your eye to a particular location, either within or outside of the frame? For example, in the figure, note that the

Figure A1. Advertisement for Matson Line cruises, *Vogue*, November 1, 1941, inside cover. Edward Steichen, photographer; Lloyd B. Meyers, art director (Bowman Deute Cummings)

combination of vertical lines (including, for example, the edges of the image, the left bikini strap, the block of text), horizontal lines (such as the platform structure or the horizon line), and diagonal lines (such as the model's thigh, the grass skirt, the flower stalks). One could argue that all of these intersecting lines lead the eye to a particular location, located on the lower portion of her body; the composition of the image reinforces this sexual reading. After describing the arrangement of lines, do a similar analysis of the use of three-dimensional space, as represented in the image. What is the relationship between a foreground (here, the kneeling model) and the background (mountain landscape)? Is there a middle ground in between the two, and how and why is your eye encouraged to move, in a spatial manner, through the image? In this case, for example, one can argue that the lack of a pronounced middle ground encourages the eye to remain in the foreground, with the model; there's no middle ground to act as a "bridge" between the foreground and background (the mountains).

Continuing with the formal analysis of the image, consider the use of light. Are there masses of light and dark throughout the image, or is the image evenly lit? The use of light can also direct how the eye moves through the image, as well as suggest the relative importance of specific aspects of the overall composition. Light may also tell you, through an analysis of shadows, what time of day the image was taken, or whether the image was made with artificial lighting (for example, if there are contradictory shadows, or none at all – though this might also suggest the sun was directly overhead). Finally, consider color: is it used, where does it appear, what is its quality? In an intentional image, such as an advertising photograph, you can be certain that art directors have thought through the use of color in connoting specific meanings about a particular product, just as art photographers choose various color processes in order to suggest differing tones for the overall work.

Stage 2: Deduction

You've now concluded your information-gathering about the image, and have mined it for absolutely all the visual information you could possibly wring from it. At this point, you should be surprised if a colleague or classmate points out a visual element that you hadn't noticed, such as the vaguely floral motif of the model's bikini. At this stage of the analysis, the deduction stage, you are still working primarily with the image and the information it suggests, rather than moving outside the image to consider history, conduct research, and think through theoretical frameworks. The goal here is to consider the image in relationship to your own subjectivity. This process usually has two aspects. First, pay attention to your "instincts" about the image, your initial "take." An initial reading of an image might be accurate, and supported by evidence, but your job is to figure out, for example, how the image is able to make its meaning clear, or connote a particular sensibility. For example, to return to Figure A1, this image is not only connoting "sex," but, one could argue, a very specific Western fantasy of the East as passive, feminized, and sexually available – what the late Edward Said identified as "Orientalism." You might "get" some or part of this interpretation almost immediately. Your job, however, is to analyze *how* this meaning is communicated through formal decisions made by the photographer, art director, and others who may have been involved in the image's creation. This is where the close looking you've done in stage one becomes useful. You need to draw on visual evidence to support any argument you might make about the image's meaning. For example, available sexuality, one could argue, is connoted through the open thighs, the parted skirt, the flower necklace half off the shoulder, the abundance of bare skin, the symbolism of blooming flowers. At the same time, the model's sexuality is rendered non-threatening, as well as "natural": though her body is open to the viewer, she discreetly averts her gaze (no confrontational or seductive looking here); we can look at her, but she can't look at us. Nearly every detail of the image connotes the "natural," whether the floral pattern on the model's bikini top, the flower in her hair, the braided mat platform, or the mountains in the background: here, her Orientalized sexuality is rendered natural, while the implied Western viewer is the "culture" to her "nature," a relationship central to the discourse of colonialism. The strongest image analyses connect the analysis and interpretation of the image to specific visual evidence.

The second aspect of the deduction stage is to engage with the image empathetically. Place yourself in the represented world. What's the weather like? Is there a breeze blowing? Would you be warm or cold, comfortable or disoriented if you were inhabiting the pictorial space? Crucially, why? This empathic exercise can be complicated, in that the image, especially an ideologically loaded advertising image, usually suggests an implied viewer, yet the implied viewer is not always, of course, the actual viewer. You need to be sensitive to how the image is asking you to interact with its pictorial space. In Figure A1, for example, the full sunshine, cozy clouds, slight breeze, and limited clothing suggest a welcoming warmth and sunlight. At the same time, however, you can be aware of what the photographer is asking you to think about the image (what can be called a preferred reading, or a dominant reading), while at the same time being aware of your own resistance (if you have any) to that preferred reading. For example one could argue that the image assumes an "implied" reader who is a middle-class North American with a potential interest in traveling to Hawaii for a vacation; one might further argue, with evidence drawn from 1940s advertising history, that the implied viewer is a white heterosexual man and, potentially, his wife. At the same time, however, let's say you are yourself of Hawaiian descent, and read this image as a colonial fantasy: despite the warmth and sunshine, you might not find the image to be so "welcoming" after all, because you find yourself rejecting the terms in which you are being "welcomed." You might perform what's called an oppositional reading of the image, one where you situate your own subjectivity in relationship to the image's dominant narrative of Hawaii as feminized playground, and identify a subjective response of irritation or refusal.

Although this stage of the image analysis asks you to consider your own subjectivity in relation to the image, you must engage with these questions with a certain degree of skepticism. As historians, you are going to be primarily interested in who the actual viewers may have been in the 1940s, when the image was in original circulation, and what readings these 1941 viewers made have made of this image; alternatively, you may be interested in the implied 1941 viewers that the image suggests. Either way, you are interested in a specific moment in history when the image was in circulation, and are generally less concerned with contemporary readings of the image, since these readings and meanings, like other historical phenomena, change over time. This information is difficult to track down of course, and in the meantime you can use your own subjective responses to the image as a set of useful tips on where you might want to go for further research.

--------- **Stage 3: Speculation** ---------

At this point, questions are probably emerging in your mind as you view the image. These questions are central to developing a research paper, since a historical essay is only as good as the research questions you have posed. The speculation stage entails two steps. The first is to use the information you have gleaned from your interaction with the image to pose further questions designed to crack open the image still further, en route to pushing you to develop ideas for further research. The second step is to develop a program of research that will allow you to further pursue questions raised by the visual evidence and, as part of this process, to develop theories and hypotheses about the social and cultural work performed by the image in the historical context of its production and circulation. First, consider the following questions in relationship to your image:

Step 1: posing questions of your image

1 When and by whom was this particular document made? What is the format of the document? Does it appear in conjunction with other images, for example in a magazine, in a museum exhibition, or on a website? Has the document been edited? Was the document published? If so, when and where and how? How do the layout, typographical details, and accompanying illustrations inform you about the purpose of the document, the author's historical and cultural position, and that of the intended audience?

2   Photographs don't create meaning all on their own; instead, a photo-graph's meaning is usually "anchored" by some other framework that encourages us to draw a particular kind of meaning from the image. A photograph's meaning is most usually directed by accompanying text (such as a caption under a news photo, or a label on a museum wall); the placement of the image in relation to other images (such as a photo-essay or an exhibition); and/or an institutional setting (such as a historical society's archive, or the university classroom). What is the larger context in which this image appears? How is the image's meaning directed by this context, through the use of text, placement, repositioning, cropping, sequencing, or other methods designed to anchor photographic meaning?

3   Who is the photographer, and why did he or she create the document? Does it even make sense to identify a single "maker"? Perhaps a "creative team" or a public relations office is a more appropriate "author" for the piece.

4   Using clues from the image itself, its form, and its content, who is the intended audience for the text? Is the audience regional? National? A particular subset of "the American people"? How do you think the text was received by this audience? How might the text be received by those for whom it was not intended?

5   How does the text reflect or mask such factors as the class, race, gender, ethnicity, or regional background of its creator? (Remember that "race" is a factor when dealing with cultural forms of people identified as "white," that "men" possess "gender," and that the North and Midwest are regions of local as well as national significance.)

6   How does the photographer describe, grapple with, or ignore contempor-aneous historical events? Why? Which cultural myths or ideologies does the author endorse or attack? Are there any oversights or "blind spots" that strike you as particularly salient? What cultural value systems does the photographer embrace?

7   From a literary perspective, does the photographer employ any generic conventions, such as visual clichés of the heroic worker or the kindly grandmother?

8   With what aspects of the text (content, form, style) can you most readily identify? Which seem most foreign to you? Why? Does the document remind you of contemporaneous or present-day cultural forms that you have encountered? How and why?

Step 2: developing hypotheses and a program of research

As a result of your engagement with the image, you now may have a number of "hunches" or hypotheses about the history and meaning of the image.

These insights are tentative, and should be phrased in the form of a research question. This is the point when you move outside the image to research the history of the image's production, circulation, or reception, as well as to offer analyses about what sorts of cultural work the image performed, and for whom, at a specific historical moment, as well as (perhaps) how these meanings changed over time, and why. Here, you go outside the image, to the larger archive, to other primary sources as well as secondary sources, to help you situate the image in a wider social and historical context. For example, in relationship to Figure A1, you might be interested in a number of different topics, such as the history of tourism in Hawaii; the history of the stereotypical representation of the "hula girl" in American popular culture; the use of images in supporting, or disrupting, US economic and political interests in Hawaii; the history of commercial photography in relationship to advertising and consumer culture in the mid-twentieth-century USA; the relationship between the US tourism industry, Hawaii, and World War II. And, of course, you will probably find yourself lacking basic historical information. For example, what is the history of the relationship between Hawaii and the United States? When, and why, did Hawaii become a state? When and why did the Hawaiian tourism industry develop? And so on.

But identifying a topic is only half the battle. The other half of developing a program of research is posing a research *question* that allows you to explore the relationship between the image, and its meaning, and the larger social and cultural context in which it circulated. You want to think about what sorts of cultural and political work the image performed in the past: how did it work to foster, or render invisible, aspects of the ever-shifting structures of power that define social and political life in all its forms? The key to asking a strong historically based question that will allow you to analyze meaning is to create questions that ask "How?" or "Why?" rather than "What?". "What" or "When" questions, such as "When did Hawaii become a state?" are useful and important for providing empirical research to support your argument, but they won't give you the analytical tools you need to frame arguments about the *meaning* of images, events, and socio-political formations in the past. To return to the list of potential topics suggested above, try and turn these "topics" into research questions, keeping in mind the visual information you have already gleaned from the image. One example of such a question might be: "How does this image work to reinforce, or disrupt, early 1940s American ideas of Hawaii's relationship to the US mainland?" Note how even this question is still a bit too broad, though it's a useful one to get you started in your research. Once you start researching, you will want to be even more specific: whose ideas will you be focusing on – art directors working on Madison Avenue? Hawaiian sovereignty activists?

Now that you have framed some initial questions, it is time to embark upon your research. As historians, you will want to consult possibly three types of external evidence, depending upon your goals. First, you might wish to consult other types of primary evidence (materials produced in the period you are investigating), such as travel brochures to Hawaii; articles in popular magazines about Hawaii c. 1941; records of Congressional debates about the status of Hawaii as a US territory; oral histories of "hula dancers" who performed in traveling shows during the period. Finding such sources can be exciting; this is the detective work of the historian. Secondly, you will want to read secondary sources, both books and journal articles, that scholars have written about aspects of your topic. Thirdly, you may wish to employ another scholar's theoretical or conceptual framework as a tool in analyzing the historical meaning of your own text. Examples here might include, for example, Joan Scott's argument concerning gender as a category of historical analysis; Judith Butler's idea of gender as an ongoing performance; Edward Said's notion of "Orientalism"; or Roland Barthes's useful distinction between connotative and denotative meaning in photographic representation.[2]

You now have the tools to analyze images as primary sources for understanding the past. How you use those tools, and to what effect, will be up to you. Good luck!

Notes

---

1   The methodology that follows mirrors, quite closely, though with some modifications, the approach outlined by Jules David Prown in his important article on material culture methodology, "Mind in Matter: An Introduction to Material Culture Theory and Method," *Winterthur Portfolio*, 17:1 (Spring 1982), 1–20. I would like to thank Jules for his seminar in American Art, where I first learned how to read visual and material culture. I would also like to thank the generations of teaching assistants in Yale's American Studies program, whose hand-outs on analyzing primary sources have also informed this essay.

2   Joan Scott, "Gender: A Useful Category of Historical Analysis," in *Gender and the Politics of History* (New York: Columbia University Press, 1988); Judith Butler, *Gender Trouble: Feminism and the Subversion of Identity* (New York: Routledge, 1990); Edward Said, *Orientalism: Western Conceptions of the Orient* (London: Routledge, 1978); and Roland Barthes, "The Rhetoric of the Image," in *Image-Music-Text*, trans. Stephen Heath (New York: Hill & Wang, 1978).

Appendix B:
List of Visual Archives

ARDIS CAMERON

──────────── **Selected Photography Sites** ────────────

George Eastman House
International Museum of Photography and Film
900 East Avenue
Rochester, NY 14607
001-585-271-3361
TTY 001-585-271-3362
<www.eastman.org/1_geninfo/1_index.htm>

The Daguerreian Society
3043 West Liberty Ave.
Pittsburgh, PA 15216
001-412-343-5525
<www.daguerre.org>

Library of Congress
Prints and Photographs Division
101 Independence Ave. SE
Madison LM 337
Washington, DC 20540
001-202-707-6394

Photographic History Collection,
National Museum of American History, Smithsonian Institution
PO Box 37012
Suite 1100, MRC 601
Washington, DC 20013
001-202-357-3270
<archivescenter@nmah.si.edu>

Still Photographs Division of the National Archives
Washington, DC
<alic@nara.gov>

University of California at Los Angeles
46 Powell Library
001-310-206-5388
<arsc@ucla.edu>

Miriam and Ira D. Wallach Division of Art, Prints, and Photographs
New York Public Library
Room 308
Fifth Avenue and 42nd Street
New York, NY 10018
001-212-930-0837
<phgref@nypl.org>

Associated Press
50 Rockefeller Plaza
New York, NY 10020
001-212-621-1500
<info@ap.org>

The Getty Center
1200 Getty Center Drive
Los Angeles, CA 90049-1679
001-310-440-7300
image requests:
<www.getty.edu/about/contact_us.html>
<info@getty.edu>

Selected Film Sites

Division of Motion Pictures and Television
Library of Congress
James Madison Building
101 Independence Ave. SE
Washington, DC 20540
001-202-707-8572

Margaret Herrick Library
Academy of Motion Picture Arts and Sciences
Fairbanks Center of Motion Picture Study
333 S. La Cienega Boulevard
Beverly Hills, CA 90211
001-310-247-3000 ext. 201
<lmehr@oscars.org>

American Museum of the Moving Image
35 Ave. at 36th Street
Astoria, NY 11106
001-718-784-4520

Harvard Film Archive
24 Quincy Street
Cambridge, MA 02139
001-617-495-4700

Northeast Historic Film
PO Box 900
85 Main Street
Bucksport, ME 04416
001-207-469-0924

Internet Archive: Moving Image Archive
<www.archive.org/movies.php>

Film and Television Archive
University of California Los Angeles
46 Powell Library
001-310-206-5388
<arsc@ucla.edu>

INDEX

Page references in italics indicate illustrations.

Mather, Increase, 286
May, Elaine Tyler, 190–1
Mayhew, Henry, 164
Mayo, Louise, 291–2
Mead, Margaret, 37
Melnick, Jeffrey, 307 n. 16
Melville, Herman, 340
   The Confidence Man, 22
   Pierre, or the Ambiguities, 42
Memorial Day massacre, Chicago, 216,
   218, 223, 236 n. 56
men, and visual detection, 5
Men and Religion Forward Movement,
   121, 126, 135–6
Mercer, Kobena, 72
Mexicans, and labor movement, 224–5
   see also *pachucos*
Mexico, and zoot-suit riots, 273–4
Meyers, Peter Hamilton, 292
middle class:
   African American, 74, 84
   and capitalism, 196–7
   and cross-class looking, 5–6, 34–6,
      149–66
   and domesticity, 9–10, 153–4, 174–5,
      178–90, 195–6, 199–200, 203,
      238–60
   and labor movement, 195–7
   and nationalism and family, 173–90,
      191–2, 202–3, 205–6
   and portrait photography, 4, 42–54
   and social reform, 6–7, 151–5, 158–9,
      161
   and standardization of identity,
      42–54
   and television sit-coms, 9, 202, 238,
      239–40, 241, 252–60
   and underclass, 33–4
Miles, Charles A., 121–2, 124, 125, 127,
   128
Miller, Arthur, *Focus*, 286, 297–306
Mills, C. Wright, 252
Mintz, Steven, and Susan Kellogg, 176
Miranda, Billy, 277
Mirzoeff, Nicholas, 13

miscegenation, 17–18, 21, 64, 82, 296
Mississippi State Sovereignty
   Commission, 17–18, 21
Mitchell, Juliet, 260 n. 1
Mitchell, Timothy, 72
Miyatake, Toyo, 183
mobility, social:
   postwar, 201
   and race, 74
   in World War II, 268
modernity, and the primitive, 29–33
Mohanty, Chandra, 115
"mongrelization," 17
Moore, Deborah Dash, 296
Moore, Joan W., 272
Morris, Errol, 349
Morton, Leah (Elizabeth Stern), 294–5
Morton, Samuel, 28, 49
motherhood:
   and class, 153–4
   and war, 181
   working mothers, 129, 186
Mullinax, H. N., *128*
Mulvey, Laura, 72, 88 n. 31, 312–13, 325
Münzenberg, Willi, 229 n. 9
Murdock, Graham, and Peter Golding,
   239
Murray, Philip, 219–20, 223
museums, and display, 37
My Favorite Husband (TV sit-com),
   261 n. 4
Mydans, Carl, 179, 183–4
Myrdal, Gunnar, 37

Nashville Centennial Exposition (1897),
   63
National Geographic, 10, 11, 311, 312–13,
   315, 354
   academic gaze, 33–4
   magazine's gaze, 318
   non-Western subject's gaze, 320–4
   photographer's gaze, 316–18, *317*
   readers' gaze, 318–19
   Western gaze, 324–7
National Housing Act (1949), 192, 244